Making Change Happen

Black and White Activists talk to Kevin Cook about Aboriginal, Union and Liberation Politics

Kevin Cook and Heather Goodall

Making Change Happen

Black and White Activists talk to Kevin Cook about

Aboriginal, Union and Liberation Politics

Kevin Cook and Heather Goodall

E PRESS

Published by ANU E Press
The Australian National University
Canberra ACT 0200, Australia
Email: anuepress@anu.edu.au
This title is also available online at http://epress.anu.edu.au

---

National Library of Australia Cataloguing-in-Publication entry

Author: Cook, Kevin, author.

Title: Making change happen : black & white activists talk to Kevin Cook about Aboriginal, union & liberation politics / Kevin Cook and Heather Goodall.

ISBN: 9781921666728 (paperback) 9781921666742 (ebook)

Subjects: Social change--Australia.
Political activists--Australia.
Aboriginal Australians--Politics and government.
Australia--Politics and government--20th century.
Australia--Social conditions--20th century.

Other Authors/Contributors: Goodall, Heather, author.

Dewey Number: 303.484

All rights reserved. No part of this publication may be reproduced, stored in a retrieval system or transmitted in any form or by any means, electronic, mechanical, photocopying or otherwise, without the prior permission of the publisher.

Cover images: Kevin Cook, 1981, by Penny Tweedie (attached) Courtesy of Wildlife agency.

Aboriginal History Incorporated

Aboriginal History Inc. is a part of the Australian Centre for Indigenous History, Research School of Social Sciences, The Australian National University and gratefully acknowledges the support of the School of History RSSS and the National Centre for Indigenous Studies, The Australian National University. Aboriginal History Inc is administered by an Editorial Board which is responsible for all unsigned material. Views and opinions expressed by the author are not necessarily shared by Board members.

The Committee of Management and the Editorial Board
Peter Read (Chair), Rani Kerin (Monographs Editor), Maria Nugent and Shino Konishi (Journal Editors), Robert Paton (Treasurer and Public Officer), Ann McGrath (Deputy Chair), Isabel McBryde, Niel Gunson, Luise Hercus, Harold Koch, Tikka Wilson, Geoff Gray, Dave Johnson, Ingereth Macfarlane, Brian Egloff, Lorena Kanellopoulos, Richard Baker, Peter Radoll.

WARNING: Readers are notified that this publication may contain names or images of deceased persons.

Contacting Aboriginal History
All correspondence should be addressed to the Editors, Aboriginal History, ACIH, School of History, RSSS, Coombs Building (9) ANU, ACT, 0200, or aboriginal.history@anu.edu.au. Sales and orders for journals and monographs, and journal subscriptions: Thelma Sims, email: Thelma.Sims@anu.edu.au, tel or fax: +61 2 6125 3269, www.aboriginalhistory.org

Cover design and layout by ANU E Press.

This edition © 2013 ANU E Press

Contents

Acknowledgements vii
An introduction to Cookie's book 1

PART 1: FOUNDATIONS
1. Growing up Koorie — in Wollongong 9
2. Life and death on the job: The Builders Labourers' Federation — rank and file democracy, 1970 to 1975 25
3. In the wider struggle: The union, gender, race and environment 45
4. Tranby, co-operatives and empowerment 61

PART 2: TRANBY 1980s
5. Aboriginal-directed education: Getting started 87
6. Exploring possibilities: Teaching and learning at Tranby 107
7. Politics and real education 123
8. Reaching out for change 145

PART 3: LAND RIGHTS NSW 1980s
9. Strategies: 1976 to 1981 175
10. Experiences: 1981 to 1982 — Street demos and bush camps 209
11. Hard decisions: 1983 to 1985 237
12. Getting land back 255

PART 4: NETWORKS 1980s
13. National networks 275
14. Onto the streets 295
15. International networks 313

PART 5: BRINGING IT ALL TOGETHER
16. Bicentennial 335
17. Beyond the Bicentennial: Victories, defeats and more struggles for change 367
18. Reflections: Networks, hubs, pathways – and leadership . . 403

Appendix 1. Interviewees 421
Appendix 2. Glossary and abbreviations 423
Appendix 3. Bibliography and further reading 427
Index 431

Acknowledgements

There are many, many people to thank for their contributions to this book. Here we can focus on some central ones.

The people who were interviewed for this book have helped Cookie to create it.

You shared your memories with Cookie in those wonderful lunches and dinners with him and Judy. In fact some of you cooked the meals! The photographs of some of those times are in Chapter 18. All of your names are in the first appendix.

We have sadly lost some of you, but your words will continue to live on these pages.

You not only contributed your time over those meals, often with lots of travel to get there, but you have been Kevin's close friends and stalwart comrades over many decades. As he has become less able to travel to talk with you, you have come to see him, keeping in touch in person or over that telephone which is still at his side.

There are some very important libraries and archives whose support has been essential to the information and the images. The Coady International Institute and the St Francis Xavier University Archives have been generous and enthusiastic in documenting this episode of innovative cooperative work. The image and holdings of the Tranby Archives, set up on Cookie's watch and built by Julia Mant and its current librarian, Rowana.

Tranby staff have always been important for Cookie to do the work he has done, and this has continued even as he became ill and had to retire from active work. Cookie particularly wants to thank Greta North, who was his PA and secretary for a long time. Tranby continues to be an exciting and stimulating environment for staff and students and both Kevin and I have been grateful to draw from that enthusiasm.

This work has been funded in part by the Rona-Tranby Foundation, which has encouraged the role of oral history and memory in giving new insights into Aboriginal stories. The Foundation's generous support allowed us to pay for air fares so that Cookie was able to talk with his long-time comrades so he make a book about the movements they shared. Roland Gridiger and the other Rona-Tranby staff have offered sustained support and interest despite the book's long gestation.

The other major contributor to funding this project has been the Maritime Union of Australia, formed by the amalgamation in the late 1980s of the Seamen's

Union and the Waterside Workers' Federation. Rod Pickette, Kevin's long-time friend, is now MUA Policy Executive Officer. These unions have been strong supporters of Tranby and of Kevin's work, and in particular, the support of Patrick Geraghty and Paddy Crumlin of the SUA and then the MUA has been vitally important.

We want to thank Margaret who has taken so much care to find photos of her life with Cookie in the early years and to share the marvelous photographs of their grown up children, Suzie and Mereki, and then the next generation, Margaret and Cookie's grandchildren, Jake, Adam, Ben and Emma.

Central to the work of actually getting this book together have been the dedicated group of Kevin's friends who have read over the (many) drafts and rummaged around old boxes to find photographs: Dave Morrissey, Chris Milne, Julia Mant, Rod Pickette, Delia Lowe, Julie House, Patty Anderson, Terry O'Shane, Chris Kerr, Barbara and Karen Flick, Jack Ah Kit, Paulie Torzillo, Brian Doolan, William Bates and Norma Walford, David Ross, Peter Thompson, Nadia Wheatley and Meredith Burgmann.

Nadia Wheatley, Peter Read and Allison Cadzow have each given excellent editorial advice. We were not able to follow all of it, however, and the faults of the book remain very much the responsibility of Cookie and myself.

Emma and Judith Torzillo gave hours of their time for great photo research. Then Judith created an image database without which we would never have managed. Both Emma and Judith have found in Cookie a role model and hero, as well as a warm friend.

There is a special thank you for Kevin's family. Joy Steep and Ronnie, Kathy Kennedy and, (while she was able), Aunty Kit all brought love and enthusiasm to Cookie's story. Joy has been a sustained support through every trauma, continuing to travel weekly to spend some time with Kevin.

And for Judy Chester's family, who have loved and cared for Cookie as their own: especially Judy's sister, Janny and her husband Tommy Ely. Judy's daughters Jody and Jannette have given warm and generous support which has been essential for Judy and for Cookie in these later years.

This book is Judy's book as much as it is Cookie's. We hope it gives a glimpse of Judy's amazing, courageous career as well as of their rich life together.

Cookie & Heather

An introduction to Cookie's book

Heather Goodall

Cookie was still an organiser in the NSW Builders Labourers when I met him first in the early 1970s. I had just started at university then, a young and inexperienced student taking history but learning far more in the demonstrations against the Vietnam War and disrupting the visits of all-white sporting teams from South Africa. Meredith Burgmann, a fellow student and experienced activist, introduced me to Kevin when she took me to the Criterion, a city pub where her political and her union mates drank.

Cookie stood out – but not because he was the centre of attention – in fact far from it. He was short and chunky, with big, twinkling eyes, a mop of unruly, curly hair, a beer in his hand and a ready laugh. What stood out was his warmth and his welcome for tentative newcomers like me. I came to realise he was always like this – part of the conversation but never running it. More often he was stirring it along – starting a story and then encouraging someone else to take it up and deliver the punchline. You'd find him passing around the beers or the smokes, drawing people into the joke from the outer edges of the crowd.

Then I seemed to bump into him in all the places I was going too – not just the political pubs but the community events around the new Aboriginal housing company which had taken over the squats in Redfern, and at plays at the new Black Theatre. Then I really got to know him better in the meetings starting up in 1972, where anti-Apartheid activists like me were being confronted with the realities of racism in Australia as Aboriginal people like Cookie and others would talk to us about what they had faced all their lives fighting work, job, housing and education discrimination. No matter how gruelling some of these conversations were – and there was lots of shouting at times – Cookie was always the same, warm and patient with people like me who didn't know much. And he seemed to enjoy what we did know, smiling, listening, keeping an eye out for someone he could introduce to someone else there, quietly putting people in touch with each other.

By 1975, Kevin had started work at Tranby, around the time I was starting a PhD. He – like others – had encouraged me to try to record the memories they knew were so powerful among rural Aboriginal communities. I'd already met some senior Aboriginal people, like Jacko Campbell from the South Coast from where Cookie also came and Isabel Flick in the north-west, who were dropping into Tranby a lot. Kevin had fostered all of this, welcoming people into the old Tranby house in Glebe, just like he used to welcome people into the building sites and the pubs. But now he was ushering them further into the classrooms of Tranby to talk to the Aboriginal students coming from all over NSW and Queensland to learn about community development. I saw him organising the teaching sessions for some of the people who were already legendary as Builders Labourers like Joe Owens and Bobby Pringle. At the same time, he was bringing into the classes these senior Aboriginal people like Jacko, Isabel and Guboo Ted Thomas. Of course when Cookie wasn't at Tranby, he could be found playing darts with students and old union mates down the road at the Toxteth pub.

Cookie didn't miss opportunities to try out what people could offer – and to encourage them to offer a bit more than they expected! He began asking me what I could do to share all these things I was learning. There was plenty to do at Tranby on all levels – not just teaching, but licking envelopes for mailouts and showing up for the demos to support the Gurindji Aboriginal workers in the Northern Territory against Lord Vesty and the other big squatters. Sometimes he had me talking to classes. And every now and again I got to pick up the oysters he loved from the nearby Pyrmont Fishmarkets. But the best times for me were the many chances to share a cup of tea with all the people he was drawing through the doors, especially his old mates, Aboriginal or white, some of them Australian and others, increasingly, from all over the rest of the world.

Cookie had me doing all sorts of things but he tried me out at teaching – I was pretty inexperienced despite the PhD. He worked out I was better at listening to memories and recording stories – he kept on asking me to sit down in the dining room with those old people over more cups of tea… and when the Rona family approached Tranby looking for a partner to build a foundation to use the family's bequest to fund Aboriginal oral history work, Cookie encouraged Isabel Flick to apply and me to help.

The Rona-Tranby fund had started from a bequest from Thomas Rona who had lost family in the Holocaust and valued the role of memories in raising awareness of how the past shaped lives in the present. The family saw parallels between the memory work done by Jewish survivors with that of Aboriginal people remembering trauma and exploring the ways it had shaped today. But they recognised that it was crucial that Aboriginal people themselves were in control. So they approached Tranby in 1990 to become a partner and Kevin welcomed them – he appreciated the best in those who came offering help, even when their politics did not necessarily match his own. So he worked with Roland Gridiger to set the fund up and organise its ground rules and accounting. The fundamental principle was that Tranby would oversee a selection committee in which Aboriginal people took the leading role looking for innovative approaches to recording and presenting Aboriginal people's many memories.

An introduction to Cookie's book

The expectation initially – from all sides – was that the stories would follow a person's life in a similar way to a conventional autobiography. But there are many stories and just as many ways of telling them among Aboriginal people – some lives are followed but they might more often be retold in the context of families and places than in conventional written biographies. Isabel Flick, for example, was comfortable with the way her life could form the backbone of a story which drew in the people in her wide family and community as well as showing how they related to the contested places of Collarenebri and the Barwon River. But as time went by, people applying for the funds from the Rona Tranby Trust began to propose different stories to tell and different ways to do it. So now the Trust has supported a range of projects, from the collections of many life stories like *Steppin' Out and Speakin' Up*, the stories of 15 women gathered by the Older Women's Network, to the stories of whole communities and places like *Yamakarra: Liza Kennedy and the Keewong Mob* from the Western Heritage Group in far west NSW and most recently the rich story of a marching band from Yarrabah in Queensland which has been made as a film.

Inevitably, people on the Tranby and the Rona sides of the Oral History trust began to see Kevin's life story as a subject for a history project. He was well-known as a unionist, as an advocate of innovative, Aboriginal-controlled adult education, highly respected as a nation-wide land rights organiser, a key player in transnational links with liberation movements and a man of exceptional integrity and dynamism. So he seemed an obvious candidate. Cookie asked me to be involved because he'd seen me work at Tranby and with many of his old friends. For the Rona-Tranby Trust – and sometimes for myself – my job was to turn Kevin's story into a life story book like Isabel's.

But Cookie was not interested in searching for the meaning of his own life. Instead, he has always focussed on what he grew up calling 'sticking fats' – sticking together with fellow activists, sharing the good and the bad in everything he was involved in – sharing not just the hopes but the hard work to reach goals and the scarce resources you had to live on to get there. Later I came to realise that many of the origins for those commitments could be found in the story of Cookie's life. But instead of telling his own story, Cookie wanted to tell the stories of the movements he had been able to play a part in and the people he has shared his life with. It was to be the story of the movements – not as abstract ideals but through the people in them and the *ways* that together those people made decisions and carried out work together.

So while Kevin didn't want to knock back the offer of funding from the Rona Trust, he wanted to use it to tell *those* sorts of story – through memories, photos and the voices of those people he had worked with. What he didn't want – and continued very strongly to refuse to be a part of – was the story of his own life as an individual – as if he had been central to the story, had caused the movements or could take credit in the end for their achievements. He wanted it to be a book about the way the people he had shared his life with had found ways – and in fact how they had *made* ways – to work together, often across obstacles and for goals that weren't well understood. But who had – together – made change happen.

So Kevin and I talked this over and we worked on ways to make that sort of book happen. Cookie was becoming sick by that stage – his energy and his movements increasingly drained by emphysema, the disease that cuts down the amount of lung space you can use to process the air you breathe into your lungs. What wasn't being affected was his commitment to his comrades and their causes – and so during the 1990s, he could still be found at work a lot at Tranby despite the fact that it was getting harder and harder. He found he was increasingly needing to work from home, helped in a million ways by his partner Judy Chester, who had been with him since the early 1980s, sharing many political campaigns as well as keeping up her own union and land rights work. Cookie was assisted too by his Tranby PA, Chrissy Kerr. At home he was just as constantly on the phone as if he was in the front office at Tranby, talking to people from all over the country, catching up on what was happening, going over ideas with the stream of people who came to visit.

We set out to record the conversations Cookie had *with* those visiting friends and comrades. We organised lunches, Judy made fabulous salads and cakes and we had lots of prawns and seafood. People came from all over the country – from Broome and Darwin and Melbourne and Cairns – and from just around Sydney – to share those meals, talk, laugh and show how much they had learned in those shared times together when they had all 'stuck fats'. Cookie brought people together, and then he, Judy and a few old friends asked some of the questions. I recorded and chipped in every now and again. There is a list of people who contributed at the end of this book. We could not record all of the many people who had stories to tell about the movements Cookie had worked in. So this book reflects the perspectives of some of those people who were close friends or who happened to be able to come to the house for lunch.

The conversations ranged far more widely than any of us had expected – in fact across all the big issues of the 1970s and 1980s and many of the undercurrents that were not so well known. Over food, a lot of tea and the occasional beer, people talked about land rights, racism, education, multiculturalism, international liberation struggles, union justice, feminism, cooperatives and the Bicentennial Long March in 1988. But what they talked over too were personal anxieties, rivalries and passions and about the funny memories – as well as why they so often turned to laughter to get over tragedy. And they talked too about the puzzle of what real leadership means and the even harder question about how to really bring very different people together to make change happen.

An introduction to Cookie's book

So this is *not* a life story. It is *not* a conventional biography with one person at the centre of the story, because that is not what Cookie has wanted it to be.

Instead, through those recordings, we have tried to make this the story of the movements of which Kevin was a part and which he fostered and sometimes created. It is not a 'complete' history – it does not try to cover the past from everyone's point of view. Rather this book records the perspectives of the people *inside* the movements with which Kevin was involved.

I have edited and spliced and cut down the long recordings, trying to keep the sense of what was said but to make the transcript work when it is read from the page. Cookie has read and reread the drafts, marking up and commenting and send them all back for changes. It has turned out to be a complex task to bring this diverse set of intersecting networks into an order which allows them to become visible in their own right as well as showing the connections between them. In each chapter we explain which people contributed to it.

The first three chapters show something about where Kevin's ideas came from about communities, networks, solidarity and 'sticking fats'. Then each of the following chapters tells the story of a phase in one of the movements through the memories of those who played key roles in them – four chapters on Tranby, three on land rights and three on the links across state and national boundaries. Then a final chapter on how it all came together in the 1988 Long March, to challenge the idea of the Bicentennial and put something much more positive and hopeful in its place.

My own story is a small part of this rich record – it is there because I was one of many non-Aboriginal people who were offered friendships and challenges – in that order! – from Kevin over many years. But it is only a small part because Cookie's networks of people are so wide and so diverse that we have struggled to bring them together in a single volume and still could not do them justice.

But, in the end, in being about these movements and the ways in which they formed and were nurtured, it has shown something of Kevin's life during these years. And it turned out that none of us knew the whole story…

PART 1
FOUNDATIONS

1. Growing up Koorie — in Wollongong

This book will focus on the movements in which Kevin has been involved, not on Kevin's life story. But — to understand those movements it is important to understand where Kevin was coming from. The communities in which Kevin grew up shaped the networks into which he was welcomed and the approaches he took in all of them.

A central foundation for Cookie was the fact that he had grown up Koorie[1] — his Wandandian family had their roots in the country of the South Coast of New South Wales (NSW). All Aboriginal communities are embedded within a context — a landscape and a web of social and political relationships. For Kevin's family and community that context in the 1940s was Wollongong, a coastal city which had grown from a fishing town into a coal mining port, but was by Kevin's time dominated by the heavy manufacturing of the steel making industry as well as by the local and deep sea fishing.

This chapter will introduce Kevin and his family, as well as what it meant to grow up Koorie in a big, working class city like Wollongong. So it will show the way Kevin's background meant that he could feel at home in so many different movements. The stories and the photos have come from Kevin and his family, in particular his sister Joy and his cousin, Kathy, who has spent a lot of time researching family history.

***

Kevin was born in 1939 and grew up at Cringila, near Wollongong on the South Coast of New South Wales. His family is from the Wandandian people, who had close relations with the Yuin language groups from the south and the Dharawal groups, whose country is broadly related to the coastal lands and waterways from the Georges River, in southern Sydney, right down to the Shoalhaven River.

Kevin's mother was Grace Speechley, the daughter of Josephine Kate Speechley, known as Granny Kate.[2] She was in turn the daughter of the celebrated Wandandian man, James Golding, a widely recognised senior man (1815–1905) and his wife,

---

1 'Koorie' is the term used by Aboriginal people of many languages in coastal and southern New South Wales and in Victoria to mean 'Aboriginal person'. Kevin spells it this way, but it can be spelt variously, sometimes as 'Koori', sometimes with the Anglicised 'oo' written to more accurately indicate its pronunciation as a short vowel, 'u' (Kuri) and sometimes, most in line with Aboriginal accents on the North Coast of NSW, with the first letter as a hard, voiced 'G', rather than a 'K'.
2 Née Golding – or Golden – 1871–1955.

Mary Carpenter, a Dharawal woman born around 1823 in Kiama and who died in 1928.³ Kate married William Speechley, an English ship builder, and they lived at Billong, near Huskisson. William himself was also well known and had been the guide for the Prince of Wales when he visited Australia and travelled to the South Coast for a tour of the Naval College at Jervis Bay in June 1920.

Grace had been born to Kate and William at Huskisson in 1911, the eighth of their ten children. Kevin was close to all Grace's sisters and brothers. Her two sisters were important to him: Mary, born in 1903, was eight years older than Grace, while Kitty, born in 1913, was two years younger. Kevin spent a lot of time with his uncle Stan, the youngest among Grace's brothers, born in 1916, who became a fisherman, on the lakes of the area and offshore, along its coastline. Another of Grace's brothers, Albert, came to Sydney to train in engineering, while a third, Ern, worked in heavy industry including the steel works and maritime trades along the coast in the port cities of Port Kembla and Nowra.

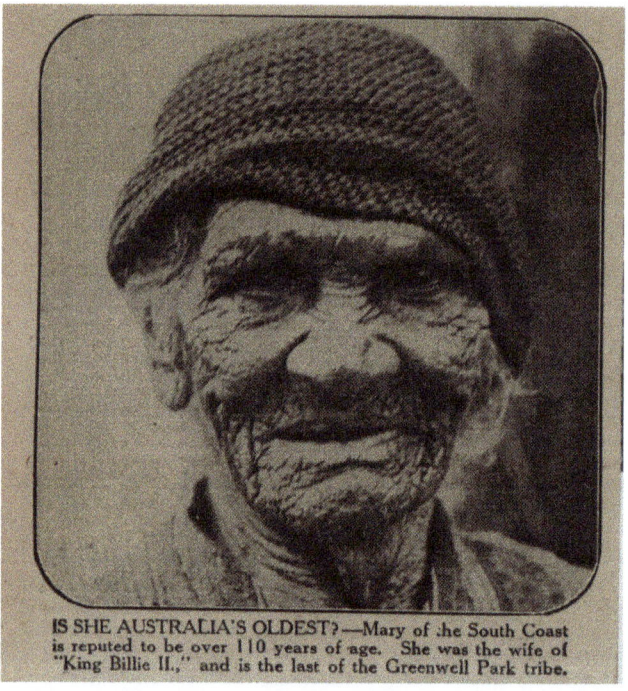

Figure 1.1: Mary Carpenter, Grace's grandmother and Cookie's great grandmother, as an elderly woman.

Courtesy Kathy Kennedy (cousin of Kevin Cook) family collection.

---

3   Family history research conducted by Kathy Kennedy, Kevin's cousin, daughter of Grace's sister Kit.

Figure 1.2: William Speechley, Granny Kate's husband and Grace's father, as an elderly man.

Courtesy Kathy Kennedy (cousin of Kevin Cook) family collection.

Figure 1.3: Kevin's Uncle Stan, Grace's youngest brother, a fisherman to whom Kevin was close all his life.

Courtesy Kathy Kennedy (cousin of Kevin Cook) family collection.

Around the campfires of holiday camps and on fishing trips, Kevin grew up listening as his older Aboriginal relations retold stories from their own early lives or the stories they had heard from their elders. The stories handed down were about conflicts as early white settlers encroached on the coastal Aboriginal land, forcing communities away from their sacred places like Gulaga Mountain and pushing them off their traditional camping grounds in some of the most beautiful places of the coast, like Wallaga Lake and the Five Islands. These iconic landscapes were taken over for farming or tourism. Kevin's aunties and uncles could tell him about their own experiences, as they grew up on the coast.

The area had a troubled history, particularly in relation to education. In the 1920s and 1930s, Aboriginal children had often been pushed out of the public schools they had been enrolled in all up and down the coast. But they did not go without a struggle! The Batemans Bay community was just one of those who fought back, with furious Aboriginal parents and grandparents, like Jane Duren, writing to the Premier, Prime Minister and even to the King to demand entry to the school system which was supposed to be 'public'. At the same time, they called for – and often received – support from local trade unions and the Labor Party to demand their children be allowed to take their rightful places in the public schools. While they did not always win these battles, the history of staunch Aboriginal resistance to this denial of civil rights and the backing, at least sometimes, of the local labour union movement, meant there was a long tradition of Aboriginal people and unions working together. This was much less common in other parts of Australia at the time, except in the similar industrialised area of Newcastle, to the north of Sydney, where again fishing, coal and steel manufacturing had created a strong line of communication between Aboriginal people and unionised workers.[4]

There had been rising pressure on Aboriginal people from the early twentieth century, because land use had changed to cropping and dairying and Aboriginal people had less and less access to their land. Then the NSW Aborigines Protection Board began removing Aboriginal children if they did not attend school, so their parents moved to live where the schools were. So increasingly, Aboriginal people in rural areas had been forced to move closer together, into what became overcrowded settlements, on reserve land set at a distance from the nearest townships in places like Roseby Park and, closer to Wollongong, at the Aboriginal reserve at Coomaditji. In the city of Wollongong itself, where Kevin's family lived in an outer suburb at Cringila, there were quite a number of Aboriginal people who all knew each other, but their homes were scattered and so they did not form an identifiable consolidated community like those in rural settlements.

But Kevin got to know his people's country well because he grew up with his mother's family. They would spend weekends and holidays out of Wollongong, particularly at places down the coast like Grace's birthplace, Huskisson, where Kevin remembers as a child being with Grace and her sisters as they gathered pippis, oysters and crabs along the shores just like they had done in their own childhoods.

Other times Kevin would pass the weekends on the boat with his uncle Stan, learning the fish, the birds and the vegetation of the lakes as well as the rocks and shoals of the coast. One of the important experiences he remembers from those years was spending time at Roseby Park, on the coast about 20 miles from Nowra. In later years, Kevin got to know well one of the Roseby Park community, Jacko Campbell. Jacko was a Dhan-gadi man originally from the Kempsey area, who lived most of his adult life on the South Coast, marrying Nan Wellington and coming to live at Roseby Park, where they raised their family. All the people in these rural settlements had strong commitments to their Aboriginal responsibilities to look after the surrounding land and waters.

---

4 Jane Duren's letter can be found in Heather Goodall 1996, *Invasion to Embassy: Land in Aboriginal politics in New South Wales, 1770-1972*, Allen & Unwin, St Leonards, NSW. The Aboriginal and working class history of Newcastle is discussed in works of John Maynard, including his 2007: *Fight for Liberty and Freedom: The Origins of Australian Aboriginal Activism*, Aboriginal Studies Press, Canberra.

Jacko had taken this responsibility very seriously, defending Aboriginal rights vigorously not only in his childhood home of Kempsey but all along the South Coast.[5]

Communities such as Huskisson and Roseby Park, like Batemans Bay further south, also had a history in seafaring, whether in coastal fishing or as crewmen joining the early whaling industries set up along the South Coast. They had welcomed the Maori seafarers and whalers who were visiting from the early years of the colony. Some stayed, marrying South Coast Aboriginal women, and their stories and traditions were woven into those that Kevin was hearing about. At the same time, he was hearing stories from his uncles about the work on the local farms, picking beans and other crops as well as the long days in the heavy iron and steel works of the towns, and about the work in coal mining in the surrounding escarpments. That meant he was hearing from an early age about the unions on the South Coast, where working people, black or white, had often been able to work together across colour lines to gain better conditions.

This tradition of working class life and organising was something Kevin learned about also from his father, as well as from the working men his mother's sisters had married. Like many Aboriginal women on the coast, including her mother, Grace married a man from outside the Aboriginal community, Carl Cook. Carl was a railway fettler, and in the early years of his marriage to Grace, he had to travel upcountry with the fettling gangs who maintained the tracks, so he was away from home quite a bit.

For a time, the whole family moved. When Kevin was young the family lived at Bowning near Yass, for three or four years while Carl 'ran the line' there. Eventually, Grace became so lonely for her sister Kit that the family moved back to Cringila and Carl worked on the railway in Wollongong.

Carl enjoyed being part of Grace's extended family, and he brought his own proud working class history into the mix. Carl's father, known widely as a good cricketer, had been a railway signalman, holding the safety of the many freight and passenger trains in his hands as he mounted the signals to direct the train drivers in all weathers and all year round.

Originally from Wollongong, Carl's father had moved to Sydney for the railway work, and Carl's two brothers, Vic and Cyril, continued to live in the inner city when Kevin was young, at Tempe and Glebe. Kevin can remember spending holidays at Carl's father's place at Rozelle, overlooking the water there, where

---

5   See later chapters. Jacko's role and commentary on 1940s to 1970s politics both north and south coasts of NSW in Goodall 1996. His work in the NSW land rights campaign is documented in the *Report on Wilcannia trip 27.11.80 – 6.12.80* / by Ted Thomas, Jack Campbell, Max Harrison and Terry Fox, representatives of the N.S.W. Land Council, AIATSIS Library, PMS 3322.

timber yards and wool stores kept the water a busy, working harbour. His uncles Vic and Cyril would come down frequently to stay with Kevin's family at Cringila, fishing and sharing the family's weekends, and Kevin would often come up to visit them, with particularly fond memories of Glebe. Cyril lived close to Harold Park Paceway, and Kevin remembers ducking off for hours to watch the trotters being trained up for the Friday night races. Grace's younger sister Kitty had married Dave Kennedy, a rigger in the steelworks at Port Kembla, a solid and careful worker, whose job was to work above the machinery where the steel was being rolled. He had always been concerned about safety in this dangerous job, and had altered his clothing, cutting out the sleeves to make sure they did not catch on anything. But Dave died tragically young when he was splashed with manufacturing acid while he was high above the rolling steel, lost his footing and fell to his death.

Figure 1.4: Kevin's parents, Grace and Carl, with his older brother, George.

Courtesy Joy Steep (sister of Kevin Cook) family collection.

Figure 1.5: Kevin and his younger brother Ron.

Courtesy Joy Steep (sister of Kevin Cook) family collection.

Figure 1.6: Kevin's class in Cringila in 1946. Kevin is on the right hand end of the back row.

Courtesy Joy Steep (sister of Kevin Cook) family collection.

Figure 1.7: Kevin (third from left) at the steel works as a gardener.

Courtesy Joy Steep (sister of Kevin Cook) family collection.

Kevin was the second of Grace and Carl's children. His big brother George was only a couple of years older than Kevin, and was his fishing and prawning partner, while Ronnie was only a few years younger, so the three boys grew up together for many years before their baby sister arrived when Kevin was 15.

The rare surviving photos from those days show Kevin and Ronnie tagging along after each other coming back from school, from Boy Scouts or from Sunday School. But these clubs and organised pastimes did not leave many memories for Kevin. Instead, it is the times fishing and digging worms for bait, the days out on the boats or watching the horses being trained which are the ones Kevin remembers. It was those times with his family and with his mates – rather than the formal schooling – that offered the real learning in Kevin's younger life.

But his Aboriginal family were not the only ones Kevin was mixing with in Cringila.

Cookie: Living in Cringila, there's every nationality on earth, plus a couple. In fact, Italians, Greeks, they were the majority of people in Cringila, it's right next to the steel works, and they all worked at the steel works. So we taught a lot of the kids to speak English. Their mother's and father's couldn't speak English. So we taught them to swear first, of course, everybody does it!

As he moved into a working life, Kevin followed the same pathways his family – and in fact all his neighbours – had followed into the heavy industry of the area. He worked in and around the steel works at Port Kembla, for example, where he was a gardener for a while.

But this was all interrupted in 1957, when Kevin was 18. Like all young men in Australia at that time, he had to register for National Service and take a medical test to see if he would be called up. The scheme operating over these years (1951–1959) involved three months full time training and then regular weekend service in the Reserve of the Commonwealth Military Force over two years.[6] Kevin was based at Holsworthy in south-western Sydney near Liverpool, but like school he was not too interested in the rules and army traditions. The one photo of him in these years shows what a good time he was having in the Army – but it was because he was sharing time with good mates, not because he enjoyed military culture.

He was AWOL a few times, heading off with mates and so he served a few stints in the military lock up during his three months training. But as he remembers it, he had a good time in the jail, because the prisoners had to serve in the Officers' Mess 'and they were having parties all the time! All with good food and drink!'

At the end of the three months' training period, Kevin returned to the workforce although he was expected to come back to the army camp regularly for weekend duties. He didn't. When the army caught up with him again, he was forced to serve another three months straight full time, in default of his missed weekends. More parties in the Officers' Mess! And once he had done that second three months, he was free of the whole thing.

Out of the army and back at work, Kevin began to think about travelling. New Zealand was a place he had been hearing about for many years from the people of the coast who had come from there or travelled there. In the early 1960s, he and a close friend, Brian Curtis, decided they would travel to New Zealand 'to have a look', so they headed over for what they thought would be a few weeks. Instead, they ended up staying 18 months, and wrote back such glowing accounts that soon Ronnie and other mates from Wollongong came over to join them. The friends travelled all over the North Island, working in places that ranged from the meat works and a wool store to apple picking. Kevin met many Maori in the North Island – both as workmates and among people he met along the road, so he came away with good memories and a real interest in going back.

---

6   *National Service, 1951–59 – Fact Sheet 163*, National Archives of Australia, <http://www.naa.gov.au/collection/fact-sheets/fs163.aspx> accessed 10 January 2013.

Figure 1.8: Kevin in New Zealand.

Courtesy Joy Steep (sister of Kevin Cook) family collection.

After coming back to Sydney, Kevin worked again in a range of jobs and shared a house with mates at Manly, a surf beach on the northern side of the harbour. Then Kevin and Carl Brisbane, one of his Manly flatmates, decided to go back to New Zealand. This time they started off again in the North Island but then travelled across the strait to Nelson on the South Island and then headed up the coast to Motueka. This time Kevin stayed a full year travelling and working, till he finally came back to Australia with even more lifelong friendships to keep him in touch.

Still living in Sydney, Kevin found jobs in a few places at once, including a long period at a paper mill where he had a job as an iron worker, and another job at a garage owned by the father of a friend. This friend was going out with a girl who in turn had a friend whom Kevin began to take out. This was Margaret Keys with whom Kevin found a relationship which brought together many of the political issues he had grown up with together with a working class lifestyle where he felt at home.

Figure 1.9: Kevin and Margaret.

Courtesy Margaret Munday family collection.

He met Margaret's family and liked them too. In particular, he formed a lifelong friendship with Margaret's father, Harry Keys, who was passionate about his politics. A hire car driver, he supported the Labor Party and in the turbulent late 1960s, there was a lot to talk over and worry about. Kevin remembers sitting up with him late into the night, 'talking politics for hours'.

Just as enthusiastic was Margaret's uncle, Bill Knott, an electrician who was a friend of many in the unions and on the Left, including a radical Anglican priest called Alf Clint. Although known in the family as 'the uncle who swore a lot', Bill took his politics very seriously. He went on to run for State Parliament in 1978, winning what had been the conservative seat of Wollondilly for Labor and holding it, through a boundary change in which it became Kiama, until he retired in 1986. Bill was another person who became Kevin's lifelong friend.

Figure 1.10: By 1969, Kevin and Margaret had married and were starting a family in Tempe, where Suzie, their first child, was born in 1970.

Courtesy Margaret Munday family collection.

Figure 1.11: Kevin's sister Joy with his daughter, Suzie.

Courtesy Margaret Munday family collection.

Figure 1.12: Mereki, Kevin and Margaret's son, was born in 1974.

Courtesy Margaret Munday family collection.

Even though Kevin and Margaret lived in Sydney, they were in constant touch with Grace and Carl and the rest of the family. Most weekends, Kevin and Margaret would head down to Berkeley, the area in Wollongong to which the family had moved, enjoying catching up with the big family, watching Joy grow up into a teenager and especially enjoying Grace's cooking – Kevin remembers they would 'eat them out of house and home!'

Figure 1.13: Grace and Carl at Berkeley.

Courtesy Joy Steep (sister of Kevin Cook) family collection.

Ronnie was often away now – he had caught the travel bug in New Zealand and travelled to the United Kingdom where he worked on oil rigs, then came back to Darwin for more oil rig work and, after the cyclone, to Western Australia. There he became a seaman and joined the Australian Seamen's Union. He would send Grace exotic postcards from wherever he was all over the world, first on the oil rigs then on the ships.

Figure 1.14: Joy's 17th birthday dinner, 1971. From left side of table: Dave (a family friend), Grace, Margaret, Kevin. On the right side, from the rear, were Judy (a friend of Joy's), Joy, Kathy Kennedy (Kevin's cousin) and another family friend.

Courtesy Joy Steep (sister of Kevin Cook) family collection.

In Sydney, Kevin and Margaret were being drawn more and more into the busy politics of the late 1960s. Margaret was active in the early women's movement, including a protest at Maroubra beach where women went topless to protest the opposition to women's presence on the beach. A tiny woman, Margaret was arrested there and charged with assault by a burly lifesaver who insisted she had manhandled him – until it was thrown out of court. Kevin remembers Margaret becoming involved in the early stages of the anti-Vietnam anti-war movement, and marching in the first Moratorium early in 1970. Kevin supported her causes, but at this time, he was trying to keep in work to support his new family too. So he was travelling a lot to find jobs, just like his father had had to do. He was in Tumut working as a rigger, putting up and removing scaffolding and machinery from building sites, when his mate Roy Bishop called him and told him there was a great job for him in Sydney…

2. Life and death on the job: The Builders Labourers' Federation — rank and file democracy, 1970 to 1975

Sydney in the 1960s and 1970s was being transformed almost overnight from a small, low city huddled round the harbour into a city of sky scrapers.[1] There were big profits to be made by the building companies if they could harness the money flowing into the city. So this new high rise cityscape was being built from scratch with short cuts and no previous experience. The workers were mostly members of the Builders Labourers' Federation (BLF) which, until then, had been a small, powerless union. A few others were in the Building Workers' Industrial Union (the BWIU). They were all as unfamiliar with this style of high rise building as the companies.

Most of these BLs (the nickname for the BLF members) had been working in small job teams on suburban house or light industry sites until the boom brought them all together for the first time in the CBD. New materials were making it possible to build bigger and higher buildings, all needing more and more workers to make it happen fast. So suddenly, these workers from the suburbs were expected to build scaffolding and carry loads up onto buildings which were 20, 30 and 40 floors high. Industrial accidents occurred sometimes in other industries Kevin had worked in. His own uncle had died on the job in the Wollongong steel industry. But in Sydney's new high rise building boom, the danger was there every day for every worker – and it was a real issue of life and death.

Cookie met it on his first day on the job.

Kevin: Roy Bishop was a key to me going onto a site and into the BLs.[2] We'd worked together as iron workers in the paper mill in Botany, but then I was working up at Tumut. Roy rang me up and said: 'I got you this fantastic job! Plenty of money. So come up here quick! Snatch it!'

So I snatched it! The next day I drove back down to Sydney. And there it was: TC Whittle's job. As a dogman!

---

1 Meredith Burgmann and Verity Burgmann 1998, *Green Bans Red Union: Environmentalism and the New South Wales Builders Labourers' Federation*, UNSW Press, Sydney.
2 The 'BLs' was the widely-used nickname for the Builders Labourers' Federation and for its members. Pronounced 'bee-ells'.

Figure 2.1: Dogman on hook at Harrietville, Victoria, 1940.

Photograph by JA Smith, 1940, republished courtesy of his grandson, 'williewonker' at <http://www.flickr.com/photos/87791108@N00/3242643681/in/photostream/>

Do you know what dogmen used to do? You were riding the loads all the way down the buildings. The crane driver was on the top but he couldn't see you all the time. He could only see the wire going over the edge. You could signal him with a rope that ran back up along the wire to a bell on the crane, but that was all you had. Some of the old blokes used to paint a line on the wire, and then they could see where you were supposed to be. They dropped one of the kibbles, that's the cement holder, on top of a double decker bus doing that one day! So the dogmen were ridin' around on the hooks and the slings – and the slings were only as thick as your finger![3]

I said to Roy: 'No! you're crazy!'

But he talked me into it. So I got the job but I'd never worked as a dogman before, in fact I'd never worked on a building site! …So I didn't know anything! I got on the kibble. It's illegal to ride but we used to ride it up in the morning save walking up the stairs. Roy had just said 'Jump on that, grab on and up you

---

3   The term 'rigger' is often mistakenly used to refer to dogmen, but as BLF members who actually did the job, like Kevin and Joe, have explained, a 'rigger' did not ride the hook, but instead erected and dismantled scaffolding and moved machinery onto and off a site.

go, I'll stay down the bottom'. So I jumped on and when I got about six foot up, I looked down and I thought 'As soon as I get off this, I'm going to walk right down them stairs and *out of here*!'

And when I got off, you could see my fingerprints in the steel, I was hanging on that tight!

***

Being in the Builders Labourers' Federation in the 1960s and 1970s was a completely new experience for workers in two ways. First, they were making buildings very different than they had ever made before, on sites where there were no amenities, using strange new techniques and working in tall, dangerous building conditions when there were few effective regulations to protect worker safety. Body hire was still being practised: workers would line up before dawn on the street and bosses would drive past and hire them for the day or by the hour – there was no job security, no conditions, no guarantees about tomorrow. Workers were plentiful, cheap and expendable. This meant that workers were being made to take high risks with no safety protection or security.

But, secondly, the new city building boom also meant that as a union, these workers had more power than ever before. The complicated steps needed to get high rise blocks up meant that workers could have a major impact on building progress if they acted together and stopped work to demand improvements. Some moments were crucial – for example, the floor for each level had to be filled with concrete at the same time, because to interrupt the pour and restart it, to do the floor in stages, would weaken the result. So if labourers downed tools in the middle of a concrete pour, not only did work have to stop at the time, but the area already poured would have to be allowed to dry and then jackhammered up again, so it could all be done in one go. So work would be held up for days. What did it mean for Kevin to be in the union in those heady days? In this chapter, Kevin talks with Joe Owens and Bobby Baker, both key activists in the NSW Builders Labourers' Federation, with Meredith Burgmann who wrote a history of those times in the BLs, with Robyn Williams, an Aboriginal activist who was one of the women who became a builders labourer and with Paul Torzillo, a friend who is now a doctor but who worked as a BL when he was a student.

Figure 2.2: Things had not changed much by 1965. This photo, taken by Valentin Sowada, shows Lance Shelton, known to other BLs as 'Blackie' or 'Sooty'. He was an Aboriginal member of the NSW BLF riding on a load in the construction of the State Office Block. The photograph is known as 'The Rigger, Sydney c. 1965'. This photograph was held in Joe Owens private collection, and he explained that this image was widely circulated among NSW BLF members in the 1960s and 1970s, particularly among those, like Kevin and Joe, who had worked as dogmen.

Photograph © Valentin Sowada and is reproduced courtesy of the Sowada family, *Yesterday's Images*.

As *Kevin* tells the story, after that very reluctant start: I ended up staying there about six or eight months. Because when we were dogmen, it was a job where you could *do* things. You had control of the crane. If you didn't lift and didn't put things where they wanted it to go, it'd hold up the job, and so you was a pretty important cog in the wheel. And the dogmen, on a whole, were pretty strong. When there wasn't any work for the dogmen, what we'd do was clean the crane down and work in and around the crane. What the builders wanted us to do was to be brickies' labourers and do other work, taking away the right of another person to have that job. So we refused.

They sacked us three times, because we wouldn't do other work that wasn't dogmen's work. The first time, I think we were out two days and Joey Owens got us our job back, plus time lost.

2. Life and death on the job: The Builders Labourers' Federation — rank and file democracy, 1970 to 1975

Figure 2.3: Joe Owens speaking at BLF rally at UTS tower site, with Bob Pringle.

Courtesy Dr Meredith Burgmann.

Joe Owens had skills that were important for dogmen because, as a young man from Wales, he had been a merchant seaman and so he knew about ropes and knots and high working places.

Joe Owens: I came into the industry in the late '60s… I was one of the few organisers who'd ever worked as a dogman. See dogman in those days … we used to ride the hook, it was a terrible thing! I'll never forget, one old doggie, old Sooty, said to me, 'You know mate in this job, you run on piss and coffee. And after a while you give the coffee away!' He was right! He was pretty well right, doggies running on booze!

Kevin: The other dogmen supported us and we got on fairly well with a lot of them. And then Roy went and become an organiser and not long after that I became an organiser too. Now the rank and file membership and the leaders of the union were one and the same. We had as much say as the president of the union. As I seen it from where I was sitting, we dictated the disputes that we'd get into. The rank and filers dictated what was going on in the union! Even to sit down and talk with the secretary of the union – Mundey – or the president, Bobby Pringle, was like a breath of fresh air.

In the Ironworkers, you didn't even see the organisers!

In the steelworks in Wollongong, we were on strike for three days, and we called out the organiser – it took him three days to get out to us! And then he went to the boss first, come out to us and said, 'Get back to work'. So we stoned him and stayed off another couple of days, never seen anybody else and we went back to work. So we didn't go on strike again.

I had to think very hard about being an organiser in the BLs. And I talked to Roy about it. But I was lucky, Tony Hatfield and Dino at a later stage, and Roy especially... They all sat down with you and talked with you, if you had any problems on the job and things like that. I'd say, 'Come out on my job, I've got a bit of a problem', so they'd come out. You weren't *alone*. I said to Pringle, he was the president of the union, 'I want you to come out' ... and he'd have to come out! He wouldn't say, 'Oh... I won't come out', he'd just come! Or I'd say to Joe Owens, 'Look, I've got a problem' and he'd come out.

Joe Owens: I was in the industry from the early '60s – not in the BLs – but in the industry – and from about the mid '60s... things began to change, you had democracy on the streets... Cookie was there, and I mean the world was *spinning* in the late '60s, early '70s... it was *spinning*! We had street marches about Vietnam, we had street marches about everything. I mean it sort of grew... into the green bans and then the Aboriginals came into it. I remember Stan Sharkey from the BWIU, bringing down a rangey old Koorie called Captain Major from the Gurindjis who were running this big wages and land rights strike in the Territory.[4] He was about six-foot three and he had feet about two foot long, never seen a fella like him! He had a crook heart so Freddy Hollows was gonna cure him and we all met him, talked about all those issues for the first time.

For us at that time it was all flying! We were the maverick wing – Mundy and meself and a couple of others – we were the maverick wing of the Communist party. Bobby Pringle was in the Labor Party, and he was out there flying... and big Pringle was the one who started bringing in the Aboriginal issues and that was when I met Cookie... He came on later as an organiser.

---

4 Joe remembered Captain Major's visit but Vincent Lingiari and a number of other Gurindji leaders also visited Sydney and spoke at union meetings.

2. Life and death on the job: The Builders Labourers' Federation — rank and file democracy, 1970 to 1975

Figure 2.4: Gurindji representatives at BLF meeting c.1967, to support Gurindji land rights campaign. Captain Major sits in front with BLF members, listening to Dexter Daniels speaking.

Courtesy Dr Meredith Burgmann.

Kevin: Yeah, I joined up in 1970 and I got to be an organiser about 18 months after. Cause you know it was only a very small union. And for so long, everybody who worked in the building industry was treated like shit. If you were a builders labourer before the end of the '60s, people would laugh at you! People used to say they were a garbage collector before they'd say they were a builders labourer.

But after Mundey and that got in, everybody was proud. Because there was a fight on, you know? To restore your confidence, to have a bit of that self esteem back. People respected the Builders Labourers! And for a builders labourer to say what buildings they're gonna build, and what buildings they're not gonna build, was never heard of! Bob Pringle was one who wasn't frightened of a fight! … I don't think anybody was! …And the bosses got the shits!

Joe: … And the trade unions in the right wing got the shits about it too!

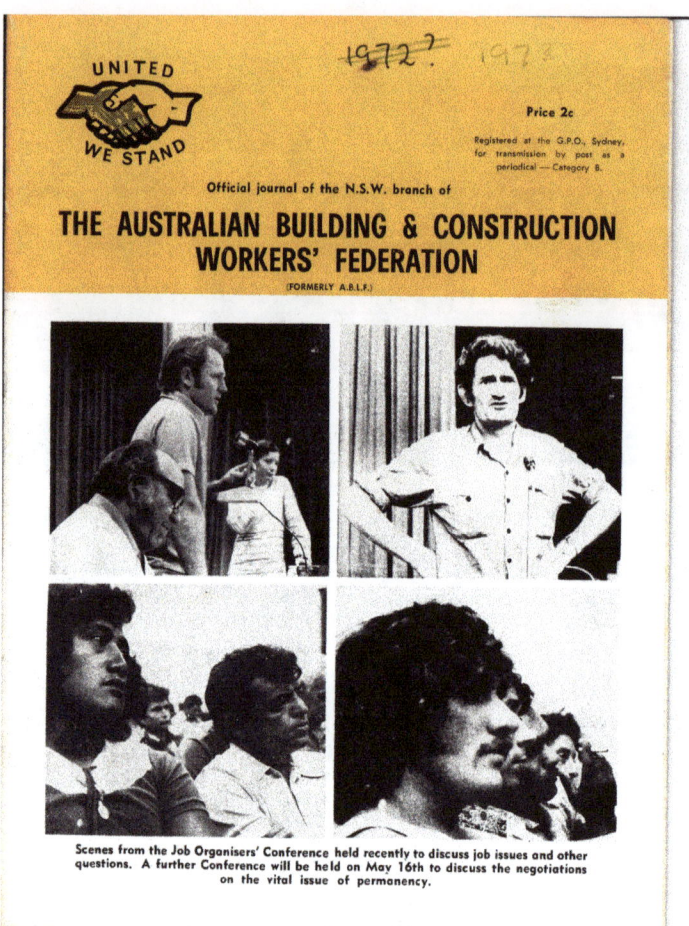

Figure 2.5: BLF Newsletter cover with Kevin Cook as organiser with Maori organiser beside him, 1973.

Courtesy Dr Meredith Burgmann.

Kevin: … And so did the developers. They just couldn't understand how much power we had! You know, take the dogmen. We'd say to them, 'We want this'. And they'd say 'No'… And we'd say, 'Okay, just wait till you've got a pour on! … We'll go home half way through it!' And see, if we did that, they'd have to let it set and then they have to jackhammer the concrete out of it once it sets… and then start all over again!

Meredith: That's actually a fairly traditional way that someone got to be an official in the BLF – by being militant on the site and then getting to know the officials and then being put on as an organiser…

2. Life and death on the job: The Builders Labourers' Federation — rank and file democracy, 1970 to 1975

Kevin: See as officials, we represented the rank and file. That's what we did, you know — we *were* part of the rank and file! And if there was any trouble on the site, well the dogmen had a lot of power, and we'd just say to the boss, 'If you don't do this, well we're going home, halfway through your concrete pour!'

Bobby Baker: Cookie and me both did the same sort of work, we were both dogmen. Kevin was working with Roy Bishop when I first bumped into him. We were working for a long time around the game before Kevin was organising, and there was all these issues that came all at the same time. See it was the tail end of the '60s, it was about money and conditions. The conditions ran into issues like safety and amenities, and then we got involved in Vietnam and then there was Apartheid, so we got involved in Apartheid. There was land rights issues and then there was issues of equal pay for women, so we got involved in equal pay for women and so it kept rolling on. Things like the green bans grew out of that attitude rather than anything else. And the attitude was, if there was something there to have a go about, well we should investigate it, and if it concerned workers, then it was our business. It wasn't to do so much with being in the Communist party. I mean, Bobby Pringle was in the Labor Party, other people weren't in anything. We seemed to think if it was an issue that a worker was involved with, then it was our business. If they were going to send workers off to war then it was our business. If there were black guys working on building sites, then it was our business what was happening there. One thing leads straight into something else.

Kevin: But the safety stuff had been hard to get up early on… when you think of all the guys that died on building sites, it must have been screaming out for something.

Bobby: Yeah it was eight dead in one year.

Kevin: That's when we decided that we wouldn't ride the hook any more.

Bobby: We had a meeting, Kevin was there and organisers like Tommy Hogan. And the bosses were saying to Tommy, 'What would you know?' Because Tommy was a brickies labourer see? So he said to me, 'You come in here, cause you know'. So he made me do it. Tommy's about six foot tall and about four foot across his shoulders, so he stood me up and said, 'You tell them', so I said, 'This is the way it is, you know there's guys getting killed'.

We said, 'Look, there's too much of that, so we're going to have one dogman up the top and one dogman down the bottom and you only ride them if you have to'. We got away with getting rid of the hook, but I wasn't all that popular down the pub.

Figure 2.6: Regent Street Redfern, injured builders labourer on job site, 1972.

Courtesy Dr Meredith Burgmann.

Kevin: Yeah, that was a lot better too. I know I nearly got killed, a couple of times on that York Street building. It was lucky I had this driver, Riley, he was a fantastic driver. But we had one time when we had about 40-foot lengths of timber and we were dropping them over the side. When we got to the right floor, there was a tray to drop the wood into. And you had to line the wood up first so you could tip it down see?

But the bell rope that I used to use to signal him had got caught in the timber and I didn't see it.

Well, when I pulled it to tell him to stop, there was nothing! And the wood hit the building, and the timber started spreading. It was about seven, eight stories up and you could see the ground through the timber. I would have went straight down with it. So I jumped out of the sling and ran down this timber, up there in the air and then I dived! Straight into the building!

I just went straight down to the pub!

2. Life and death on the job: The Builders Labourers' Federation — rank and file democracy, 1970 to 1975

Bobby: Yeah that's right, it was that sort of thing. I mean it was funny – if you didn't get hurt.

See the issues of safety were important. There was nothing there. The jobs had no amenities, no facilities, nothing: if you got hurt, bad luck, and if the ambulance didn't get there quick enough you know, you could bleed to death, even if you'd just done something really simple. So we had a long campaign to get a first aid officer on the job and, and that was a fairly heavy campaign. I mean it was simple things, like I want a tap. You're working with reinforcing steel or something and you're trying to do it, and you give yourself a gash with it. Well if you do a really bad job of yourself, there's no one there at least to put a bandage on it, or do something, hang on to you till the ambulance got there. So they were fairly long and hard campaigns. The idea I suppose from quite a lot of companies at the time was really that, you know builders labourers were cheap and you could get hundreds of them. They didn't stand there waiting for you to die, but they didn't show a lot of sympathy if anybody got hurt.

Kevin: It was like they thought: 'There's plenty more builders labourers! We'll just pick'em up…'. And they didn't like you going home when someone did get killed or injured either.

Bobby: No, they weren't happy about that! And if someone got killed, we'd go around to the job and you'd collect as much money as you could off the blokes, because compo took a while. You'd go to the boss and you'd say, 'The guys gave us 200, so we want you to give us 200', and mostly they'd give it to you, well, sometimes. Most of them would sign a cheque. One guy leaned against a hand rail on a building to push a load, and the hand rail went and he fell. He had six kids. So we went around, Kevin was one of the guys going around getting money, because his wife would have waited at least three months before she ever got anything at all.

The real problems with the building industry were those types of things, but when you solved those problems, other problems didn't look impossible. We didn't win them all. We tried to stop them putting up the monorail, and never won that! But you know, you'd just have a go!

Just like the conditions of the big jobs in the booming economy were new, the way decisions were made in the BLF was new. With so many rank and file workers as officials, and with such active contact between union office holders and jobsites, making decisions was always a matter of debate and discussion. Kevin took many lessons away with him about how working people built up confidence in their organisation.

Kevin: Well you'd talk to the workers first, and sometimes they'd say, 'Oh no, we're not gonna do that' and so you'd sit down and talk to them. The Manly job was like that. There were these tall buildings that meant a lot of work for builders labourers, but residents and people on the beach didn't like the shadows. A lot of the blokes on the site weren't long in the union... couple of them were Maori fellas. We had two or three meetings, and they said 'No'. Then they called another meeting... they called it themselves... and they brought in the tradesmen. They had meetings amongst themselves at lunchtimes and at different times and then they decided that they wanted to get some expert advice. So we took Colin James the architect up there.. and after they'd talked it out some more. In the end *they* made the decision that they were going to put this ban on! ... and the people from Manly were pretty okay about that! But the workers missed out on 12 months work.

Paul Torzillo: Was it tougher in the places where there were mostly migrant workers? Where they weren't speaking English easily?

Kevin: No. We had interpreters ... we had people translating ... Vini Perez was one ... and he interpreted meetings...

Joe: The BWIU did a bit of it ...but we did more!

We went round the concrete yards and those Italians come with us, to talk about the issues at the concrete yards. Them sort of blokes appreciated it. They reckoned, 'Well them blokes are doing a little bit for us, they want us to know what's going on. They don't want us to just stick our hands up and not know what did we vote for'.

Bobby Baker: You had to look at the historic thing I suppose: first off we got wages, then we got safety and conditions on jobs. I mean, there was nowhere to get changed on a job, you'd be working in the middle of Sydney, you'd get covered in crap and you went home like that. So those were the first issues, once you did those, you had some trust, the guys trusted you and we had mass meetings. We very rarely did any large issues without mass meetings, and because probably about 70 per cent of our membership were migrants we made an effort to get stuff written up in at least three or four languages and try and get interpreters to meetings. By putting the whole of the issue before workers, and then asking what they thought, they trusted us really. If we said, 'We think we should stop work in support of some people trying to keep a bit of bush on the harbour', there'd be muttering, even the office people were saying 'Bloody silver tails!', but the point is, it was the issue rather than the people. And so they support you, it was okay. And then we'd say, 'Okay we want a 24 hour stoppage over Apartheid in South Africa'. We'd explain what's happening there. We probably had more mass meetings than any other union in history. Kevin'd tell you, he went to plenty of them.

2. Life and death on the job: The Builders Labourers' Federation — rank and file democracy, 1970 to 1975

Kevin: But I've seen it where people wanted to put on bans where the workers on the job voted against it. They come to a mass meeting, put their claims to the mass meeting and I've sat beside a real good mate of mine, Roy Bishop, where we've voted differently, on the ban, and got up walked out, went to the pub and had a couple of beers together. You know it was that sort of thing, if you got beat at a meeting it was a political decision, you know, a political decision. So it didn't fracture the union in any way, which was really good. Some you won, some you lost.

The union was very democratic. It showed a lot of people, especially me, what could be done by very small amount of people if they all stuck fats. And those principles have carried on, all the way through to working with Aboriginal people in the early land rights campaign. When Gallagher's mob came in and used the federal union to take over NSW, not one person defected from that original BLF group and many more hundreds come on board. And they didn't get paid. They were just in it for the principle. That's why it never got defeated. They were a very strong, close knit group of people!

Joe: The other thing was, mate, you can look back on it as a bit of a golden age even though History can never repeat itself. But it was a time when people weren't *afraid* to tackle issues! In those years, we weren't afraid to tackle issues. And it was also a time when we were used to strikes. And we've never been a pattycake industry, you know we were hard! and it was a hard industry, so you weren't afraid to raise the issues.

And there was a great deal of trust, because while we got all the fame and fortune came to us because of the green bans, there was a fucking lot of hard industrial work went on down below you know, the fight for dirt money! You'd had to fight for height money! You'd had to fight to stop somebody getting sacked! We'd had to fight for all that sort of stuff, long before Super[annuation] ever came in.

So while the other stuff got all the prominence and publicity, the day to day stuff was the thing that they trusted you for. I'll never forget a bloke tellin' me that! It was after we went on strike for about four weeks to get the same margin of skill. This was in 1970 and if anybody'd asked me in 1968 would you ever hold the industry out for four weeks, I'd have said no, we couldn't! But we did then! We held it out. And there were very few scabbed on us.

Paul: Do you think being successful on those struggles round conditions and pay, that fact that you took the bosses on, do you think that helped you when you had to come to the social issues?

Kevin: You wouldn't have got the support if you didn't do that…

Making Change Happen

Joe: It's a bit like talking to a 60-year-old building worker and saying, 'Look mate, things've got to change' and him saying to you, 'Fuck, mate, We've done it like this for 60 years! ...You're old enough to know we rode the hook! What was fuckin' wrong with that?'

Fuck! Six blokes got killed in four months! Did people think we didn't think about it!

The old blokes don't want to listen to you... I was talking with these old scaffolders a few years ago and I said, 'Things had to get better than what they were...'. And one old bloke was heckling me all the time and I said, 'You and me worked on the fuckin' Commonwealth Offices, long before it became Chifley Tower, when that doggie went down. I was on the beam watching him go down, and I watched him hit a concrete fucking truck, his arm came off. And I come down and fuckin' spewed and *you* spewed with me!' And he said, 'Yeah I remember that Joe'.

Figure 2.7: Wall graffiti at Woolloomooloo – the BLs seen as the only protection for existing low-income residents against high rise apartment blocks.

Courtesy Dr Meredith Burgmann.

2. Life and death on the job: The Builders Labourers' Federation — rank and file democracy, 1970 to 1975

But they just want to tell you about the good old days! And I say there was fuck all good about the 'good old days'! Because it had to get better! Nothing ever happens easy does it?

The 1970s saw many university students taking up casual work as BLs, attracted by the militancy and the camaraderie in the NSW BLF. Paul Torzillo was one, working as a BL in his holidays from medical school. The 'worker-student' alliance was closest to reality at least for a while in the BLF. But the conditions were no better for middle class students like Paul than they were for everyone else in the industry.

Paul: It was important to remember just how dangerous the building industry was in those days. When I was a student in the '70s and working at the abattoirs, I have a vivid memory of going to a funeral service for that young bloke who was an organiser who fell off a building site and died in the '70s. You spoke at the service for him, Joe, about the building industry and how dangerous it was…

Joe: Yeah, that was Dave Shaw. He fell off scaffolding… his father came to see me about a month after. His family were well off. His father just came around and he knocked at the door, he said 'I'm Dave's father'. I'd seen him at the funeral, and I said, 'Oh yeah, come in…'. He'd lost his son and he just wanted to know what had happened, what was he like… And I said, 'I don't have to tell you any lies, mate, he was one of the fuckin greatest!'

Kevin: He was a nice bloke wasn't he.

Joe: …And a *good* bloke… he was a front liner! In that time, we were all on the front line… and that was what Dave was like. He was a nice, decent young bloke. I don't think he ever belonged to the building industry, cause he wasn't like us… well he wasn't a brawler!

Kevin: But he wouldn't take a backwards step either, he had a lot of guts…

There were some very different experiences for Koories working in a union like the BLF from those they might have had in other unions, and particularly the rural Australian Workers' Union (AWU) where many Aboriginal workers were in unions as shearers and rousabouts. The ethnic mix in the city unions was very different – the building industry particularly included many recently arrived migrants. And the lines of racial segregation were not so rigid in the city as they were in the bush, so the BLF took an important role in supporting many of the Aboriginal initiatives in the early 1970s.

Kevin: I think the Koories who'd been involved with the union found that racism's not only just Koories but it was blokes on the jobs. You know the bosses were callin' Italians 'wogs'... and that soon stopped! We sacked a couple of bosses, you know, got rid of the foremen, for doin' that!

Joe: Yeah, it was a big issue. I'll tell you how it worked... sections of the industry was based on your nationality. We only had half a dozen concrete yards. The biggest one was Martin and Gasparini who were all Italian. If you went into earthworks, it was all Greeks. Do you remember there used to be a pick up in Newtown... at six in the morning these big young Greek blokes'd be all there... the pick up [body hire] for casual labour was all on in those days...

And if you went into formwork, you had Yugoslavs. Cookie, do you remember the brawl on in St Martin's Tower, between the Yugoslavs and the Croatians? because that war was on then... But you got South Americans, Spanish ... they were all in form work. You got into steel fixing it was all the same...

When you got into rigging and scaffolding and dogging, you had mostly the home grown mob... blokes like me that went into that 'cause I was an ex-seaman and I knew about ropes. And that was one of the ways I learnt about racism. In my first week ever, when I was a young seaman, and I was in South Africa, I went to a bar with these Lascars, off a P&O boat. We went into a black bar... and the coppers beat ME up! This was back in the '50s. I was the wrong bloke in the wrong bar... they beat the living shit out of me! And I went back to the ship and... Well... these lascar blokes got me back to the ship! ... and I had a broken arm and collar bone and ... the old Bosun said to me 'What the fuckin' hell happened to you?' and I said, 'I got bashed by the coppers down at...' and he said, 'What were you doing drinking in the fuckin darkies bar?' And I said 'Well *you* never said anything to me!'

I was about 18. I'll never forget that! Beaten because I was in the blacks' bar!

Judy Chester: Usually its blacks beaten up 'cause they're in the white bar!

Joe: Oh well if you were black and you went into a white bar you got *killed*! I just got beaten up! They would have got killed!

Paul: With a lot of the membership born overseas you can't romanticise people's identification too much, you couldn't assume that they'd know much about Aborigines or be interested. It would have been a tough problem to deal with, explaining any sort of issues at all, let alone black ones. Did they think 'Oh well, fuck them, we're working hard', or did they identify, or was it a bit of a mixed bag?

Kevin: I think the bosses played right into our hands, because, on a building site, most of the bosses, whether they be foremen, leading hands, thought they were a cut above everybody else and they'd go along and say, 'Get out of here you wog bastards' and all of that, and the Builders Labourers' union got onto that, and started pulling the bosses up and in fact sacking the bosses for being racist.

So that built the migrant people up too, no longer could the boss come up and call an Italian a wog, in a detrimental way. He might say, 'Hey you wog bastard' if he was a mate of his, but on no account could he do that if he was angry or had the shits, he just couldn't do it, because he'd get the sack. That made it a lot easier when you were talking about black issues, it was a social issue the same as not calling migrants 'wogs' on the site. And the bosses done that a hell of a lot and the migrants got very, very angry.

Bobby Baker: Yeah, we certainly had Greeks and Italians and other people marching in the land rights marches. Kevin's right about that. They all saw themselves as downtrodden in some way, one way or another, they were called 'wogs' or whatever and they didn't like it, naturally! So if you said the black fellows are being pooped on, they says, 'Fine, I'll come along to help you'. So Cookie's right, but it was a very cliquey union, it truly was, but there was a lot of work put in, it doesn't happen just over night. We had interpreters at every meeting. I think we had some of our stuff put out in about five languages. We made it clear what we were on about, so if we wanted people to go to land rights marches, we didn't just say, 'Get along there!' We said, 'You're going there because this, this and this'. So when they went they knew what they were doing, they weren't just wandering along, waving things and not knowing what they were talking about.

Kevin: And we had a lot of migrant organisers through the years too, that helped a lot.

Paul: Cookie, later on you had lots of contacts with migrant groups. Did that start then, when you got those contacts in the BLs?

Kevin: Yeah, through the Builders Labourers. And especially the Greek Communist party, the Italian Communist party, FILEF,[5] Panucci's mob, the Italian Education mob… So that was all a lead up you know. When I went to Tranby I still had those contacts and so we brought them in on Tranby. And we had incredibly good communication with a lot of the migrant groups … and you can see in the 1988 march… where they put on a show to raise money for us… You should have seen how many different groups they had on!…

---

5   Federazione Italiana Lavoratori Emigrati e le Loro Famiglie.

Making Change Happen

Figure 2.8: As the BLF presence became more widely felt, the federal Builders Labourers' Union developed an alliance with the Master Builders' Association to intervene and take over the NSW Branch by supporting deregulation of the NSW Branch from the Arbitration System. The conflict led to bloodshed and violence on the job with both police and rival federal BLs targeting NSW Builders Labourers' activists. One result was Bob Pringle being bashed.

Courtesy Dr Meredith Burgmann.

2. Life and death on the job: The Builders Labourers' Federation — rank and file democracy, 1970 to 1975

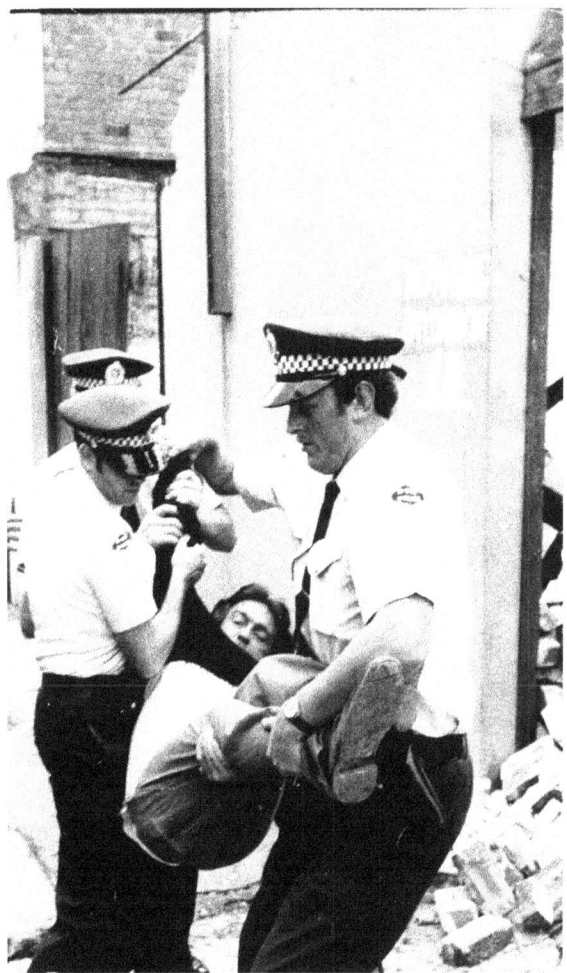

Figure 2.9: Another result of this conflict was Joe Owens being arrested.

Courtesy Dr Meredith Burgmann.

Kevin's time as a BL – and as an organiser – taught him many things, even beyond the many contacts he made with groups like the migrants. Some of these lessons reinforced what he had known from growing up in the Koorie community, like the importance of sharing and the value of face-to-face communication. Others came from these completely new industrial conditions on the city building sites in the 1970s. As distressing as struggles over trying to get living wages had always been in many industries, the dangerous life and death conditions faced by BLs everyday of the week created a deep bond of comradeship and loyalty which cemented everything Cookie knew about the advantages of acting together. 'Sticking fats' took on a whole new meaning when you had just seen someone fall from a load at the top of a building and be torn apart by the impact as they hit the footpath 20 storeys below. You knew you had to act together to get that changed. Just as important was the extraordinary experiment which the BLF had conducted in those brief years of rank-and-file control, with limited tenure of office, so union officials went back to the job when their term was finished. No other union was run like this, and it meant there was no gap between the leadership and the members of the union. For Cookie, it was another powerful lesson about how to organise to get things done – it was by leading from the grass roots. So these two lessons were ones which Kevin remembers in particular as the ones he carried with him into all his later work.

3. In the wider struggle: The union, gender, race and environment

The new ways to organise the union that the Builders Labourers developed to meet the new conditions they faced on the job were not the only thing they experimented with. One of the big changes the union made was to look *outwards*. The Builders Labourers' Federation began to see itself not just as a more powerful union in the building industry, but as a force in the society that was changing all around them in the 1970s. Unionists like Joe Owens, Bob Pringle and Jack Mundey believed the union had a responsibility to express their members' views about the environments that the building industry changed, but as well about the issues that affected all unions and citizens, like the work and conditions of women and the questions of war and peace, like the Vietnam conflict. The BLs argued that the struggle against the bosses was not isolated from the politics of the society they lived in – at work and at home.

One of the first things that the New South Wales BLF were able to introduce within the union which had an impact outside was that from mid 1971, the union actively opened up for women to join it and work on job sites in the suburbs and the city. This was often something that the previously all-male workers on some of the sites did not find easy, and the union was involved in the job site meetings where union members thrashed the issue out. Women often took part in militant struggles for better conditions and safety along with their fellow workers. Some of these women unionists were Aboriginal, like Wendy Stringer and her twin sister Robyn Williams, and they became close friends with Kevin. Wendy was involved in a bitter 18 week strike at Hoxton Park over demands that the poor conditions at the site warranted a site allowance. The company eventually settled the claim but demanded a new set of workers, although they were to be union members, including a woman.

As *Robyn Williams* remembers it: So, Crow Industries said, in the court, that they would have a replacement with another woman. So, guess what? Out I went. Guess what? They knew! They knew they'd been screwed, but not quite sure how. So, there I stayed. They had to accept me on that job! I stayed there until that job closed down. Then I went into the city and worked on a big one, Rawson Place. And later on there was a big strike on. It was just a very bloody fun time! We worked hard. We all drank hard!

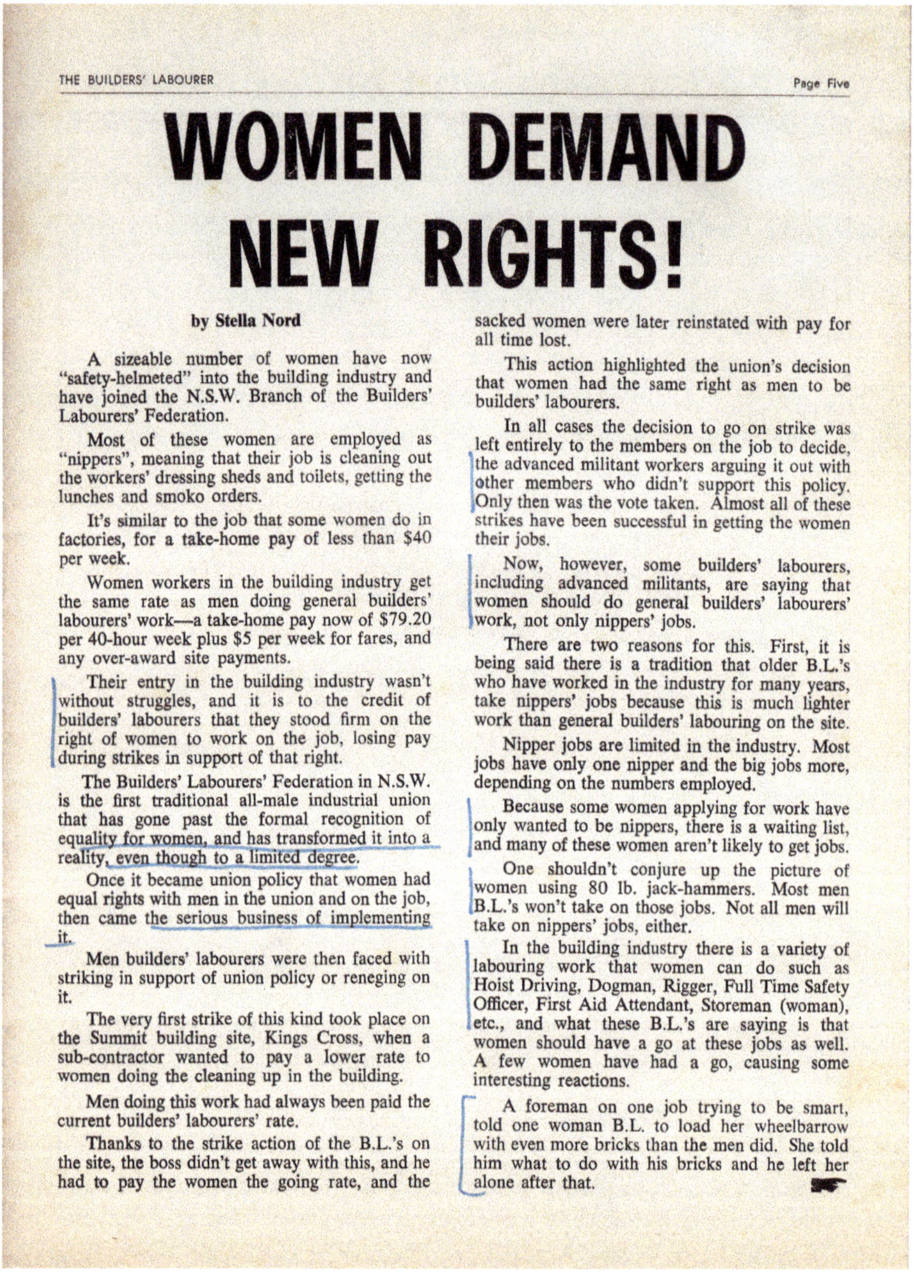

THE BUILDERS' LABOURER   Page Five

WOMEN DEMAND NEW RIGHTS!

by Stella Nord

A sizeable number of women have now "safety-helmeted" into the building industry and have joined the N.S.W. Branch of the Builders' Labourers' Federation.

Most of these women are employed as "nippers", meaning that their job is cleaning out the workers' dressing sheds and toilets, getting the lunches and smoko orders.

It's similar to the job that some women do in factories, for a take-home pay of less than $40 per week.

Women workers in the building industry get the same rate as men doing general builders' labourers' work—a take-home pay now of $79.20 per 40-hour week plus $5 per week for fares, and any over-award site payments.

Their entry in the building industry wasn't without struggles, and it is to the credit of builders' labourers that they stood firm on the right of women to work on the job, losing pay during strikes in support of that right.

The Builders' Labourers' Federation in N.S.W. is the first traditional all-male industrial union that has gone past the formal recognition of equality for women, and has transformed it into a reality, even though to a limited degree.

Once it became union policy that women had equal rights with men in the union and on the job, then came the serious business of implementing it.

Men builders' labourers were then faced with striking in support of union policy or reneging on it.

The very first strike of this kind took place on the Summit building site, Kings Cross, when a sub-contractor wanted to pay a lower rate to women doing the cleaning up in the building.

Men doing this work had always been paid the current builders' labourers' rate.

Thanks to the strike action of the B.L.'s on the site, the boss didn't get away with this, and he had to pay the women the going rate, and the sacked women were later reinstated with pay for all time lost.

This action highlighted the union's decision that women had the same right as men to be builders' labourers.

In all cases the decision to go on strike was left entirely to the members on the job to decide, the advanced militant workers arguing it out with other members who didn't support this policy. Only then was the vote taken. Almost all of these strikes have been successful in getting the women their jobs.

Now, however, some builders' labourers, including advanced militants, are saying that women should do general builders' labourers' work, not only nippers' jobs.

There are two reasons for this. First, it is being said there is a tradition that older B.L.'s who have worked in the industry for many years, take nippers' jobs because this is much lighter work than general builders' labouring on the site.

Nipper jobs are limited in the industry. Most jobs have only one nipper and the big jobs more, depending on the numbers employed.

Because some women applying for work have only wanted to be nippers, there is a waiting list, and many of these women aren't likely to get jobs.

One shouldn't conjure up the picture of women using 80 lb. jack-hammers. Most men B.L.'s won't take on those jobs. Not all men will take on nippers' jobs, either.

In the building industry there is a variety of labouring work that women can do such as Hoist Driving, Dogman, Rigger, Full Time Safety Officer, First Aid Attendant, Storeman (woman), etc., and what these B.L.'s are saying is that women should have a go at these jobs as well. A few women have had a go, causing some interesting reactions.

A foreman on one job trying to be smart, told one woman B.L. to load her wheelbarrow with even more bricks than the men did. She told him what to do with his bricks and he left her alone after that.

Figure 3.1: BLF Newsletter 1973 – 'Women demand new rights'.

Courtesy Dr Meredith Burgmann.

3. In the wider struggle: The union, gender, race and environment

Figure 3.2: Sekai Holland in anti-apartheid demonstration, copy of an ASIO surveillance photograph, hence the annotations.

Courtesy Dr Meredith Burgmann.

Another of the women who joined up to be a builders labourer was Sekai Holland, a Zimbabwean who was studying journalism in Sydney, where she had married an Australian, Jim Holland. Sekai became a key advocate in the anti-Apartheid struggles of 1971, addressing Builders Labourers' meetings on the demands by South African activists that Australia break off sporting ties with South Africa.

The Builders Labourers' Union became actively involved in the campaigns against the Springbok sporting tours.

Kevin learnt a great deal from Sekai and from meeting members of the South African exiles community in Sydney who were part of the protests against the sporting contacts. Union members took part in the demonstrations to disrupt the Rugby games and Bob Pringle was arrested and fined for trying to saw down the Sydney Cricket Ground's aluminium goal posts.

Figure 3.3: The South African government had stated that the Springbok jersey, symbol of the Apartheid nation, would never be worn by a non-European. Some Springbok jerseys were, however, smuggled to the opponents of the all-white South African football team's visit. This photo shows a defiant group of Aboriginal activists – Gary Foley (left), Billy Craigie and his sister, Lyn Thompson (pregnant with her daughter Yeena) – dressed in these smuggled Springbok jerseys at Lyn and Peter Thompson's home at Eberly Street Randwick, close to the Sydney Cricket Ground where the football games were held.

Courtesy Peter Thompson collection.

Kevin had come to know well many of the other members of the protests. Meredith Burgmann, a fellow member of the Australian Labor Party (ALP) with Kevin and one of the supporters of the BLF, played a high profile role as well in the games disruption.

Kevin also spent time with the group of young Aboriginal activists in Bondi and Redfern who had come to know Sekai well and who were prominent in the demands that racist sporting teams be rejected by the Australian public. Gary Foley, Gary Williams, Lyn Thompson and her husband Peter were to become people with whom Kevin was to build long term friendships as well as sharing many political campaigns over the coming years

Kevin's interest in the campaign against white South African Apartheid was framed by the continuing opposition to the Vietnam War. This opposition was shared among both BLF members and Aboriginal activists. The Vietnamese people's struggle to free themselves from the remains of French colonial control and then the newly imposed American imperialism struck a particular resonance for Aboriginal people, who saw themselves still suffering from their colonisation by the British and later by the Australian state. So national liberation struggles around the world held great interest for Aboriginal activists and this included the large newly-decolonised nations like China. The Australian Government had refused to recognise the People's Republic of China after its liberation in 1949 and this denial continued into the early 1970s.

Aboriginal activists (supported by unionists) took a leading role in breaking that barrier when they formed the first ever Australian delegation to the People's Republic of China in 1972. They were interested in the Chinese government position as an opponent of imperialism but also in the conditions and demands of the many national minorities within China, whose conditions of encapsulation as minorities within a powerful state could also be compared to those of Aboriginal people. Terry Widders, an Anewan man from Armidale and a student at Sydney University in linguistics and Chinese language, took part in the group and in later travel to Japan to learn more about indigenous minorities there.

The currents of emerging Aboriginal and union politics continued to intersect in Kevin's life. This was nowhere more evident than in the Builders Labourers' Federation involvement with the booming building developments planned for Redfern. This was the suburb in inner city Sydney where Aboriginal people had been settling in large numbers from the 1950s as they left rural areas to escape racism and to look for better work and education opportunities in the city. The target of the developers was an area covering two streets of derelict houses, known as 'The Block', near Redfern Railway Station. These shells of houses sheltered many homeless Aboriginal people, particularly *goomies*, the term used in Aboriginal English for people addicted to methylated spirits. The building boom which was bringing so many builders labourers together in the city was also displacing working class people, low income families and the Aboriginal residents of suburbs like Redfern. The pressure to make Aboriginal people move out of the inner city, to make way for development, was felt both in the streets and in the rising numbers of demolitions of old houses. This is where the BLF had a direct stake because they were the labourers who were being called on to knock down Aboriginal people's houses.

Figure 3.4: Another development was the emergence of the shopfront Aboriginal Legal Service, in which Gary Williams and Lyn Thompson participated.

Courtesy Gary Foley Collection.

The sale of the Block to developers for offices or apartments would not only take the shelter of homeless people but it would remove the potential for decent, low cost housing to be built and offered to Aboriginal residents. The BLF members banned any demolition or construction work on the site which effectively ended the plans to purchase it for development. In response, in a landmark decision, the incoming ALP federal government funded the purchase of the Block by an Aboriginal-controlled corporation, the Aboriginal Housing Company.

Joe: The BLs said they wouldn't demolish the Block cause Aborigines were living on it. Then when the (federal) money went into Redfern – that really boomed up some Aboriginal things about blacks. That Housing Company – they wanted to do all that building!

THE BUILDERS' LABOURER   Page Thirty-three

BL's back Aborigine housing scheme

This story on an Aboriginal Community Housing Scheme is taken from the Communist Party weekly, the Tribune.
The story was written by Denis Freney.

* *

Sydney branch president, Bob Pringle, commenting on the project said that in the past builders' labourers had often been accused of blocking progress when they placed black bans on certain jobs.

"Developers and their champion, Premier Askin, have been vitriolic in their attacks on us.

"We are waiting to hear what they have to say about our building programme for the Aboriginals," he said.

The Redfern (Sydney) Aboriginal Community Housing Scheme may well become a hallmark not only for the Black community (especially in towns and cities), but for urban planning as a whole.

The scheme will cover 65 houses in the block bounded by Louis, Caroline, Eveleigh and Vine Streets, Redfern.

The back fences of most of the houses will be pulled down and the laneway torn up to create a lawn-covered recreation area. There are two factories in the block. One will be converted into a hall-workshop-gym and cultural centre, while the other will house a pre-school which will be run by Aboriginal mothers in the community with trained help, and a medical centre linked with the Aboriginal Medical Service, with fulltime nursing staff and a detoxication unit, to help alcoholics overcome their addiction.

Bob Pringle

The corner store will become a co-operative shop, selling food at cheap prices.

The whole project will be managed by an elected co-operative committee. Low rental will be charged on the accommodation provided, to repay the promised Federal Government loan (not grant).

One of the major difficulties the community will face will be the chronic unemployment and job discrimination suffered by Aborigines. Already, however, 10 young Blacks are working as builders' labourers on the reconstruction work. It is hoped to employ many other young Blacks on the work (at present only seven houses are being renovated), and that they will get steady jobs in the industry, and also learn skills, both on job, and also in a job and crafts training centre to be established in the block.

Good housing; steady, well-paid employment; a growing pride in the community and in Aboriginal culture and traditions; a well-fed and medically cared-for community: those are the goals of the Redfern Aboriginal Community.

The Redfern Aboriginal Housing Project developed out of the struggle and dedication of some Black militants and their White supporters.

It is difficult to know where to begin the story.

Perhaps it is best to start in 1971, when the Aboriginal Legal Service was getting off the ground, largely as a response to the police harassment of Aborigines in Redfern and other inner-city suburbs.

The rural depression had resulted in something of a mass exodus of Aborigines to Sydney — and particularly to Redfern.

Some Redfern police had been notorious for their random discrimination in arresting Aborigines just before and just after 10 p.m., particularly on Friday and Saturday nights. Many believe this was done simply to build up the police tally — in an easy collection.

Figure 3.5: BLF newsletter 1973 – 'BLs back Aborigine housing scheme'.

Courtesy Dr Meredith Burgmann.

Kevin: Bob Bellear was involved in all that. I went down to see Jim Cavanagh … he was the new Labor minister once Whitlam got in, in '72. Cavanagh was a South Australian senator and he'd been a BWIU[1] union official. We went down there and he was the one who bought the Block, he was the one who give them the money to buy the Block, and Pringle played a very good role in that! But also Jack Mundey and you, Joe, because you were principals in the union. Without your say-so, he couldn't do anything…

Joe: But Bob Pringle was the frontline bloke in those Aboriginal issues… oh we might have been part of it but I'll tell you what mate …I knew Pringle for all up 30 years… 'cause I knew him when we were rank and filers …If you tried to buck Pringle, she was a hard fight that one! He brawled! The other thing too was there was a lot of tension in Bobby too towards the end because he'd had a terrible accident in the '60s up in Moree. He was working on a steel job and he fell. … He came back after all that injury and a lot of that come back was because of that willpower he had! That was part of Bobby's politics, he was such a stubborn fella, if he got the idea in his head, you wouldn't shift him! You had to accommodate it in some way!

Kevin: But he was good when he was working with the Aboriginal groups too, because he'd never put up anything. He'd always listen to what they were saying, and he'd back 'em up. And he'd come back to the union, and he'd say 'This is what they want!' You know he didn't say, 'This is what I want' or 'This is what I told them' or anything like that. He was good like that… and he said to me, 'Now you're here, *you* look after them!' But you know, I always sat down and talked to him all the time. He was an inspiration wasn't he?

Joe: He was! And he was the only white who was on the Black Caucus for the Tent Embassy. 'Cause we went down there and some of us were moving in when there was a lot of wrestling going on. And he said, 'Keep out. Keep out of it! Let them do it. They've gotta do it!' And he just told us to keep out of it, they've gotta fight for themselves. You know I'll tell you one thing about Pringle… *he* was the first bloke who brought the green bans on. It was over Kelly's Bush, but when it came up to the Executive, I thought what the fuck's he on about? This is about blue rinse fucking middle class sheilas who are out at Kelly's Bush? What's that got to do with us? 'Cause I went out to see it, and there was a bloke called Bobby Lavender from the FEDFA[2] who was there with Bob Pringle, and I'm lookin around and I'm thinking, 'It's a nice fuckin' place … but what am I doing here?' I could understand the Rocks, but I couldn't understand Kelly's Bush! And Jack went along with it, and Jack became the figurehead for it and

---

1 Building Workers' Industrial Union.
2 The Federated Engine Drivers and Firemen's Association.

justifiably so, because Jack articulated it so well, but Pringle was the bloke who brought it into the union. And that's the thing that's not known much, and he never ever said it afterwards!

Kevin: Everyone in the union knew it!

The Builders Labourers' Federation had been involved in supporting Aboriginal campaigns by displaying flags and signs in highly visible places on city building sites and by attending demonstrations. Kevin's friend Roy Bishop was one who was in a series of conflicts with his bosses because he kept putting up a huge Aboriginal flag (then only newly designed) on a crane on a tall city site in 1971, to advertise the coming demonstrations in support of Aboriginal land rights. The march was called Ningla-Ana which was said to mean 'Hungry for our Land' in the Pitjantjara language from Central Australia.

Kevin: The Aboriginal Housing Company got started in Redfern when the coppers come down and tried to evict people in these old places on Eveleigh Street. They were squatters, some of them were *goomies* and homeless people who had nowhere else to go. The coppers were trying to get them out cause the developers wanted to have them vacant so they could pull the whole block down. Bob Bellear had been a seaman, but he was studying law by then, and he got involved in it. Then so did Paul Coe, another Aboriginal law student at the time and they brought the new Legal Service… They were younger Koories who wanted better legal rights for people in Redfern. So they stopped the coppers from evicting the tenants, and then they got the unions involved to stop the demolitions. Then they got a group of people to go down to talk to the federal minister, Cavanagh, in the new Whitlam Government and he said yeah, he'd buy it!

Kevin – as the only Aboriginal organiser – was automatically given the 'Aboriginal Portfolio', so he worked with Pringle and the Redfern activists like Bob Bellear and others to support their call for funds from the federal government. More directly, he then worked with the community to set up the Housing Company under local Aboriginal control and employing many black workers. And as a Builders Labourer, Kevin ensured that the Housing Company from the very start offered decent conditions and wages, which was what the union had been fighting for. So Kevin was invited onto the Board of the Housing Company. He had the job of liaising between the Aboriginal Housing Company and the BLF and with other unions in the building industry, like the BWIU and the FEDFA.[3]

---

3   Bob Bellear's account of this important process is in his book: Robert W Bellear (ed) 1976, *Black Housing Book*, Amber Press, Sydney. Extracts from it can be found at the Redfern Oral History site, <http://redfernoralhistory.org/OralHistory/BobBellear/tabid/150/Default.aspx> as can Kaye Bellear's account of the establishment of the Housing Company and the broader Redfern politics of the day, <http://redfernoralhistory.org/OralHistory/KayeBellear/tabid/165/Default.aspx> accessed 10 January 2013.

Making Change Happen

Figure 3.6: Aboriginal BLs on Redfern Aboriginal Housing Company site.

Courtesy Oral History of Redfern website.

Joe: The Left in the federal Labor Party in those days had much more influence that it ever has now. You had Jim Cairns and Tom Uren… Cavanaugh was a bit of a slow boat to China but he was *there* when it all came about! And there was a young bloke from South Australia, Peter Duncan, helping him.

Paul: I was around Redfern a lot in the early '70s. I was a medical student then and I was volunteering for the new Aboriginal Medical Service. I'd used to go round the area on Thursday nights with Lyn Thompson who was a field officer then. The Empress pub was such a focus for everyone… it seemed to be where the police versus the community battles all got fought out. Every night at ten o'clock the coppers'd come down and just pick people up in the streets. I've got a vivid memory of young blokes outside the pub at ten o'clock, you know 15 or 16, and they would have all been sparring to get ready and then they'd take the coppers on! They'd been dancing around in the streets, practicing their shots… you know they'd all get busted, but they'd have taken the coppers on… and you know they'd all be busted but they'd all have five minutes of taking the coppers on! And then everyone would go up to that Redfern police station … Kaye Bellear was there and Bob, and they used to have these students… and like even Abschol, like Eric Wilson, you know I'd see him there when I was there on a Thursday night, and that group of Christians, like Carla Cranny, who hung around with Ted Kennedy and Dick Buchhorn and those people and they'd be there... There was a lot of activity... And I remember Pringle was there a lot along with those young black activists like Billy Craigie and Bob Bellear.

Kevin: Yeah, that was happening at the same time as the housing company... We'd go to a meeting in Redfern, on something like South Africa, and they often asked people to go back to the Empress. It was on a Friday night... And as you walked out of there, if you were black the coppers'd just throw you in the van whether you were drunk or not ... See they had to get a quota! And they got their quota alright!

Bobby: It's interesting you say that because my recollection of that period of issues around the apartheid stuff, but particularly Eveleigh Street and the Housing Company, is that in fact, most of the work was the back room stuff. To his credit, Pringle was very careful, about putting in a lot of yakka but not getting up at a meeting and instructing what the strategy will be. And like you say, Kevin, about the BLs when we did the tents and things for the Tent Embassy that was that as far as we were concerned. Kevin came in – or anybody else came in – and asked us, we'd supply, but we wouldn't direct. It wasn't our business, it wasn't whitefellas' business. It was blacks' business. So if they wanted a hand we'd give them a hand, but we didn't tell anybody what to do.

The Housing Company allowed real spaces not just for the people who were down and out and squatting and needed low cost housing. It also made real spaces for people to take part in the cultural revival that was going on among the Aboriginal community in the early 1970s and for black and white activists to share experiences and build networks.

Kevin: When the Block was first set up it was for itinerant people, to save their money, then go out and get mainstream accommodation and that did happen a bit. But then, you know, people love living in that area so they started to stay.

Meredith: I was thinking about the building though. I was just realising how much influence the BLs must have had on the way the actual building process got set up, the renovation process.

Kevin: No, no, I didn't have that at all, it happened within the Aboriginal community, yeah. That was one of the things that Pringle was really good on, allowing that process to happen. He always used to say people have got to have the right to be wrong, that was one of his sayings. Really, he probably was the best person to be involved from the union. 'Cause he was less sort of bossy than Jack and Joe.

Figure 3.7: Tent Embassy erected, Canberra.

Courtesy Peter Thompson Collection.

And Pringle knew all the people there too, that was the other thing, he knew Bob Bellear and he knew most of the others, you know, Coe and all of that, through other things. So he was very good. I was there three months as an organiser with him and then I took over the Aboriginal portfolio from Bob. But you know I used to always sit there and talk to him about it because he knew the place a lot better than I did. Then I've got mixed up with Black Theatre, and that was with Betty Fisher, that was really good.

Black Theatre was another arena in which Kevin's union involvement intersected with his growing involvement with activist Aboriginal politics. He was drawn into the newly developing theatre group – in which Aboriginal people challenged white Australian cultural dominance in a series of innovative and adventurous plays and street theatre performances. Cookie got involved partly because his friends among the BLF, like Tom Hogan, had a close friendship with the Aboriginal jazz singer, Betty Fisher, and she became Black Theatre's director. Then the theatre company needed space, and so once more the BLF defence of Aboriginal people's right to space in Redfern was an important support as the new group fought to find a place in Redfern to rehearse and perform. But in this group Kevin met new people again – like the established actors Bob Maza, Justine Saunders and Zac Martin, and the committed activist Lester Bostock, from the North Coast of NSW, who had been first studying and then teaching at Tranby Co-operative College in Glebe. Black Theatre produced and circulated many memorable plays, television and filmic productions in the early 1970s. Yet, although it was less publicised, a critically important role played by Black Theatre was as a meeting place, in which actors, political activists, unionists and filmmakers could meet, socialise and plan projects. This was a time when there were few meeting places in Redfern other than pubs so having an alcohol-free and relaxed space to meet in was rare and, for many people, it was very welcome.[4]

Meredith: I can remember going to so many things at Black Theatre, it was really vibrant. Cookie, you used to get me down there. Although mind you, Betty Fisher terrified me: she didn't take too well to white fellas! But there were some great plays on there. Like the one with Bryan Brown in it, *Here Comes the Nigger* – written by Gerry Bostok – where Bryan Brown played the shit – he was the red-necked brother. It was the first time I'd ever seen Bryan Brown act and it was one of the most gripping performances I've ever seen.

Kevin: I thought the best actor there – the best non-Aboriginal actor – was Max Cullen. He was incredible, he was a copper in one, you know they had about seven or eight different parts, but he was a copper in one act. And I come in late or I'd gone out and come back, and there he was backstage, he and his mate were slapping each other across the face you know and psyching themselves up for the part.

Meredith: That's what Bryan Brown was doing too in the play and then what shocked me was at the end, when it was all over, all the Koories came down and just had a beer with him and a chat! I said, 'How can you do that when he was so horrible?' It was real method acting the whole play, well it was early '70s, that's when it was all really happening…

Kevin: With that Max Cullen, too, you could see the hate in him and next minute he'd go out and come back in and he'd have another part and everybody liked him. But I reckon he was a fantastic actor.

Meredith: And I saw *The Cake Man* too, 'cause you used to make certain I was dragged along to everything. But the other important thing about Black Theatre was it was a really important social meeting place at the time. I reckon, I think a lot of informal political activity went on there, and because of the sort of welcoming way in which Cookie ran it and you know once you got past Betty Fisher, there was this sort of relaxed atmosphere.

---

4   ADB Online: Anna Cole and Wendy Lewis 1996, 'Bettie Fisher (c.1939 - 1976)', *Australian Dictionary of Biography*, vol 14, MUP: 170-171. ABC Messagestick, 'Best Foot Forward' interview with Lester Bostock and Gerry Bostock, 30 May 2004, *Redfern Oral History*, <http://redfernoralhistory.org/Enterprises/BlackTheatre> accessed 10 January 2013.

Kevin: She was an incredible person. Betty was a great singer, and probably one of the best Aboriginal actors. And Justine Saunders and all of those people were there too. Then they formed the Redfern group. One or two people from each of the organisations met once a month to discuss what was happening, both in Redfern and outside. And that was a good political rallying place and we had a lot of support, from the people that visited Black Theatre. Like when we painted Black Theatre out completely ourselves. The people who came and helped us were all the builders labourers, architects, like Colin James and his students and all the people who worked with Black Theatre. They painted it out and then they got the Aboriginal Dance Group there too – they gave them space when they had no space. So there was a hive of activity there you know.

Meredith: Yeah, I know. That's what I mean, it was a totally social place. If you went there, there was always something going on. And then there was the great wedding of the year, remember when Tom Hogan married Betty Fisher and all the builders labourers were there. We had a bit of an argument about who had behaved the worst, the builders labourers or the Koories. The builders labourers won.

Kevin: That was a funny night, I've never laughed so much in all my life. I never had a drink that night.

Meredith: True? Why not?

Kevin: I just watched.

Meredith: You got drunk on atmosphere!

***

The NSW BLF was destroyed in 1975.

Employers like the Master Builders' Association (MBA) had been forced to make many concessions to the NSW BLF when it had demanded safety for workers and for environmentally responsible buildings. So the MBA struck a deal with the federal Builders Labourers, a body based in Melbourne, which had been deregistered because of financial and political difficulties. The federal Builders Labourers agreed to take over the NSW branch of the union in exchange for employer support from the MBA for the registration of the federal union. The NSW branch executive, lead by Bobby Pringle, decided to fight it out in the courts, but the court cases went against them. Despite widespread members' support for the NSW branch leadership within the union, the federal union took over, denied union tickets to the NSW leadership and this left all the key activists out of a job. Kevin's involvement with the Aboriginal community in Redfern as well as in his own area meant he had ways to use his union experience and networks in a new way. But he found there were real differences in being a Tranby advocate who negotiated widely across the whole labour movement compared to his old role as a union organiser within one union.

Kevin: No, it couldn't go on forever, they wouldn't have allowed it... I was really lucky, because while I was working as a Builders Labourer, I was also involved in the Aboriginal issues. But there was a number of people in the Builders Labourers who lived day and night just for being in the Builders Labourers: outside of that, they didn't have anything. They'd watched it go from being a shit job to something you could be proud of. So it hurt them when Gallagher's mob took over and forced them out. You did feel a little bit of the oxygen went out of you. It was fantastic to belong to the Builders Labourers, especially as an organiser. I thought it was anyway, and I think a lot of other people did too: people who were on the executive, people who were the rank and filers, they felt great! It could kill people if that's all they had, they never recovered. But a lot of people went onto other things. They had to – because they had to work. You couldn't get a job in the building industry.

Bobby: They tore all our union tickets up and because there was a no ticket, no start, it suited the bosses. Obviously we weren't their favourite people anyway, so they didn't care. I was in a pub once and Gallagher offered me a ticket but I said, 'Stick it up your bum', and he said, 'Oh, morals, you can't eat morals'. Basically I suppose there were about 20 of us that they barred completely, wouldn't let us anywhere near a building site. And Kevin's right, he had somewhere to go, he had something to lock himself into. I went and started working on the maritime and finished up in the big shit fight with the AWU. Other people just sat down and put their hands in the air and didn't know what to do with themselves.

And of course, I used to spend a bit of time over at Tranby, annoying them!

***

As this last conversation between Kevin and Bobby Baker suggests, the end of the NSW Builders Labourers' Federation was a disaster for some people in which they were excluded from the work they knew and from the new form of the union, leaving them little in their lives. But many people tried to pick up the pieces and make new lives for themselves. For all of them, they brought with them many valuable experiences from the NSW Builders Labourers which never left them. And for Cookie, these experiences were to give him resources to build a new – and even wider – set of networks.

4. Tranby, co-operatives and empowerment

The first time Kevin heard about Tranby College was when he was still a builders labourer and met the Reverend Alf Clint. Alf had enjoyed strong union support over many years. When Kevin met him, Alf was continuing to get on a lot better with unionists and communists than he did with the church hierarchy!

As *Kevin* tells the story: Yeah, old Alf Clint wrote a letter to the union about getting some finances for Tranby College,[1] and I think it was Pringle said 'Ring Kevin, he'll deal with it!' So he come in to see me and we had a strike on so I said look, 'I'll have to make it tomorrow', you know, I apologised to him. And he said, 'What milk bar will I meet you at?' and I said 'To be quite truthful, I don't know a milk bar'. And he said, 'What about the Sussex Hotel?' and I said 'I know that'. So I went up there and I was shouting him, I shouted him all afternoon! I thought it was a couple of beers and off he'd go after our meeting. But no he stayed there all night! And he knew more of the Builders Labourers than I did! And so we got to talking, he needed money for the college, and so I went to the executive and we got some money for him. So then I went over and seen the place at Tranby to see what he'd done. And after a while I got onto the Board of Directors.

There were other things too. Dexter Daniels come down from Darwin and they were fighting that land rights fight up there. And so the union got behind that. There was a lot of behind the scenes things, you know, like raising money for the food and to take people down to the Tent Embassy in Canberra in 1972. That was all raised through some of the unions.

We used to go to meetings together after that, Alf and me, and I said 'Why aren't you wearing your collar? We'll get more money if you wear the collar'. I learned a lot about him then when I was going to those meetings with him. He was a funny guy. He'd started off working in a co-op store in Balmain in the 1920s or so. He heard Bishop Bergmann[2] preach, and he started talking to him and he ended up being a Bush Brother. But he said to the church, 'Before I join up, there's one thing I have to ask of you. I want to hold my ALP ticket and my AWU union ticket'. And they allowed that. So he went up and he used to preach at the mines around Lithgow and Portland.

---

1 Alf had been supported by the church to set up co-operatives for community development and economic advancement in Papua New Guinea and later in northern Australia. He worked predominantly in Australia with Aboriginal communities, establishing cooperatives not only in Queensland but in the northern rivers area of New South Wales. In 1957 he established a co-operative training centre for Aboriginal co-operative members in Tranby, a Glebe house donated to the Anglican Church for this purpose by the family of Justice Robert Hope, who remained an active member of the Tranby Board of Directors, and whom Kevin was to consult frequently, see Chapter 5.

2 Bishop Ernest Bergmann (1885-1967) was the High Anglican Bishop of Goulburn, and was known as the Red Bishop because of his strong social justice sympathies. He was the grandfather of Kevin's close friend and political ally, Meredith Burgmann.

Figure 4.1: Aboriginal Australian Fellowship May Day float.

Courtesy Tranby Archives.

Joe Owens knew Alf well in the union: Yeah, I remember those stories about Alf too. Let me put it this way, the Moscow wing of the Communist party thought the sun shone out of Alf's arse, cause Alf was very keen on the Soviet Union. That was one thing we had to keep away from when we were talking with Alf, us blokes like me and Mundey, cause you'd cop a mouthful off him![3] … I never forget a yarn with the ex-leader of the Miners, who was telling me that the Miners' Federation supported Alf no end. Alf was shifted to some parish up in the coal fields where they were gonna give him the arse cause he hadn't enough customers! The old bishops down here were lookin' to get rid of him. So all these left-wing miners went to church every fucking day and night, singing fucking hymns! Half of the bastards were communists! singing hymns! And the place was packed!! And they were all coming up … fuck me dead! They're getting more here than they're gettin' in the Anglican Cathedral! But it was humourous! And when it was all over they'd go out with Alf and they'd all get on the piss! …

Kevin: That's what he told me too, he used to have church on Sundays and then Lenin meetings on Sunday night!

Joe: When that big strike was on, when that miner got killed at Rothbury … that was way back in the mists of time, Alf was there! That old Miners' Union bloke said 'Clint was there you know, he was very young, when the coppers shot the miner'.

---

3   Alf remained in sympathy with the Moscow-affiliated Socialist Party of Australia, which broke away from the Communist Party of Australia, to which Joe and Jack Mundey belonged.

Kevin: Yeah, he never backed down, Alf!

Joe: Alf was a hard bloke to knock back for support… Alf could drink with the best of them! Fuck me, didn't he'd get on the piss! But he was a hard bloke to knock back!!

Kevin: Bill Knott was around that mining area too, he was in the Electricians' union, the only communist and this was when they *hated* communists! Bill was a union rep, he even ran for parliament as a communist, out there. He's another funny bloke. But Alf could walk that thin line between all the unions, whether it was the AWU, the BLF or the BWIU. He had a good rapport with the Seamen's Union too, especially with Eliot V Elliott.

In 1975, after the union battles, Kevin took some time away from the city. But Alf Clint hadn't forgotten him.

Kevin: After Gallagher come in and destroyed the New South Wales Builders Labourers' Federation, I went home and went fishing at Lake Illawarra with my uncle. We were professional fishing and I was down there for about four months, on the prawns. We didn't make any money, but we had a good time. I know you might say we drank all the profits, but you couldn't drink when you'd go out on the boat. Too dangerous! I learnt all about the prawns, about fishing and Stan taught me how to row.

So I was working down in Wollongong fishing and Bill Knot, Margaret's uncle, who was a mate of Alf's, came around to my place at Berkeley and said, 'Alf wants to see you up in Sydney'. So I come back up.

Alf said he wanted me to be a student and to work! I said that was alright. But then Alf said he couldn't pay me anything. I said, 'Look, I'm just fishing for fucking nothing, I'd might as well come up!'

So I was going to spend about three days a week in class. Now the third day I was there, Alf came up to me and said, 'Would you unlock tomorrow morning? I have to go away', I said 'Yeah'. So he give me this big bunch of keys and I unlocked the next day.

Then I came to class the morning *after* and everyone's standing outside. I said, 'What's the matter?' 'Keys!', they said. Now, I still had the keys, I'd taken them home. I thought Alf would have another set. But Alf wasn't there!

Alf rang up the next day and said, 'I'm in Cairns – I want you to look after the place until I get back'. And that was it! He was gone two weeks!

Kevin's move to Tranby surprised many of his friends. City-based students and activists like me knew that co-operatives had originated in radical workers organisations in the 19th century, but we thought that today, co-operatives were mainly associated with church charities, or very individualised credit unions, or big commercial bodies for rural producers like the Dairy Farmers' Co-operative. We didn't know much about the community co-operatives Alf had helped set up in Papua New Guinea, the Torres Strait Islands or Queensland, all run by local people to fight racism and discrimination in employment. And we didn't know anything about the international network that Alf had connected Tranby to, which had started up as a fishworkers co-operative in Antigonish on the west coast of Canada. This had blossomed into Coady International Institute which had supported co-operatives in India, Africa and Latin America. The co-operatives in India were often run by indigenous people, known as *Adivasi*, or by economically-marginalised low caste or untouchable groups. In South Africa, co-operatives had been one of the only political organisations that were legal for Africans living under Apartheid. And in Latin America, this co-operative movement had pioneered 'liberation theology' and 'action research' where local people made all the decisions. But we didn't know any of that, so we didn't understand at all why Kevin would have wanted to get involved, except that he had known Alf for a while through the union and this was a steady job for a while.

But Alf had seen something in Cookie that he really wanted for Tranby.

Joe Owens talked with Cookie about this: Now I'm not pissin' in your pocket, Kevin, but you knew how to organise! That was the thing – Cookie knew how to organise! And Alf wanted that! He realised for that place to grow that he needed to get people in to organise so he went looking! And Cookie did it for 'im! You knew how to do it, Kevin, you brought in all your experience from the union!

And that was the way it worked! Kevin did use the union contacts that he already had to shape what he could do at Tranby. He drew on the people he knew from the BLF who were good communicators to teach the students about organising and industrial law. And he expanded his own union training, enrolling in a class at TUTA, the Trade Union Training Authority, when it opened its doors at Albury in 1977. There he met Serge Serino, a union organiser in the FEDFA[4] and found they shared a lot of interests, as well as sparking Kevin's warm memories of the Italian kids he had known at Wollongong and the Italians he had worked with in the BLF. Serge was another one who came to teach at Tranby, and introduced Cookie to his friend and fellow political activist, Frank Panucci, a trade union researcher working at the same time in Italian-Australian cultural and political organisations. In this way, Kevin built up wide ranging networks which all brought an extraordinary set of innovative and enthusiastic teachers into Tranby's classrooms.

But he found that although he could build on his trade union background, he had to change the way he approached people now that he was an advocate for

---

4 The Federated Engine Drivers and Firemen's Association.

Tranby to the whole union movement. Unionists treated him differently because now he was no longer representing just the BLF but was representing Tranby. So Cookie had to build relationships with right-wing as well as left-wing unionists, in a way that had never been needed before.

But whatever political position his allies took, Kevin was always interested in them as people. He called on the doctor, Paul Torzillo, for example to come with him when he went on Tranby business to see Pat Clancy, the Federal Secretary of the BWIU[5] and aligned with the Moscow-affiliated Socialist Party of Australia (SPA). Paul was on the Board at Tranby by then, but he still wasn't quite sure what Cookie wanted him to do in this meeting with Pat Clancy. It turned out Kevin wanted Paul there in case Clancy talked about his heart problems and his eyesight – he was worried that Pat Clancy would not go to see a doctor otherwise.

As *Kevin* recalls it: Yeah, I took Paul along because I knew Clancy was sick, and I wanted to give him the chance to ask Paul any extra advice that he might have needed. Pat Clancy was another one who was always good with Tranby. He supported us because he'd been close friends with Alf. And I had no troubles either, you know, with other people like with Tom McDonald or Stan Sharkey in the BWIU, even though we might have taken very different positions in the unions. Stan Sharkey was the main instigator in setting up the National Aboriginal Trade Union body, TUCAR.

Bobby Baker, from the BLF, thought it was Tranby that brought very disparate unionists together: You shouldn't have had any trouble anyway with any of that mob Cookie. They all had differences of opinion about which line of the Communist party you happened to be following, but on issues like Tranby or issues like the land rights, there were no real differences of opinion really.

Kevin agreed: Even when we set up the Black Defence Group, there were a couple of trade unionists that helped out, like Meredith Burgmann from the Academics Union and Rod Pickette from the ATEA [Australian Theatrical and Amusement Employees Association]. Also, it helped no end when we sat down and talked with a couple of key people about setting up what was the best way of doing it, who to get involved. As soon as we started it up it just clicked. We got a lot of gains through that and that was through the association with the Builders Labourers. But once you left the union, it was a fine line you had to walk between the unions that you were directly involved in, who'd been supportive when you were a builders labourer, and the other unions. You couldn't be seen as part of one camp and that was very hard, but we managed that pretty well I think. Which is really good.

A lot of the BLs found a welcome at Tranby, and they contributed to the teaching there about politics and organisation – as well as stirring up some debates!

---

5 Building Workers' Industrial Union.

Joe Owens recalled: I ended up over at Tranby a lot after the union folded. Remember when old Alf give me the dump when the kids went on strike, do you remember that one? The kids were whinging about something ... Alf got me in as a teacher and I was teaching public speaking. That was before we all got any money (for teaching). And we had Russ Herman coming over with a camera and taking pictures of the kids and showing them how to speak... and how to present themselves on the camera... And Alf thought it was great! But anyway the kids had a blue about something, might have been about the tucker or something...

Figure 4.2: Rod Pickette, with his son, 2011. Rod was an organiser with the Australian Theatrical and Amusement Employees Association in the 1970s and active in the NSW ALP. He is now National Policy Officer in the Maritime Union of Australia.

Courtesy Rod Pickette family collection.

Kevin: No, it was about the showers! And you know that strike got it fixed! So the students won!

Joe: But Alf was held in great respect... Take Charlie Oliver from the AWU. ... I actually got on well with Charlie Oliver. There were some things I didn't like about Charlie but I liked *him*. Now he never got on with the Builders Labourers.[6] But I'll never forget if you mentioned Alf Clint's name, mate! The decks were cleared! If Charlie Oliver was there, you'd get all the support you cared for!

---

6 Because as a member of the right-wing faction of the ALP, Oliver did not like dealing with communists in the BLF.

This broad commitment to Tranby from unions of all persuasions was the result of years of Alf's hard work in building strong working relationships – partly in the pubs but just as much through building interactions with unions, so Aboriginal students could take their place beside unionists to learn not just the trade but the politics of organising! Paddy Crumlin, the General Secretary of the Maritime Union of Australia and a member of the Tranby Board in the 1980s, talked with Kevin about Tranby's links with the Seamen's Union.

Figure 4.3: Paddy Crumlin, a member of the Seamen's Union in the 1970s and now General Secretary of the Maritime Union of Australia.

Courtesy Maritime Union of Australia.

Paddy Crumlin: Tranby's been a thing in the Seamen's Union for about 50 years. When you're on a ship, you often sponsor young guys, you know scholarships, that sort of thing, going right back. It was a real connection.

Tranby went a long way back with the Seamen and the Wharfies and the Miners in the early days. Alf must have had fantastic respect, you know, even I heard about him even though I was a lot younger and never bumped into him. Even just his ability to communicate issues! And to knock around and be involved with communists. He had a big connection through the party, before all the splits in the '70s.

Seamen had their political rolling funds and political issues and political and industrial issues. Ships like the *Iron Monarch* would agree to keep a sponsorship going for an individual and would pay money out on a regular basis. We were involved in Abschol, too. The Wharfies and the Seamen were involved in a program that helped young Aboriginal boys get jobs in the industry, like up at Weipa there was a program that got six young guys on up there as seamen and a deck boy. Alf was a good friend of Eliot V Elliott[7] the general secretary of the Seamen's Union. Eliot used to go and tell the Seamen, he'd say 'Well we need more money for more scholarships, butchers, bakers and candle stick makers!' There was a lot of butchers and bakers in those days, hands on trades. That was late '50s, early '60s.

For the rank and file it wasn't just about money. For example Jack Hassam, he was a seaman on a 60 miler that ran between Sydney and Newcastle. Jack was living down at Millers Point, and sort of home every night. The union said, 'Do we want to send someone down to be a director, at Tranby?' Well Jack was a rank and file member, a knock around sort of a bloke, and that's how Jack ended up down there on the Tranby Board. He's a terrific bloke. Hands on and that was the sort of connection between the workers themselves. And after that there was Pat Sweetenson.

I was talking to Patrick Geraghty about it. He said Elliott was a great mate of Alf. They all knew Alf as that sort of knock-around bloke who loved a beer and could get a message across and was part of that progressive broad front. It was a real big thing the co-operative thing, getting things going, and doing it in a knock-around sort of a way. That was the connection I think with the Seamen, a *political* connection with a bit of knowledge about Tranby because of Alf and then you Cookie!

To have exposure pretty early in anyone's political development to something like Tranby was tremendously important. It's had a political impact – on a whole generation of Aboriginal and non-Aboriginal leadership in terms of Indigenous issues. I mean it's absolutely unique, almost irreplaceable. You know, everyone speaks from your own perspective, but, in my political development, in *my* understanding of issues, that's what Tranby's been.

Yeah, so a lot of it comes back to you mate, no doubt about it, like Geraghty said, 'He was a genius that Alf, he found the little bloke, he found Cookie!' 'Well, Cookie found him probably more like it', that's what I said to Geraghty!

As well as supporting rural co-operatives and organising work placements, Tranby had a series of courses running to train co-operative members about how to manage their local businesses and manage the co-operative process.

---

7   Eliot V Elliott, the General Secretary of the Australian Seamen's Union from 1941 to 1978.

Kevin was interviewed about this early teaching program in 1996 by Russ Herman, an old BLF friend as well as a filmmaker. As Joe had mentioned, Russ was another union person who Cookie had pulled in to teach at Tranby. In the interview, Kevin explained what Tranby was like for him at first:[8]

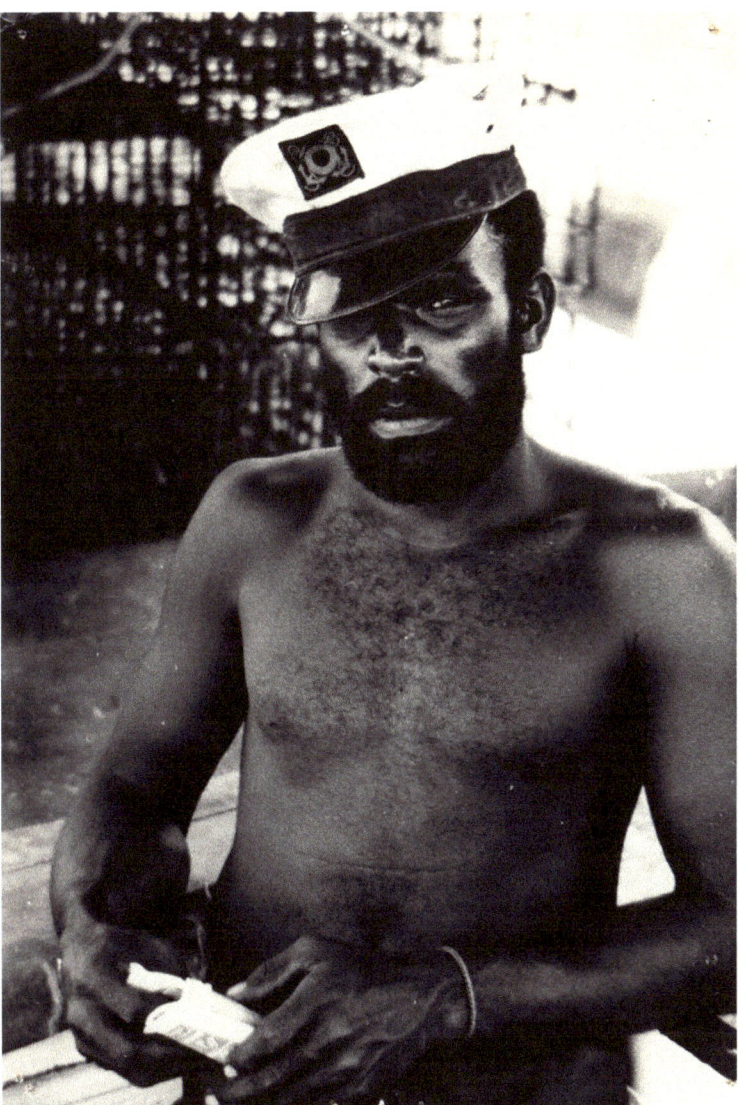

Figure 4.4: Tranby apprentice seaman. As Paddy Crumlin describes, the role of the Seamen's and later Maritime unions, in sustaining contact with Tranby, was crucial in setting up such apprenticeships.

Courtesy Tranby Archives.

---

8 Russ Herman, 1996, in one of a series of documentary interviews to compile a history of Tranby Co-operative College.

Figure 4.5: Pat Geraghty, long time leader of the Seamen's Union of Australia and a strong supporter of Alf Clint and the Tranby apprenticeships for Aboriginal seamen.

Courtesy Maritime Union of Australia.

Kevin: When I first came up to work at Tranby, we only had one course then. It was called the Co-operative Course and it was about running small businesses, using the co-operative principles. There were about 15 students when I was here. We had one paid teacher, the rest of our teachers were from St Scholasticas down the road, the Catholic College – they'd send up teachers. But it wasn't a very good arrangement because if one of their other colleges was short of people, then those teachers would go there and then they'd send somebody else up to us. So we had no continuity. But if they didn't do it, then we'd have no teachers to teach. So the arrangement wasn't the best but we got through with it.

The problem with having the one course, we had people who'd had very little or no schooling to people who had gone right through the schooling system. So that the range of education background was very wide. When the teacher would come in, he'd have to teach literacy and numeracy to some students, and try to carry on the full-time course as well. So it was very hard on teachers, but we didn't have the money to employ teachers to come in and teach literacy and numeracy.

Figure 4.6: Courses at Tranby: teaching 'co-operation'.

Courtesy Tranby Archives.

Figure 4.7: Courses at Tranby: class including Lester Bostock (then a student).

Courtesy Tranby Archives.

Working with Alf was exciting: he knew an amazing lot of people from the clergy to prime ministers, to trade union leaders, to miners on the coal face. He had a very good rapport with workers. That's where his ministry lay: before he came to Tranby he was with the working class. So that all of the contacts he'd built up through the union movement, plus then all of the contacts I'd built up through the union movement, kept Tranby in good stead when we had to call on support from those unions.

And we did call on them on a lot of occasions in the early days because we weren't funded. In the few years before I came on board, the place had closed down three times because of lack of funding. So that the trade union movement played a very big role, along with church groups, in funding Tranby in the early days.

By 1977, I was doing trips all over the place for Alf and for Tranby. One of the funniest ones was my first trip to Brisbane, Ayr, Cairns and then back home. I didn't know what to expect, I didn't know too many people because it was Alf who knew everybody. He gave me a note saying you have to go and see these people. First I went to Ayr and I stayed with a family who were Pentecostals. I'd never heard of Pentecostalism before, I've only been to the mainstream churches.

4. Tranby, co-operatives and empowerment

So I went to church there with them and I sat down between two large women. I didn't know what to expect, I looked up and they had a kind of a stage there with drums and guitars. The minister was yelling in a loud voice and they started singing and then everybody started to sway backwards and forwards. Of course, I wasn't in rhythm, I was just sitting there in between these two large women, so I was getting knocked around. I had to start swinging too. I've never been in a situation in church where people are singing, with drums and electric guitars. And then another woman started to run down the aisle and said, 'I've been saved, I've been saved!' And I was taken aback, you know!

And when we went out I talked to the people who I was staying with and they said, 'Oh, that's a very quiet service, Kevin', they said, 'you should come tonight'. Well I had to decline because I didn't know what to expect!

Next day I was off again up to Tully by train. Before I left Sydney, Alf had been telling me about the rainfall at Tully and especially about the large snakes. When I got to Tully it was about four o'clock in the morning and when I tried to get a cab into town, the station master said, 'If you get a cab into town, nothing's open. You might as well sleep on the station'. So I just slept on one of the seats. And when I woke up, before I opened up my eyes I could feel this nice warm thing on the middle of my chest. And it took me 15 to 20 minutes before I opened my eyes. And as I opened my eyes I swiped, cause I thought it was a snake! And it turned out it was only a little kitten. I tried to call the cat back but it wouldn't come, it ran away!

But in all of those places, the people were trying to work out how to run their organisations and co-ops and some of them were sending students down to Tranby.

The meaning of co-operatives was debated in Australia just as it was in many other places. Kevin was grappling with this, not only in his first years in Tranby but later on. He talked this over with Russ Herman, explaining in this 1996 interview that co-operatives continued to offer important principles.

Russ: The co-operative was considered – certainly by Alf Clint – to be the answer for an Aboriginal community. Today, co-ops aren't so popular anymore. What do you think about the concept?

Kevin: Well I believe co-operatives are the closest thing to the way we live as Aboriginal people – we are communal owners. The co-operative is set up on those principles that are the principles that Aboriginal people live by. That's why we thought that the co-operative way, the co-operative principles in small business, is the way that Aboriginal people should go.

Making Change Happen

Figure 4.8: Co-operative enterprises in communities: Robert Bolt, member Numbahging sugar cane co-operative with cane, Cabbage Tree Island, North Coast NSW.

Courtesy Tranby Archives.

Figure 4.9: Co-operative stores in communities: Numbahging store co-operative, Cabbage Tree Island, North Coast NSW.

Courtesy Tranby Archives.

Russ: But isn't there a lot of pressure from the general community these days, against co-operatives?

Kevin: No. I think the ideas are still there and important. Even if the organisation is forced to be registered as a company, under the federal government's laws, it can still operate *as* a co-operative because it's still one member, one vote. It's not how much money you put into it, it's one-member-one-vote.

So even if it's a company or they're registered under any other criteria, it seems to me that the majority of Aboriginal organisations still use their own principles, which is the co-operative principle which is one person one vote, its communal ownership.

So co-operatives aren't a new thing in Aboriginal communities. I think that communal living is the way forward. I think that we have to share our resources. If we don't, because of unemployment, there'll be an even larger division between the haves and the have-nots. But if we own things communally then we can trade communally, then there's not a big issue about unemployment.

I think one of the big stigmas attached to unemployment and the dole is that it's so individual – especially for Aboriginal people. Aboriginal people have to be doing something that is the betterment for their own community. If they don't do it they feel that they're not important, they're not worthwhile, and that's where you get drinking and other social problems.

Cookie at Coady: In touch with the world

Alf had begun to talk with Kevin about the Antigonish movement in Canada and its international network soon after he arrived in 1976. By that time, Tranby Co-operative was concentrating not on setting up new cooperatives but, from the mid 1960s, on bringing Aboriginal people from remote areas. As funds allowed, people had come from the co-operatives in the Torres Strait Islands, Papua New Guinea, Samoa, Vanuatu and other Pacific Islands to the college for courses and for the summer school. Alf had organised for a Tranby student, Charles French, to go to Coady in 1964 and French had returned to take up further tertiary studies. There had been attention to communicating with far-flung cooperatives since then, with the newsletter *Milli Milli*, but there had been no-one travelling to study at Coady since Charles French had been there.

Alf wanted Kevin to see how international co-operatives had been developing in those years since 1964. Finally, in 1979, Kevin agreed to enroll at Coady for a semester – it was to be his first trip overseas since he had been working in New Zealand.

Kevin's time at Coady has been a mystery to his friends in Australia until recently. He would have been happy to tell us, but none of us thought to ask. As I have learned from talking to others[9] who had worked closely with Cookie before and after he went to Canada, we had all assumed that he had been having an interesting time but mainly as a break away from the hectic politics and networking he had faced in Australia. Personally, I had thought he had done some abstract courses on bookkeeping or communication strategies. It was only as we worked on this book together that I learnt how wrong I had been. As we talked more about his time at Coady, it became clear that it had been a tremendously important experience for him.

---

9   Like Meredith Burgmann, Barbara Flick and Brian Doolan.

4. Tranby, co-operatives and empowerment

Figure 4.10: Charles French, 1964, Tranby student who was awarded a UN scholarship with support from Tranby and Sydney University to enroll for a semester at Coady International College, St Francis Xavier University.

Courtesy Tranby Archives.

Figure 4.11: Cookie just before he left for Coady – mid-1979.

Courtesy Heather Goodall.

Figure 4.12: Coady International Institute had flourished by building links between working and minority peoples co-operatives in the developing world. This 1962 graduation photograph shows the wide range of people who were by then participating in the co-operative training at Coady.

Courtesy St Francis Xavier University Archives.

Figure 4.13: In India, in 1986, a priest speaks at a development symposium organised jointly by Coady and the Cochin diocese.

Courtesy St Francis Xavier University Archives.

By the time Cookie headed for Canada in 1979, there had been a growing numbers of co-operatives in developing countries since the 1950s. More recently, in the 1970s, there had been a revival of co-operatives in the west. So Coady International College at Antigonish was now offering courses in Community Development as well as in Co-operative Studies. These changes had echoed the new experiences which Coady staff had been having as they travelled to the many co-operatives in their network, from India and Africa to Latin America. This shift had fuelled further developments in the Coady philosophy to make it much more cross-cultural and ecumenical. During 1979, the same year that Cookie studied there, the Institute commemorated Moses Coady by arguing that he was 'light years' ahead of his time:

> Almost fifty years ago, he warned of poisoning our earth and our waters ... He urged scientific thinking in a generation when men and women were often inclined or directed to parochial notions, hearsay and superficial catchwords ... He was breaking windows in musty institutions many years before Pope John was opening windows to allow fresh breezes to blow through. ... He said that one could not speak of Catholic co-operation or Protestant co-operation, of Buddhist, Mohammedan, Shinto or Hebrew economics any more than one could speaker of Quaker chemistry or Mormon mathematics. ... He fought for the concept of one world of humans.

Kevin chose the Community Development course, in line with his main interest, but he mixed freely with the students in the Co-operative course too, as well as the staff in the Institute, particularly those who had worked in Latin America. Students were accommodated on the campus at St Francis Xavier University where Coady was based. Here they lived in dormitories with individual bedrooms but shared living and cooking spaces, so there was lots of everyday socialising and networking. It was late summer as the semester got started, and Kevin found the classes useful, learning more about the history of the early United Kingdom workers' co-operatives like Rochdale, which had supported workers' employment and opposed slavery in the United States, despite suffering economic disadvantage. It was their commitment to principle over economic security which Kevin told me he had really valued.

Most important to his experience, however, were the participants who had come to the International Institute. They were all activists in community-oriented co-operatives, rather than in any of the large corporate or State-controlled ones. These were people working in and for communities, who found what they wanted in the co-operative structure, which enabled economic self-reliance based on democratic decision-making. Each of the participants had come from co-operatives which emphasised self-reliance above dependence and principle over profits.

Figure 4.14: Kevin's graduation photo, 1979, showing his whole Coady class. Kevin is sitting third from the right in the front row.
The people with whom he became close friends included: Front Row: G. Asirvadam (India – 3rd from left); Second Row: Maria Cwata (Zimbabwe – 1st on left); Third Row: Dr Angelina Roche (India – 8th from left), Ruth Mpisaunga (Zimbabwe - 7th from right), Alice Thiongo (Kenya – 6th from right), Sophie Mazibuko (South Africa – 5th from right); Back Row: Joe Mullor (India – 3rd from right), Griffiths Zahala (South Africa – 2nd from right), James Ross (Liberia – on extreme right).

Courtesy St Francis Xavier University Archives.

Cookie found there were three major areas – India, Latin America and Africa – which had sent students, although there were also individuals from Ireland, from Canada and of course Kevin from Australia. All of them worked in community-focused co-operatives, however small or large. And Cookie became close friends with people from each area.

The students from India were largely from the southern states of Karnataka, Andra Pradesh and Kerala. But one, Father Joe Mulloor, was from Bihar State in the north of India, and in close contact with the nearby forest-dependent indigenous communities, known in India as *Adivasi*. Kevin spent a lot of time with Joe Mulloor, discussing his work with local people. Today, he pays him the ultimate tribute when he says: 'Joe was my mate'.

A southern Indian student Kevin spent time with was Dr Angelina Roche, a medical doctor also from Karnataka but living near the western coastal city of Mangalore. Another close friend was G Asirvadam, who lived just a bit further east in central forested areas but these were over the border in the State of Andra Pradesh. Here Asirvadam led the Kadapa District Agricultural Labourers co-operative. He was a committed activist which showed when all the students were asked to record their 'Interests' in the Coady Year Book. Most wrote down hobbies like music and gardening. But Asirvadam recorded his 'Interests' as 'Socio-economic upliftment of low caste people'. He was campaigning against debt bondage among agricultural workers, many of whom were living in virtual slavery trying to pay off enormous debts they had accrued just trying to feed their families. Kevin saw Asirvadam's role in union and class terms.

Kevin: Asirvadam was like a union organiser – working with people who were share-farmers and owed money to farmers and other landowners – they never got out of debt. It starts off with a low amount of money they have to pay back, and then it builds up. … He bought some people out of debt himself to get them free!

It shows the closeness in which the students all shared their daily lives, that Asirvadam was also remembered because he shaved himself – and others if they wanted to try it out – with a razor. Not with a blade in a handle but with just the bare safety razor blade held nimbly between thumb and forefinger, as the student newsletter showed in a sketch. He shaved Cookie – 'And he did a great job of it too!' Cookie laughed as he remembered, 'He kept on sharpening it!'

***

The second group were those from Latin America, and Kevin spent a lot of time with some students from Guyana and Belize. 'St Xavier's was always sending people out all the time to South America and they'd come back and talk to us about it.' He remembers their approach in communities, which was to organise study circles among co-operative members to analyse the problems they faced and develop strategies to solve these problems, step by step, then put them into practice. Their attempts would then be evaluated, again in the co-operative group discussions, reassessed and refined so they could be tried again. This strategy for development and research is now familiar as 'action research', but in the 1970s, this was pioneering work. Hearing about it left a deep impression on Kevin – he remembers realising this was an approach to community development which would carry people with it.

The third and very important group for Kevin were the students from Africa. He was good friends with James Ross from Liberia in western Africa, but the people he was particularly close to were those from Zimbabwe (formerly Rhodesia) and South Africa.

Making Change Happen

Students from the class of '79

Figure 4.15: James Ross from Liberia is the tall man in the check shirt in this photograph of the Class of '79, taken from the Coady International Institute Newsletter, February 1980.

Courtesy St Francis Xavier University Archives.

***

Cookie shared not only classes with these African students but also the day-to-day living and cooking routines of the dormitory.

Cookie remembers: There was a good mix of people there, especially the South Africans. And especially the women from South Africa. The women used to have a time to cook every day, at about 6pm or 7pm. There was me and an Irishman, Bill Walsh, and these women from South Africa, Monica Mosala and Sophie Mazibuko, and Maria Cwata from Zimbabwe. Everyone used to throw in some money and the women would go once a week to the market and when they came back – eight or nine women – they'd all be walking back up the hill with the food balanced on their heads!! They'd cross the road and the cars would stop 10 or 20 metres back from them out of respect and not wanting to hit them or frighten them. The University was the lifeblood of the town!

Because of the struggle against Apartheid in South Africa at that time, with co-operatives being one of the few black organisations which were allowed to exist at all, each of these southern Africans was intensely politicised.

As *Cookie* remembers: I had already been involved in the anti-Apartheid stuff in Australia. And I took with me – and I wore it! – an ANC T-shirt. One of the

South African blokes I spent a lot of time with wanted that shirt badly. I didn't want to give it up – because I liked it and it meant a lot to me too – but mainly because I was worried about what would happen to this bloke if he wore it over there (or maybe even when he had it through Customs). But this bloke was persistent and in the end I gave it to him – I dunno what he did with it! He couldn't have worn it! He'd have got shot!

They all told him about their lives in South Africa under Apartheid and in Rhodesia under white-minority rule. Cookie met up with Sophie some years later, when she came over to Australia, representing the ANC – the African National Congress – Nelson Mandela's party which was waging the struggle against the South African regime. When they were at Coady together in 1979, Sophie would tell Kevin about how she used to sneak out at night in South Africa to go to ANC meetings – when the organisation was illegal and she would have been jailed or worse if she had been caught. Just from talking with these activists over cooking and dinner, Kevin says he came away with 'a bigger picture'. It is significant that he interpreted all the work of the students he was close to – including the priests and nuns – in class terms as he did with Asirvadam, whom he said was 'just like a union organiser' as he went about organising and freeing debt-bonded labourers. Overall, Kevin summed up his fellow students by saying: 'All of these people had a good understanding of politics. All of them worked on the left.'

The course itself aimed to maximise the communication between participants. The main project over the whole semester was for students to apply some of the course's resources and approaches to a community development problem they were working on in their home countries and to which they would return. Kevin chose the gaining of land rights as a strategy for empowerment of Aboriginal people in NSW. These projects were shared and discussed among students at various points through the semester and Kevin was able to talk over his ideas for strategies and key goals. The assignment has long gone, but Kevin remembers those conversations vividly. The key goal he came to settle on during these discussions was that the land rights movement in NSW should concentrate on the inalienability of title – land should not be able to be sold so that land rights gains would be protected. He remembers the next important goals to have been the democratic membership of the land holding bodies, which might come to be called Land Councils, and the regional nature of representation, so the problems of alienation of leaders from their communities, which he had seen to happen in State-level centralised bodies like the Aboriginal Lands Trust, would not occur. Apart from the advice and critiques he received from other students, Kevin remembers ruefully that the South Africans expected that Aboriginal people in Australia would achieve their goals of empowerment long before the people of South Africa had achieved freedom.

From these many discussions, Kevin brought back to Tranby a strengthened interest in co-operative organisation to achieve social change through economic empowerment and particularly through education, drawing on the Frierian community-driven approaches from South America. Despite their many differences, Kevin was struck by how all of his fellow students were focused on empowerment – and their support and enthusiasm for each other convinced him of the importance of sharing ideas and networking with activists around the developing world.

Kevin: They were about empowerment! That was the critical thing for all of them, about empowering communities!

***

Kevin feels that the lessons he took most seriously to heart were in the debriefing session at the end of the course. The Coady staff stressed that all of the students were going back to difficult conditions where their ideas and visions would not necessarily be welcomed.

As *Cookie* remembers: They gave us a three day briefing about all the pitfalls about coming back with new ideas and trying to get them put into practice. They said, 'Don't try to do it all at once or in a hurry'. This was really important for the people like the Kenyans, who were going back to a church situation.

Cookie says the biggest lesson for him was that: 'You have to bring people along with you – you can't lead by being out in front.'

Over the next decades, he brought this approach both to his work in education with Tranby and as a land rights activist. He tried to work by carrying people along with him. In the development of the land rights movement and then the advice he was able to give on the structure of the Act[10] and the Interim Land Council, he felt he had fulfilled many of the goals he had set during that time in Canada in 1979.

---

10 *Aboriginal Land Rights Act 1983* (NSW).

PART 2
TRANBY 1980s

5. Aboriginal-directed education: Getting started

'Cause at the time you could see something growing, it was like there was something there shimmering, just waiting for someone to feed it and help it grow. Because at that time there wasn't anything like that, I don't think, in Australia.

Robert Stanley, Tranby graduate and staffer 1980

Transitions

Kevin returned from Canada early in 1980, bringing new confidence in the directions he wanted to head for community learning and development. At the same time, he kept in mind that Coady advice to make sure he carried his colleagues and comrades along with him in whatever he did. This chapter traces out the first impact of that strong sense of direction which Cookie had brought back. To do this, the chapter has drawn on Kevin's memories and those of the people who contributed to the development of Tranby from 1980, when Cookie returned from the Coady International Institute, to around 1983. The contributors are introduced further throughout the chapter and include Julie House, Robert Stanley, Brian Doolan and Paul Torzillo.

***

Cookie continued to have a strong conviction that co-operative organisation was important for communities because it encouraged equality in decision-making as well as setting the stage for economic self-sufficiency. And he was thinking about justice in urban areas as well as in rural ones. So when a chance came up to support a co-operative in the Sydney area, he encouraged the Tranby Board to grab it.

Tranby had been approached by Aboriginal communities in western Sydney to help to set up a co-operative factory producing boomerangs based on a method used by local man, Harry Cooley (see Fig 5.2 on left, in the co-operative factory) who had been crafting them at home for some years. This coincided with the offer being made by the NSW Department of Community Services (DACS) of short term funding to trial co-operatives. DACS insisted on professional management and a clear commercial goal to be met in order for funding to continue but the Tranby Board gave their auspices to the project.

Figure 5.1: The boomerang-making team working in the co-operative factory.

Courtesy Julie House.

Harry Cooley was to be joined by two younger men, including Rodney, pictured here working in the co-operative factory.

Searching for a sympathetic manager with relevant experience, Kevin found Julie House, a young woman who had been working on co-operative organisation with rural communities in Thailand.

Julie understood the community goals of achieving self-reliance through meaningful work and the project began with enthusiasm from the community board, although they were frustrated that the factory could only offer employment for three people.

Once the three workers had refined the machining steps, however, it became clear how labour intensive the process was. First the boomerangs needed to be cut out, then sanded perfectly to be ready for screen printing or heat-stamping to print or burn the design onto them, and then finally they were lacquered to finish them off.

5. Aboriginal-directed education: Getting started

Figure 5.2: Finished boomerangs with Harry's signature.

Courtesy Julie House.

While the three men were working in the factory, Julie was knocking on door after door of the city's tourism shops and art agencies, to show them samples of the boomerangs and negotiate a wholesale price. After a while, it was obvious to everyone that the factory was not going to be able to generate enough income to pay wages. These New South Wales machine-produced boomerangs – although designed and made entirely by Aboriginal workers – needed many hours work to produce but were facing stiff competition from low priced but hand-made boomerangs and other artefacts being marketed at that time from Queensland. So their wholesale price was continually undercut by the competing Queensland goods. Reluctantly, the workers and the community board decided the co-operative would have to wind up, selling off its machinery once it became clear it could not gain further funding or run independently.

The difficulties of the co-operative were a lesson to everyone at Tranby that the key to empowering city communities had to be aimed at adult education to increase Aboriginal competitiveness and professional skills. Aboriginal people had suffered through decades of discriminatory education. The education department had allowed NSW public schools to be officially racially segregated till the late 1940s and then the department continued to allow *de facto* segregation until the early 1970s.[1] Many Aboriginal people from country areas had been badly short changed when they had left school without literacy or numeracy skills, but they were increasingly taking on the management of community organisations as they tried to support community goals in urban areas.

***

Robert Stanley grew up in Moree and his experience of NSW state education was typical of what so many Aboriginal people had had to put up with before they came to Tranby. After a positive experience in a primary school where all the students were Aboriginal, Robert went into the Moree High School, with many more white students. He found it a major culture shock, and was unhappy there, although he stayed longer than many other Aboriginal students. Robert finished his Intermediate Certificate and left school at 16, working in an apprenticeship making rural tools and then in ringbarking contract teams. He had been thinking of coming down to Sydney to further his education but as he said in an interview with filmmaker Russ Herman: 'I didn't like that idea. I've never been past Narrabri before that so I didn't like the idea of the Big Smoke.' His mother encouraged him to enlist in the army, in which he served inside Australia for two years, and once he had returned to civilian life in 1979 he decided to make the leap to come to Tranby College to study.

---

1 JJ Fletcher 1989, *Clean, Clad and Courteous: A History of Aboriginal Education in NSW*, Southwood Press, Sydney; Goodall 1996.

Robert: I done the year here at Tranby and at the end of the year then I went back to Moree. Then in January 1980, Reverend Clint wrote me a letter asking me would I like to work here. I jumped at the chance and started work here on the February 6 …then in April of that year, Reverend Clint died. We made Kevin Cook the acting General Secretary and under Kevin's guidance actually we did have a bit more freedom than we had had before. Cause with Reverend Clint, all the letters and everything we had was addressed to his place, so we didn't see any of that. He was working here, but all the correspondence and everything went to his place out the other side of Manly there, which I thought was a bit odd. And he was the sole person that made all the decisions.

Then Kevin took over the role, he was voted in by the Board and he had the full support of the staff, which wasn't many but he had the backing of all of us. When I first started I was like an organiser, but we didn't have an accountant at the time so I was doing the books and just about everything. We didn't have many staff, especially in the office and at that time, you know, we was lucky to get paid. So you couldn't really get staff to stay here under those conditions.

But I thought it was great. 'Cause at the time you could see something growing, it was like there was something there shimmering, just waiting for someone to feed it and help it grow. Because at that time there wasn't anything like that, I don't think, in Australia.

There were other institutions there for Aboriginal people, but they were run by non-Aboriginal people. The Aboriginal people had no say in it. When I came here, this was the first place where I seen where they was making their own decisions. And we didn't have government funding so we had no-one to answer to – so we just went ahead and did what we wanted, not what the government or non-Aboriginal people wanted. This was the first time we done it, something that the Aboriginal people themselves wanted.

Then we got Brian Doolan. He was in Wilcannia at the time, so Kevin asked him to come down here to Tranby. Brian come here in 1981 and he was really good. He was instrumental in setting up the College as it is today. Before Alf died, the College here was based on teaching about co-operatives, so all the subjects were things like the Credit Union. It was just the one course which didn't suit all the students because they was all at different levels. …Our teachers was all voluntary. Most of them came from St Scholasticas Girls' School. Only thing we could offer them was a feed, on the good days! And most of them were nuns, which wasn't too bad.

1981 was the last year we had that Co-operative Course. At that time there was an HSC class in East Sydney Tech, which was all Aboriginal. Half way through the year, '81, that course was abandoned (by the Tech). I don't know what happened. But Terry Widders was here at Tranby at the time, so Terry went up and got those students and we brought them back here to Tranby. In 1982 we started the Tertiary Preparation course and Terry wrote the program. So then we jumped from about 20 to 25 students a year in 1981, right up to about 110, 120 students in 1982.

Until Brian came along, we didn't have a Director of Studies. We'd made that position when Brian came here. There was only one little thing wrong, we didn't have any money. So most of the time we'd sort of help Brian with his rent.

We only had this old building here at Tranby, and the back part was hostels. We were virtually nursing each other! By 1983 we had four courses running: the basic skills education, a more advanced general education and then business studies, and then the Tertiary Prep course. So it was a lively old time at Tranby, for that first year.

All along we was eyeing off that building next door but they wanted half a million for it – we was lucky to provide meals, let alone buy a building for half a million!

Rethinking learning at Tranby

Kevin was interested in expanding the educational activities of the College to meet the changing needs of the urban and rural Aboriginal communities and he began looking for teaching staff who were interested too. He invited Brian Doolan to join the Co-operative as a teacher and to help to reshape the ways Tranby delivered education. When Kevin talked with Brian for this book, they discussed how the decisions they had made together about new courses and teaching methods.

Brian had most recently been living at Wilcannia in far western NSW, with his wife Kathy Bannister and their baby son Luke. He had trained as a teacher in the Catholic education system, but he was more attracted to community and adult learning than to formal institutions like schools. So he had worked with Father Ted Kennedy in his radical ministry to alcoholics in Redfern. Brian and Kathy had then moved to Wilcannia where Brian was employed by the Wiimpatjaa community to teach in their adult learning centre. Kevin asked him what he felt he'd learnt in those situations that he found useful when he came to Tranby.

Brian: The thing I learnt at Wilcannia was an awareness that there were no answers. As far as I'm concerned – actually none! If there were to be ways that were going to be successful, they would be articulated by Aboriginal people.

I think the other thing I learnt was because I was coming in as well through the Redfern experience with Ted Kennedy who worked with the *goomies* there.² So when I went to Wilcannia, I learnt about the overpowering impact that grog was having in the community. Of course I knew a bit about it already, but the experience actually in the community made it obvious that it was so totally debilitating and that it affected every aspect of what anyone was trying to do. Whether it was their involvement in a housing company, a medical service, an education centre, or whatever. And yet, despite the horrors of grog there were people who were still willing to stand up and try and set up education centres and medical services and legal services.

And so there were these amazing people right throughout, certainly in that stage. At Wilcannia, of course, I was exposed to people like Foxy Williams and Mrs Elsie Jones and others like them. And then at Menindee, I met Tartu – old Will Webster – and all those other people, who were amazing people in themselves.

When I first came to Tranby in '80 I think, there was one course that was repeated a couple of times a year. It was basically a course that sat around the notion of co-operatives. This meant of course that the funding base was unclear, to say the least.

Kevin: We didn't have a funding base!

Brian: It was pretty much hand to mouth. There were some individuals that seemed to get an enormous amount out of the courses. But there were a lot of other people who were participating in the classes but had other agendas. They were doing it because they wanted to be in Sydney or they wanted to be away from where they were coming from. They wanted to be away from problems, away from family or whatever. There was a group of young gay people who, I think, who found it comfortable to be around Tranby. They felt like it wasn't judgemental and they didn't have to face all those sort of problems that they might have had to face back home with families and things like that.

So there were lots of reasons for people being there. I found when I came from Wilcannia to Tranby was that there were so many reasons that people wanted to do things that it was a bit confusing but it was also very enabling. There were lots of options.

And historically, too, it hit a period when there were people in the bureaucracies who had been supporters of the Movement from the early '70s, with the Tent Embassy and those sorts of things. There were people like Evan Sutton

---

2   *Goomies* is the NSW Aboriginal term for people addicted to alcohol and methylated spirits.

and Sue Rutter in Commonwealth Education and Keith Campbell in TAFE,[3] Tim Hornibrook's boss. When an idea like Tranby or even the notion of this Aboriginal-controlled educational institution came along, they were able to push the buttons very quickly to give some support. And so when I came, I found lots of opportunities and all these possibilities.

I think one of the things we really wanted to do was to get a firm funding base for a post-secondary Aboriginal-controlled or Aboriginal-run institution. And that meant a couple of things. It meant firstly, pulling together some sort of curriculum that was recognisable for people in educational institutions and schools so they could say, 'Well, that sort of thing makes sense'. It was still very loose. It was centred around things like a co-operative studies course, a general education and then a tertiary education preparatory course that would create a bridge, a school to university or school to TAFE process.

Kevin: And Aboriginal Studies. It might sound strange that an Aboriginal institution would teach Aboriginal Studies to their students. But we had a lot of students who came from varied backgrounds. People have been taken away from their mothers and fathers and their communities and lived with non-Aboriginal people, and didn't know their history. We had people who have been brought up in very isolated communities, and didn't know the wider implications of the Aboriginal struggles. Aboriginal Studies was a very, very important issue for Aboriginal people. And so it was one of our core subjects – in fact it overlapped all of our subjects. I think that Aboriginal Studies and the way it's taught at Tranby is very important to the philosophy of the place.

Brian: Then of course was the input of senior people from the community like Jacko Campbell. He saw opportunities for things like the National Parks training course. It meant that people like the Suttons and the Campbells and the Rutters in those bureaucratic positions became allies. Kevin and I were able to talk to them and they'd say, 'Yeah, we want to support this'. Then they'd put together the bureaucratic package.

And the package often involved, say, from TAFE, 'We can give you X hundred teaching hours'. Tranby could then allocate those hours to certain teachers so they could come in and run those things. Or Commonwealth Ed would say, 'If you have X number of students we can give you this much' and we had to negotiate each year. Or they'd say, 'We can give you X dollars per head' which would help support the administrative arm of the College, the finance manager, all that kind of thing.

So when I came there I saw enormous opportunities. And all of those opportunities, of course, centred around Cookie's presence.

---

3   Technical and Further Education.

5. Aboriginal-directed education: Getting started

Figure 5.3: Jacko Campbell at Tranby, key member of the Board of Directors.

Courtesy Tranby Archives.

Figure 5.4: Cookie on the phone – as always. His desk was in the 'front office' which he shared with all the administration staff and the visitors – before they headed off to the dining room for a cup of tea.

Courtesy Tranby Archives.

He gave the place the validity to act as an Aboriginal-controlled centre for education. People found Cookie's presence enabled them to do things, and they weren't necessarily doing things just about Tranby. They were involved in the land rights movements, the New South Wales Aboriginal Land Council, they had links with trade unions. There was this enabling force called Kevin Cook who validated all these different things that people were doing. And they criss-crossed around his desk and his telephone and that happened to sit, very fortunately, in Tranby. Which I think allowed the growth of the Tranby as one of the many initiatives that were centring around him in those days. So that was my take on it!

Kevin: But I think, too, the way it got done is that we hired some pretty important people in that field. Kathy Campbell came from Victoria where she had a very good reputation working in secondary education with adults. And it was very progressive, it had to be progressive because the Aboriginal people wouldn't have stayed. We tried to make it as interesting as possible and we did that by acquiring an incredibly good bunch of people. But they were often only able to stay a short period of time, say two years. Or sometimes, like Brian, about four or five years. Was that how long you lasted? Before he had to go out and get a real job and earn some money so that he could support his wife and kid! And that was the downfall of the place because as I saw it we didn't have that continuity all the way through which we would have liked because of the lack of money. But it also brought a number of other people in at very crucial times with very, you know, different ideas. So it'd bubble and – you know – start up again!

Brian: I think, too, there was a level of honesty amongst the people who came in around then. Nobody came with the answer. Everyone acknowledged that we didn't have a way of interacting with Aboriginal kids or interacting with young adults, or older adults, that provided a satisfactory education experience for them outside of a totally Aboriginal setting. I think there were some really interesting questions raised and good people came around, Chris Milne and Heather Goodall and Dave Morrissey and Paula Ware, Kathy Campbell. We were asking: 'How do people learn?' How do young adults learn, with all these different things pulling at them, home experiences, maybe grog problems?

Kevin: Drug problems, fights about homosexuality, all sorts of problems. They wanted to get away.

Brian: Yeah, that's right. All those young gays that came around Tranby were fantastic, creative and wonderful young people. All those people who came to teach, no-one really knew how to do it, but everyone was willing to give it a go. To give it a go with very scarce resources. I think people were stimulated and interested by the idea more than anything, because obviously we couldn't pay them much! And they didn't get a lot of prestige. Certainly not in the short term.

Kevin: How many years did you drive a cab when you first came to Tranby because we couldn't pay you? Robert Stanley and myself were sharing a wage with Brian. The three of us shared two wages.

Brian: And the wage came from union donations and from selling buttons and collecting on the corner. When I came originally the wage came through Operation Aborigine, the fundraiser out the back. And through unions.

Kevin: Those Gooriala buttons were incredibly good, you know. Not the old version that looked like a sad charity – that was earlier! The Gooriala ones never had any writing on them. It was a Dick Roughsey designed badge: the Mornington Island and the Aurukun people were down for a conference so they stayed at Tranby. And they gave us permission to use the dreaming. I got a badge when I was over in Canada. People in England, Italy, everywhere'd collect them! These Tranby badges were seen all over the world!

Figure 5.5: Kevin and the Board developed an innovative funding raising strategy which departed from previous 'charity' collection approaches. Tranby announced the Gooriala (Rainbow Serpent) campaign – drawing on cultural expression to develop the Gooriala image and performance.

Courtesy Tranby Archives.

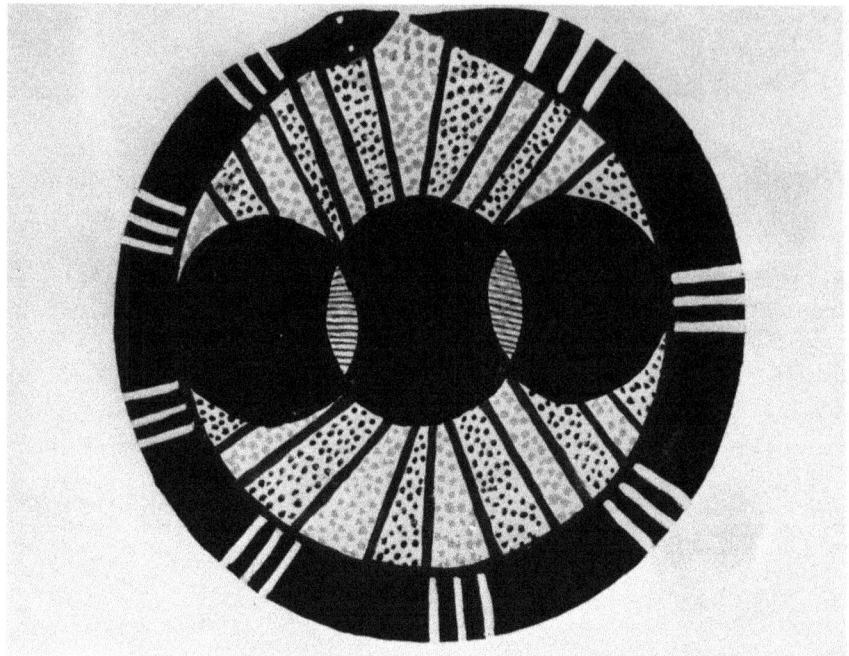

Figure 5.6: Gooriala badge.

Courtesy Tranby Archives.

But we never knew if we'd have enough money to cover wages! Once we had three weeks wages left and with no income we said that we'd have to close down most of the operations. People were going to go on the dole. People were going to go out and get second jobs. I know Kathy Campbell went out and got a job teaching English as a second language.

But at the end of the second week, a woman down the road from Tranby had died and left money to Tranby in their will. So we were able to pay wages and that happened on a couple of occasions. We had nothing. The next minute we had $100,000.

Brian: That's right. Remember I got that job at Granville TAFE, at nights, going and teaching literacy for two hours. I also had a job out at Long Bay Gaol. Which was terrific because I got to meet all that mob from Brewarrina out at Long Bay. Do creative writing.

Kevin: That's right, yeah.

5. Aboriginal-directed education: Getting started

Figure 5.7: Kathy Campbell and Wally Mussing.

Courtesy Tranby Archives.

Brian: There was that week where we went into the front room, took the tea pot and the plates. Remember that donation? People would bring donations for the poor Aborigines in the outback. But they'd bring all this stuff and then Tranby had no funds to post it out. I remember once when we literally had no money. Partly as a bit of a joke – just laughing – Cookie grabbed a teapot and I grabbed a couple of plates and we said: 'That's it for this week!' That must have been '81, '82, something like that?

Kevin: The way we got our first funding from the Commonwealth, was that Brian and I went to see Holding, before he became a minister, at some federal Select Committee on Aboriginal Education.

Brian: Yeah, it was in 1983, down near Circular Quay. There was you and Terry Widders and I. One of the people sitting across the other side was Susan Ryan, we knew who she was. But there was this other bloke, Clyde Holding. And I certainly had no idea who he was. He was just a name at the other end of the table. Then the election happened, Labor got in and we get this phone call.

Kevin: Yeah, to come down and see him. He was the new Minister for Aboriginal Affairs! Brian and I were doing cartwheels around Tranby. Whistling and singing. We run down there and he promised the world.

Brian: We met him down in Martin Place. There's some Commonwealth offices and we went in there. He promised us so much. Well, it's probably a pittance really, these days. But it was the first real financial help and we thought might be some longer term financial base for Tranby. We were so happy, we came out and we walked down the street and we went to what for us was a really expensive restaurant. It's probably just a better class of fish and chip shop. Shouted ourselves a big meal! We thought: 'Oh, well, we've done it here!' Holding said, 'We think Tranby is a really good idea. We like the idea of an Aboriginal-controlled adult education facility. We want to back it, and in the short term here's some money to underwrite it'. And it might have been $100,000 or $200,000. It wasn't enormous. But to us…

Kevin: And then we didn't get it!

Brian: That's right. But we were very happy about the notion of *almost* getting it. Holding didn't actually have the bureaucratic mechanism to allow that to happen.

Kevin: When we did get the money it was about a third of what he said he was going to give us and we still couldn't pay the wages! But before that funding from the federal government, it wasn't funny, we'd go along and we wouldn't know whether we could pay wages each week.

Brian: The other thing is that my memory of the period is that Tranby as an educational experience wasn't all a raging success. I mean it was an honest attempt by a bunch of people to provide that education environment and content for a very diverse group of younger people who were there for a whole range of reasons. And only a few of those reasons actually had anything to do with the education.

So there were some spectacular failures. There were young people who might have been attending classes at Tranby, but then they got caught up in other things or in grog problems, formed relationships which turned violent. Sometimes within the college group. I remember once when we had the hostel out the back, we actually had to ask a couple of people to leave. You know, it wasn't as though they walked into this hallowed area that changed things.

What it was – it was a *hub* of things. It didn't necessarily change their experiences, but there were some people who flowered. I'm not sure if that's because of anything we did. When most people flower it's usually because of the individual and they just take that opportunity. I remember young guys in the National Parks course particularly. And some of those guys who went back to the South Coast and were doing park ranger stuff and were incredibly successful.

Kevin: And we had a lot of people go into the public service. And one of our ex-students used to run the examinations for the public service board and she used to come out to Tranby, put our students through. You look through the public service now and there's a lot of our ex-students in there in incredibly good roles.

Brian: And if you look at the broader, political context you see the importance of the experiences they had. I remember the education department protest when the assistant secretary or someone at Bourke had made some racist slurs. It was the students at Tranby that organised the demonstration calling for her removal. They actually went on to occupy the offices of the department. Now I think for a kid from Collarenebri that's come to Sydney and to then be involved in confronting what had been seen as the white stronghold, the Department of Education. And not only confronting it but basically thumbing their noses at it by occupying the building. And then being able to negotiate, to be able to say, we're going to walk out based on these ten conditions. l thought it was an enormously liberating experience.

Kevin: Yeah, it was good. It empowered those students. And a lot of them have gone back and worked within their own community. And that's the beauty of it. You mightn't see their name in lights, but they're working on their local group and playing a very important role. They can read their financial statements so they can have an input how the money is spent. If you can't read the financial statement, you haven't got a chance in telling your community how they can direct their money. And that's why, before Aboriginal people were educated, white people were able to dictate where Aboriginal people would spend their money. It was crazy. And that's the other thing that Tranby done a good job at.

Overall, I don't think I got really frustrated at anything in those days at Tranby. If something didn't work then it might have been the wrong time or the wrong place, so you'd come back to that at a different stage and try something new. And you'd keep going on something else. Life's too short to hold grudges.

Working with the Board

Paul Torzillo has been introduced in earlier chapters as a medical student who worked as a builders labourer during his holidays where he got to know Kevin. Paul became a respiratory physician at Royal Prince Alfred Hospital and continued to be involved with Aboriginal medical issues and broader community development in NSW. Then he worked in the Pitjantjatjara Freehold Lands in Central Australia as a doctor with the Aboriginal-controlled Nganampa Health Service in 1984 and 1985, and has continued to be its Medical Director. Cookie asked him to become a member of the Tranby Board of Directors in 1986 and he remained on the board till Cookie retired in 2002.

Kevin talked with Paul and Brian about the role of the Board of Directors.

Kevin: I think a lot of the credit for what Tranby did could go to the Board of Directors. We had people in there for a long time, like John Short, an accountant working for Qantas. John and his wife met Alf Clint when they were younger and built up a relationship with him. John was there as chairman for years and years. Peru Permal, was another guy. They didn't come into Tranby and say, 'I'm on the board of directors, what's happening?' They sat back and listened to what the people were saying to them. We had Paddy Crumblin, from the Seamen's Union and then there was you, Paulie, you used to be the chief doctor for Tranby. Many weekends, some of our students were crook. We had to get people into hospital. First port of call was Paulie.

Brian: In the early days you had Justice Bob Hope, Bob Bellear, Michael Knott.

Kevin: Those type of people were incredibly good and stiffened up the organisation. They'd look at what you were doing. They looked at the money pretty critically – like Michael Knott. We had this old car and we were trying to trade it. He looked at the finances and said, 'No, we can't do it!' And straight away that was okay, because we knew he'd really looked into it. They were really fair.

Brian: But they were flexible enough to be able to cope with the sort of changes that you were bringing in. In the early eighties there was such a huge change in the educational structure of the place, from one course running repeatedly, to three different courses at least and the other offshoots like Black Books, and huge extra numbers of people. And all that complicated business trying to stretch the money, and the board coped pretty well.

Paul: I've got a slightly different view of how the Board worked. Some things that were obvious to me were that the Board relied very heavily on Cookie's directions and views about what was going on. I think that was pretty clear both in minor issues and philosophically.

But there were a few things going on at the same time. One thing was that in my observation, Cookie often used board meetings as a way of generally pulling in influential white support for the Aboriginal movement in general, not just for Tranby. So one set of discussions at the board meetings would be about things in which Tranby was in fact not directly involved, say, Tranby might be supporting this issue but not actually taking part. There might need to be a political response to what the government was doing in education for example. Or it might have been the visit of some international activist from South Africa… or it might be a general issue about trade unions. And Cookie would be saying, 'Well, I think we should send a letter supporting this move…' or 'The Tranby students are intending to go this political demonstration or that event...' and then there'd follow a general discussion about why Cookie thought this was important... It was often a political education session for influential white people on the board, for example conservatives like Bob Hope, and to some extent Peru. And Cookie would be making sure he was pulling in the trade union people who were there. Very often that wasn't hard, because they were already on side. But there was often a bit of shoring it up, with ongoing information and news about these issues, and I thought a lot of the time it was general education about the general Aboriginal scene or even the progressive left movement.

And then the second thing that was going on was involving Tranby in mainstream or progressive left political action. That meant the big political movements and events that were happening, like changes in the industrial laws, the waterfront, the whole waterfront issues, the whole of that actually got discussed at board meetings... In a way, Cookie was able to link the Aboriginal scene to the issues about workers' rights, I think. And part of that was to have these issues discussed at Tranby board meetings.

Another way of doing that was through the constituents or the makeup of the Board. The Board was just a remarkable spread of people with vastly different backgrounds, even different political perspectives from a pretty conservative judge going through to union activists. And even shop steward level activists, not just people like Paddy Crumlin who was a Federal Secretary. And then there was Peru Perumal with his progressive background that was international, there were members of his family who had been politicians in countries overseas, but who worked in a fairly middle class environment. And on the other hand there were these key Aboriginal people who were mixing with them. So it was a really heterogeneous mix of people but discussing all these issues where generally people were carried along. There might have been a criticism of having a Board that had influential white people on it, but a real advantage was that you had all these people of different backgrounds who could pull in all sorts of support, especially the trade unions, but it made Aboriginal affairs and Tranby a part of mainstream politics and not a side issue, and that was important.

I think the third thing that was going on that was important... and is probably even more important now in retrospect – was it was a real public display of financial integrity. So here was a group of people, some of whom were successful business people, one of them was a judge, experienced trade unionists, they were not people who were going to let some sort of dodgey audit or financial scam happen. And when you look around at the sort of catastrophic way that some of the organisations have been managed and at some of the financial ripoffs that were going on then. It was incredibly important to have that very public display of financial integrity.

In practice, it meant that the place was run honestly, but secondly, there were a lot of people from outside the scene who got to look at the audited books every month and clearly nothing shonky was going to go on. Now at the time I thought that was a minor issue.

When I look back on it, it was actually really important because it was a very upfront, transparent look at how the organisation was run. Which was different from a lot of other organisations where clearly there was a lot of money was being ripped off by key people. So this made Tranby very different. And it was a real problem for the place when that situation broke down temporarily in 2002.

Cookie: To me, Bob Hope was pretty progressive. I used to go and sit down and talk to him about lots of issues. We owned a property in northern Queensland and the people up there wanted to renew their lease and they wanted a long term lease. And being a judge, he knew the pitfalls. I sat down and talked to him for a long time about it over a number of weeks. And in the end he drew up the lease for us, and we took it to our solicitors, and said 'This is what we want, and anything that you think should be included we'll sit down and talk to you about it'. And the lease was for a 50 year lease with a 50 year option. And that's a very long term lease, and I think we charged the community $2.00 per year. And the property's worth millions and millions of dollars. It's an old banana plantation. To get that kind of experience and knowledge to me was incredible. And you could sit down and feel easy about what you were doing.

And all of the people on the Board of Directors had their own expertise. Peru was an architect. He did a lot of work over the years at Tranby for nothing. He didn't talk about it, but whenever we needed anything done, I'd just go up and talk to him about it and he'd get it done. And the people from the trade union movement like Dick Scott. He was the chairman of the board at Tranby for years. After he retired I used to go up and see him, I'd take my lunch up and he'd have a cup of coffee and I used to stay there for about half an hour…

And Mawley, the BWIU rep, he was another bloke from Newcastle, he played a very good role at Tranby. The BWIU altogether played a really important role at the College, with Stan Sharkey and Pat Clancy. Then you had the Seamen's Union, Pat Sweetenson and Jack Hassan … They told me that Jack Hassan was going to be a director… and I'm looking for Jack Hassan the fighter, I knew he worked on the wharves! But this was the white Jack Hassan! Now Sweetenson and Hassan were rank and filers, and they played a really important role. The people on the Board of Directors never ever got any kudos! Like Paulie here. We'd wake Paul up in the middle of the night to get our students into hospital or to come and have a look at one of them if they were sick.

The Aboriginal people who were on the Board were important, and I'd sit down and talk to them on the different issues, especially on land and really important issues like that. Jacko Campbell was someone I relied on a hell of a lot. And I'd go to board meetings with the knowledge that I'd spoken to them before, and I knew what they were thinking. People like Sylvia Scot, Bob Bellear, Cliff Foley, Robert Stanley, and old Wally Mussing when he was alive. People like that. It was incredible just to be able to sit down and get their views, to get a really good picture. And to make sure I wasn't running away with what I thought was right all the time. And then before meetings I used to go outside the Board of Directors on certain issues and talk to other Aboriginal people on certain issues and get their views, and then come back and bring it to the Board… and put it up before our Board. And nine times out of ten they'd pass it.

Isabel Flick was really important. She wasn't on the Board till really late, but I used to talk to her a lot about issues that were coming up at the Board. Then she went onto the Board later on, taking Delia Low's place. Nan Campbell, Jacko's wife and Delia's mother, was another one I relied on, she had a lot of knowledge. She wasn't on the Board but I talked to her a lot. And those are the sort of people who even though they weren't on the Board directly, they were as much the decision makers as the Board of Directors I think.

Figure 5.8: Regie on the switch.

Courtesy Tranby Archives.

There'd be a lot of people were just dropping into the front office and talking over their plans and projects. Just on the land rights issue in NSW, say, people were all the time coming through and they'd use Tranby as a meeting place. We said they could use our facilities, you know have a cup of coffee, if they had meetings in town they'd go into town, come back. And so we had students who'd be involved with them and individual [members of the] Board of Directors, if they were around, were involved with them also. And then you had people like Johnny Ah Kit,[4] Paddy Dodson, David Ross, all interstate people, they'd come down and be around. Terry O'Shane, he'd been involved with Tranby before I was, through Alf Clint. Joe McGinness. He was another person who used to spend a lot of time at Tranby. I'd be talking to him to get advice, he'd be talking to students. He wrote his book down here. He come down here and stayed at our place for a couple of months, and he used the Tranby facilities and the Tranby people like Chris Kerr. Now Isabel Flick and people like her were able to use Chrissy too. Isabel used to say, 'Oh, I don't know how to do this…' and Chris'd be on the phone getting it done! And any typing that they needed to be done, Chris'd get that done. They used to use my office. And Joe McGinness got a bit of typing done too for his book. And that was really good for our staff to be able to say, 'Oh yeah I knew them…' and for our students too… See that's paying respects to their elders and to people who they looked up to…

---

4   John Ah Kit, referred to mostly by Kevin as 'Jack' or just 'Ah Kit'.

6. Exploring possibilities: Teaching and learning at Tranby

This chapter is about how the teachers Kevin brought into Tranby tried to experiment further with teaching and learning. The contributors include: Terry Widders, Chris Milne, Isabel Flick, Karen Flick and myself, Heather Goodall, as interviewer.

Terry Widders is an Indigenous researcher and teacher from Armidale on the northern tablelands of New South Wales. After he had finished his Honours degree in Linguistics at Macquarie University in 1980, he and his wife Margaret had gone to Japan where Terry was studying Japanese language so he could learn more about the history and politics of the Ainu and other indigenous minorities elsewhere in China and east Asia. In this interview, Terry talked with me, Heather Goodall, because I had taught with him in the Tertiary Preparation Course Terry had managed at Tranby in the early years of the 1980s.

Terry: It begins with a letter that I received when I was in Japan from Brian Doolan in 1981. So I was in Hokkaido, in Sapporo the main city: 'Heard you were around and you'd finished your initial studies… Would you be interested in calling in to see us here at Tranby when you get back?' So… I did. And another reason was I had to get some work! Never forget the work!

Brian's letter said Tranby had changed since Alf had died and so on, and they were working on a new kind of model. I didn't know at that stage what it was but…

So early '82, I went around and they were talking about a system of TAFE[1]-type contracts for positions and the idea was to develop something 'core' at Tranby. They still had the old business studies unit if I remember correctly, that had been a long running thing from the co-operative days. And then there was talk about becoming an educational *institution*. But then how you *could* be, that was what the conversation was all about. I think I lobbed in there with a number of other people, like Chris Milne, and perhaps Dave Morrissey … he was perhaps later but it was about how to develop a kind of presence in, for example, Parks and Wildlife, as you'd say today, developing an Indigenous perspective in the curriculum…

But at the beginning it was much more focused then on the people who were going to be taking these courses. My working ideas or assumptions were firstly a sort of cultural capital idea, where rather than have a program of development

---

1 Technical and Further Education.

for a category of people, bright or otherwise, the idea was instead that people are already bright in themselves, it's a question of cultivating individuals, in their own pathways. The other assumption was that that this could have a community base of sorts, so it was related to a community idea outside of Tranby as well as Tranby itself becoming a kind of re-created community education centre. What that could be was still to be worked out. It wasn't going to be a hub of a co-operative type of structure as such, but the principles were still continuing, hence the Business Studies course...

So, there we were, and then a couple of things happened, just off the cuff as it were. One little wet day, not too far into '82, we got this call from some head teacher at East Sydney Tech, who said 'There's an Aboriginal class who are doing a tertiary preparatory certificate'... but it wasn't very clear over the phone ... 'some of them have left, they're in a classroom of their own, the course is probably not going to continue, would you come over to talk to them?' I thought 'Come over and talk to *who*? About what?!'

So I went over. It was really wet! And it was really archetypal, gloomy institutional architecture ... and there in the smallest room right down at the very back of this miserable, damp institution... there they were, all sitting around like little wet fowls! ... And there was about seven of them and that was the point, that the number was too small for the course to continue. But it was in the context of, well, seven of whom! They could have joined another class! I thought isn't there another class running? But they said no, this is a class for Aboriginal people! And I thought, 'What an institution!' But anyway, Robert Smith, from Western Australia, was the kind of spokesperson. And he explained that, in effect, they'd been abandoned! And the head teacher was dealing with it in an administrative way, by saying, 'Well, we just don't have the numbers to continue, and we *aren't* going to continue! And so would Tranby do something with them!'

So, 'Well', we thought, 'what *can* you do with seven bedraggled little numbers eh?' And they probably looked at us and thought, 'Well, who are *these* people!'

Anyway, it was pretty much on the spot that we said, 'Well why don't you come back to Tranby with us and we'll have a course there?' And so we did! It was a bit like little henny penny the red hen!

So we said 'Well if they're here, we'll need to have a tertiary prep course!' There'd been some talk about it, but it wasn't really being planned yet. But this sort of personified it! They walked in the front door! And said 'We're it!'

So that did then crystallise the idea. Then the talk was about *how* it was going to happen, not *was* it going to happen. And on the spot, I think I became the head teacher of the Tertiary Preparation Course! Not that I knew how to be a head teacher of anything! I was still practicing sounds in Japanese at that time, and wondering who the Ainu were!

So then we put up a proposal on the basis that it was already there happening, we've got a core group, and so we said, 'We want to run a tertiary preparation course here, and look who we've got to do it!' And the other thing was to recruit others to build up the numbers. So apart from being the head teacher and all that, in practical terms, we just got so many hours paid by TAFE. Then after that I remember walking around in a 5 km radius of Tranby, especially into the Redfern and South Sydney area and knocking on doors. Or we were talking to people in the Business Studies course and saying 'You wouldn't happen to have a sister or a cousin who was interested in this would you?' There were a number of other young women, mainly young women, who had been somewhere about in the TAFE system, just nibbling on the edges of a potential, tertiary type course. There were three or four like that, one who wanted to become a nurse.

Of the original seven, I think about four eventually stayed, and this other six or seven or so came on board. It was '83 when it eventually kicked off! I think we started somewhat informally in '82, got them registered as being part of a course. But I think we started off with the TAFE year in the beginning of '83…

Only in retrospect did I see how it was *running*. We were more interested in what it could become. There were two things we needed to think about. One was the educational framework thing: and that had settled into place. This was a legitimate framework, we could do it. We had a class. That was one thing. So that was part of the becoming process, that's the pathway it took…

But the other thing was that it was all very cash poor. It was the casualised labour problem. You could only be paid for so many hours: of course there was so much work there you could stay 24 hours if you liked! But you could still only be paid for so many hours, ten hours, 15 hours or however many it was from TAFE. And that wasn't enough to live on! At least for me, I was freshly back and we had to find a place to live and pay rent and Margaret had come back to finish her last year at University. So it was a balance between the practical, and what you needed to do that, and how far we could push the opportunity of setting up something like what was then called the 'TEPC', the Tertiary Education Preparatory Course. So that – for me at least – was the balance between those two things.

Figure 6.1: Brian at his desk in the 'back office' – the tiny room which became the teaching preparation space sometimes for six or seven people at a time – and, when Lyn Riley Mundine was there – the occasional baby!

Courtesy Tranby Archives.

And I think then it was also up to Kevin and Brian, doing the *talk* with TAFE people, and union people, to gather the broader support for it. There was Tim Hornibrook, from the NSW education department, who talked more about people and possibilities than about programs, whereas others talked more about programs and dollars… although they might also have talked about possibilities! So what we were talking about with TAFE was what it connected with, the bigger planning and bigger structural possibilities. Because if we were going to *become* something, we need to become something on a firmer basis, not just TAFE hours. We needed three year funding, we needed to get hooked up with the department. So that was more the preoccupation of Kevin and Brian at that time I think.

Another arm was the possibility that Dave Morrissey and Chris Milne were raising, they were talking about Black Books becoming not just a business, but a repository, not only of people and their life experiences, but as that was *written*, as that was a focus of Indigenous literature and other kinds of literature. Kathy Campbell was already there and had a community development role. She was a bouncy type of person and it was her bounce and ideas that, along with Kevin and Brian, that shaped these meta-programs.

So we had this sort of committee, people like Kevin, Brian and Kathy, they could make the *talk* of possibilities, and then there was this next layer of people, like Chris and you and me and Dave and others, who sort of scrambled into the rabbit warren almost, figuratively of course, because we were trying to find pathways of specificity. And so these specificities then began to take shape, like the Black Books thing and the TEPC thing. And then these others kept talking, Kevin and Kathy and others, they kept talking and they were asking: 'How do we give this thing a shape in the community as well?' So this was really getting started in '83, in a process of 'becoming' as much as being clearly formed.

But the other thing just for me was having enough money to live on. Just by chance this was the first year that that Aboriginal History course started at Macquarie, with Eric Wilmot and Michael Williams. Unfortunately Eric went to the Institute for Aboriginal Studies! I rang Michael up to wish him well, this was in February… And he asked me if I wanted a job as a casual tutor! Well, I did take it on, it gave me a bit more of an economic base. And what made it useful at least in my head was that I could see that here was the University base and over here was the Tranby/TEPC base. It allowed me to work on what possible ways you could see someone going from here to there, if they wanted to.

But that was just one pathway. There were other bridges to develop, to community organisations as they were becoming, there were public service positions people might have wanted to go into, it related to what they wanted, like that young woman who said: 'I want to become a nurse.' So then what we tried to do was to link her up specifically with people in nursing faculties and shape the course to fit what she would need. So it was individually tailored…

We were trying to create the TEPC structure that would give the students themselves the capacity and the information to go where they wanted to go. That's what we thought was the thing that was most important for that type of a course, rather than you finish a course first and then try to fill out forms about what you might want to do. What we were trying to do was very much the cultivation of individuals, so it was very intensive. It might have missed the mark many times but there were good intentions and plenty of energy!

Looking from the community

Isabel Flick was a key activist in north-west NSW, living in Collarenebri but travelling widely and well known as an advocate for better educational opportunities as well as land rights. She knew many of Tranby's country students because she had seen them in their community and family settings, and she knew the way that rural schools had undermined their confidence and failed them in any real education. As she watched those same students at Tranby, like Brendan and Jacqui, she saw the gains they made in practical knowledge and in confidence. She talked with Kevin about her impressions.

Figure 6.2: Isabel Flick sitting with a group of Tranby students – playing cards was a great way to break the ice.

Courtesy Chris Milne.

Isabel: I was surprised with Brendan last night at the Tranby Graduation: he got up and spoke … he was very nervous but he did the job really well. And I thought, for people like him and Jacqui, you know, that's what Tranby is all about, eh? It's given them a life, and it's given them education. And the self confidence.

Kevin: That young Cheryl too, she spoke like a professional last night. When she first started Tranby, she couldn't even look at you. She was that shy. I congratulated her and she said: 'I was really nervous!' But like I told her, I couldn't tell that at the time! It was excellent.

Isabel: That's where it gives us satisfaction, you know, to think that that's really happened. And we've watched Jacqui grow there. Its been one of the best things she ever did. Then that time when young Tommy got kicked out, you'd think it was the end of the world for him. He thought I was going to really back him up. But I said, 'Oh well, you couldn't have been doing the right thing'. And he started giving me a story. And then his sister came in and she told him off. And she said, 'Well, you weren't doing the right thing. You just go away and get your act together'. And he did too. And when he came back he really put his head down.

Kevin: Yeah, see they're not barred for life when they're told, 'Go and get your act together!' He mucked around for a whole year.

Isabel: Yes. He was so cocksure sure of himself wasn't he? But then he was right after that eh?

Now, the way those classes worked were of so much benefit too. Tranby had community people like me in there talking to the students. When they dealt with the Deaths in Custody reports I was able to tell them how that came about. About how Tranby College was the place that we had the first meeting to say, 'Can we get a Royal Commission into Deaths In Custody?' And they didn't even know that.

And it wasn't just students at Tranby either. The nicest experience that I've had in my time was this little Koorie girl at the St Scholastics Catholic school up the road. She hung around Tranby until she saw me and then she said, 'Oh, Aunty I just wondered if you'd come down there and help me. I'm doing this reconciliation thing, and I can't seem to get a lot of support. I know Aden Ridgeway's coming and Linda Burney but I'd like to get some Elders to come. And I thought I'd ask you'.

So I ended up doing that. I thought 'Oh, I hate this because I'm here, for the first time. I'm going to a Catholic school, and getting involved with Catholics'. But it turned out to be a really nice day. When I told them about how I learnt what a clothes-horse was, when I was apprenticed out and I thought it was a real horse, these kids in the classroom just busted themselves laughing! And then when I was telling them how my Mum's family was all sent away and a lot of the things that happened to us in between that, and they were saying, 'We don't understand'. One little girl said, 'Why did they go to a reserve? Where's a reserve? Where do you see a reserve?'

When then that young Koorie girl comes back to me after, and said, 'Well Aunt, you know what happened? The other Koorie kids don't talk to me now. Because they don't believe in reconciliation'. And I said: 'Oh, that's fine, you're starting to work in black politics now. You're going to be a stronger gin than me when you're finished, because now what have you got to say when people tell you, they don't believe in reconciliation? You can say, 'Oh well, lots of people don't. Some people do. But I've got my own opinion'. I said, 'You go on from there. I think you'll be a really good little ambassador for black people'.

Figure 6.3: Isabel and her sister, Rose Fernando, with their niece, Jacqui Mason when she graduated from her Tranby course.

Courtesy Chris Milne.

She said, 'Oh, I will say that too. I'm going over to New Zealand for this youth conference soon. And I said, 'Well, there you go. You're right into it, and you're 15'. She told me, 'I wouldn't be like you. I don't think I'll ever be like you'. I said, 'You're going to be better because you're going to have a good education, if you decide you're going to have a good education. You might decide you're going to get drunk and have babies and all that'. 'Oh, no', she said. 'No.'

And I said, 'Well, that's the decision you've got to make, only you can do that. If you need help or you want to talk to someone, there'll be someone here at Tranby to help you'. 'Really?' she said. So she got that support straight away. And that's why I think that was the most wonderful experience that I've had. Here's a young kid coming to me at Tranby and saying: 'How do I handle it?' And when she left she was really saying, 'Oh Aunty, I'm going to do this and I'm going to do that'. She said, 'I really feel better now. Thank you Aunty, I really feel better'.

Linking to the community

The teaching staff were also very conscious of trying to shape the course structures so as to take advantage of the community connections that Tranby offered as well as to make learning support available to community people who came to Tranby for political and social reasons. Here Terry Widders talked about how he saw the emerging college-based programs relating to the early idea of education *in* the community.

Terry: Well, Kathy Campbell as a community development person was there talking about community education in this meta way. And then we had all these people coming through Tranby all the time, people from Joe McGinness and Terry O'Shane from North Queensland to the north-west NSW mob, either just stopping over or dropping in on their way to a meeting. So there was still a fairly regular stream of people and so it was very much a lived expression: people would come and talk there, offload their agenda and talk about whatever they were on about, or what they were doing, like Joe in the north … So that whole 'ambience', if you like, of educational courses was still there, but we were asking, 'Where do you find a specific kind of a context for doing that?' and of course it had be balanced with the economic practicalities, 'What wherewithal did you have to do what you were thinking about doing?'

Figure 6.4: Cookie with Tranby students, 1985.

Courtesy Chris Milne.

So it was a wider idea than the old co-operative idea, where you set up a co-operative here and work out from that, build a bakery or whatever. This broader idea involved asking, 'What would be the kind of framework?' Would it be land rights in NSW? Or self-determination or autonomy at a local level? But you needed people to do that as well. 'So how do you actually *do* this?' This was my recollection of it anyway…

So if you've got TEPC and Business Studies… what else could you do to cultivate individuals who were already doing that work in the community? Like Karen Flick? At Tranby, you'd see people like Karen at that time who were not just standing still, they were actually already going, trying to gee up a whole region… like the whole of the north-west at the time… So there was another version of the little wet fowls if you like – another version of the people who wanted to do something and were looking for pathways.

For these people out in the community, how do you support them? To be in accord with that broader, community dynamic? And what's the structure you might set up? Do you set up a central community committee?

Well in a way, it was already there, just through the way Cookie and others *knew* people, whether it was the South Coast, the north-west, or across the whole country. But at the same time, I think it was always also a question of: 'Well, it's a great idea, and you might put them up at a base here, but what's going to pay the wages for the next month, and the month after that? What's going to pay for the renovations that the place needed just to keep going?' So those things were running at the same time too. It was a matter of setting up a base, financially as well as with practical programs.

And the thing I remember coming up in a practical kind of way was the women's group called NOW in western Sydney, with Robyn Williams. That developed through 1984, it was a lot about reflections on life experience for many of the people in it, so it was a pretty open weave set of possibilities.

And certainly things at Tranby were becoming a bit shaped up because of the structure out of which it came, like TAFE and its courses and accreditation and that sort of thing. But woven through that were all these other individuals, like Karen Flick and Joe McGinness and the other visitors. So the question for us all was, 'How do you get a grip on that in other ways than have a cup of tea and a talk?' Because the parts of that new structure at Tranby, the administration, Black Books, classes, getting funding… was all taking up a fair bit of time of the relatively limited numbers of people who were there. Well, I thought that one way to engage with all the people around like Karen and Joe was really just to *offer*: just offer support and let them decide what they needed or wanted…

Tranby and young people from the bush

Karen Flick was one of the young people living in the bush who came into contact with Kevin Cook and Tranby through her family taking part in the country meetings in which Kevin and Tranby were involved. Her practical education and opportunity to take part in politics was through Cookie and Tranby. In this section, Karen is talking with Kevin about her experience of Tranby and its backing of her work and learning.

Karen: I think the first things that I remember to do with Tranby and with you Cookie was I always heard your name around the house up in Wee Waa. Kevin Cook this, yeah, and Kevin Cook that! And if you want to get anything done well all we got to do is ring up Kevin Cook. And as a kid, I never knew who this Kevin Cook was you know!

So as I'm growing up, I started to go to all the meetings with Mum and Dad and Aunty Iz and all that mob, and that's when I got to meet you. We were setting up the first state land council, before the Act, it was the organising, campaigning body. Those were meetings where you'd go to just sit down and have a yarn with people and get strength from each other. We'd be talking about the issues and working out where we wanted to go with it, to come up with a bit of a strategy about stuff. Those were bush meetings or, you know meetings at somebody's house or, or whatever and a couple of the ones that I remember were the regular ones at Dubbo out at the farm. But also the ones down at Menindee on the mission there and, people would just come from all over the place, and, and also when we first set up the North Western Regional Land Council at Angledool.

Cookie was a key player for us in terms of finding the dollars to allow people to meet and sit down and yarn. But it wasn't just the dollar side of it, it was also, for me anyway, to provide a bit of solidarity and a strategic approach so that we who are out there in the bush knew that we had some other contacts and that there was support elsewhere. So for us, for me anyway, Cookie was somebody who was able to bring a lot of different people together, and, you know facilitate those meetings and allow that discussion to happen.

So through Cookie and Tranby, we'd be connecting up with people like Jacko Campbell and Nan Campbell and that mob from the South Coast, so it wasn't very many people but it was a good solid group of hard core people who would get up and have a go. And these are also the people I think who also did things in their own communities. You know who challenged all the time and never gave up. It was also about sitting down with your family, so you'd have kids there running around, or you'd have old people, or you'd have a game of cards, and everybody would just be there sitting around. So you'd have all these political discussions and meetings but it was in the right kind of atmosphere and I think that's what worked a lot.

I remember at one of the Dubbo meetings and Cookie approached me about going to the Kimberleys for some Federation of Land Council meeting, and I think I just said yes. I mean I didn't even know where I was going or what the hell I was going to do there, and…

Kevin: I had a pretty good approach, I just said 'You're going to the Kimberleys…'!

Karen: I said 'yes' because it showed me that somebody else had some faith in me and trusted me to do that and so I felt pretty proud about it.

I remember when I went up to the Kimberleys, I like it so much because of two things. One was catching that red eye flight from Sydney to Perth. You stopped at all those places along the way in the middle of the night. Then, flying into Kununurra you see those huge rocks, and I was seeing the country for the first time from up here. It looked just like I could see the spirit in the land, you know you could see those giant sleeping lizards or you could see something had happened there. That for me really connected with country. It was like all those discussions that we'd been having in those bush meetings, about how connecting with country was so important.

But the other thing about going to the Kimberleys was that I was welcomed there and I was welcomed through Cookie's name. So then we got off up there and there was this other old fella from Cairns, he's come across from the North Queensland Land Council. And he was talking about Kevin Cook this and Kevin Cook that as well, so it was obvious the name was around the place. And then I met Johnny Watson for the first time and, Jimmy Bindary at Kununurra and that was just absolutely amazing.

The meeting was in language most of the time, it wasn't a big meeting but there were big issues going on, it was after Noonkanbah and it was around the same time as the Argyle Diamond Mine fight, so people were really concerned about those particular issues and how the company was treating them. So the Federation of Land Councils played a fairly big role in that. And Cookie's association with that travelled all across the country. I actually talked to Johnny Watson about this, many years after when I actually went up there to work. When I first met him that time, he'd sleep right there and I'd be over here and he was sort of looking out for me and making sure that I was okay. When I talked to him years later he said, 'I looked after you because of Cookie', because he knew Cookie and he respected him and he knew that there was this thing called the Federation of Land Councils was a pretty solid organisation.

***

Those of us who were teachers at Tranby were often, like myself, Heather Goodall, university graduates with a strong interest in Aboriginal politics – but not a lot of teaching experience or even qualifications. Kevin had invited us to come on board because he liked our enthusiasm and our politics – but he wanted to reshape the learning at Tranby too. Apart from Brian, most of us had not thought about how to pass on the knowledge we had gained over the years at schools and universities, much less about how we could learn from students. And the Tranby students, as Karen and Isabel have explained, had a wealth of life experiences between them all. So we needed to learn from each other – but when we started at Tranby, we did not have many ideas of how to make that happen.

Figure 6.5: Chris Milne in 1984, while he was teaching at Tranby.

Courtesy Chris Milne.

Chris Milne came to Tranby soon after Brian and Terry started. Chris had a degree in economics and was working on a NSW government research project with Lyall Munro jnr in Redfern, about identifying Aboriginal children in out-of home care. Brian brought some students to talk to Chris about the project and then, seeing an opportunity to fill a real gap in Tranby's teaching capacity, Brian asked Chris if he would come to Tranby to do some teaching in statistics.

This worked well with Kevin's goal to make sure the College could teach both the politics of economy but also the basic numeracy needed to run a co-operative or a community business. So before long, Chris was given the role of organising Business Studies and maths, numeracy and economics across all the programs, and later the first computing courses. And then it wasn't long again before Chris was involved in excursions and the wider activities of students.

Like Brian and Kevin, Chris found the College had created a welcoming space for its students. He remembered that a number of young gay Aboriginal students came to Sydney and felt accepted at Tranby, whereas they had been uncomfortable in their home communities, which highlights one of the contradictions of the times. But Tranby was not without its own tensions. One of the issues which demanded attention from everyone was gender. Kevin's experience in the Builders Labourers' Federation had already showed him the strengths of women's presence in a union, and in education, women were more highly visible than in other industries. But at Tranby initially, as Chris pointed out, there was a largely male leadership until Helen Boyle became Director of Studies, in the mid 1980s, after Brian Doolan had left to take up work in Central Australia. Helen's role was not an easy one for many of the men in the organisation: Chris saw it as one of the costs of change for many of them, both personally and politically. But the examples of Isabel and other strong women involved in Tranby were crucial in establishing it as an environment where women's voices could be heard. The effectiveness of that voice is clear in the next chapter in which Karen Flick talks with Kevin about the campaign to end black deaths in custody. Karen, herself from NSW, Rose Stack the Tranby librarian and Helen Boyle, the Director of Studies, both from Western Australia, and Rose Wanganeen, a Tranby teacher from South Australia, all took extensive roles, with Isabel herself, in shaping that campaign tirelessly.

While these currents were all important parts of the way Tranby offered new learning experiences for both students and staff, we all felt the need to think about our 'teaching' – and how we were not confident that we were much good at it. The importance of the link between communities and the College, and the role of political activism in college teaching, were fundamental to the way things changed, but as well, we as teachers had to change too.

Chris remembers that many of us – who had degrees but no teaching qualifications – relied on our own classroom experiences, however unhappy they might have been. I was certainly one who did that at Tranby in 1983. I can remember that, the more worried I became that I wasn't teaching well in my first few months of teaching Tertiary Prep history, the more I fell back on the most authoritarian of my school memories – asking students to rote learn dates or 'causes and effects'. Brian Doolan realised that we all needed to get some training, and he enrolled the lot of us in a TAFE Graduate Diploma in Adult Community Education, starting in August 1983. We discovered the working class traditions of English trade union education, but which had been reshaped in the light of community education movements in Latin America and Africa in the 1960s. So we were pushed over the edge – pretty eagerly – into experiments in 'participant-directed learning'. We were suddenly able to restructure the Tranby programs so they reflected students' interests and took off from students' knowledge. For staff like me, and for some students, this was a breathtaking relief! But for other students, it was a frustrating time when there seemed to be no scaffolding and no direction to the learning we were offering. As Chris too remembers, for many of the Tranby students their expectation was that to be credible, Tranby should be like school. They wanted to be catching up on what they had missed at school, not being forced to leap off into a new direction.

In time, things settled down a bit – the feedback from students and the recognition that each student had their own learning style all helped to make teachers more receptive to really learning from students. There is a whole other book here to be explored... with more student voices! But that will have to wait till later.

7. Politics and real education

The last two chapters looked at the emergence of formal educational courses on site at Tranby. Over the same time, as Karen Flick pointed out, Kevin was involved in the political campaigning for land rights across the state, culminating in the achievement of the New South Wales Land Rights Act in 1983.[1] These different tracks – education and politics – are often seen separately. But they worked together in the way Kevin and his comrades understood real learning could take place through Tranby, as they explain in this chapter.

In the first section of this chapter, Kevin and Brian Doolan talk over the way they saw education and politics interacting at Tranby. Then three of the key areas of this interaction are sketched out. The first is TUCAR, the Trade Union Committee on Aboriginal Rights, a strategic body which Kevin set up before he went to Coady although it continued to play a key role in both the college and in political activity after his return. Then there are two examples of the approaches to engaging politics which really developed after Kevin's time in Canada. One is the incorporation of senior Aboriginal people into the teaching program at Tranby as a way to support their political roles. The other is the campaign to end black deaths in custody, which drew strongly for its eastern Australian campaign on the infrastructure and support it received from Tranby.

The chapter draws on the memories and voices of many people – sometimes those of people who worked at Tranby and taught in the programs, while others are from the community members who took part in the courses or who, just as importantly, used Tranby as a base for some of their powerful mobilisations in the 1980s against racism and prejudice in the law, education, land, employment and housing.

While there were different themes among the people and movements who came through the door at Tranby – the common ground was that Kevin made a space for all of them, with the only demand being that the activists in turn make time for Tranby students to come, to talk and to listen to the way things worked.

He also encouraged them to talk with each other – in TUCAR for example, Kevin was able to bring together trade unionists from widely different commitments in working class politics, like communists and the right wing of the Australian Labor Party – far more widely than he would have been able to do from inside one union. Among the Aboriginal people as well, he was able to foster strong friendships between key people who would otherwise have been separated by long distances and the pressures of local campaigns, such as the friendships

---

1 *Aboriginal Land Rights Act 1983* (NSW).

between Jacko Campbell from Roseby Park on the South Coast with Isabel Flick, from inland Collarenebri. Or between Isabel and Joe McGinness, from far North Queensland. As they all shared desks, shared meals and had unhurried talks together over shared cups of tea in the Tranby sun, all these people built up lasting connections.

Figure 7.1: Judy Chester, Cookie and Kevin Tory, each with a key role in TUCAR, were here carrying an Aboriginal flag at a land rights demonstration.

Courtesy Judy Chester family collection.

The person who helped to make it all work – alongside Kevin – was Judy Chester. Kevin and Margaret had split up by the time Kevin began work at Tranby and for a few years he was a single dad when Susie and Mereki came to stay. Then he met Judy. She was a Wiradjuri woman from Wellington who came to Sydney as a young girl when her family had to move to the city for medical treatment. She married in the area and raised her three children, Jodi, Peter and Jannette, around Liverpool in the 'new' suburb of Green Valley. Judy first came in contact with Tranby when local, grass-roots Aboriginal women began calling for a program that met their desires to re-enter the education process. They contacted Tranby, which sent teachers like Terry Widders to work with the local women to set up a totally new program they called 'NOW'. This was so successful, the idea was later taken up by TAFE and, under the NOW banner, offered to women in many different areas. A bit later on, when her marriage broke down, Judy moved with her children into the inner city.

Judy got back in touch with Tranby and after a while she and Cookie began what was to become a lifelong relationship. Judy kept on extending her education, which led to her work with Tranby in its Action Development Unit and then as an organiser for the Public Sector Union where she made strong new friends. Just as important for her was her role as the partner in Cookie's life. She formed close, generous friendships with all the people Cookie brought together through Tranby and their shared political work. Together, they kept what they laughed about as the 'Elastic House' – their home and their warm companionship was always able to be expanded to fit whoever needed them.

Shared visions

Brian Doolan: I'd met some amazing people when I was at Wilcannia, who despite the tough conditions they faced, were still willing to stand up and try to set up the education centres and the medical services. Coming to Tranby, I had the real privilege of seeing these people and others like them from all over the place coming through, people like Jacko Campbell, Merv and Shirley Penrith, Barbara Flick and Tombo Winters, standing up saying: 'Now we want to get on with achieving our rights!' There was a very strong sense of rights which was an incredibly exciting thing. And it was interesting that it was around that desk where Kevin was sitting and around his telephone, that a lot of those people criss-crossed with one another. It was that whole enabling environment.

I think you could have walked into Tranby and said, 'I want to start the next shot for Mars', Cookie's response probably would have been, 'Yeah, okay, now how are we going to? What are you going to do?'

It wouldn't be, 'Yes, I'm going to back you' necessarily. It certainly wouldn't have been, 'Oh yeah, okay, this is how you do it', because it was never directional. It would have been something like, 'Gee, that's really interesting'. And if you could show a bit of nous about how you talked about it and how you were planning it, then Cookie would back it at that point. And that would sort of validate it.

And so if somebody else walked in and said, 'They're mad', his response would be, 'Well, you know, we're all mad'. It wouldn't be necessarily that they're not mad – you don't put people down for being mad!

So I come back to this whole enabling thing that Kevin has allowed. He has played a validating role because he holds a position that people respect. So if Cookie says, 'Yeah, it's alright' or 'Yeah, that person's okay', that carries enormous weight because there's such high respect for him throughout the community. And I don't just mean the Aboriginal community – I mean throughout the broadest community! In the trade union movement, in parliament amongst politicians, amongst the community groups, amongst activists. He has been able to validate a whole lot of initiatives that may well have died had they not got that sort of validation and that support.

As an example, I think the Deaths in Custody movement was one where there was a really important issue but there were only a few people involved in trying to raise it. And the fact that Cookie was known to be a friend of those people, was showing support for those people, was allowing meetings to go on at Tranby and giving the resources of the organisation and was from time to time lending his own time to go along and help organise things, helped the growth enormously. And it doesn't mean that Cookie started it. He didn't. Other people started it. But he *enabled* it.

There was the same thing with Black Books, the idea of setting up an Aboriginal-controlled book shop which would supply texts to schools so that schools could run Aboriginal Studies courses. I'm bloody sure Kevin's never had the experience of setting up a book chain. But he *enabled* that to happen. He didn't straight away say, 'Oh, no, that's too much' or 'No, our strategy is we've got to focus on X, Y or Z'. It's, 'Yeah, if there are some people that want to seriously give that a go, well, use the front room over there and off you go!' He allowed it to happen.

The whole Trade Union Committee on Aboriginal Rights was a similar thing. There were a lot of people in trade unions who, out of a sense of good will, a sense of justice, a sense of fairness, wanted to support Aboriginal people and the Aboriginal struggles in their different forms. But they found it really difficult to hook into the Koorie community. They found a bridge in TUCAR and Cookie, who was somebody who would say, 'Yeah, you're not the enemy. In fact you're an ally'. And, 'Yeah if you want to organise that demo or you want to organise that meeting or you want to organise that committee and the fundraiser or whatever, you can give it a go'.

So he enabled it and sort of gave it validation. So that they could say, 'Yes, it's not just us floating off on our own white fellow idea. We have a link to the Aboriginal movement'. And that link very importantly had credibility. Because there were other people also who were trying to provide links who didn't necessarily have the credibility that Kevin had.

They're just a couple of examples that have quickly come to mind. And of course also, most importantly, was the whole land rights movement in the period of the preparation of the Green Paper. The fact that Tranby was able to act as a base for rural Aboriginal people from lots of parts of the state, from Broken Hill, Wilcannia, Menindee, Collarenebri, Moree, from the South Coast and up north, all the different places. That people had a point they could come to.

They had a choice in that, of course. There was also the Redfern base around the legal service and other places. But many people chose to use Tranby as their point of reference, as the base from which they would work when they came to Sydney. It was the point from which they would go to Parliament House or go to the Select Committee hearing or organise the demonstration or whatever. Again that was just an example of Cookie resourcing, allowing, things to happen. He was not leading, you know. Although a lot of people would say, 'Kevin's our leader' or 'Kevin's in charge'. And I remember Cookie's response to that as always being, 'Oh, bullshit!' But certainly his role was in *allowing* it to happen and giving it some resources, giving it a resource base as it developed. And always encouraging the discussion. He encouraged the honest discussion, the hard discussions about *how* it was developing.

What do you think about all of that Cookie? How do you see all those things fitting together? Or didn't they?

Kevin: They did. They did fit together and they did quite well. Because there's a lot of people who come here who weren't exposed to different things. And I always said this, is that when the Tranby Board or when TUCAR were meeting at Tranby, the students would be involved because they'd see white people coming into the organisation, sitting down and they could sit in there with them. And they could see that the white people weren't leading the discussions. At the TUCAR meetings, the Aboriginal people would lead the discussions and the trade union movement would back them. That's what we asked them to do. We said, 'We need the backing of the trade union movement. This is the organisation we believe that can get our message across and hopefully that the unions can get behind and so to push our message'. And that's what I wanted students to see at Tranby, and lots of them did see it.

The churches were another supporter that we had, the Australian Council of Churches (ACC). We had some of the meetings of the Aboriginal Advisory body for that ACC at Tranby. You had people like Terry O'Shane, Johnny Ah Kit,[2] Gary Foley – people from all over Australia were on the Australia Council of Churches Aboriginal Committee. We didn't agree with what the churches were doing 100 per cent, and they didn't agree with us. But we got along fine as long as we didn't go behind their back to do anything. We'd say, 'This is what we're going to say!' And you know, it might be against the church policy. But the next day we'd be meeting in there, nothing said, you know. That was our

---

2 John Ah Kit, whom Kevin more usually called 'Jack' or 'Ah Kit'.

prerogative. We could go against them and they could go against us. So I think that's the way it worked and it worked really well. And Tranby students got to see some of that as well. So that's how the politics fitted in with the education centre work.

Brian: Students used to watch that, even if they weren't directly involved in it. It was just part of the atmosphere.

Kevin: Yeah, and that's what I'm saying. For our students, where they came from in a lot of country areas, it was 'us' and 'them'. They didn't have a good relationship with any white person. But by the time they left Tranby, a couple of them had made very strong friends with white people and they took them back to their country and showed them around – and they're still really close knit. That was good because it showed that you could work together. And Aboriginal people like Isabel Flick had four or five people behind her from Tranby, black and white, and she got a hell of a lot of work done in country areas. She got on with some of the white people because she didn't take a backwards step! So she got people around her. I think that was what Tranby was all about in those days. We had some very influential people like Isabel working with us.

TUCAR

Figure 7.2: Dick Scott at an early Tranby meeting.

Courtesy Tranby Archives.

7. Politics and real education

Setting up the Trade Union Committee on Aboriginal Rights (TUCAR) created a way that the Aboriginal political movements could interact with the broader community – in this case through the trade unions – as well as providing a space for sharing information. As Kevin was well aware in 1975, there had been many unions which had had a long involvement with Tranby, like the fund-raising and on-the-job training programs carried out for years by the Seamen's Union. But times had changed. Aboriginal activists were more assertive about their need and right to speak for their own community goals, and they often shook off white support, feeling it would be controlling and exploitative. So unions which had been sympathetic, began to worry about whether they were being paternalistic and they had become more confused about how to offer support.

Kevin saw the need to foster a new space for communication between Aboriginal people and the trade unions. He had good friends who were active unionists, like Rod Pickette in the ATEA (Australian Theatrical and Amusement Employees Association) and Meredith Burgmann in the Union of Academic Staff Associations (later the National Tertiary Education Union – NTEU). Together they imagined a body based at Tranby which would offer that space. They talked over a number of names and decided on TUCAR – it was a pronouncible acronym and its role was clear. Kevin took Meredith to talk with Alf, still the General Secretary, in around 1977 and with his support, Meredith, Rod and Kevin set up TUCAR.

As Brian Doolan had observed, unions 'found a bridge in TUCAR and in Cookie' which allowed them to connect to broader Aboriginal and Islander communities. There was enough initial interest to form a committee and negotiate a space for it in the NSW Trades and Labour Council building in Sussex Street. Kevin could draw on his old comrades from the Builders Labourers' Federation and sympathetic unions like the Construction, Forestry, Mining and Energy Union (CFMEU) while Rod could mobilise the arts and media unions and Meredith had access to the large body of sympathetic academics across the country. TUCAR was aimed at informing unions about Aboriginal goals and seeking union support for Aboriginal campaigns.

The key to TUCAR's effectiveness was, however, the seniority of the union delegates who included a stellar array of the most well known unionists in the state. The participants went far beyond the networks around left-wing unions which Kevin himself had developed in the BLF, linked to the Left of the ALP and the majority of the membership of the Communist Party of Australia who had split with Moscow after the invasion of Czechoslovakia in 1968. As well, however, TUCAR included the networks which Alf Clint had nurtured with the Communist-led unions which stayed with the Moscow line, like the Seamen's Union of Australia and the Miners' Union. And it brought in some powerful right-wing Labor Party unions, who were sympathetic to Aboriginal rights regardless of their politics. A key example was Charlie Oliver, the General Secretary of the Australian Workers' Union (AWU), a right-wing union which had always covered rural Aboriginal workers like shearers and rousabouts, but which had often failed to take public stands in support of Aboriginal issues. Oliver, however, became unshakable in his commitment to support Tranby however difficult the issue might be.

Figure 7.3: Charlie Oliver with Desmond Tutu.

Courtesy Tranby Archives.

With time, TUCAR needed a full time worker and with funds raised by the union affiliation fees, it employed a series of Aboriginal organisers including Lee Silva and later Kevin Tory, an Aboriginal man from North Coast NSW who brought with him not only a background in Aboriginal politics but a legacy of proud anti-colonial activism from his father's Indian parents. New faces joined the committee and support group, including Hannah Middleton, an industrial relations academic who had became the honorary secretary of TUCAR by 1981.

The support that unions could offer was considerable. A good example was the continuing problem of housing. Families being forced to pay rents for substandard housing on government reserves was a recurring problem, highlighted by a community-wide rent strike at Purfleet in Taree in 1960 but repeated many times since then. To this was added the frustration which many Aboriginal people felt when they had tried to purchase the houses they paid rent on for years, believing after confusing discussions with state government officials, that they were paying off the purchase price of the land. TUCAR took up such issues, lending union weight to the public calls for a rapid hand over of government housing to such long term Aboriginal householders.[3] At many other times, TUCAR coordinated mailouts and fundraising, offering political, moral and financial support to similar local and regional campaigns.

Just as important as what unions put in was the information sharing process. TUCAR meetings as Meredith, Rod and Kevin have described, often involved Kevin and other Aboriginal speakers giving union representatives sketches of current issues in various communities and an analysis of the overall progress in gaining better state legislation. These thumbnail sketches found their way back into union newsletters and work site meetings, building up a stronger and better informed link between Aboriginal and union movements at grass roots level, not just between delegates. It was particularly important that this flow of information had operated in terms of land rights because there was such a lot of local information which had seldom circulated outside the Aboriginal community before, as the previous chapter has made clear. Because Kevin had been mobilising this circulation of information about the ongoing land campaign since 1977 – and particularly since 1980 when the Wran Government had set up a Select Committee to inquire into the needs for land among Aboriginal people in NSW – there was a strong awareness of this issue. Trade union support was called on at many times, but the critical one was in 1981, when the Select Committee had strongly recommended action to fulfil land rights demands but the Wran Government seemed disinclined to act. Kevin takes up this story in conversation with fellow TUCAR founder, Rod Pickette.

Kevin: Well it looked like the recommendations were just going to sit there and Wran wasn't going to do anything with them…

Rod: So on May 11, 1981, we got up this deputation from TUCAR unions to Neville Wran, to try to get him moving on implementing the recommendations of the Select Committee. Because it looked a lot like the Labor government was just going to ignore its own committee recommendations, or water down the land rights stuff by mainly focusing on education and housing. So we called on the unions who'd been interested and active in TUCAR and organised this meeting with Wran.

Kevin: We expected about five unions didn't we? The Premier's office said we could have six. And we got about 15! Among others, we had Stan Sharkey from the BWIU,[4] Col Cooper from Telecom, Hannah Middleton, from TUCAR, plus Pat Geraghty from the Seamen's Union and Dick Scott from the Metalworkers!

---

3   TUCAR minutes, 21 February 1978.
4   Building Workers' Industrial Union.

And of course there was Charlie Oliver. He was on the Right in the ALP and – in ordinary union politics, you didn't hear anything coming from him, you know? – you wouldn't know which way he was thinking. But from our point of view at TUCAR or Tranby, anything that we asked for, we got! We asked him for support to go to Wran at that meeting. When he walked in, Wran was very surprised! 'Cause old Charlie used to pull a lot of weight with the Labor Party, not just at the state level but at the federal level too. Maybe more than Neville Wran, who was the Premier of the state!

Rod: I remember it sort of shook them out of a bit of lethargy, didn't it? Just the standing of all those people who came along. The government, particularly Wran's minders, were taken aback. They hadn't expected this sort of breadth of concern.

Kevin: Yeah. And we only told them the unions that were coming. We didn't tell them which *people* were coming! And then when we all rocked up – they were running! His minders were running!!

Looking back, Kevin talked with Terry O'Shane about the role of TUCAR in the overall mobilisation of unions to support Aboriginal campaigns, including the Bicentennial in 1988.

Kevin: TUCAR played a good role, linking up with the trade unions. Kevin Tory and I would go down to see Martin Ferguson, when he was on the ACTU,[5] and he'd say, 'Don't give us anything we can't do first up'. So we said 'Employment' and so he worked for an Aboriginal person to be employed on all the Labour Councils, in every state.

But if he couldn't do something he'd say so. He'd say: 'I can't help you there, that'd split the trade union movement, but you should go ahead and do it.' And he'd tell us which unions he thought would back whatever it was, and who to see there. So he was really helpful that way. Jennie George was another one. One of the things that came out of it was we were able to get people from the Federation of Land Councils to address the ACTU.

But when you think about it, you might say 'Oh well, we done that', or 'We got that done' – as if it was easy. But it was really hard work, you know – for TUCAR! We used to have meetings once a fortnight to build that trade union support up. Remember that? And then it started going real well. After the big demonstrations in '88, everybody wanted to be our friend, you know? They said, 'How did youse organise that?' We said, 'Oh, it's pretty easy'.

---

5   Australian Council of Trade Unions.

Leaders and elders

Kevin's family life, then his work in unions and in co-operatives meant that he built up strong relationships with senior community leaders – older people with both knowledge and passion who remained active in their communities but wanted to have a say in the bigger debates as well. Each of these people were frequent visitors to the college and all the students became familiar with them and had access to them, which ensured they were mentors on many informal levels. Each of them also had a role in fostering particular programs or campaigns which spilled over into the students' lives, contributing to their formal or their informal educational experience while at the college.

One person Kevin had known was Jacko Campbell, from Roseby Park where he had settled although he still had family in Kempsey. Jacko was part of a strong network of South Coast elders and activists. His wife Nan and their daughter Delia were activists in their own right, while others like Guboo Ted Thomas, from Wallaga Lake, had shared memories with Jacko of life at Sydney's Salt Pan Creek during the Depression. Others again, like the younger couple, Mervyn and Shirley Penrith, also from Wallaga, had become allies of Jacko as he battled for decent housing in the early 1970s. Often accompanied by Terry Fox, then a Catholic priest, and with assistance from Merv Nixon, from the South Coast Trades and Labour Council, these South Coast Aboriginal people were frequent visitors to Tranby, building on their South Coast kinship with Kevin to develop strong relationships with Tranby staff and students.

Joe McGinness was another old friend of Kevin's. Joe had been a stalwart as the President of FCAATSI (Federal Council for the Advancement of Aborigines and Torres Strait Islanders) in the 1960s, uniting Aboriginal activists from across the country. He himself had come from Darwin, where he worked as a wharfie, and travelled to North Queensland with the Army, leaving that port for overseas service during World War Two. He was demobilised in Cairns and remained there, continuing his maritime work and marrying into a local Aboriginal family.

He became one of the key activists in Queensland and federal activism, campaigning for civil rights and for land rights. Joe continued to be particularly interested in union and co-operative ventures, advising Tranby on its bakery and other co-operative ventures in North Queensland. He visited Tranby with another North Queensland activist and unionist, Terry O'Shane, where Kevin met them before he was sent by Alf to North Queensland to visit the Tranby co-operatives there. Kevin stayed with Joe when he was there, and in return Joe stayed in with Kevin whenever he came to Sydney.

Figure 7.4: Nan Campbell (left) with her sister and other South Coast women.

Courtesy Heather Goodall.

Figure 7.5: Joe McGinness and Cookie at Tranby.

Courtesy Tranby Archives.

Over the years after Kevin and Margaret had separated, Kevin's accommodation had often been rough, so when Joe first started coming down to Sydney regularly, he would stay in the student accommodation at the back of the Glebe classrooms or at the Tranby-managed hostel in the Rocks. Later on, as Kevin set up a much more comfortable household with Judy, Joe would stay with them. Either way, Joe was often at Tranby, and his warm, broad smile became a welcome sight for students and visitors to the College over many years. When an area of land at Clump Mountain near Mission Beach, south of Cairns, was bequeathed to Tranby, Joe took up a position on the Board and continued to advise Tranby on the running of the property which remains part of Tranby to this day.

The third key community elder whom Kevin drew in to be a frequent visitor and mentor at Tranby was Isabel Flick, the Gamilaraay woman from Collarenebri, whose observations on the effect Tranby had on students coming from the community were included in the previous chapter. Isabel became a commanding presence at Tranby during the later 1980s and 1990s, well known to students and drawing great strength and resources from the students and staff at the college. Isabel had worked in a city hospital for some years in the early 1970s, where she met Paul Torzillo when he was training in medicine and before he had joined the Board at Tranby. But Isabel had only vaguely heard of Tranby by the time she returned to the bush in the late 1970s. She explained how she then became closely involved with Tranby in the early 1980s during the campaigns for land and for an end to black deaths in custody.

Black Deaths in Custody

The campaign to end black deaths in custody is a good example of the type of campaign which Tranby was able to support and which in turn was an important learning resource for students. The story is told here by Karen Flick, who is Isabel's niece, and by Isabel herself. Both were involved in the support of the Murray family after Eddie Murray was found dead in police custody in Wee Waa in 1981. When talking with Kevin, they explained how they saw Tranby getting involved in supporting the initial political activism around land which was occurring in Wee Waa when Eddie died, and then how the College became a resource base for the campaign to assist Eddie's family and to try to win justice for the many people who had died in similarly suspicious circumstances.

Karen had been living in Wee Waa in 1981, and remembers the planning which was going into organising an occupation to reclaim a centrally-placed camping ground for Aboriginal cotton seasonal workers in the chipping season, from which the local council had just barred them. The Aboriginal workers from all over the state had annually camped at Tulladunna, just on the edge of town and next to the river, from which they could easily be hired each morning for the long day's work of chipping out the choking weeds which grow around young cotton plants. The council argued this was an 'unsightly' camp and wanted the workers to be moved to a newly created Aboriginal Reserve, eight kilometres out of town. The Aboriginal protesters saw this as part of the wider issue of land rights and hoped an occupation would bring publicity and stop the council before the summer chipping season began.

Karen: We had been talking about land matters I guess around Wee Was for a long time, and then the council started to close down some of the camping areas saying it was unhealthy or something like that, it was not fit for people and the water was buggered up. But *they* had buggered the water up themselves, through the run off of the chemicals they used on the cotton! So we campaigned around the land issue – it was about challenging the local council that Tulladunna had to be left open because for people who come there and work, seasonally on the cotton chipping, that was the place that they would stay. So, we had a responsibility to keep Tulladunna open.

Kevin: We'd heard about this occupation from the Flick family and we organised the Tranby bus to go up. We had a few students from Collarenebri at that time, like Chittles (Colin Thorne) and some other students that Isabel had been sending down. And we had some lawyers and Madeline McGrady, the Aboriginal filmmaker coming too, to document the occupation.

Karen: Yeah that's right, you were all coming up anyway from Sydney and the South Coast to support the June land rights occupation. Then Eddie Murray was killed in June and that involved our family and the Murray family big time obviously. I remember the day that Helen Murray, his sister, came around and said to Mum and Aunty Iz, 'You got to come! You got to come! Eddie's dead', so they just jumped in the car and went up there. And then all the other things that happened after that, it was very intense, it was very difficult to go through that, anytime anyway.

There were a whole lot of other questions that needed to be asked so we decided that we would go ahead with having the sit-in at Tulladunna. It was a bigger picture – it was about whether somebody could come there and be able to get some employment and be safe at the end of it all.

Kevin: We camped there, the nights we were there for that weekend occupation, I remember how cold it was, in the middle of winter.

Karen: Yeah, and it was getting pretty hostile wasn't it.

7. Politics and real education

Figure 7.6: Isabel Flick speaking at a Black Deaths in Custody rally.

Courtesy Tranby Archives.

Kevin: That's right – that car come that night. Tried to run over the tents. One of the Koorie lads from Tranby was sleeping in it. He jumped up and chased the car, banged on it with his fists on the windows… I thought he'd be knocked ass over head, jeez he was close to getting knocked over.

Karen: Yeah, and it was all that small town stuff, you know, that was really raw and red for me. Because all we were doing was sitting on our country, standing up for our rights and challenging the authorities about the death and what had happened.

Karen's Aunty Isabel stayed with the Murray family after Eddie's death, and she was with the family through the first half of the inquest held in Wee Waa. It became clear during that hearing that the police had serious problems with their accounts of which officers had been on duty the day Eddie Murray died. One was shown to have been misleading the court in his evidence. The second part of the inquest was due to be heard in Sydney.

Isabel: When the Coroner's Court was going to be shifted down to Sydney, we realised then that the Murray family wasn't going to get the kind of support that we were hoping. They were so upset, you know, they needed to be taken to and from the court and looked after all the time, because they were in a sick state really. And we were the ones trying to do all of that. So we said: 'Oh, we'll have to contact Kevin and see what he can do'. At the time, the Murray family didn't know about Tranby.

And so it worked out that Kevin had a bus there to meet us at the train. 'Cause on the trip down, we were all sitting up on the train all through the night, and we were all pretty knocked out by the time we got here. And then I was thinking about how hard it was that we had to get down here to the court, and this is the mother and father of the boy that's been killed and their family. We weren't worried about ourselves, we were just thinking: 'How can we make it better for them?' And then Kevin sorted it all out for us, met us at the railway. And took us over to Tranby with this big breakfast ready and everybody was able to freshen up a bit and go on down to the Coroner's Court there. So, that sort of eliminated a lot of worry for us with that.

Really since that time we built up a good sort of communication thing, and if I run into some kind of problem out there I could always ring Kevin and he'd be running around like a scalded chook too, but he'd always find someway to handle my stuff as well, and then we'd analyse it a bit later. So I reckon we had a really good little unit to keep us going.

Because after the inquest, with that 'Open' verdict, we couldn't just let it go. We wanted to go on and try to push to find out what really happened. But to go on to try to set up the push for a Royal Commission into the Deaths in Custody was a pretty full-on sort of decision for us. It made it better because we knew we had that support here in Sydney at Tranby. And then when we were talking to the lawyers, well, it just sort of automatically happened, Kevin did all the lawyer stuff, and getting them together and we just had to come down and talk at the meetings, and say: 'Can it happen?'

Karen: I came to Sydney not long after that, and was working at Tranby, and got involved with the Black Deaths in Custody Committee… there was some activity already, because there had been John Pat's death in September the year before, in WA, so it must have been 1980. And, I remember when we came down for the inquest, we were asked to talk at the next rally about John Pat's death, which was September. I remember Aunty Iz and I came down to speak at it. I remember going to the rally with Aunty Iz and Madeline mob was there with her camera.

And I talked to people about that. I talk to Mum and Dad and I talk to Aunty Iz and I talk to Leila and Yabbu [Eddie Murray's parents] about whether I should get involved, because I'd be talking about their issues, so I was conscious of making sure that it was all okay. And, they said fine yes, be involved, you know. And, once again the resources of Tranby and Cookie supporting all of that was what, and during all that time, once again I think I continually sought counsel from Cookie, because there were some hard issues that we were going through.

Karen: I mean we were talking about challenging the entire judicial system about what's going on in the jails and that, because that's what it was…

Kevin: Federally, not just in the state, you were talking about the whole federal system right across.

Karen: And then trying to play a support role, cause then we were also getting information about all the other deaths that had occurred, or things that were happening and that sort of stuff. So then playing a support role and an advocacy role for families.

Judy Chester: The committee itself was mainly all women, I think that's important to say that.

Karen: Yeah it was Rose Stack, who was the librarian at Tranby and Rose Wanganeen from South Australia, Helen Boyle from WA who'd just started as Director of Studies at Tranby and me. It was Helen and Rose Stack who had set up this little committee before I came on board. They were both from Western Australia, Rose Wanganeen was from South Australia and then me from NSW.

Kevin: The four of you were really the main force. So you stretched right across the country.

Karen: But it was important to remember that we had to work on so many levels. Some of the things the committee needed to do were about challenging the legal system on this level, then there's informing people about the issue through the media on that other level, it's about supporting families on another level, it's about changing the way things are on a day to day level, so all that sort of stuff was happening. And then just trying to gather a small support group to be able to keep doing whatever you were doing and having the annual rally or go and having fund raising and all that sort of stuff.

Kevin: That was the biggest thing, the fund raising wasn't it.

Karen: 'Cause you needed to have resources. All that communication took time. And I remember that incredible emotional demand on you, that support of the families, of the people involved in all these tragedies and trying to work out how to cope with it.

Kevin: I remember being at the second part of Eddie Murray's inquest at Glebe. The family broke down and just sobbed and sobbed and you know it just broke your heart. It was the worse thing watching them, seeing how it affected them…

Judy Chester: They took it really hard, they had to keep reliving it, go there every day talking about it, and they didn't actually get to bury their family and get on with their lives. … Day in and day out.

Karen: And this is going back to the land issues and everything else that we were involved in, there was a role for everyone. We said, 'Yes you can participate but in terms of the public face, it's *our* responsibility, it's our obligation to raise those issues and to be the spokesperson in the media'. It was important for a lot of different reasons, it was important for families to know that 'Yeah them black fellas down there, they're staying true to what they said and they're doing the talking'. And it was important for the wider public to know that this was a black issue that we were dealing with, it affected everybody but it was a black issue, these were black deaths in custody and that's what we were campaigning against.

And it was important for us, for me anyway, to make sure politicians heard black voices, cause they can easily be dismissive you know, and I remember talking to Gerry Hand, Clyde Holding, two of the federal ministers we went through during that period. They were fairly dismissive until we began to show there was not just one case – and we were building on it all the time, showing them – 'Here's another case, and here's *another* one'. … So that built the case, at the Royal Commission.

So when we finally got the announcement it was in 1988. The government said, 'We'll have the Royal Commission' – but it was fairly broad, it was to be an investigation into other issues associated with it too. I didn't quite know what that meant. I was at your place Cookie, remember? And I rang up John Terry and said, 'Well, how should we respond to this?' He knew what I was thinking about and he said, 'Well you acknowledge it. You say, "This is a good thing but – we're also going to be closely monitoring what you're doing and how you're doing it"'.

After I'd rung John Terry, then I rang the media and told them what I was going to say. It was a learning curve, wasn't it? It had to build up a lot of people in a very short time!…

And Kevin, you used to know a lot of lawyers. Remember we had to get all them lawyers to advise us, they all worked for nothing too. It was all those connections that you had Cookie, and it was the media connections you know and the other support through the unions and things like that that allowed us to continue. So there was a lot of other sorts of support that we were able to get as a committee, apart from Cookie's just overall endorsement of the whole thing. That was important but it was about being able to have a place to do those things, have those meetings, have those discussions, but also resourcing all those other bits and pieces. So that was important.

Isabel kept up the conversations at Tranby – giving back that support in the teaching she gave again and again to new generations of students:

Isabel: I really enjoyed going into the classes at Tranby to talk to the students these last few years [in the 1990s]. When they dealt with the Deaths in Custody reports in their Legal Studies course, I was able to tell them how that came about. That Tranby College was the place that we had that first meeting to say: Can we get a Royal Commission into Deaths in Custody?

And you know, they didn't even know that. Because I said to them: 'How do you think the Deaths in Custody Royal Commission came about?' And the students said: 'Oh well, the government was getting worried about all the deaths in custody and so they decided to do something about it.' And I said: 'Oh, hang on. No, that's not the way it happened at all. It was people like us that had to do terrible things like march down the street, shout out about the police killing blacks.'

And so I could tell them how we camped on Tulladunna for a week. And we were really under threat there. But, as I was saying, we had the real contact with Tranby if something went wrong. We knew that that was the only organisation we could call on. And so I explained exactly how hard it was to camp that full week there, even though they had a sign saying: 'Campers will be prosecuted'. We dared them to prosecute.

Figure 7.7: Tranby students at rally at Sydney Town Hall.

Courtesy Tranby Archives.

So just getting that Royal Commission going was hard enough. Because we used to come down and march and have our rallies down at the Rocks and that went on for a couple of years before we finally got it happening. But we were very lucky that we had the base of Tranby all the time. Without that we would never have got anything going in that Royal Commission.

And even the court itself, when the commission was in session, you know Tranby supported that all the way through. The students used to go in and listen and so they were learning as well. A lot of them didn't know a lot of the things that were happening. So it was another education to them really. And what I said to those young Tranby people was, 'It's up to you now to carry on the monitoring of those Royal Commission recommendations. And if those recommendations are not being implemented then you got to ask why not and how can we deal with it'. I would like to see them set up their own Watch Committees in their communities.

Over this time, Kevin and Judy were themselves involved in a wide range of political networks and activities, like the nuclear disarmament movement and the overall directions of the Australian Labor Party. But at the same time, they were building the relationship that would last them all their lives.

Figure 7.8: Judy and Cookie.

Courtesy Judy Chester family collection.

8. Reaching out for change

'Outreach' or 'extension' are words which often seem to be the defining characteristics of Adult Education, but these words keep the focus on a central institution. The Co-operative for Aborigines, although housed at Tranby, had instead always seen itself as belonging in communities. The Tranby building in inner city Glebe was only one part of a much wider network. So for Tranby, 'outreach' had many different meanings.

This chapter has been written by drawing on Kevin's memories in conversation with some of the people who explored and invented and developed those different types of 'outreach'.

Black Books

Black Books was a Tranby outreach program – but it was really in reverse. It was Tranby – as a community organisation – reaching *into* the educational institutions of the state. As Tranby's knowledge of the secondary education system deepened, and as Aboriginal Studies entered the mainstream curriculum, it became clear to Kevin and others at Tranby that the resources had to get much better in schools if the existing teachers were to be able to deliver the new curriculum. Many of Tranby's staff and students were drawn on to develop better resources for school education by reviewing books which could be used as the basis for Aboriginal Studies teaching and learning.

Kevin: This Black Books idea got started with Kathy Campbell. Kathy'd come from Victoria where her father was a union organiser. Her politics clashed with his and so she did her university training at Armidale where she worked on the campaign that successfully got an ALP candidate up for the first time in that electorate. She went back to Victoria and worked in schools where there was a large migrant group and the schools were very progressive in that time. Then she came to Sydney, because her husband worked for a newspaper as an editor and we were looking for teachers, so we grabbed her! She had a lot of great ideas!

Figure 8.1: Cookie and Black Books staffer, Cathy (another one, not Kathy Campbell).

Courtesy Tranby Archives.

We used to go over to Stanmore where the teachers were doing courses on Aboriginal Studies. That was a Department of Education place where they sent teachers for inservicing. I was a speaker over there and Kathy came over with us. And we started talking to teachers. All the time they were saying to us they were going through their school libraries and there was nothing for them, or they'd been reading through stuff and they didn't think it was right. So we come back and Kathy started working on how we'd set up an information centre. That's what it started out to be really. And the bookshop idea sort of developed from that.

Kathy approached Dave Morrissey, who was an anthropology honours student when he first became involved with Tranby, initially to help in the Land Rights Support Group. In this group, white students and others took some of the organising burden off Aboriginal activists by picking up the jobs like, for example, seeking support for the campaign from non-Indigenous organisations or of publicising Aboriginal rallies. Later the Land Rights Support Group published the early land claims to assist the campaign for further political reform. Having graduated by then, Kevin asked Dave to work with a specific community, at Nambucca Heads, in their attempt to secure their land, using other legislation. At the same time he was doing anthropological work on land claims for the Central Land Council in the Northern Territory.

Dave: Kathy Campbell came to me in 1981. This was the time when Aboriginal Studies was just getting going in the NSW curriculum, and she wanted Black Books to be able to cater for the school libraries and history programs. What Kathy needed was someone to actually vet the books that Black Books was going to list in its catalogue. The whole premise was that the books that Black Books would have on sale would be *worth* having on sale.

Kevin: So she got Dave to read through the books we wanted to put on the catalogue to come out from this information centre. And the thing was, while Dave was reading the books to make sure they were factual, Kathy'd be on the phone to the communities the books were written about, making sure that it was alright, you know that everything in the book was okay? We said that if it was written about a community or a person, then we'd have to get in touch with that community or person before we'd sell the book. And that's what gave us a really big plus in front of all other bookshops, 'cause people could trust that what they were buying was alright by Aboriginal people.

Figure 8.2: Black Books team: Maria McKell (second from left in Uluru T-shirt) was highly experienced in book management after many years at Gleebooks, with Karen Flick, Matt Davies and a volunteer at Black Books.

Courtesy Tranby Archives.

Dave: Many of the school libraries had some books but they were all old. Ones like AW Reed's *Legends of Australia* were still around. None of them so totally offensive, but all of them were pretty useless. And a lot of the newer ones were too academic. So you can't give the Year 6 kids the same book you'd give to a university student. But the teachers wouldn't know till they got it on the shelf. So then it's not much use. Kathy asked me to help her by reading the books and putting together the catalogue, while she was putting together the shop. I read all the books she wanted, about 110 in the first catalogue. Went through them and put the catalogue together and it enabled Black Books to start marketing to schools. We were able to tailor orders for them.

That would have been from mid '81. Then I guess about early '82 we started trying to sell books in a more serious way. And Kathy then moved on to do something else, and so I was persuaded to stay. I was only there about a year or so and then I think Maria Mackell came in from Gleebooks and other people came into help run the show and there was a CDP[1] employee in there too and we had students reviewing for us.

Kevin: And there was that great volunteer, Joyce Lambkin, she came every day for years.

Judy Chester: And we used to do the proof reading you know? The women in the NOW program out at Liverpool. Dave Morrissey would come out when he was teaching in the course with all these books and hand them out and say 'read 'em'. So we'd read them and just write what we thought of the book. So we were the reviewers for Black Books! ... It's still really missed, Black Books, I used to go and buy all my presents there for kids.

***

Tranby conducted far more outreach programs which involved Tranby actively working with communities to create learning environments *in* communities. Here are three examples – the NOW course and urban women's training, the Sites course and National Parks, and the land council training in bookkeeping and management. These were all different but they shared two fundamental principles which grounded all Tranby projects and which were the guiding principles Kevin used to measure what made up *real* education.

The first principle was that each course was established because the communities involved approached Tranby – at no stage did Tranby decide they knew best what was needed. As each example shows, the ways that those connections were made were through the rich networks that Tranby – and in particular Kevin – had fostered.

---

1   Community Development Program funding for Aboriginal [and other] trainees.

And the other principle was that each course was aimed at empowering individuals and communities to take more active control of their lives, sometimes economically but always politically.

This was the way Kevin (talking about the land council training courses, see below) understood education in the community.

Kevin: People out there with little basic schooling who have got enormous talent to organise in their local area. It could be Little Athletics or local football. … and they haven't got, in inverted commas, the 'educational background', but they *run* it, you know? If you ask them, and talk to them, they've got no self confidence in themselves to be able to put themselves up as, you know, 'I can do this, I can do that…' but after doing courses at Tranby, they went from strength to strength! And they were involved in a lot of the educational organisations, like the AECGs,[2] local TAFE courses… Tranby went out to the communities because what we found was that with those sort of people, if you took them away from the community, well the community'd be lost. And so those people were trained in their own environment, and the community people who relied on those people still had access to them…

This meant that for Kevin, Tranby, would be available and accessible for everyone in a community, not only for one faction or family. As he explained.

Kevin: Tranby has been a comfortable place for people to come and just meet up because it's always been neutral. And we've always tried to keep it that way. Any of the Aboriginal groups that come up for support we always give them support. We don't interfere with anybody else. And they don't interfere with us, which is great. Because if you go into an area there's always three to four different groups, and we have to be able to work with the whole lot of them – or you know, the college would fold. So you can't take sides really. And we work with incredible people… you know, the mind boggles. And doing all this, our students who are there they get that knowledge and it makes them far better people.

***

The first example of Tranby's community-based education is the NOW course for Aboriginal women which ran in western Sydney. Terry Widders (Chapter 6) had remembered this course as the most exciting example of community education he was involved in. There were other Tranby courses like it in country areas but this example is important because it shows the interest Tranby had in thinking about the many Aboriginal people who lived in the city *as* communities, as well as offering courses for those in the bush.

---

2   Aboriginal Educational Consultative Groups.

The NOW course was also notable because this was when Cookie met Judy Chester, introduced in the previous chapter, who became his lifelong partner and comrade.

Tranby became involved in this program because Robyn Williams – who lived out near Liverpool and had once been a builders labourer – had known Kevin when he was the Aboriginal organiser in the BLF. So she was confident that he actually would listen to what they wanted and respond seriously to the women's request for a course that suited *them*.

The NOW course: Urban outreach

The story is told here by Judy Chester.

Judy: Our course got going at Liverpool because Robyn Williams was doing the outreach programs for TAFE back then and she said, 'Well what do you girls want?' And we all said, 'Well we just want a taste of *education*!' We'd all been locked up with our kids for years, our self-esteem was down around our bootlaces!

And we had to fight tooth and nail with the AECG over that because they said it wasn't accredited! But we got it! It was called the Aboriginal Women's 'NOW' program, we were the pilot course. And now the NOW program is still going, its for migrant women and for other women… its just wonderful! A couple of old girls went and had a demo at Blacktown TAFE because they wanted to go on the second program! They said, 'No. You've *done* it!'

And Kevin was my teacher! Tranby was very involved in it.

Kevin: Robyn come out and asked us could we write up a course. And so we wrote up a course that had Aboriginal Studies in it and Co-operative Studies…

Judy: Terry Widders was our Aboriginal Studies teacher… and he had to wear shorts! That was his uniform. And so you had to get there early 'cause old Myrtle Kinchela, she used to be at the front! That's the only time she never ever went to sleep in class was when Terry was teaching! You ask him! They used to make him wear shorts, even in the winter time. They said, 'We'll shut the door and turn the heaters on!' But he was a good teacher – they loved it!

Figure 8.3: Brian Doolan – an enthusiastic planner of community education.

Courtesy Tranby Archives.

Kevin: Brian Doolan was out there teaching…

Judy: …And Cookie with his garbage can for an ashtray! They used the local teachers to do the woodwork and metalwork, cause we had to do that, that was part of it… and I think Dave Morrissey did a bit teaching and Chris Milne.

Kevin: It had all sorts of topics, it covered a lot. We taught quite a few parts and my part of the program was the Co-operative movement…

But basically it was a *start* to education for the women out there.

Judy: And most of those women went on and done some fantastic stuff. Nola Woods was on the course, and Helen James – that's old Tom Williams' sister from La Per – and there was me and my sister Janny Ely. There was about 15 of us wasn't there?

Kevin: ...And I think every one of them started furthering their education. One of them was writing a book. Even Janny herself, she got a lot out of it...

Judy: Yeah, look at her now. From the NOW course all those years ago, today she's got her uni degree and *she's* running community-based courses out there for TAFE.

The NOW course aimed at catering for the needs of *all* women, of whatever age and pre-existing knowledge, which meant the classes reflected the strong role of older women in families and local Aboriginal communities. Judy used this and other opportunities to stay in close touch with her family, and in particular with Nanna Latham, in Wellington, despite the fact that Judy's family had moved to the city.

The Sites Course: Jacko Campbell taking on National Parks

The courses for parks rangers and sites protection officers reflect the way community leaders like Jacko Campbell shaped the way Tranby approached teaching. As the land rights movement gathered momentum, the early legislation to protect Aboriginal sites fell under National Parks and Wildlife Service (NPWS) jurisdiction. Some National Parks staff, like Howard Cramer and Sharon Sullivan, were sympathetic to Indigenous interests, but overall the institution had few Aboriginal staff and few links to Aboriginal communities. The NPWS tended to act without any consultation with Aboriginal communities.

Elders like Jacko were incensed that despite Indigenous demands for land rights having finally forced some action to protect sites, the control over their sites' management and interpretation was still in the hands of white government officials. Jacko seized the opportunity of offering sites training through Tranby, with an anthropologist like Dave Morrissey tutoring, as a chance to push for greater Aboriginal cultural control over significant sites.

Kevin: Jacko Campbell wanted us to train Aboriginal sites officers or rangers. He hated the National Parks didn't he. He reckoned they were insensitive and basically he wanted Aboriginal people to be able to run things themselves.

Dave: National Parks ran their training at the time out of Goulburn, what was then Goulburn CAE.[3] The idea was to put these six blokes, two from Wallaga Lake, two from Jerringa and two from Wreck Bay, through the National Parks and Wildlife Service course at Goulburn. But they needed a bit of a boost to get through it, a bit of tutoring, so I was asked to take that on. There was all those hassles in that sort of model of education where the students had to go down to the Goulburn College for periods and go home and practise it and so on. And they had a lot of schooling required, written assignments and essays. Now they actually did the official course: really all I was doing was a bit of extra back up and tuition on how they get their assignments done so they could get through the proper course. So Tranby didn't get separate accreditation, it was the mainstream accreditation.

That was the first phase and then the second phase was that Jacko wanted to get something both more expansive and more appropriate. So those guys would have late '81 into early '83 and, by then the land councils were being set up, so by '84 or so there were regional land councils being set up and we figured that having sites officers based in the land councils would be a useful thing to do.

Figure 8.4: Sites Course students learn from Guboo Teddy Thomas.

Courtesy Tranby Archives.

---

3   College of Advanced Education.

Figure 8.5: The class in the Sites Course at Tranby with Dave Morrissey in the back row.

Courtesy Tranby Archives.

Figure 8.6: Site Recorders, Lake Mungo Trip with Wiimpatja elder Alice Kelly, far western NSW.

Courtesy David Morrissey.

Kevin: We worked it out and organised it through Tranby. Jacko was still the driving force behind it because we said that every regional council should have a person employed there who could do the site survey for the region. We wanted to have laws that wouldn't allow the Department of Roads, or Telstra or anyone, to go anywhere without firstly going through the land council to find someone to check that what they wanted to do was alright in terms of protecting sites and important places. So that if there was a road to be dug, well that person would be employed, or the land council would be employed, they send out their sites bloke, and money should go back into the local land council or the regional land council, whoever employed them, so that they can you know cover their wages.

Dave: That was the plan. And the State Land Council which was then an office in the back streets of Redfern, they backed it and put in some dough and so did the then office of Aboriginal Affairs.

Kevin: So they all backed it and we designed a course, so each regional land council employed two people and give them a Toyota and an office to work out of and so on. Some of them were actually working for the local land council like La Perouse for example, where the regional land council wasn't organised enough to do it yet, so La Perouse took it up as a local issue. Some of them worked and some of it didn't.

Dave: I was still doing a bit of work for the CLC[4] in the Territory, so I went for about six or eight months going up, up for two weeks, back for one, up for two weeks back for one, with site work in the Western Desert, up to three months. So, we put together a course and it probably would have been over '84 and '85 I think we ran that course. It was a separately accredited course, running out of Tranby and in cooperation with the State Land Council. We got it accredited with TAFE. We put together a course with about five modules a year and it was based on recognising sites and what to do to record them and being able to organise yourself to work within management plans, how to write a basic management plan for a site. And some field trips. Lake Mungo was a good trip and another trip up the coast, and another one down the coast, so we did a few regional trips so they could get to look at other types of sites. And we got a lot of cooperation from Sharon Sullivan, who was in charge of National Parks down there on the South Coast. So they organised to get the doors to open up down the coast. And we got Ray Kelly, the Aboriginal sites officer with NPWS to help us. He was up on the North Coast. And Jeanette Hope gave us support out there in the west, where she was running the Willandra Lakes Research stuff.

Kevin: Yeah. But it was a good course wasn't it, incredibly good.

---

4 Central Land Council.

Dave: Oh yeah, it was good, the problem was, the idea was to have people come down and do some course work, go back and practise it. But they weren't getting the support, because the Aboriginal land councils were actually under such pressure it was hard for them to actually function properly. So some of our students would get back and find their bloody Toyota had gone. Or they'd get back and find their office had been left, and they didn't have enough power at the local level so the land councils didn't have the administrative capacity to actually support them in the work they were doing.

Kevin: But a lot of them did really well. Autry Dennison at Toomelah was one who was doing great for years before he passed away. And some of them are still going.

Dave: Yeah he's alright, and some of the others too. Badger Bates did the sites course too…

Kevin: Yeah, he was a participant, he was the one from the Far Western Regional Council. See they had one person from each regional land council… So they had 13 on the course… A couple of them fell over, but that's to be expected in any course… But the majority of them who did the course went back and they were employed by the regional land councils or the local land councils… and I think a couple of them are still going.

Dave: In fact one bloke who's still running out of that is Barry Moore – still has tours of the Wreck Bay, showing people bush tucker. I think he's their official Aboriginal ranger down there now, so he carried that one forward after he finished the course.

Kevin: Barry went back down to Wreck Bay and he worked as a ranger down there with the land council. And then he set up his own program down there, and he's been going for quite some years now… He's got a program down there where people go down and he takes them all around Wreck Bay, shows them sites, shows them food and resources… And he's doing that now! … That's after he got trained with Tranby. He'd never have done that before.

Dave: I think the stuff that used to worry them was the writing side of it, because there's a lot of that.

Kevin: Yeah, that killed everybody. But talking to people who were doing the course – and talking to their communities – they said they couldn't believe the improvement in the guys when they went back to work. So I think a lot of people were looking at that course, not only in NSW but interstate, and it could have been taken up interstate. But the money wasn't available to run a second course.

Dave: And, by that stage some of the land councils had started to come unstuck, because they weren't handling their money well...

Land councils training courses

The final example of Tranby's role in developing education *within* communities is the courses run for and with land council members. By 1985 many communities in NSW were in distress as they struggled to cope with implementing the new Land Rights Act[5] without adequate training in either legal or financial training. Tranby began to run courses which responded to that community concern. The language of the Act had intimidated many people, so Kevin asked John Terry to help put together a 'plain English' version and to design a course that would allow people to understand it and learn how to use it. John was a lawyer who had previously worked for a long time with the Western Aboriginal Legal Service living at Wilcannia and Walgett and was by then working for the NSW State Land Council in Sydney. His skills and experience – and his sense of humour – made him an ideal person to work with people at community level. For other types of support, Kevin was able to draw on younger staff like Chris Milne, who had been teaching mathematics, but also the older accountants like John Short, who had been such stalwart supporters of the co-operative. One of the outstanding results from these courses was showing members of the community how to do the detailed searching of Lands Department maps to identify the land which met the Act's criteria as being available for claim. One of the people who was most effective in using this new skill was Judy Chester's sister, Janny, who with other members of the Gandangara Land Council, was able to identify many hectares of claimable land around Menai which ultimately passed to the land council. (See Chapter 12.)

Judy Chester takes up the story again here because she was involved in these courses as both a local land council member at Gandangara as well as with her growing connections to Tranby as a graduate from the NOW course.

Judy Chester: Those courses that Tranby got going after the Land Rights Act came out were really important. There was no training and everyone's going, 'Oh this one's ripping off that one'. So Tranby went out and did the plain English version of the Land Rights Act, and they did the Uniform Accounting System. Janny was only talking about it the other day… about the skills that people on the ground got from Tranby. … She said Tranby used to pick up that role but now, she said it's getting harder and harder to do community education these days…

---

5   *Aboriginal Land Rights Act 1983* (NSW).

Dave: I think two things were happening in parallel: we were discovering that the site curators in our training course were getting mucked around because their land councils were falling apart. In some of them, people were running off with the money and they were spending it as if it was private cash because they'd never had any private cash. And at the same time the land council were aware of the problems and trying to put a better system in. So somehow there must have been a conversation about putting our heads together and doing something about it.

Kevin: Yeah, people were getting into trouble because some communities didn't have any organisation, they only had the land council, so it had the only black-controlled money that was going in the community. So people would die and their relations'd say, 'Oh the land council can help us bury them' and they didn't understand what the money was to be used for.

Dave: There were certainly categories of spending outside the Act which were inherently worthwhile doing, which made it hard for the land councils not to respond to that type of appeal.

Kevin: And then the government was jumping up and down about people thieving and stuff like that, they just didn't understand what their role was, you know, that's why those courses were really, really good. Really good.

Dave: There were also some of the land councils of course had been seized by one family or one side of town, and the other side wants to know how to knock them off. So, although we didn't go in with that intention, we were often training the second generation to knock off the first.

Kevin: But what we said was, 'When you go out there, don't get involved!' Because one day they'd be fighting with one another and you take sides, next minute they'd all be together, and they blame you, you know. So we said no one could take sides of anything like that.

Dave: A lot of the workshops would end up with someone coming in and saying, 'So-and-so did this or that, is that allowed or not?' And often this and this and this were totally *not* allowed! So we have to say 'Well we can't comment on the specifics...', but we'd try and go on and tell them what they could and couldn't do.

Kevin: And we'd try to talk to as many people across land councils as we could, and we'd hold workshops that brought in people from different land councils in the region.

Dave: Yeah, we'd hire a motel and fill it up with people from land councils and ourselves. I guess we really were addressing the local land councils rather than the regional land councils, under the totally untestable assumption if they were able to do things right at the local level it would work better at the regional level. I don't know if it happened or not.

Kevin: Well I think it did, because there's a lot of good things that have happened, you know. You know people have got land now, that they'd never have had that without the land councils getting better informed about how to find land to claim.

Dave: Yeah, because then there was a mechanism set up to identify what might be claimable land, without logging claims on it. Some of that vacant Crown land that was tucked away in parks and forest reserves and those stock routes are the sort of places that have been identified and could be claimed as land claims once people knew how.

***

The land council training programs led to new ideas about how to fund community training for development. The idea to create the Action Development Unit is described firstly here by Dave Morrissey in conversation with Kevin. He saw it as an attempt to set up an Aboriginal-controlled consultancy which could tender successfully for funds which were otherwise going to non-Aboriginal consultants. But for Kevin, the fundamental goal was training and community empowerment. The word 'action' in the title echoed the 'action research' approach that Tranby staff embraced – where research of any sort was aimed at making practical changes which would be trialled in communities, evaluated, improved and then used in the next round of development. Then Judy Chester takes up the story. She was employed in a number of the Action Development Unit projects with a commitment to making the training and research translate into change on the ground. Both of the courses she talked about here with Kevin led to these types of changes for individuals or for communities – either across the state or very close to home.

Taking outreach even further: The Action Development Unit

Dave: After the second sites course had wrapped up, we started to do the training with the land councils. And that was the point where we figured if communities could sort out their own development strategies, that sort of third world development idea I guess, it would be a useful thing to do. So we set up a development unit to work towards that. At that stage there was the possibility of government funding to support community projects and to help get them running. The government was prepared to fund all sorts of white run consultancies to do that work, so we thought we could try and run this as a sort of Tranby owned consultancy that could support communities to work out their own development strategies.

This was a pretty unheard of idea at that stage, around 1986 or '87. One of the motivations was Tranby needed to be able to bring in money to fund its broader education programs. And the only way to get money was to do consultancies, and the only way to do consultancies was to have an entity, and, the idea of the development unit was used to give it some sort of spin or position I guess. We called it the ADU, the Action Development Unit. In retrospect, we went about it in a way that was perhaps too much project by project rather than working first to put in infrastructure and capacity building… What we were saying with the ADU was, 'Okay let's get a little business going that can earn a bit of money, pay for it's own way and in the meantime look for ways to help the community…'.

Kevin: …Through training.

Dave: …Exactly – through training. I was really there to do capacity building at the community or say regional levels, so it was more an extension of what had worked or not worked with the land council training.

Kevin: Judy worked with the ADU on the housing work. That was a good training program, wasn't it Jude?

Judy: Yes, the Real Estate Institute used to come in and run it in conjunction with Tranby, and they used to bring people from the housing co-ops from all over the state, and run workshops on how to maintain your houses and how to collect rent and basic stuff like that. I used to do all the arrangement of the travel and accommodation for them. We'd put them up in a motel at Redfern that had conference facilities so they'd all be together. And it was close to the city if anyone wanted to go out. There'd be a talk and they might have to do exercises and some of them brought down materials and books from their co-ops.

I think they'd spend the first day sitting around talking to each other about all their problems! And when you listened to all of them, it was like hearing the same story from every different town. People not paying rent and all that. And they'd just sit down and hash it all out. I think the Real Estate Institute got a lot out of it to tell you the truth, because I don't think they ever had to deal with issues like this! And they stuck with Tranby for years didn't they? Running courses. And they thought it was quite relevant and important, eh? I thought the courses were really good. And the people from the housing co-ops that come down were passionate about doing the right thing, you know? This was why it was so good for them to come together cause they used to network with each other…

Kevin: And that course went all over NSW. It wasn't just held in Sydney. And it wasn't just basic. It enabled people to nearly become a real estate agent. And in the end an Aboriginal woman got her qualifications and ran the course, a woman from the North Coast. She ran the courses instead of the guy from the Real Estate Institute.

And another big project for the ADU was the one about local government that we did with Jenny Onyx from Kuring-gai College. What started all of that was that the local councils were getting into trouble. The Aboriginal people were saying that the councils weren't doing the right thing about the reserves. The local councils were saying that's not for us to do anything about, that's for the federal government. So there were lots of fights between local government, local councils and Aboriginal communities. So that's when the tender went out and we won the tender.

Judy: I was working at the ADU at the time. What they did was they had six communities didn't they Kevin? And they had to look at the way or the amount that Aboriginal people used local government facilities, like the library and the baby health centre… And what Dave did was he employed someone from each community to do the survey and do the work. And Janny was the person employed in the Liverpool area to be the researcher. I forget what communities they used… But there were six of them. Moree was one… Nowra on the South Coast.

Kevin: And in the end, when we finished and drew up the conclusion, it turned out that the local councils did not employ Aboriginal people. And they were the highest employers in country areas! You might get one or two Aboriginal people who were working on the roads or something like that. But that was all!

And so we got onto the local councils to start employing Aboriginal people. And so Tranby come under Leichhardt Council so we said, 'Well, if we're going to ask Moree Local Council to employ Aboriginal people, why not ask Leichhardt Council to employ Aboriginal people?' So we got together with the Italian community reps on the council and we put it up to the council that we wanted them to employ two people and they said yes.

Changing local government

The potential for Tranby to make real changes in the local government area of Leichhardt could only be made a reality because of the strong relationship which Kevin – and Tranby – had built up with local community organisations.

An important one was FILEF,[6] an organisation built up by Italian Australians who formed a large part of the Leichhardt population. Here Kevin talks with Frank Panucci, the union researcher to whom Serge Serino had introduced him, about their long friendship and the politics on which it was built.

Frank: I met Cookie first through old friends of mine – activists and unionists like Hal Alexander and Serge Serino who talked to me about Kevin and some of the work he was doing, it must have been late '70s early '80s I think. Then after that I started to get involved in FILEF which is an Italian organisation. Most of the people in FILEF were community-based people and a lot of them were workers and members of unions. But what brought them to FILEF was the community-based activities and stuff around issues – it was always a rights based organisation. So we did day-to-day bread-and-butter stuff within the community but also the broader issues. FILEF's basic tenets when it was set up by Carlo Levi in Italy was basically to ensure that Italian migrants overseas were not subjects within their new societies but protagonists of its transformation. It was an organisation that was interested in ensuring that Italians and people of Italian origin, played an active role in the way this country moved forward, towards the more progressive, open, equitable country that we all wanted it to be.

And obviously one of the issues that came up, because it's a progressive, left-wing organisation, was the issue about Indigenous issues in Australia and what the migrant organisation do around those issues and, so we thought about who we could go and talk to about it. So the first port of call basically was Kevin Cook, and we sat down and start talking to Kevin.

Kevin: I got introduced to Frank through Hal. We hit it off pretty well! I just related it to living in Wollongong, and growing up with so many Italians.

But I think that what we were saying is that if we were fair dinkum, then we had to get a broad base, and FILEF was an organisation that was forward thinking, it was out doing things in their community.

Frank: I suppose more than anything, those first meetings were more about us learning what Indigenous issues were about in Australia and I suppose to cut through a lot of mythology about it – mythology both in the sense of what is the public representation of it, but also the mythology of left-wing views of what Indigenous issues were – because that's where our background was, our training. We could see there were similarities between the migrant experience and the Indigenous experience, which were related to issues of racism and structural discrimination and issues like that. But I think it became pretty clear to most of us – and we went through a pretty steep learning curve! – that the similarities between the issues were, in a sense, at the tangent. We went

---

6   Federazione Italiana Lavoratori Emigrati e le Loro Famiglie.

through experiences which had the same label in certain aspects in our lives – experiences of racism and structural discrimination. But the fundamental issues about the rights of Indigenous people – as people who suffered colonisation and dispossession – had nothing to do with our experience, in terms of how we moved into this country and participated in this country. It meant there were real differences in the way that the forces that control this country, then and still now, reacted to migrants and Indigenous people.

So if a dispossessed owner of lands in this country turns around and says, 'Well it's easy for you cause you can pack your bags and go but this is my country!' then I suppose it's that kind of stuff that actually changes you. It changed things for me and I think for an organisation like FILEF where it placed the whole issue of Indigenous issues into the broader social struggle within Australia. From the mid '80s we incorporated it into our actions, into the way that we saw Australia: unless you addressed Indigenous issues that you would never actually achieve the transformation of this country that we wanted. So it transcended Indigenous issues for us, because it actually transforms the way that we dealt with community generally.

And I think that at FILEF we did that for a while and to a great extent that was because of having a reference point like Kevin and Tranby. Whenever we felt the need to talk about something, we knew we could pick up a phone to call Kevin at Tranby and the advice we would get, it would be a measured counsel which would not be an imposition on us.

Kevin: But the other thing was that FILEF was working at the council – Vera from FILEF was the Multicultural Officer there. Leichhardt Council had this 'Multicultural Committee' and they were trying to put Aboriginal people in with it. So Vera rang me up and she said, 'You better get up here or you'll be lobbed in with us', I said 'What do you mean?' and she said, 'They're calling you "multicultural"!'

And so I run up there and we sat down had a meeting with the council and we said, 'We are *not* migrants!' And the migrants backed us up 100 per cent. See, we got the support of FILEF and then, that's swayed the other people of the group to see that we'd be one out. So we called for two groups, the Aboriginal group and the rest, the Multicultural group, and we wanted our own separate organisation or advisory committee. And that's how we got the Advisory group and through that was how we got the people employed there.

See at the time, what they were trying to do was to get more people employed on the council but we never had one Aboriginal person employed in it! I hadn't seen one person within the council! So, we went to Hand, Larry Hand and Kate Butler. So we got one person employed as an assistant in their printery, cause the council did their own printing that time, so we got one person in there. Then they wanted to put another person into the parks. And we said, 'No, we want a position like a trainee town clerk'. And I think at first they laughed! So we said, 'Well, we don't want any position until that's filled'. And so we fought for two years and in the end they gave it to us! It was Larry Hand and a number of other people on the council backed us up and said 'Righto'. So we got people employed then as trainee town clerks. Jeannie Townsend was employed as the community development officer…

And the flag flies next to the Italian flag with the Australian flag at Leichhardt Council, every day. Wonderful, I love driving past there, looking up there…

Judy: and then they got a regular Aboriginal Advisory Committee that used to meet.

Kevin: Yeah it used to meet at Tranby, and I was the chairperson. And it was the only committee of council that was chaired by someone who wasn't a councillor. And I think that was really good in itself. And so that there's a number of councils now that have got Aboriginal Advisory Committees. I don't know if they're chaired by the Aboriginal people or not.

Judy: Now Marrickville Council is… Lester Bostock and Ann Weldon are there… and the City of Sydney and Liverpool… so it's happening, it's happening…

Reaching out into the global community

The international contacts which first Alf Clint and then Kevin brought with them were fostered in the Tranby environment. Such an extraordinary international network allowed teaching to take place with an international perspective as well as ensuring that this global outlook contributed to the political campaigns which drew support from the College. Brian and Kevin talk here about how they saw these international contacts developing.

Tranby was able to build on many different networks – Kevin's own South Coast background and his time in New Zealand had given him many contacts with Maori communities in NZ and in Australia. Then his Builders Labourers' network and his time in the Coady International Institue in Canada had cemented his connections with African activist organisations like the African National Congress (ANC) at the same time as it introduced him to Adivasi and working class movements from India and to South American liberation networks.

Alf Clint had also had long standing friendships and co-operative networks with fellow co-operative members in Indonesia, Papua New Guinea and the Pacific from where students had come to Tranby in the past and had remained in contact. He was a close friend of Walter Lini, who became the first Prime Minister of independent Vanuatu (and a co-religionist of Alf's) and of Barak Sope, a key minister in Lini's government. Kevin not only carried on Tranby's support for Lini and Sope, who came to stay frequently when he was in Sydney, but went on to build a strong alliance with Hilda Lini, younger sister of Walter and an outspoken advocate for a nuclear free Pacific and with the independence leaders of Kanaky (New Caledonia) and the Free Papua movement among West Papuans.

And finally through the rapidly expanding global education networks of indigenous peoples, Tranby and Kevin in the later 1970s had made connections with First Nations organisations in Canada and the United States. Kevin was to build on these networks outside Tranby for his work with the land rights movement, but as well there were key activists and educators from all these places who were invited in through the doors at Tranby to engage with students and the broader Tranby community.

Kevin: Tranby's international links came about because Walter Lini, the leader of the Vanuatu liberation movement, and Alf Clint were friends. A lot of Aboriginal people in Australia have got links to the mob from Vanuatu because they were the ones kidnapped and 'blackbirded' into Australia as indentured workers. So Barak Sope stayed at Tranby and that allowed a number of people from Vanuatu to come over and talk to him about fundraising for independence. That's how they started to raise money for him.

Brian: So through those old international links, you got people like Barak Sope and Walter Lini.

Kevin: And all across the Pacific. Walter's sister, Hilda Lini was at the University of the South Pacific in Fiji and she used to stay too – only we put her up at your place! Any of the conferences we went to, we always had a very good relationship with the people of Vanuatu.

Brian: And there was Joy Balazo, with the nuclear free mob from the Philippines.

Kevin: And that was through the trade union movement too, not to mention the personal friendship with Joy Balazo who was employed by the Australian Council of Churches. Kevin Tory and me went to a number of meetings with her. She was only new and we took her around and introduced her to all the trade unions. She's a very good speaker. They were having problems with people in Melbourne and they come up to the Tranby camp at Minto and we went out there to speak with trade union people with her, just to see if we could ease the situation a bit. We played roles like that with Joy. And a number of Aboriginal people like Kevin Tory went over to the Philippines. They played really good roles while they were there.

Figure 8.7: Joyce Williams, Judy's aunty from Wellington, had travelled to meet Desmond Tutu.

Courtesy Tranby Archives.

Figure 8.8: Oliver Tambo speaking in Tranby College dining room.

Courtesy Tranby Archives.

Brian: But didn't you end up with the South African ANC leaders, Bishop Desmond Tutu, Oliver Tambo, coming through Tranby too?

Kevin: I'd had contacts with those people going all the way back to my BLF days… and then at Coady in Canada, there had been ANC people there I was really good friends with…

Then when Eddie Funde of the ANC first came to Australia, Meredith Burgmann introduced me to him and he got me on the ANC executive in Sydney. I used to go to meetings and I introduced him to a lot of people. I said to him that everybody that comes out here, doesn't matter who it is, only ever goes to the east coast. They go to Sydney, Brisbane, Melbourne and no-one else sees them. We're really lucky in Sydney. But people in the Northern Territory, people in Western Australia, people in South Australia, they never get to see international people. So, the ANC brought a dance group out and they went here, there and everywhere, it was a really good program. Aboriginal people got a lot out of it and so did the dancers because the old blokes showed them some traditional dances. So we got to know a lot of the ANC people. It was an incredibly big thing when we hosted Oliver Tambo and Bishop Tutu. When he come, he come to Tranby. Just amazing people. They come in, and five minutes later you're sitting down talking to them as if you knew them for years. We've had incredibly well-known people at Tranby but they've always been treated the same way as anybody else. And, you know, like you've got Judy's aunt, Joycie Williams, going up and saying to Bishop Tutu, and saying, 'My name's Joycie Williams from Wellington, take my photograph'. They responded!

Judy: And the kids! They were in awe of him. He just had a presence about him. And Oliver Tambo too. Just to get the chance to meet those types of people was incredible.

Brian: So those Pacific connections came out of the old co-operative movement. But a whole lot of others came out of your political work, Cookie, like the anti-Apartheid movement, and the Maori. And then your involvement with the ANC and other Africans as well as the Indians – from India – and the South Americans at Coady in Canada? Then later on again though Education with the First Nations mob in the USA and Canada too?

Kevin: Yeah, we had the American Indians, when they come out here. And the Maoris, too, we did a lot of work with them, like with the Building Bridges concerts. Every time we had our Building Bridges concerts, the Maori people were there, they'd be building the scaffolds or they'd be doing food. We had their presence in everything we done.

Judy: What about that big ceremony we had up with the Maori people, all these Maori politicians and kids came over from Bondi and performed dances.

Kevin: There was an art exhibition at the museum. Before they could show it, they had to do their ceremony, and we was up there eating breakfast at five o'clock in the morning.

Judy: These kids lived in Bondi, and they were singing their songs and doing their dances. They were really strong with their culture. And it just blew these old fellows away, didn't it, Cookie? It was amazing. I'm glad we didn't miss out on that.

Kevin: Yeah, it was great.

Judy: The exhibition was fantastic too. They're very good artists and had marvellous carvings.

Brian: With those international connections, with the ANC its political goals and its rights agenda were all clear. But with the Pacific mob, at the heart of the nuclear free demands, was actually an indigenous issue, but a lot of the white fellows involved didn't recognise that. There were common agendas, weren't there, in a lot of these groups, about land rights for indigenous peoples and similar ones. Which is why they could sit down and very quickly identify with us and talk with us.

Kevin: Yeah but with the Fijians it was a really complicated situation when the Coup was on in 1987. It was difficult wasn't it? You had the issue about indigenous people and their rights but at the same time you had the trade unions and the Labour Party issue and the question about democratic organisation for all Fijians, indigenous, Indian or anyone else. The coup wasn't just about indigenous rights but about deeper issues. But the leaders of the coup made that out to be the point of the coup. Other indigenous Fijians who were members of the trade unions, the Labour Party and other organisations, like the churches, were locked out of the decision-making.

Karen Flick came into the Tranby network just as these international links were really building up and she explains how young people like her were affected by this new environment.

Karen: The great thing about being around Tranby was having access to some resources that freed you up to have your discussions that you needed to have and develop those strategies… Tranby has always been a bit more than just a meeting place. It was a place that allowed ideas to grow and develop. Allowed people to say whatever they wanted to say, supported a whole lot of people who would not have access to any other forum. And also opened us young Murris up to meeting a whole range of people, not just other countries, but other … other struggles, you know. And for me, that was the Maoris, it was the mob from Vanuatu, the Philippines, from Kanaky, the whole of the South Pacific, and Asia and also Africa of course.

It was just amazing being able to connect with those people like Hilda Lini from Vanuatu and Susan Ounei from Kanaky. I remember the early meetings that we had with all the mob from the South Pacific and, of course, they also had connections with Tranby and with Kevin Cook through the old co-op thing, so there's a link there again. So we could meet with people from other struggles and of course we met all the people involved with the peace movement.

Figure 8.9: Visiting indigenous Philippinos, including Joy Balazo, on left, who organised the international tour.

Courtesy Tranby Archives.

It was the timing too. There were a lot of things happening at that time in the Pacific, about nuclear testing and a nuclear free Pacific. But the focus for indigenous movements, and from my perspective, was that there's no nuclear free Pacific without independence and so it was very much that line of pushing independence because then we would have a say about our own country, and our own situation. And then that was also the peace and justice line, you know you can't have peace without justice in these countries. I ended up being a representative on a forum organised with Bev Symons from the Nuclear-Free and Independent Pacific movement and Vivien Abrahams from the Women for Peace and Freedom. Cookie put me onto that committee initially, and I kept going to it… couldn't stand one or two of the women but they did a lot of solid work, it was just their approach that was a bit hard to take. And so I was at that Peace and Justice conference and that's where I met a whole range of other women from the Pacific, from Kanaky and New Zealand and some women from the Marianas, Tuvalu and those places going under water now. So you could see a range of issues and I always had counsel from Cookie on that too, you know. So it was a really good time for me to be around.

Changes

High pressure and continuing scarce funds meant that most people could only stay at the college as their main employment for a couple of years. But they were invariably strongly influenced by their experiences there, often in ways they did not recognise till later on. In this section, Terry Widders and David Morrissey talk about the points where they decided to move on from Tranby, in 1985 and 1988 respectively. At the same time, new staff were being drawn in who would work with Kevin to take up the ideas circulating in the co-operative and generate new courses in the 1990s, like the Community Development course and the Legal Studies course, as Chris Kerr discusses Tranby in the 1990s with Kevin in Chapter 17. In that final chapter also, Brian Doolan and Terry Widders evaluate the key influences Tranby had on their later lives. But here, Terry and then Dave Morrissey consider the pressures on staff which shaped their decisions to move into work outside Tranby.

Terry Widders: By the end of '84 the course at Macquarie Uni was again about to be run. It had taken an 'off year' in 1984, after running as an experiment in '83. Then they rested it and were going to decide to run it again if it seemed like a good idea, which it did, as it made money by bringing in lots of students!…

For me, on a personal note, it was getting increasingly difficult. We'd had our first child at the end of '83, and the expenses became pretty constant after that, but at Tranby I was still a casual TAFE hourly-paid teacher and that was tricky, because I needed to work elsewhere. I had a few extra hours teaching in the NOW course out in the Western Suburbs, but for our family I needed to have a change and get something a bit firmer as a base, just to be able to cover living costs.

I think Tranby was just on the cusp of three year funding at the end of '84. I was beginning to see a pattern of possibilities for my own pathways in that Tranby and wider context… so what could I do specifically? By the end of '83 we'd had that first TEPC graduation, it had been relatively successful; those small wet birds had become quite good little flyers… and had taken off! And we were into our second intake. But for me, it was a great idea but I couldn't really keep going at that income rate.

Another sort of thing was if they were going to get firmer funding, that was good, but how would we formalise that? That funding would be for specific positions, and would I fit into that? What sort of structure would emerge? And the third factor was how were decisions being reached? Was an agenda of what *needed to be done*, steering the direction we went in? Were those everyday needs and demands becoming dominant? In retrospect I can see it was what Kevin had to do, just to get things done… It reminded me a bit … not that I'd had a lot of experience … but reminded me of union meetings… where you organised the factions… or in this case the Board members … to get things firmed up, because next day Kevin had to front someone, somewhere, to say 'This is what we've decided to do… and we need to get the funds to do it…'.

Well for me, I took the decision that that wasn't what I wanted to do. I still wanted to stay pretty much 'open weave', to focus on supporting and cultivating the people like Karen Flick who were getting active in the community, to reach further out into community development. I was worried about the centralisation that was going on since the late '70s in particular, the corporatisation of Aboriginal communities, in fact the whole creation of that idea of 'community' and the mushrooming of so many organisations. I saw all that as a problem… It just takes up so much time and energy to attend to that … Because I still had a left-over from the experience of trying to practise community development up in the northern tablelands, New England area in the last '60s and early '70s. I thought they could do more of that… But there were many practical questions they had to address at Tranby and I'm sure Kevin saw that much more clearly than I.

So there were several factors playing on my mind. And it came to a bit of a crisis at the end of '84 because I was offered a year's contract at Macquarie… so I thought should I follow that up? Could it live alongside the Tranby work? Did I totally agree with what I thought was rather a 'managed outcome' model of how things were working at Tranby? So it was a balance of things, of which directions to go, money, pathways for me and what I wanted to do myself… So like most things it was complicated at the time but it was late '84 when I decided to resign and focus on the Macquarie work.

***

Dave Morrissey: I think what I really learnt from working in that ADU was that we got used to listening to people. It didn't really show up to me till after I'd left. By 1988, Chris Milne and I had been around for a while and we were really burning out. So we moved onto setting up our own consultancy business. What we found later on, was that the people we were working with were saying, 'Well you're a bit different from the other people we've dealt with because you actually listening to what we said'. So even though the character of what Chris and I were doing was moving away from Aboriginal Affairs, we found that we still benefited from having learnt in those years that it was vitally important to be *listening* to what people were saying and to let them have enough autonomy over what they're doing so they have some ownership of it. And we actually carried that right through, the business is still running. That realisation of the importance of listening to people was probably the main thing that we picked up from our Tranby ADU work and were able to carry on with. Just knowing that if you impose a regime on the people you're working with, it's not likely to be sustainable, so, you got to sit back and *listen* to what you actually want, actively interpret the way they want to do things.

And overall, you know, what I remember about Tranby was that there were so many schemes going on in that front room at Tranby, keeping up with even ten per cent of them was hard. Half of them died in the bum but the other half came off, with all sorts of odd results!

Kevin: Well, you know like there was always something happening, there was never a dull moment.

PART 3
LAND RIGHTS NSW 1980s

9. Strategies: 1976 to 1981

By 1976, the campaign for Aboriginal land rights in the state of New South Wales badly needed a kick start.

There had been a long history of land rights demands in eastern Australia from at least the 1860s, and they had been escalating ever since, most often on a local or state level.[1] But by the early 1970s, the attention of Aboriginal people all over Australia had become focused on the national stage as the way to achieve land justice. The states had slipped from view.

This was because in 1972 the growing sense that a change of the national government – from the long reign of the conservative Robert Menzies to the Labor Party under Gough Whitlam – was going to happen had led the Aboriginal Tent Embassy to be established on the lawns of Federal Parliament. This increased the pressure on Whitlam and soon after his party finally won power in December 1972, the new government declared it would act rapidly on how best to achieve national land rights. But it soon became clear that the federal government would not be able to legislate to change state land laws. These remained under the sole control of state governments according to the Australian constitution. So the federal ALP concentrated on the laws it could change – those in the Northern Territory and the smaller Australian Capital Territory around Canberra and a naval base at Jervis Bay on the NSW South Coast. And Aboriginal people everywhere still focused on that campaign, in the hope that a good outcome in the Northern Territory would lead eventually to strong models for each of the states.

The NSW Aborigines Act was amended to form an 'Aboriginal Lands Trust' in 1973, in response to the rising Aboriginal interest in ownership of their land.[2] This amendment did not, however, pass real ownership of land to Aboriginal people. Instead, it simply renamed the existing nine member Aboriginal Advisory Council – previously an appointed body of Aboriginal people but from 1973 to be all elected – as trustees of all Crown lands reserved for the use of Aborigines. There were widespread demonstrations by Aboriginal people in 1973 opposing the creation of this 'Trust' and demanding instead the full handover of all remaining reserves as well as other lands of significance to Aboriginal people. These remaining reserves amounted only to 4300 hectares but the Trust was also to be empowered to submit claims to areas of 'vacant Crown land' deemed 'claimable' by the Minister for Lands. More than 250 claims

---

1 Meredith Wilke 1985, *Aboriginal Land Rights in NSW*, Alternative Publishing Cooperative Limited in association with Black Books, Sydney; Goodall 1996; Morris 1989.
2 *Aborigines Act 1969* (NSW); *Aborigines (Amendment) Act 1973* (NSW).

were submitted by the Lands Trust but these were mainly in the latter years of its existence, in the late 1970s, under pressure from unhappy communities who saw the main area of the Trust's activity to be approving the revocation of reserves to suit the government's agenda.[3]

When the Whitlam Government was ousted in December 1975, with the Bill for the NT Land Rights Act drafted and before parliament – but not passed – there was an even greater campaign applied to force the incoming conservative Fraser Government to honour the Labor Party commitments to the Aboriginal communities of the NT. Fraser watered down the Bill, giving even more concessions to the white graziers and miners, but eventually passed the amended Bill in 1976.[4]

But that left the question of what next? Shopfront and service organisations, like the Aboriginal Legal Service and the Aboriginal Medical Service, had flourished under the new funding from the federal Whitlam Government as well, of course, as the Aboriginal Housing Company in which Cookie and the Builders Labourers had been involved. While the Legal Service kept on looking for possibilities for legal challenges on the land issue, they had little time and few resources to follow these up in a big campaign.

It was now clear that each state would have to pass its own land rights bill – but this would mean re-building momentum for a new campaign for each state.

The initiative was taken, as has often been the case, by local communities. Aboriginal people around the state had been watching the process in the Northern Territory of communities explaining their connections to land with a formal claim. They had begun looking at how they could express their interests in land in the same way.

The first group to do this was the network of Gamilaraay people with a relationship to what had been the Aboriginal managed reserve at Terry Hie Hie, south-east of Moree. They had been forced away from the land and the Reserve had been revoked and they now lived in nearby towns like Boggabilla (where they had been sent when Terry Hie Hie was closed) and Moree. But in May 1977, they came together to demand that the Reserve be restored to them, as the first step in a recognition of their ownership over a wider area of land to which they had traditionally held the custodial rights. Their letter with documents supporting their claim was widely passed around among Aboriginal people, who were starting to consider how they too could make a claim on the land that was important to them.

---

3   Wilkie 1985: 9.
4   *Aboriginal Land Rights (Northern Territory) Act 1976* (Cwlth).

9. Strategies: 1976 to 1981

Kevin was just becoming established at Tranby at that time, and knew some of the people involved in the Terry Hie Hie claim. In the communities he knew best, on the South Coast of NSW, Aboriginal people were watching Terry Hie Hie closely and eagerly talking over the possibilities of making their own claims.

***

This chapter starts in 1977 when the campaign for land rights in New South Wales began to change gear. It looks at the choices made by activist groups to refocus land rights campaigning onto the potential of state legislation. These included choosing strategies like direct action, building alliances and making changes to party policy to force governments to take action. Then the chapter follows the story of how these strategies worked over the next few years to push the ALP government to focus on land rights in the hearings of its Select Committee, chaired by Maurie Keane, which took evidence in urban and later in rural areas. When the Select Committee reported in August 1980, Aboriginal and non-Aboriginal activists intensified their campaign for land rights in rural as well as urban areas. They expected that the Labor government would follow the Select Committee recommendations. These called for the government to begin extensive and in-depth consultations about how legislation could best respond to the deep desire for land which had been expressed to the Select Committee hearings.

Chapter 10 looks at this campaign from late 1981 to the end of 1982. A key experience for activists and communities in this period was the bush camp, a new type of political gathering for people in NSW which was modelled on meetings about land in the Northern Territory but then developed to meet local, NSW conditions. This type of meeting allowed NSW Aboriginal people to strengthen alliances across regional and personal differences. The outcome was that the campaign for rights to land began to build goals which were wider than any single piece of legislation.

Then, in Chapter 11 we explore the ways Kevin and his close friends like Barbara Flick and William Bates confronted the difficult decisions when a NSW government offered a Land Rights Act in 1983 which fell far short of Aboriginal goals. They had to decide whether and how to participate in a structure they believed to be flawed. The chapter then takes an in-depth look at two examples in which communities established local land councils, one in the city and one in the country. These were not organisations initiated from the top down, but instead were created by people organising at the grass roots level to build organisations which would meet what were often widely differing local goals and needs.

Finally, in Chapter 12 we look at how people went about actually getting land back in the early years of the Act – by either claim or by purchase. Both strategies meant that Aboriginal people had to gain very new skills very rapidly and they needed to have strong networks of support.

1977 to 1978: Kick start strategies

This section draws on Kevin's discussions with Rod Pickette, an organiser in the Australian Theatrical and Amusement Employees Association (ATEA) and Meredith Burgmann, in the National Tertiary Education Union, both unionists who Cookie had come to know well as a Builders Labourer and with Barbara Flick, a good friend and Yuwalarai woman from Collarenebri. Kevin had first met Barbara during the anti-Apartheid campaigns when she had come to Sydney to study nursing at the Children's Hospital and later to enrol in a Bachelor of Education at the University of Sydney. Barbara remembered that she had left the university disillusioned after a lecture in her politics course on the Wee Waa cotton strike in which no Aboriginal perspectives were acknowledged. Although the strike had been organised by her father Joe Flick, with Barbara and many others actively involved, no Aboriginal voices had been recognised in the university account. Frustrated, Barbara had deferred her studies, moving into an activist role in community organisations like the Western Aboriginal Legal Service.

Direct action: Black Defence, the 1977 Land Rights Conference and land claims

The Black Defence Group was an idea that came out of the atmosphere of protest and action campaigns that Kevin and his friends had been involved in during the previous few years. There were many occasions when small groups of people – who could be organised quickly to come and stand in a picket line or make up a deputation – could make a big difference. Some of Kevin's friends in the unions and others he was meeting in his first years at Tranby were eager to take on these active roles and it helped to make it sound like a 'real' organisation if it had a name. So the 'Black Defence Group' came into being.

As *Kevin* explained in the discussion with Rod: It was a motley crew when we first started off the Black Defence Group. Marcia Langton, myself, you Rod and Toni Smith – that red-headed girl who used to ride the motorbike. There were other Aboriginal women like Barbara Flick and her Auntie Isabel. There was Nellie Anairs and Lorraine Fitzpatrick. Then there was Meredith Burgmann who used to come to the meetings and you did too, Heather and so did Paulie Torzillo when he could. But I always said, after working for the Builders Labourers: you can achieve a helluva lot with a very few people. As long as everyone *stuck fats*. That's an old saying from playing marbles. It means as long as they're together! *Stick fats*. And we did! On Saturday nights, you know, we used to be out pasting up posters for demonstrations!

Rod Pickette laughed: We sounded like a pretty dangerous organisation, didn't we! [laughter] The Black Defence Group. I think they thought it was something like the Black Panthers in the US. Little did they know there was half a dozen people meeting in a telephone box. [laughter] It just shows it's amazing what you can do, you know, with a small group of people just focusing on the right sort of issues at the right time. You could easily get a lot moving.

But as *Kevin* pointed out, it was helpful to sound impressive: We used to ring up the Aboriginal Affairs, we'd say, 'Look, we want that report!' [or whatever it was]. They'd say, 'Who's this?' And we'd say, '*Black Defence*! You just send it to Box so-and-so in Redfern'. [laughter] 'Who are you?', they'd want to know. 'Don't you worry who we are', we'd say. 'Just send the stuff in the mail!'

But as time went by, the Black Defence Group formed a nucleus of reliable people who provided the infrastructure for organising grass roots support for Aboriginal goals around land.

Kevin: Marcia Langton had a lot to do with the Black Defence Group, where you know we used to sit around and talk. Land was always the issue, everything could come back and there'd be land. I think without the Black Defence Group, organising that 1977 Land Rights Conference, you might have gone another five or ten years without anything happening. There had to be someone who took up that issue. You know, everybody was talking about it, because the NSW Lands Trust wasn't *doing* anything. So people hated the Lands Trust with venom!

Perhaps the most important event was the 1977 Land Rights Conference, which was the first time for decades that Aboriginal people had come together to talk about their goals for land in many different regions of the state. It was held in Redfern on the October Labour Day long weekend, celebrating the eight hour day, and more importantly when the Aboriginal Football Knockout was on. This is a major sporting and cultural festival organised wholly within the Aboriginal community and which is held each year on the October long weekend, hosted by the victors of the previous year's knockout, researched now by Heidi Norman. In 1977 it was going to be held in Sydney because the Redfern All-Blacks had won the previous year. Marcia Langton (a key member of the Black Defence Group) and Cookie decided this would be a good opportunity to allow people from all the different regions across the state to share their goals about land. In previous decades, people had preferred to organise regionally and the land rights campaigns of the 1920s, for example, about which John Maynard has written, tended to be organised by the coastal regions, while those in the 1930s were based at Cumeragunja on the Murray River. The campaigns around rent and then land in the 1960s and early 1970s had arisen from conditions on the North Coast of NSW and had built up their momentum there.[5]

So the Football Knockout in 1977 was an important opportunity to bring people together to talk about what might happen in NSW now the Northern Territory Land Rights Act had finally been passed.[6] The Black Defence Group provided workers for support: Meredith Burgmann handled registrations from rural areas and kept the books for the conference, Rod Pickette organised union sponsorship and others like Barbara Flick and myself pasted up posters and licked envelopes for mailouts. It was an extraordinary event as Rod Pickette recalled.

Rod: That was spectacular when you think about it now. It was a pretty dramatic achievement even if that'd been all that happened. What amazed me about that was the wide representation. Just about every area was represented there. And it seemed to bring all these people, and it was the really respected community leaders from every area around NSW. And they were all speaking in the same language, you know.

Kevin pointed out that the football games themselves, always an important social event, had been set aside by some people so they could come to the conference instead to talk about land.

Kevin: It was funny, because at the same time there was the football knockouts on. And a lot of people didn't go to the Knockout for the first time, you know. They wanted to come to the Land Rights Conference instead. It was that big an issue. 'Cause at that time the Land Trust (the NSW government management group) were doing terrible things to people. That's when they were selling off bits and pieces of land.

They tried to sell off the old reserve at Terry Hie Hie near Moree. There was another place near Penrith in western Sydney, called Llanillo. Rod and I went out there, as part of the Black Defence Group, to meet the community reps. They got that land, too. They stopped the Lands Trust getting rid of Llanillo. The Lands Trust tried to sell other land off too, but we stopped them selling that as well, which was good!

---

5   Heidi Norman 2013 (forthcoming), *From Activism to Enterprise: A Political History of the NSW Aboriginal Lands Rights Act, 1983*, Aboriginal Studies Press, Canberra; Maynard 2007; Goodall 1996.
6   *Aboriginal Land Rights (Northern Territory) Act 1976* (Cwlth).

Rod remembered the galvanising effect it seemed to have on the western Sydney Aboriginal community who were trying to stop the sale of Llanillo to feel they had some support.

Rod: It seemed to be so empowering for them, you know, that they suddenly had an organisation backing them. Yeah, it was bloody good to see.

The conference called for the full scale recognition of Aboriginal rights to land, set up the New South Wales Aboriginal Land Council and demanded the abolition of the Aboriginal Lands Trust. A working group of 11 people was elected, all well known for their past campaigning against government control through bodies like the Lands Trust, although they did represent coastal areas more strongly than western ones. This working group included Kevin Cook as convenor and later chairperson, Joyce Clague as secretary, Kevin Gilbert on publicity, Alice Briggs as treasurer, Alan Woods as initial chair, Camela Potter, Trudy Longbottom, Betty Tighe, Ray Kelly, Jack Campbell, and Ted Thomas.

As Kevin explained, the 1977 Land Rights Conference was a turning point.

Kevin: That Land Rights Conference really got things going again. We set up that NSW Land Council from that, and people started traveling around, talking about land.

The 1977 land council born out of the Land Rights Conference in Redfern gave a platform for the first time to all the regional interests in NSW to meet and express their views about land. But all the travelling round 'talking about land' was done from 1977 to 1983 out of people's own pockets, with pension money and hard earned wages paying for petrol and food to camp out. This was the way that people from the South Coast like Jacko Campbell and Ted Thomas could get to bush meetings at Angledool or Menindee, on the Darling River. And it was the way that people like Aunty Phoebe Mumbler and Jessie Williams from Nambucca Heads on the coast could cross the mountains to be at a land rights meeting in Dubbo. There they met up with other people from across the state, all of them on limited means, travelling on public transport with pensioner concessions or in old cars and sharing petrol money. At the meeting they camped out or stayed in hostels, and were fed with cups of billy tea and sandwiches made up in the kitchens of the Aboriginal community members of the town.

Making Change Happen

Figure 9.1: 1977 Redfern Land Rights Conference, Black Theatre, Marcia Langton and Bob Bellear.

Courtesy Peter Thompson.

Figure 9.2: 1977 Redfern Land Rights Conference: Mick Miller and Cookie.

Courtesy Peter Thompson.

Figure 9.3: Percy Mumbulla (left), Gail Lovelock (from Armidale) and Gerry Bostock (right).

Courtesy Peter Thompson.

One of the ways the land council acted as a turning point was in stimulating still more communities to formulate their land demands as a claim which they could lodge with the state government. The very fact that these claims were made then created growing pressure on the new Wran Government to set up a process which could hear and recognise the claims.

After Terry Hie Hie, the next two claims to be written up and lodged were the Jerringa claim over Roseby Park, in February 1978, with Jacko Campbell as community representative, and the Yuin claim, over Wallaga Lake in June 1978, with Ted Thomas as signatory. These three documents set out clearly and powerfully – in maps and words – the long held demands of these communities for land justice, with their claims based on traditional culture but also on historical association and economic need. They were strong grounds on which to launch a campaign for the recognition of land rights under NSW law.

Making Change Happen

Building alliances, 1977: Unions, churches and beyond...

Kevin thought hard about planning to achieve changes. He has described how this planning was applied to the land rights campaigning. He talks here with Barbara Flick about developing strategies and working them through in practice.

Kevin: When we had the Black Defence Group, we sat down and we analysed where our support for land rights could come from. The only two areas that it could come from was the trade union movement and the churches, as progressive groups. We started out with the Trade Union Committee for Aboriginal Rights, TUCAR, and that was easy to set up because most of the people who were on the Black Defence Group were also trade unionists. (See discussion in Chapter 7 about politics and Tranby.)

And we also wanted to set up an organisation to go out and see if we could influence the churches. Then we started to get involved with the Australian Council of Churches. They already had an Advisory group, with Bob Bellear as Chairman. After he stood down as chairman, Foley took over and I went onto the group in Bob's place. Then when Foley stood down, I took over as Chair. I must've been there six years or something like that. So Black Defence played a role in getting that support from the churches through the ACC as well as from the trade unions through TUCAR and that support was one of the things that helped us get land rights.

Barbara: I know you kept on working with the unions all through that time. How did you get on with the Communist party mob then?

Kevin: They had a few people still in positions in the union. I got on terrifically with all of the factions. See there was two parties then, the Australian Communist Party and the SPA, the Socialist Party of Australia. I had mates in both camps. But I think the strangest connection for me was Charlie Oliver, from the AWU, who was on the Right. Now he played a very good role later on, in 1981, in getting the unions to see Wran.

Barbara: There was a lot of talking going on with the churches. And I went to some meetings with Kevin. But he certainly went to a lot more than I did. And speaking on campuses, university campuses, we did some of that work together. But then again, he did much more than I did. So it was really a busy time in trying to reach as many people as possible, through trade unions, through workers, through the churches, the student groups. None of it would have happened unless we were able to convince all of those people that it was justice that we were talking about.

9. Strategies: 1976 to 1981

And I suppose it was the '70s was a period of time when the world started to think about justice, because many things were affecting people personally. Like the war in Vietnam. And the television screens that showed images of civil rights actions in the United States, and the Women's Movement, things were happening. So I think the country was getting used to people expressing their needs and being articulate about it.

And this is what grew out of Tranby College at that time that Kevin was involved.

Kevin: Dick Scott from the Metal Workers – the AMWU – was an example of that. The Australian Manufacturing Workers' Union is a huge union but he'd been associated with Tranby for years. A great guy, you know, really nice bloke. And an Anglican, a Christian Anglican in Alf's camp, you know, who done a lot for Tranby and who done a hell of a lot for the land rights.

Penno – Mervyn Penrith – used to come up from the South Coast with Jack Campbell, and we'd say: 'Ok, there's a meeting on tonight, come out'. We got a lot of support from the churches that we went to. The Quakers were always good. And the Manly-Warringah Support Group started up after that. People who were working with us then from that group are still working with us now. It was a great support for the land rights campaign.

So it was an incredible set of connections, but it not only did Aboriginal people good, but it's also done non-Aboriginal people good. Because the people who supported the land rights, a lot of them are still actively involved in support groups, in Tranby, or some Aboriginal organisations. Now they're getting to go down to, you know, the South Coast, and they know where to go, where not to go. They go out west now. You know, a lot of people went to the handback of Mutawintji, you know. So then, that's something else that was done through land rights.

Barbara: And remember Margaret Roadknight was a great supporter. She used to come to the university campuses with us, and entertain and liven up the crowd.

Kevin: I carried her guitar.

Barbara: I have a photo of you carrying her guitar! It was fairly early days for people and that was a really good thing for her to do. She'd come along with her guitar, and she was really popular on campus at the time. She'd lend her support to our fundraisers and dances and encourage people to be active. So we got really good bands for nothing, like Mental as Anything. And do you remember Chips MacInolty doing posters for us. And the Tin Sheds at Sydney Uni.

Kevin: The non-Aboriginal support, it was really great. People played a very vital role in the introduction of the land rights legislation. Like the Land Rights

Support Group – Dave Morrissey organised that and he got lots of people together to help out – like they'd paste up posters or lick envelopes or type or print off books. And you talk to them, and you say: 'You're part of history. You helped in that area!'

It's just amazing how so much can be done by so little mob of people. I learnt that in the Builders Labourers. We used strategies from everybody I think. It's amazing… what I thought was quite funny, a lot of people ask me: 'Who's giving you all this information?' 'How are youse doing it so good?' And we thought we were bumbling along and everyone else thought we were going really great. And we were doing it ourselves, which was good!

Barbara had a key role in introducing people from the South Coast, like Jacko Campbell and Mervyn Penrith to her relations and friends on the Darling River, a story which will be taken up in the next Chapter, 'Experiences'.

Making changes to policy: ALP Conference, June 1978 leads to Select Committee

But first, the other strategic step which flowed directly out of the 1977 Land Rights Conference was the attempt to work from inside the Labor Party to change its Platform which would then put pressure on the Labor government to make real changes in policy. With the evidence of the already-submitted Terry Hie Hie claim and with drafting of the Jerringa and Wallaga Lake claims underway, activists like Kevin were looking for ways to put pressure on the Labor Party to respond.

To follow up this part of the story, Kevin talked with Rod Pickette and Meredith Burgmann, both members of the ALP with a keen interest in the formal structures which brought motions up to the Annual Conference which was where the Party Platform was decided.

Rod Pickette has explained how he saw his role in supporting land rights within the ALP.

Rod: When you think back to 20 years ago when land rights was the issue – it really was very central. Other things were seen to hang off that. I saw my role to be a white fella supporting Aboriginal land rights, because I thought that unless there was a way of ensuring that Aboriginal people still have rights and ownership over land, then the other things – like the culture – won't have the same chance of surviving as a living thing. I still think it's absolutely as important today as it was then. It's all very well for everyone to be educated to a standard or to have jobs with equal access, but that's not sufficient. It was really a renewal of the call for self-determination, it seems to me.

9. Strategies: 1976 to 1981

Figure 9.4: Walking along the beach to lay the wreaths into Botany Bay.

Courtesy Heather Goodall.

The situation after the fall of the Whitlam Government was that the NSW activists had to shift the focus from the federal government back to the state government, which was then held by the ALP. Kevin's assessment of the support from state Labor politicians was that those who had been longest involved were his old friend Bill Knox, then George Peterson, Frank Walker and Maurie Keane. While others in the ALP were sympathetic, it was these four whom he expected to be the most informed and consistent supporters. He was pessimistic about the commitment of the rest of the party members, because, as he said: 'The Labor Party, they only pay lip-service to it.'

The unions, whom he had begun to draw in through the TUCAR structure, were an influential extra-parliamentary support, but the parties to the left of the ALP were more varied in their attitude. Rod pointed out that the Communist Party of Australia had not taken the issue up as a major campaign, although individuals within the party were strong supporters. But he felt that 'It took the Communist party a long time to actually grab the land rights movement. Inside the party, it didn't actually ever form a significant issue'.

Kevin felt this was because Aboriginal people had not joined the party.

Kevin: There would only have been a few Aboriginal members. There was Louise West. But that's one thing about how the community saw it. Like I remember we were going down the South Coast with old Jacko, and you know what a wonderful bloke he was. But then someone said, 'Oh, I think so-and-so is in the Communist party'. And Jacko and them all reeled back – like it was 'Shock, horror!' And I said, 'What's the difference between them and Merv Nixon, you all work with him?' And they said, 'Oh well, he's a white fella!'

But if you were black, there was a stigma about being in the Communist party. My uncle was in the Communist party in Wollongong years ago. See, I think people were at uni when they were joining the Communist party, or at work in the unions and joining the Communist party. Very few Aboriginal people ever were at the uni and there were very few people in jobs! And so they just didn't do it!

The smaller Socialist Workers' Party had been much more evident but as Kevin pointed out, their support for the Aboriginal movement was even more reluctantly received.

Kevin: … That was because they tried to take the issues and run with them rather than supporting the Aboriginal people, and that was a problem, you know. People got a bit scared of them doing that. And that's why they stayed well clear of them.

9. Strategies: 1976 to 1981

Figure 9.5: Rod Pickette with son Maka and daughter Akidi.

Courtesy Rod Pickette family collection.

Overall, Kevin argued, 'There wasn't a political party that got behind Aboriginal land rights at the time'.

So changing the ALP Platform was a priority. Meredith Burgmann was a long time member of the ALP. She is speaking to Kevin and to Rod as she describes the frustrations of even trying to get Aboriginal ALP members like Kevin onto the Aboriginal Affairs working party.

Meredith: In a number of the things that we were involved with – you were it! You were the only black! And which is why, getting on to the Labor Party work, Kevin was used absolutely unashamedly. Do you know remember when we got you on the Aboriginal Affairs Policy Committee, but they kept saying 'How many branch meetings has he been to?' And I said, 'He's the only Aborigine on the Aboriginal Affairs Committee, don't you think it's a good idea to have him there?'

But it was a real issue for them! We actually had to have that discussion. They weren't too bad though, they pretty quickly understood the politics of it and put him on and having him there was really, really critical. Because it legitimised all the things that he was working on, suddenly. The fact that there was a structural connection was really important, because there were no Aborigines involved in the Labor Party at all until then. Bob Bellear wasn't really actively involved until a bit after you and people like Joycie Clague and others had been members but hadn't been on the policy-making committees.

Rod: Yeah, I can remember being on that Aboriginal Policy group, Cookie was on it already, and then after that Bob Bellear was the Chair. And the only other person I remembered that was on it was Alan Duncan, who was involved in Aboriginal education for all those years. And there were two or three other people who were not Aboriginal.

Now the Right faction had the numbers in the Party, but the funny thing is, they just didn't grasp the importance of the Aboriginal Policy Committee. On the Policy Committee we'd actually done quite a lot of work – we looked at all the Northern Territory stuff. That was 1976, and we looked at the federal Act that affected the Northern Territory. I was co-opted onto the committee when that was going on. And we got help from people we knew who could explain the federal Act and the other laws to us. So basically we were a bit amateurish in a way, because we didn't get a lot of senior professional advice. But nevertheless we tried to pull together all the best ideas we could about what land rights really meant.

Kevin: We were mainly on about *communal inalienable freehold title,* it was a really new way of holding title to land.

Rod: Yeah, it was the words that it turned on. I think that's why there was such a scare. When it got to the state conference in June '78, half the conference probably didn't realise what they were actually voting for. I remember that conference well, I was there because I was the Theatrical Employees Union delegate. Despite all the work we'd put in at the committee, there still wasn't any guarantee that any policy recommendation you put up would actually make it to the floor of the conference. And then if it didn't get voted on during the conference, it would just have to wait another year or so to try to get put up again. But there was probably also an element of support.

It was a growing public issue. There's no question about that. And so a lot of people were very sympathetic. And I think particularly the church organisations and other organisations like that. It was a bit of a contradiction, you know. People would find their natural conservatism and their racism was sort of pushing them to say 'No'. But other elements of them, like their Christian ethics or something would say, 'Okay, we've got to support this', so there was an element of sympathy there. So even though people mightn't have understood what they were really doing, nevertheless we were able to get some support.

9. Strategies: 1976 to 1981

Kevin: We'd done a pretty good job in that committee in the short time that we were around. But at that conference I think it was very late in the session. Nearly the last thing on the agenda.

Rod: In fact I think we had to do some hard work to actually make sure it got up, you know, because so many of those Policy Committee reports would just never get up. Because of the time limitations, and the shenanigans that used to go on there. So I think there was a lot of behind-the-scenes lobbying. If I remember rightly it was way down on the agenda because Aboriginal Affairs, you know, wasn't going to be at the forefront of the issues on the day. But a bit of work got done to make sure that it actually got through at that time. Because I think it would have got kinda lost if it hadn't got up at that time. Nobody would be working on it. So all that energy would have dissipated. That was at the height of all the work on the committee and it would have been really hard to get it up to that peak again.

Kevin: We actually got it up on to the agenda I think through the unions.

Rod: Yes. It was people like Dick Scott. I'm pretty sure it was those big union delegations and of course Charlie Oliver. You can see how the political alliances there were so critical really to getting it through. But it would have been different if it had just been seen as a Left union thing – because in those days the party was running at about 65 per cent right wing and about 35 per cent left wing delegates. So – because this was something that was seen as a fairly radical policy – if that had been seen as coming only from the left wing it probably would have got rolled just on factional lines.

Kevin: It wouldn't have even got up.

Rod: No, that's right. It wouldn't have even got onto the agenda, let alone get passed. But, you know, it got through that process and got put up at the conference and got voted on.

Kevin: And once it got on the floor, people then probably didn't want to be seen as racist. And it just went through pretty easy. Bob Bellear was the main instrument in getting that through, he moved it and he made a great speech. Because not too many people on the committee would go against him. Not only because his arguments were incredibly good. But as well they didn't like to be looked to be racist or silly.

Rod: Bob was probably seen as more centre figure – he wouldn't have been seen as a fringe left-wing sort of militant. Bob was studying law at the same time and so he had the right credentials. If it had been, say, Gary Foley or someone, maybe it wouldn't have happened, you know. Once Bob had moved it, I don't think there was virtually any opposition to it. I don't recall one speaker actually getting up and opposing it. There have been some questions about the balance of the report or something, that you know needed more emphasis on some other thing, but I can't honestly remember who actually spoke even about that.

Kevin: No. And I think a few of the unions that were members of TUCAR spoke for the motion. So the role of TUCAR was pretty important in mobilising people for that, eh?

Now once that policy change had been made in June '78, we had something to push the Labor Party on. To catch up with their own policy!

And we started having marches as well as the meetings in the bush. And then from one of the marches, I think I was there in parliament with you Rod and other people too, after the 1978 election, when Maurie Keene asked Wran that Dorothy Dix question about the land rights issue, about whether or not the government was going to act on the Report. But it was only after everybody was yelling and screaming at him, you know, 'Why don't you get something done about that platform'. That's when he got up and asked the Dorothy Dix question. And that set it moving about getting the Select Committee into Aboriginal Affairs.

Rod: So the sequence was: the Land Rights Conference, then the period of agitation and working through the Labor Party, then that meant that after the election, the Select Committee got up.

Kevin: That's right. The Select Committee only got set up because that policy was already there.

Rod: But still the Select Committee was really the Wran Government's attempt to head off land rights because they were concerned that the policy was vastly more radical than I think they'd ever expected to get through a NSW Labor Party conference. So then the Select Committee was set up as a way of dissipating the push for land rights, because it had health and education and everything else in it too... So that was one time when TUCAR organised its people to gather in Maurie Keene's office to go to Wran. The Select Committee had already been established, and Maurie was Chair, but it was inquiring into everything, wasn't it? It had to look at education, housing, health.

Kevin: And land rights was running a poor last!

Rod: It was way down the list, that's right. And it seems like Keane was given the writing instructions to put these other things up on the top of the agenda and don't let this land rights thing run too far ahead.

Kevin: So we needed pressure to put land rights back up onto the top of the agenda again.

9. Strategies: 1976 to 1981

1978: Turning points

The Tranby base was important because it had links into rural Aboriginal communities along the North Coast – where the Co-operatives were based – and on the South Coast, from where Kevin's networks had developed, as well as in urban Aboriginal communities. And as we have just seen, it was a crucial focus for drawing in city resources and allies. But the land council's working group was far more representative of city and coastal people than of those in the far west and if the movement was going to represent views from all over the state it needed to extend its geographic range.

There were other developing resource bases in rural NSW which allowed this to happen. The Western Aboriginal Legal Service (WALS) which covered the whole western half of the state, had broken away from the Sydney-based Aboriginal Legal Service (ALS) in 1977. By 1978, WALS had consolidated its main office in Dubbo, from which it supported the active, experienced field officers living in Brewarrina, Wilcannia, Broken Hill, Menindee and Dareton. Barbara Flick began visiting the far west in 1978 and then became the coordinator of WALS in 1979. She was able to bring together the north-western communities, where she had grown up, with those of the far west. For this whole region, WALS was now providing strong and committed legal staff, eager to back up local political demands with innovative legal strategies on land and heritage. Barbara here is talking with Kevin about her early introduction to the far west.

Barbara: I think in '78 was the first time I really went back out west to Wilcannia to that dance we held to raise money for the Peter Tobin[7] law scholarship and I started to really make some links with those people out there. And by the end of '79 to '80 I really wanted to go back out there, so I took it when the opportunity came along. And it was that the political base had been fairly well developed in Sydney with Cookie's contacts in the trade unions, and with Marcia Langton and also with the politicians like those guys from the South Coast – Bill Knott, George Peterson and to some extent Frank Walker. So the base in Sydney was fairly strong. … There were lots of interesting people in the north-west and the west and the South Coast.

---

7   Peter Tobin was a legal student at Sydney University who had been involved in the late 1960s and early 1970s in support for Aboriginal communities and in the establishment of the Aboriginal Legal Service (ALS). On graduating, he became the first lawyer to take up a country post with the ALS, working with field officers Tombo Winters and Stephen Gordon in the newly-opened Brewarrina Legal Service office in 1973. Peter was killed in a plane crash in Cuba in 1977 and Aboriginal activists like Tombo, Stephen, William Bates, George Rose and Isabel Flick established a scholarship to assist Aboriginal people to study law. A number of these people were later involved in WALS.

I think that with me going to an organisation that worked in the west, and Cookie, you being in one in the city, we were able to provide resources and mix between the two groups.

And to try to use those joint resources to do what people were telling us had to be done. It wasn't just the people down the South Coast who were talking about legislation for land rights in NSW, it was people from the west and from Sydney and from the North Coast. But we seem to have had an organisational base to bring all that together. And we also insisted on making sure that what we did was the initiative of older people. We were just younger in those days and so we were given instructions and were able to do that kind of work.

In 1978 too, there was a major political campaign over the Wilcannia Common, which focused the attention of many local people on the potential of combined legal and political action to achieve some control over their land again. Peter Thompson talked to Cookie about this event. Peter is an archaeologist originally from Moree. He is one of the few non-Aboriginal people with a continuing, close relationship to the Aboriginal community. He had been married to Lynne Craigie, a Gamilaraay woman from Moree who had since died. Lynne and Peter had a daughter, Yeena. In 1978, Peter was living in Wilcannia with his partner, Edna Hunter, from the Aboriginal community there, and they were raising their son, Warlpa, and Edna's granddaughter, Emily.

Peter: We had a big thing about the Wilcannia Common in 1978 I think when John Terry was out there as the lawyer for the Western Aboriginal Legal Service. There was a 10,000 acre Common being neglected. In the middle of it is a big lake, and it floods when the river floods, so, the Commons are meant to be run in a way which would allow flexibility without overtaxing it in the fertile years. This hadn't been run that way probably ever but certainly not for 20 or 30 years. And in the '76 flood, it flooded this lake and then when it went down there was a beautiful pasture there for months and months and months like pasture you wouldn't see around Wilcannia, more likely to see around Wellington or something. So butchers in Adelaide had heard about this and they were just trucking their cattle up there to depasture on the free agistment, because there was this huge unregulated Common.

So they ended up having a bit of a crisis about it, and the Western Lands Commission ordered an inquiry by the Local Land Board. Now John Terry wanted to put in a submission about it, because people used to hunt on there and there's lots of burials around the sand dune around the edge of it. So John Terry was there, and he got interested I think because Jack Cromby had been ordered by the Common chairperson of the Common's trust to do a muster, and he'd never been paid properly. So that's how JT got involved. His first entry was to take up Jack's wages claim and then all this other stuff started to develop as he talked to people, about the burials around there that all these cattle are treading on and, you know that's the only place we can go and hunt without getting hunted off. And so we put in quite a lot in the submission about that. I think that was '78 and I think that was one of the issues that was bought up when the select committee came in '79. It had helped to focus people's attention on a recent battle about land and hunting and culture.

Kevin: They knew a lot about it, didn't they, you know. People weren't coming into the land rights campaigns with no knowledge at all. There had been that campaign and then there were several meetings all in that area and they all focused in on that land, just land, land, land. Not anything else, they couldn't be side tracked you know.

After that 1977 Land Rights Conference in Sydney meeting we pretty soon started going out into the bush. And I think the first time that I met you Peter was when I went up to Wilcannia, after that '77 meeting. I remember when I slept out under the verandah outside of your joint. I was scared of snakes.

Peter: …I probably wouldn't let you in the house! And there was more snakes inside anyway!

Kevin: I didn't know that! I was outside 'cause it was really hot and I said I'd sleep there on that bed frame you had outside. I was going to sleep in the car, but it was too hot, but where you had the bed, there was a bit of a breeze, so I slept there. I think Father Carter was up there too.

Peter: Well he came to Wilcannia in '78. And that's when we started organising the Western Regional Land Council.

Kevin: So I talked to you, Edna Hunter, Batesy [William Bates], Crow [Mervyn Williams], he was the Chairman of the regional land council so it must have been going when I was there. And Brian Doolan was working up there too. But I think Barbara Flick was the link, she'd gone up to work at the Western Aboriginal Legal Service in Dubbo, and I can remember her saying you have to go and see Peter Thompson. So I come out there, and I've started to cry! I just couldn't understand why people would live in a place that was so hot! And it had no sea!!

Although Kevin was travelling in 1978 on land council business, he had Tranby and its students in mind – and finally came to see how they felt about being in Sydney, so far away from home. But not only that – he found the Tranby networks really did extend across the state:

Kevin: It wasn't till the students started coming down to Tranby from Bourke that I fully understood what it meant by that commitment to their country.

You know people would leave Tranby Thursday afternoon to go home for the weekend at Bourke, and I'd say, 'What do you want to go all that way for? Why would you go home?'

'Oh Kevin', they'd say, 'we have fun!'

They might be fighting in the pub you know, but they'd say to me, 'Yeah, but its *my* country!'

They wouldn't leave it for the world. And some of them, you know, might have got offered a really high powered job in Sydney, but they still would have wanted to stay in Bourke or in Wilcannia or in Moree.

I went up there more or less on land council business at that time, but while I was up there I'd try to get students for Tranby. And old Alf had kept telling me about this bloke at Wilcannia. Johnny Quayle. He was the one who was involved in setting up of the first brickworks, you know. He was up there when we was running around with the land council in 1978, but he didn't get involved.

Peter: That's right. Alf would have known him because Johnny had been a student at Tranby. That's sort of typical of the connections between Tranby and lots of places in the bush, isn't it. When you see somebody like Johnny Quayle who's pretty important in community development, you often find out that they'd been to Tranby.

While Kevin was there in 1978, he, Peter, Barbara and others would talk over the directions in which land rights organisation might go in NSW. As well as their own local experiences, they had been watching developments in the Northern Territory since 1973 and had learned lessons from what they saw. They saw a really important role for the regional land councils but not in the same way as these bodies had developed in the Northern Territory. The discussion which follows gives an insight into how the regional land councils were imagined before the NSW Land Rights Act existed.

Kevin: Remember when we used to sit down, Pete, and try and work out what the best way to go forward was with this land council idea? And we'd talk about what the structure would be – should be – like. We didn't want it to be like the Northern Territory, they only had two regions. We said, 'What is it we really want to do? Is it just land rights, or is it a wider thing than land rights?'

And it was to organise people, that was one of the main things, so that you could ring up and get your message across to the largest number of Aboriginal people in New South Wales that's possible.

And we thought concentrating on the regional land councils was the best way of going about it. You'd still have local land councils and a state body, but the regional land councils would be the focus. So that if you wanted someone to go on tour, you could have a central position within the region, where they'd go and all of the regional community would come in. Also because we were expecting we'd be going into new ventures, so if they were setting up motels or something like that in one local area, then any problems that one area had, they could come together with another area in the region who were going to buy a little motel then tell them what all the problems would be and how to find the solutions before they went into it. So that they wouldn't have that problem. Or in any industry that they were going to set up in that area, the regional council could be the place where they'd all be able to sit down from across that area, so that the locals wouldn't be doing the same thing and competing against one another. If they all wanted to get into it, they could get into it on a regional basis, or, they could go in it by themselves. But the whole region would know what they're doing.

Figure 9.6: Joe Flick, Isabel Walford Flick, Paul Torzillo, Jacqui Mason 'Labor Party policy says YES!'

Courtesy Heather Goodall.

So when all the regions come together as a state body, it's a lot easier to get that information out. It might even be hosting, say, music bands going through, so that they could go to each region. They'd get a large number of people there, make money for the regional land council and then go off into the other regions. So it wasn't just on land issues, it was the whole economic issue.

And it can still be done, if they organise themselves properly. That's why the regional land council was set up.

Peter: Well, in the bush, at Wilcannia, we'd been toying around with things, and the housing was one of the first to get going with the Paakantji Housing Company. Wilcannia was trying to do it a bit differently through Paakantji and not getting anywhere! But the way that it was different was to find answers in people's culture and so it meant reconnecting with the past and people's own history and culture and language and land and all those issues. I think that was probably important. The other one was that people out there were very unconcerned about material things. So they weren't focusing on getting the flash house, or stuff like that. When they were getting organised, it always seemed to come back to basic issues of survival like fishing, hunting and the need for land to do those things and just extending that to protecting sites and culture. So it was pretty easy for people to focus on land issues out there, probably easier than in other regions, where they could think 'Oh yeah, we might be able to start this business', or that factory.

And then, after the Wilcannia Common, there as a couple of issues came up, one of them, one of them was protecting the grave on Kinchega National Park. This must be around '82 I suppose. The National Parks Service had a road going across the top of this old grave and they didn't want to move the road. So Barbara Flick at the legal service, I think it would be just before the land councils got going, the Land Rights *Act* land councils, but the Western *Regional* Land Council was already going. She got the lawyers looking up what we could do and they decided to use the section of the Crimes Act[8] that stopped medical students from mucking around with corpses, you know you have to treat human remains with dignity. And so we threatened to take National Parks to the court under the Crimes Act and they very soon found that it was necessary to change the road a bit, put an island up in the middle!

So that was one issue, and the other one was Telecom with the tower on Coonanberi Mountain. We found out about that a week before they were going to air lift the tower out there with helicopters. So we just launched this little campaign, and were successful, eh! We wrote letters to various ministers I think and said it was sacred site and the tower just couldn't be done.

So it was won by asserting the muscle, I suppose, of the regional land council. That was the other reason why the regional land council was important, it gave, it gave leadership opportunities. Some of the other structures didn't. You had the legal service, which gave leadership opportunities in a fairly structured way in an organisation over the whole of western New South Wales, and prior to that

---

8   *Crimes Act 1900* (NSW).

all of New South Wales. And that structure and scale meant that people were competing against each other to be directors. But because the land council at that time wasn't a corporation, it allowed people to co-operate and get their co-operative leadership working. I think that was important too.

And finally none of those issues, like no land issue, no culture issue, no hunting or fishing issue was strictly speaking a local one. It affected people beyond the local area and so, you know, it linked people across the region and allowed people to operate, or this organisation allowed people to operate at that level. The big issues at that level were land, culture and fishing and hunting. They weren't housing, they weren't sewerage, they weren't running a petrol station or something, all of those were local issues. So that once people organised at a regional then land became an obvious focus.

The campaign kick start happens: 1978 to 1981

Once the ALP Conference in June had voted to change ALP policy – and particularly to demand land rights for Aboriginal people – the pressure was on the Wran Government to put this new policy into action. Even with a new mandate after the election was won, Premier Neville Wran appeared to be reluctant to initiate any policy change and it was only after a lot of pressure that Maurie Keane, Member for Woronora in southern Sydney, moved in October 1978 that an inquiry should be established into the current state of Aboriginal affairs. Land was low on the agenda in this proposal, which was initially going to look first at health, housing and education before it turned to land. But through November, pressure was brought to bear on Wran by trade unions and the churches, encouraged by high profile Aboriginal figures like Bob Bellear but particularly mobilised by the behind-the-scenes organising from TUCAR and Tranby, orchestrated by Kevin and his colleagues. In February 1979, the Select Committee began to take evidence in its first hearings at Wallaga Lake and Roseby Park, where there were strong statements from Aboriginal witnesses demanding that Land be the priority for the inquiry. There were few further rural hearings during 1979, but it continued to come under heavy pressure from the NSW Land Council to focus on Land.

***

During 1979, Kevin went to Coady in the second half of the year, but the campaigning for land was accelerating across the state. Communities were preparing land claims in Wilcannia in the far west, Bodalla on the South Coast, Warangesda in the south-west, La Perouse in Sydney, Toomelah in the north-west and Nambucca Heads on the North Coast.

***

When Kevin returned from Canada, he had spent six months talking over the strategies for gaining NSW land rights with the community activists at Coady from Africa, India and Latin America, giving an even wider context for the conversations he had been having with Barbara, Peter, Jacko and others in Australia. As well his already strong commitment to be working at grass roots level, he had an even stronger awareness of the importance of taking people along with him in whatever goals he had.

The land claim from Bodalla was lodged early in 1980 and the others began to flow, all increasing the pressure on the Select Committee to focus on land. The land council held a large community meeting at Dubbo in May, with people attending from the north and south coast and from right across the west. This was an unprecedented gathering of Aboriginal people from regions who were not normally able to be in touch with one another. Among their resolutions calling on the state government to fulfil its Platform to recognise Aboriginal rights to land, the Aboriginal Land Council demanded speaking rights at the coming ALP conference in June. They gained this demand, and two South Coast activists, Mervyn Penrith and Max Harrison, spoke movingly at the state conference demanding urgent action on land rights.

The Select Committee's approach had changed in response to this pressure, holding more rural hearings. Its brief was not whether land rights should be granted, as this decision had already been cemented by the change in the party's platform in 1978. Rather it's brief was *how* to implement it. In August 1980, the Committee brought down its first report, the Interim Report on Aboriginal Land Rights. Meredith Wilkie's careful assessment is that the Report acknowledged four significant principles (although some of its recommendations did not follow these through fully). These principles were self-determination, prior ownership, right to full compensation and cultural integrity.[9] It recommended:

1. scrapping all existing legislation;

2. allow claims to be lodged on any area of Crown land that was defined as open to claim;

3. establishing a three tiered structure with decision making at local and regional level land councils, while the 'upper' state-level land council was to act as a forum rather than a centralised decision-making body;

---

9   Wilkie 1985: 23.

4. a Land Fund for land purchases (in recognition of the high proportion of state land already alienated over 200 years of colonisation) to be drawn from 7.5 per cent Land Tax for 14 years.

While this report was generally received favourably by Aboriginal people in NSW, the Aboriginal Land Council was cautious – it argued this was only a first step towards what should be a broader recognition of land rights. But it agreed to work on with the report as a basis if there were immediate and wide consultations with Aboriginal people across the state on how to implement the recommendations and an immediate freeze on the alienation of all Crown land, to allow claims to be prepared.

Neville Wran was reluctant to take action on the Committee's report, arguing its recommendations would be hard to implement. In October 1980, he established a 'Cabinet Committee of Review' which was widely seen as a delaying mechanism. His promises of wide consultation did not eventuate. In September 1981 he announced the – unasked for – establishment of a Department of Aboriginal Affairs which was again widely seen as a distraction from the continuing demand for urgent implementation of the Select Committee's recommendations – as a minimum – leading to a wider land rights law.[10]

The Aboriginal Land Council held a major meeting in November 1980 and resolved to counter Wran's delaying tactics by embarking on its own consultation program, with members committing to travel round the state asking local communities what they saw as the best ways to implement land rights. With some funding support from the Australian Council of Churches Aboriginal Affairs Committee, chaired by Cookie, the South Coast elders like Jacko Campbell and Ted Thomas, accompanied by Mervyn and Shirley Penrith, began to travel from community to community, gathering Aboriginal views and recommendations. Their trips continued into 1981, and then in April, the Select Committee released its second and final report, on health, education and state-federal relations. Its major advice however, was that rapid implementation of its recommendations on land rights was essential to the success of any of its recommendations on other themes.

The land council meeting in November 1980 had been to organise people, Kevin felt, to give people a chance to decide what their next steps would be. Barbara Flick and Kevin talked about their sense of where things were going then:

Barbara: I think we'd decided by then that the Select Committee report was strong enough to put pressure on for legislation to be introduced in the State Parliament. And I think that that was… although there'd been a lot of political activity before, it needed to become more focused and to try and work out a

---

10   Wilkie 1985: 36.

real role for the responsibilities. And how to be accountable, back to the old people… to make sure that the struggle wasn't just for younger people to go on and build power bases, that it was to try and work out, how do we now try and influence legislation to realise the dreams of what older people had? And it had to become more formalised, and I think it was at that time that you took on formally the role of chairperson in a different way. And that we supported you, Kevin, and the other executive officers of the organisation. Peter Thompson was around at that stage and we started to think about what claims people had already talked about and that had been around for a long time. We wanted to work towards documenting those claims that people had had in their minds for a long time.

Kevin: And that's when the Land Rights Support Group helped get that book out… the NSW Aboriginal Land Claims Book. On the South Coast and the far South Coast they had already drawn up their claims. Jacko Campbell was one of the first, with the Jerringa claim for Roseby Park. And Wallaga Lakes. I've always admired the people down at Wallaga Lakes – their old reserve covered an area of land where the council came in and sold it off. The council had cut a road through it and sold part of the property, the same as what they did at Orient Point, Jacko's home at Roseby Park. In the Wallaga Lake land claim the border came right up to the houses. So in the claim they didn't claim the full reserve, they claimed just up to people's houses, and then they put it in… They wanted first option to buy the houses if they ever come up for sale. But they didn't claim them! And I still say that first document that was drawn up had very conservative claims by Aboriginal people.

Barbara: But there was an incredible solidarity. Everything was happening at once. There was the barricades in Glebe about the expressway. So those links with the old Builders Labourers like Jack Mundey and Bobby Pringle were reinforced all the time. And people were really beginning to understand that the struggle was a struggle of the people. So it had made it clear how important solidarity was right across all of those issues, which were about building a better life for everybody. So I think all those links had held to build political strategies shared across all those movements at the time.

Kevin: But I think the land rights campaign was the best organised group that I'd seen, and that's including the Builders Labourers!

Barbara: We were very disciplined. And a lot of it was because you were at Tranby Cookie. There were many times when there were long-term feuds happening between individuals but Cookie, you could often fix them up in a way nobody else could do, because everybody else carried baggage, you know, from one side or the other. But Tranby really was independent and non-aligned, and I think it's true that you also were that way. One of the strangest things about you, Cookie, is that I don't think I've ever heard you run anybody down. And not put up with it very much when anybody else wants to do that. So, I think that was important at the time that people saw you as being independent and somebody who thought for himself and wasn't tied by all of those long-term family feuds or regional feuds that happen constantly.

Kevin: I think those old feuds were a great waste of energy and manpower. That was one of the things that would've killed us, if any infighting would've broken out. I think we would've been gone right from the first.

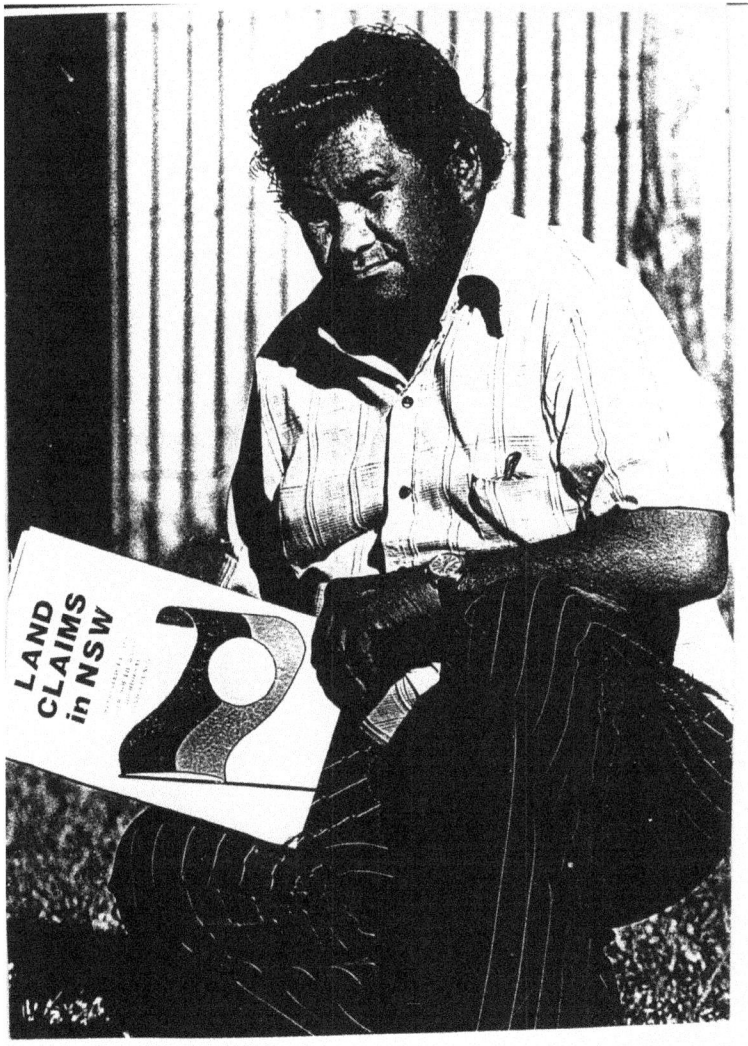

Figure 9.7: Tombo Winters, Brewarrina, with Land Rights Claims book.

Courtesy Tranby Archives.

Making Change Happen

Figure 9.8: Aboriginal people travelling to connect up across the state: Pearl Gibbs, South Coast women, Tudi Longbottom (La Per), Isabel Walford Flick (Wee Waa and Dubbo) and Leila Murray (Wee Waa) at Farm in Dubbo, talking about land rights.

Courtesy Barbara Flick family collection.

Figure 9.9: Meeting in Dubbo, about land rights with Guboo Ted Thomas (South Coast), Phoebe Mumbler (Nambucca Heads, North Coast) and Terry Fox.

Courtesy Tranby Archives.

Barbara: There weren't many people around who didn't have strong alliances — whether it be with the region or with the bush or with the city or with the way in which things happened. But Cookie you were one of the few people that was the voice of reason and would work through things with individuals and with groups to make sure that everybody went along the same path.

Kevin: Well, we did have some sticky times didn't we? Some things we could never mend, but some of these things we got over pretty quickly.

I think we learnt a lot about other people just by working together... I don't think you know people personally. I think you know how they work under different conditions, and how to get the best out of those people. I've got a lot of admiration for people like Tombo Winters with what they did with the first years of the land rights.

And I think people knew it was important to stick together, because if we didn't stick together, we would've been gone very quickly. And the government would've been laughing at us. No, I think overall, it was a very good show of the solidarity and I still believe people are reaping the benefits now. You know, communities, they've got land. They would never ever been able to afford the land that they got. And you know if they sit down and start working out where to from here, I think there's a lot more to be gained from the land rights struggle in NSW. If that happens then we're better off. And that's all it was, to make sure that Aboriginal people's standards were lifted. If our standards lift then everybody else's standards have lifted. Because we still don't own very many shops or many farms. We don't own very many hotels. And non-Aboriginal people will benefit from our struggles.

***

Through an election campaign in September 1981, Wran continued to delay, and 1982 shaped up as a key year in the expression of Aboriginal goals for land justice in NSW.

The next chapter gives some insights into the experiences of the activists in the campaigns in 1982 and 1983 to pressure the government to fulfil its land rights policy. The bush meetings in NSW allowed for shared discussions about strategies for achieving cultural and social goals through land. This had results which were more important than only forcing the government to act, as it finally did in 1983. By the time the Act came into being, there was a far more solid and shared consensus among Aboriginal communities in many regions about what access to and control over some land might offer them.

Figure 9.10: Another visualisation of the shared pressure on Aboriginal people across the country. In this demonstration against uranium mining contrary to Aboriginal wishes in the Northern Territory, a representative from the Northern Land Council digs up some symbolic earth in Macquarie Street, opposite the offices of the mining company, Energy Resources Australia, operating on Aboriginal land at the Ranger site.

Courtesy Heather Goodall.

9. Strategies: 1976 to 1981

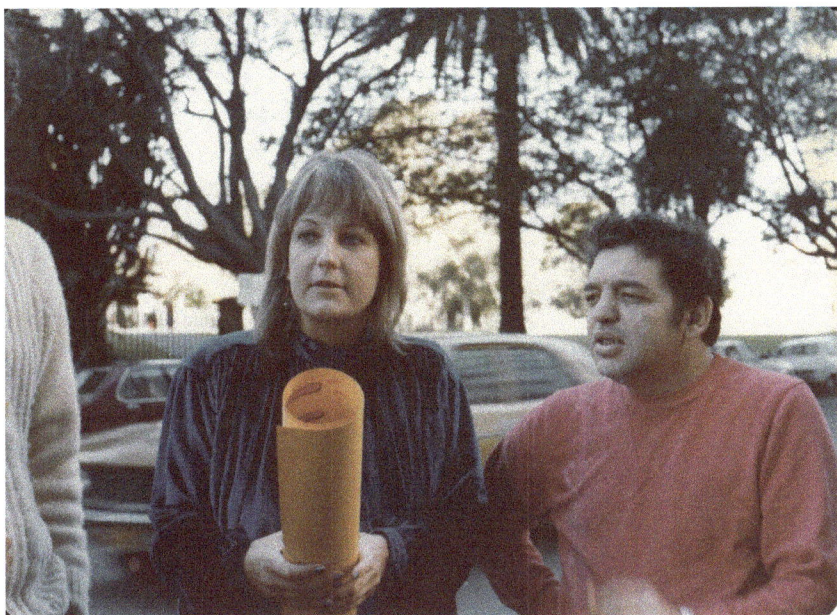

Figure 9.11: Meredith Burgmann and Kevin Cook, in crowd of supporters against the Ranger mine.

Courtesy Heather Goodall.

Figure 9.12: Bob Bellear throws the load of symbolic soil into the foyer of the Energy Resources Australia office building.

Courtesy Heather Goodall.

10. Experiences: 1981 to 1982— Street demos and bush camps

> They wanted a piece of land that was theirs. And that was what made me sit up and take notice of how we couldn't stuff it up.
>
> Kevin Cook on the Menindee Meeting, 5 December 1981

The state election in mid September 1981 brought Neville Wran's Labor Government back into power – but it gave no real sign that the land rights issue would be advanced in the coming term. Aboriginal activists escalated their campaign to force the government into action, however reluctant the Premier himself appeared to be.

This campaign took some well-worn paths, with deputations, petitions and demonstrations. Street marches had been an important way to publicise land issues and a memorable one had been in July 1980, before the Select Committee's First Report, when the Aboriginal Legal Service demanded support for its legal challenge to the state on the grounds of continuing and unceded Aboriginal sovereignty. A hired train, the Moree Special, had brought people from the north-west to march on Parliament and they had been met with a warm welcome at Central Station.

This strategy was one used to put pressure on this second Wran Government in 1982 as well, with a major march planned by the NSW Land Council (the political organising body set up after the 1977 Land Rights conference) which would draw people from all over the state to march down the city streets to demand land rights laws urgently.

The most striking innovation of the NSW Land Council campaign however was to create welcoming spaces for Aboriginal people to talk to each other. These were the bush meetings which became the hallmark of that year of mobilisation. Rather than the old style formal meetings in halls – like the 1977 Land Rights Conference had been – the Land Council concentrated now on building communication in rural areas, between communities and between regions. This strategy of creating time and conditions for Aboriginal people to meet and talk over goals and develop strategies had been seen to work in remote areas – often associated with ceremonial meetings, the opportunity to develop common political strategies had paid off in the 1945 Pilbara Strike and then during the early 1970s in the Northern Territory land rights campaigns. Before 1981, it had seldom taken place in New South Wales. But the bush meeting idea made it clear that Aboriginal relations to land were the foundation for talking and planning for the future.

Figure 10.1: Tombo Winters (from Brewarrina) and Joe Flick (from Wee Waa and Collarenebri) meet the specially hired train, the *Moree Special* at Central Station, July 1981.

Courtesy Heather Goodall.

The one hope in that second Wran Government was that although the establishment of a Department of Aboriginal Affairs, announced in September 1981, was unwanted, the new minister, Frank Walker, appeared to be serious about addressing land questions. Walker, from the Left of the ALP and previously Attorney General but not involved in Aboriginal Affairs, nevertheless initiated discussions in Sydney with Aboriginal organisations to determine their priorities and particularly to seek their views on land rights. Although he did not initiate the extensive consultations with Aboriginal people which the Select Committee had recommended, Walker's interest made the bush meetings even more important because they allowed communities to discuss and if necessary argue out all the options so they had common positions to take to Walker and the government. Finally, after two years of frustration, these discussions seemed to bear fruit just before Christmas in December 1982 when Walker issued a 'Green Paper' on land rights, a document understood to be virtually a draft for the new legislation.

This chapter, 'Experiences' does not trace in detail the events from the 1981 election through to the Green Paper. Instead, it gives the perspective of the Aboriginal participants on the kinds of campaigning they did – in both the bush meetings and the street demonstrations – in which *they* stimulated and supported effective and widespread discussions across the state about what land rights might actually mean to Aboriginal people on the ground. This made visible the processes of real exchange and cross-generational input into planning about land to which the government could have had access for its 1983 Land Rights Bill – but in which it had failed to take part.

Figure 10.2: Greg Davis, Land Rights March, July 1981.

Courtesy Heather Goodall.

Figure 10.3: Alice Briggs (Taree) at Land Rights March, July 1981.

Courtesy Heather Goodall.

Figure 10.4: Land Rights March, July 1981 led to rally at Parliament House – Gary Williams speaking.

Courtesy Heather Goodall.

10. Experiences: 1981 to 1982—Street demos and bush camps

The Aboriginal Land Council Sydney march, 30 October 1981

The NSW Aboriginal Land Council organised a large rally and march in Sydney in October 1981, when it was looking very unlikely that the Wran Government was going to take action on land after the election. The Land Rights Support Group, a loosely-structured network of interested volunteers, some teachers from Tranby and a range of other community groups, were called on to paste up posters and screenprint the yellow T-shirts that the land council handed out to all and sundry on the day of the march.

Here Karen and Barbara Flick, sisters but living in different towns in country NSW, talk about their views of this experience.

Karen: We came down to Sydney for those land rights rallies. I remember Dave Morrissey was with the Land Rights Support Group then, with his little canvas bag with the flag on. We had that big rally where we took all the curries and everything over to Black Theatre and gave everyone a big feed there. Then we had the march.

Cookie played a fairly key role in that again for two reasons. Firstly was because it was calling for land rights but also it was about being able to mobilise this support group, down here, that allowed people from the country to come there and be a part of it. That's what I think you need as well. You need to have that assistance. It's a bit more than sympathy, because those people are also committed to doing the right thing.

It was real support. We know that they'd go in and support you, that they'd stand on the sideline but that they would do everything that you wanted within reason to back you up. Dave Morrissey and the people like that, they'd put their hand in their pocket all the time, they'd take people home to their place and billet them out, they'd go around do the cooking, do the washing up, be the drivers, so that it made it as easy as possible for those people who come down from the country areas to actually participate in that meeting.

You know those country people would come up to me and say, 'Look this is the best meeting we've ever been too, we didn't have to do anything other than go to the meeting and sit down there and talk'. I think that's what we tried to plan to do, we'd sit around before the rally or the meeting and say, 'These people are going to come there, they've got little or no resources in their home towns, what we have to do is to show them they've got support down here'.

And they did that. Exceptionally well!

Figure 10.5: Frank Walker, newly appointed Minister for Aboriginal Affairs in the Wran Labor Government, speaks at Land Rights rally. Supports call for implementation of the Select Committee Report Recommendations on Land.

Courtesy Heather Goodall.

Kevin encouraged Tranby students to take part in the overall land rights support process with mixed results. Overall however he saw it as a key part of the development of their confidence, and that was the goal, whether or not it happened through the land rights campaign.

Kevin: There are some students who are very, very involved in land rights. And then other students are not. Until they start learning about it, you know. It's part of history, you know. Unless you know the history, you're not going to be involved in it. We used to get some students who'd come out and paste up. Not too many, eh? We always gave them the opportunity – [laughter] Briany Bates from Bourke was one. He was good. And there was Chittles – Colin Thorne from Collarenebri. But see Chittles'd never been involved in anything like that before.

We had those four-gallon drums of that glue, you know, in those days, it was before computers, you know. I think Dave Morrissey had run off the posters. We took the Tranby bus. It had a little door that opened in the middle and we'd have to get out and put the thing up. It was the most exercise any of those students got in three years at Tranby! [laughter]

But it's funny, you know, to see some of the students, when they come in to Tranby at first they'd have their heads down. Not looking left or right. And six months later they walk in and take over the office and using your telephone! You have to get a stick to knock 'em out of the office. It was always great to see how they'd change!

Figure 10.6: 'Land Rights NOW!' The banners had become more urgent …

Courtesy Heather Goodall.

Figure 10.7: … And now much more culturally assertive – this sign was written in Paakantji, reflecting the high proportion of people who had come down to join the rally from far western NSW along the Darling River, from Wilcannia, Menindee and Broken Hill along with those from the coast. Many have extensive knowledge of their own language and an active language teaching program had begun in the schools. In this photo, Percy Mumbulla from the South Coast is shown speaking in front of a Paakantji sign reading: 'We Are on Our *OWN* Land!' The people standing near him include Kevin Cook, Paul Coe, Karen Flick and Guboo Ted Thomas.

Courtesy Heather Goodall.

From the time of the election, even though Aboriginal people were not confident that Wran would take any action on land rights, the opposition from rural farming and mining industry groups began to escalate. Despite the Select Committee recommendations, which had been very moderate, there was a rising campaign of fear mongering. Accusations were made repeatedly – as there had been against the Northern Territory Land Rights Act – that Aboriginal people were going to take landowners' 'backyards' – including suburban backyards. These advertising campaigns were aimed particularly at voters in urban areas, where the majority of NSW citizens lived and where sympathy for land rights was likely to be strongest. So the campaigns by industry groups led to widespread urban anxiety among whites about the outcomes of any land rights legislation. This rising hostility was the atmosphere in October 1981 when the big Land Council march was held and it was one of the reasons so many country people – including senior country people – made the long trip down to Sydney to be at the march.

***

Barbara: They were incredible times because lots of old people came and marched. They felt that they were able to participate in what could have been seen as fairly radical type of activity. I think that was a really important element at the time…

Figure 10.8: Barbara Flick speaks at rally while Kevin talks to Maurie Keane, chairman of the Select Committee Report.

Courtesy Heather Goodall.

And from all over the state, they found a way to express their involvement in this campaign, and to support what people like Kevin were trying to achieve. That was a really strong vote of confidence, for those old people to come down to Sydney to march on State Parliament and to make some statements.

Kevin: And that gives you heart. Unless that had happened, I wouldn't have been able to keep going! I used to think about it when we were being boo-ed and hissed at some of those rallies we spoke at, at the universities and in other places. When you sat down and talked to some of them old people, they'd just said: 'Don't worry about that. You're doing a fantastic job.'

And then half the time, the people who were hissing and boo-ing would came straight up to you, after the meeting, or a couple of days later. And they'd have their arm around you and say: 'Look, I'm sorry but, you know, you knew what was going on.' That didn't stop it hurtin' at the time!

But the people who give you that support, that's what made it all worthwhile.

The Menindee meeting, 5 December 1981

One of the first of the big bush meetings was early in December, in which the western Aboriginal communities came together to form a regional council – again on the model of the Northern Territory structures but with the intention of operating more effectively and more widely than had been the case in the Territory.

Barbara Flick had been working actively with Kevin since her move to Dubbo to coordinate the Western Aboriginal Legal Service (WALS) in 1979. She was living with Stephen Fitzpatrick, a WALS lawyer and she and Stephen were sharing a rented farmhouse out of town with a number of other lawyers for the service. It was here that some early Land Council meetings had been held. The location out of town was a clear benefit, but the meeting at Menindee, an old Protection Board-managed station to which many people on the Darling River had a close personal and historic attachment, took the process to a new level. Even though many people travelled up and down the Darling from where they were now living, once they had arrived at Menindee they felt at home in those surroundings. This meant those people who felt this security were able to confidently welcome others who came from further away, like Barbara and her relations from the north-western areas, or Jacko Campbell and Kevin from the South Coast.

Barbara: What I think was interesting was that at the Menindee meeting, the old people like *Thartu* – Big Will Webster – were really supportive.

Kevin: I remember that old woman who got up and spoke – Tibby Briar. She spoke for about four to five minutes and she was really articulate and I thought it was incredibly well-researched. Coming from Wilcannia where there is hardly anywhere to get the information from. When she spoke you'd think that she'd been to every meeting for the last ten years down in Sydney. And she had her heart into it! I listened to her for about ten minutes and I thought butter wouldn't melt in this woman's mouth. And then she said: 'And they can all go and get fucked!' I just burst out laughing. And she was serious eh? But she was really on the ball, she knew exactly what she wanted to say. And she was getting angrier and angrier.

That was a great meeting.

Barbara: Tibby was real active about this for years. She was the one who took me and Maureen O'Donnell down to Wentworth to take the skulls out of the museum, the Wentworth Museum. And she had been involved in diverting the road at Kinchega National Park so that it didn't go where the people were buried. So she was an old campaigner. I think it was really good at that stage because we still had a lot of the old people around us. A lot have died in the ten years since then. But in the early '80s, we still had people like Big Will Webster, Tibby, May Barlow, Jacko Campbell, to give instruction to us.

Kevin: And we didn't do anything off our own bat, which was really great because there was a lot of responsibility in pushing the land rights issue. The older people would say: 'This is what you have to do.' And all we did was to do their bidding. It wasn't us jumping up and down and saying: 'We're going to get you land rights, and this is the way we're going to do it.' It was *them* telling us what to do! We'd go back and work on it, and then coming back to the next meeting and say: 'This is what we've done. What's our next step?'

Barbara: And I remember in particular that meeting at Menindee Mission, because Kevin coming out there was a big deal to them. It wasn't the done thing! You know, the people in the regions travelled around and worked in the bush for their mob, but people who were based in Sydney, and acted state-wide, it's really difficult and we didn't see them much. But Cookie was one of the few people who was able to move around the state and people felt comfortable. There's a great black and white photograph that I have of you Cookie and Big Will and William Bates, under the bough shade at Menindee Mission. To me this is what that time meant, what that whole period meant.

They say you can't have your head in the clouds if your feet aren't on the ground. And there was also a lot of pressure, I think, at the time from various individuals who wanted to turn this into some kind of money-making deal. Or they would've liked to negotiate with Cookie about how to set-up the power base so that might benefit them, not mentioning any names! So I think that Cookie was watched over for that period of time to see how he'd go. And he made people feel confident that this was a serious thing, and that we were going to get some results. There was always a feeling that this was going to take us somewhere!

Figure 10.9: Bush meeting, Menindee, 1982, to establish the Western Regional Land Council, a campaigning body set up a year before the Land Rights Act was passed.

Courtesy Barbara Flick family collection.

Figure 10.10: At the Menindee meeting: Kevin Cook speaking, left, *Thartu* (Big Will) Webster (standing, centre) and William Bates (seated, right).

Courtesy Barbara Flick family collection.

When we started the hard negotiations with Frank Walker and we realised the reality of compromise and negotiation with state government, we might've been a bit flat. I know we worried a lot about whether we were part of those before who had sold-out our mob. I certainly felt like that from time-to-time. And we took a lot of pressure, but I think Kevin probably took more than the rest of us, but he handled it very well. I don't know how, but he seemed to be able to make really big people sit down and shut up.

Kevin: That's because I was five foot nothing! And I'm still five foot nothing!

Barbara: Maybe! [laughter]

Those bush meetings were important, because there was everyone there and there were opportunities to talk outside the meetings as well as in them. People could sit around the camps and talk, while they were getting stuff ready and then later on when they were making Johnny cakes around the campfire … And kids were there. Any age could come. It wasn't sort of 'delegates only' type meeting or conference, you know.

Kevin: That Menindee meeting had everything. It had the atmosphere. It had kids. It had old people. People from the cities, from country towns all over New South Wales. And just by smelling what they were cooking, you could nearly tell where they came from. You know, like the goanna was there, the kangaroo, emu was from this other place, you know. And you just stuffed yourself full of really great food. But you know, some people had hardly been out of Wilcannia. But they were so articulate, the way they spoke. And they knew exactly what they wanted.

They wanted a piece of land that was *theirs*. And that was what made me sit up and take notice of how we couldn't stuff it up.

William Bates

William Bates is a man with Malyangapa, Wadikali, Pantjikali and Paakantji connections who has taken a major and sustained role in land and heritage campaigning in western New South Wales. Here he talks with Kevin about the Menindee meeting.

William: We set the Regional up before the Act – we were at the Menindee Mission… and you were there, talkin' on some of them tapes, Cookie… we was always taping them meetings…

That's when we was fighting first to get a Land Rights Act and then after a while we were trying to work out what should be the contents of it. We formed a land council and a working committee to start pushing and dealing with the government. That's when Frank Walker started talking to us. Peter Thompson was always there with us too, you know, pushing with us.

Kevin: It was a really very *disciplined* dispute… nobody got out of hand, and it went for six years…

William: John Terry was at that Menindee meeting too, when we set up the Region. He was the lawyer working with WALS but he was doing land council work for us then. We was talking about how we wanted the Region to work. What it was meant to do was to concentrate on land. And we wanted to give people a chance to talk it over face to face. The most central place for people to have meetings was Menindee Mission, and we'd get two or three hundred people there at times. Big lots of people.

Kevin: When I first started getting into politics, if people had a big meeting they might have it in a hall or something. There wasn't so many big meetings on the riverbank or out in the bush. The people in the west got that going really strongly in the land rights campaigns. They were not just focused on the Land Rights Act, but about getting *land* back.

William: Oh yeah, I'd rather meet under the trees on the riverbank any day than sit in a hall or inside a building. And I mean even today.

Kevin: Well Menindee started it all up didn't it, really? Like cooking up and food and all that! Like everyone'd smell something cooking they'd go over and have a try of that and then on to the next one. Bachelors like me, well I'd be into *all* of the tucker!

William: Yeah, we had food in the hole, *hungis*[1] sometimes. Eric Wilson, one of the WALS lawyers, he'd be there in his little Renault, driving around!

Kevin: William you used to get all the meat didn't you?

William: … After they sacked Bill Galvin![2]

Kevin: …[laughter]… Yeah! That's right, he was the cop there then and he used to throw it in the back of the copper's car, didn't he, the paddy wagon? And he pulled up and threw it out to you! The first time he done it I was like … speechless!

---

1   Maori term for the type of cooking mentioned – buried in a hole, surrounded by hot stones and sealed to steam.
2   Galvin was a police officer in the far western region, before becoming NSW State Police Aboriginal Liaison Officer. Western Aboriginal people got on well with him and he reciprocated by assisting to hunt bush tucker.

William: Yeah, we'd built that old bough shed there at the mission and that old copper, Bill Galvin, used to come out and make sure we was okay. And if there was any whitefellas over the other side of the river there gettin' cheeky, well he'd chase 'em away. And he'd ask us if we wanted meat. And if we said yes, well he'd go and get meat for us! I think his boss, the Sergeant there, told him after a while, he said, 'You're not allowed to go and do that!' He used to get the kangaroos and throw 'em in the back of the police van. But old *Thartu*, Willie Webster told him: 'Don't you take no notice of them fellas!', he said, 'I'm the boss of national parks! If you want to go and get meat for us, you can go and *do* it!'

It used to be good those big bush meetings…

Kevin: No-one drank while the meetings were on, eh? I never seen anyone drinking while the meeting was on.

William: No, that's right. And there was lots of old people likes of Vinno Quayle used to be there, old Aunty Lulla. And Aunty Tibby, she'd be at *every* meeting! And old *Thartu*!

Kevin: Yeah, the old fella, he used to come along to every meeting.

William: A lot of old people, old Aunty Lotte Williams. Yeah, the old people liked those bush meetings all right. If you went out and left them in town or didn't help them to get out there, they'd be into you! That's when we formed the first regional land council in the state there at Menindee round at the time. One of the photos I've got at home is *Thurru Miiki* [Edna Hunter] in the corner of the oval there in Wilcannia, and we've got this little bark hut set up there. And she was laying in there, looking at me, and we had a sign on it sayin': 'Western Regional Land Council Office'!

Kevin: And those meetings were a way of catching up too, like when Isabel Flick from Collarenebri was catching up with all her old mates from Wilcannia and people'd come up from the South Coast… You know there was a lot of strong friendships forged in those days! And they're still going on!

William: Yeah! I remember them old people sitting there all day doing this [acts out dealing cards] … dealin' 'em out!

I had one of them cyclone beds, I was laying back on it watching them… And when they were finished and I sat up on it… Isabel got up there and was rubbing her knees and saying 'Oh jees I'm stiff!' And someone said, 'Get up and let that old woman sit down!' And I said: 'That old woman needs to walk around and stretch her legs! She's been sitting round with her legs folded *all* day!' And she looked at me and bust out laughin'!

Making Change Happen

Kevin: Yeah they could play, couldn't they, eh!

William: Some of the photos we got on the wall there, at the cultural centre, they got little notes under them saying 'Aboriginal People having meeting'. Meeting alright! Well, they'd be talkin' alright! About all sorts of things and land too.

But say, like Aunty Nancy! I used to rouse on her: 'Next time you come out, you leave that pack of cards at home!' 'No way!', she'd say! The photographs'd say the people there having a meeting, but they'd be doin' *this*! [hand actions of dealing cards] [laughter]

Figure 10.11: Core protesters with Aboriginal flag at the bush camp at Tulladunna in Wee Waa, 1981, where the council had decreed that no one – meaning no Aboriginal people – could camp there. From left, Joe Flick and his wife Isabel Walford Flick, from Wee Waa, Julie Whitton from Toomelah, Boggabilla, Barbara Flick, Joe and Isabel's daughter.

Courtesy Heather Goodall.

10. Experiences: 1981 to 1982—Street demos and bush camps

Peter Thompson

Peter Thompson here talks with Kevin about the Menindee meeting in December 1981.

Kevin: Well those meetings in the west were incredibly good meetings, and dry too. Well, kind of – but there wasn't too many people broke the curfew. There was only about four or five people really who drank at Menindee. A couple from Bourke, I seem to remember turning up at the meeting, but they'd had a drink before they got there. They didn't drink actually at the meeting.

Peter: No there wasn't much breaking of the curfew at all. And it hadn't been done much before at all, to have dry meetings. It was a bit of a struggle, and it hasn't happened much since then either.

Kevin: And you'd see everybody shuffling around, you know going to different camp fires to get different sorts of food, goanna and kangaroo…

And see, what we were doing was, we'd have these meetings, then anything that come out of the meetings, we'd take it back to Sydney, do all the Minutes and if any action was needed, then we do that action. Then, if we could get anything done, we'd be on the phone, and ringing up and letting people know what we'd done. It was a pretty good way of doing business. By the next meeting, when you were asked, 'What have youse done, what are you going to do?', you'd be able to say: 'This is what we've done'. And I think the politics were really getting into it then.

One thing was, when I think back about those bush meetings, I think it was a great strategy of having the meetings in country areas, so that people could get an idea of what they wanted.

Peter: Yeah and out on the land that they've had some ties with, like old Menindee Mission and Pooncarie. It helped to put people's mind in the right frame. And we had an older generation there then. People like old Willy Webster and Tibby Briar…

Kevin: And they weren't scared to talk you know.

Peter: Yeah, that's right.

Bushy Kirby, he was another old fellow, he come up from Murrin Bridge and Alice Bugmy. And those people, you know they have been holding back on their hunger for something like this I think, just waiting for it to happen.

These meetings were just the right thing in the right time, at the right place. We had three meetings altogether I think. One at Pooncarie, and two at Menindee, all before the Land Rights Act.

Kevin: Yeah, those old people were all into it in a very big way. And from other places too, all those old people like Gary Willams' mother, Jessie Williams from Nambucca, and those women from La Per, Trudie Longbottom, Mrs Simms and Louise West, when she was alive. ... There was about eight or nine, they go everywhere for a land council meeting. And they were the backbone, you know, they all knew their history.

Peter: And that energy that was there in '81, '82!

And it survived the Land Rights Act, you know. At least for the first seven years of it anyway in the Western Region. It was that energy that gave people the ability to keep focusing on land, even though if we didn't have lots and lots of money, but other areas might have been spending it on day-to-day things. So that the impetus survived in the west and you had a visionary leadership, in people like William Bates. And so in the Western Region, they just spent the money on land. They never spent it on anything else, just land.

The Angledool meeting, July 1982

After a series of meetings on the coast and in Dubbo over the early months of 1982, with further meetings with government, the people of north-western NSW, along the upper Darling, held a meeting at Angledool to set up a regional land council. This was an important meeting, firstly because it was on the land that was such an important part of the family histories of so many people in the north-west. Even more important was the opportunity this gave for older people in those local communities to express their views about land and encourage younger people to act on their behalf to carry on the campaign.

The Angledool area crossed over the boundaries which had marked the bitter split which had occurred in the legal service when the Western Aboriginal Legal Service (WALS) had broken away from the Sydney-based Aboriginal Legal Service (ALS) in 1978, largely because the western communities were critical of the way power had become centralised in the Sydney ALS office. This split has been discussed earlier in Chapter 9, which looked at how the legal and political support of the WALS team had assisted emerging land rights movement in the western areas of the state.

10. Experiences: 1981 to 1982—Street demos and bush camps

Figure 10.12: The bush camp meeting at Angledool 1982, to form the North Western Regional Land Council, again before the Act was passed. The photograph shows George Rose Snr around the campfire with young men from Walgett.

Courtesy Barbara Flick family collection.

The split in the legal service meant firstly that Walgett and areas to the east, like Collarenebri, Moree and Boggabilla, had remained within the ALS structure, served by ALS lawyers based in Sydney. Those which had split away to form the WALS were the communities to the west of Walgett, like Brewarrina, Bourke and Wilcannia. They had set up a base office in Dubbo to support the Aboriginal Field Officers and other staff living in the townships in the western half of the state.

Yet even the division between the WALS and the ALS did not fully explain the polarisation in this region. Most of the Field Officers in both services on the upper Darling were close relations who hailed from Angledool. The split in the legal services had in fact cut across a large and influential family of activists and spokespeople who took different sides not just on the question of criticism of the Sydney-based legal service but on questions like strategic unity. Tombo Winters in Brewarrina and George Rose in Walgett were first cousins and the Flick family in Collarenebri were just as closely related because Isabel Walford,

Barbara and Karen Flick's mother, was also a first cousin to Tombo and George. This meant that Barbara and Karen were nieces to them both. So the decision by George Rose to remain outside the WALS while his cousin Tombo and niece Barbara were so closely associated with it had reflected underlying family tensions as well as organisational issues.

This had made the Angledool meeting all the harder to organise and it made the dynamics of managing it harder still. Yet everyone came along, as Karen Flick, Tombo, Barbara, Kevin, Paul Torzillo and others describe in the following conversation.

Karen: I remember those bush meetings where you'd just go to sit down and have a yarn with people and get strength from each other and you know, talk about the issues and work out where you wanted to go with it, to come up with a bit of a strategy. Before the Land Rights Act eh? And so those were bush meetings or, you know meetings at somebody's house or, or whatever and a couple of the ones that I remember were the regular ones at Dubbo out at the farm. That's what it was like when we first set up the North West Regional Land Council at Angledool.

Cookie was a key player in doing that, because not only did he find the dollars to allow people to meet and sit down but – beyond only the dollar side of it – also, for me anyway, he provide a bit of solidarity and a strategic approach, so we who are out there in the bush knew that we had some other contacts and there was support elsewhere.

So for me anyway, Cookie was somebody who was able to bring a lot of different people together and facilitate those meetings and allow that discussion to happen. And it meant we'd be connecting up with people like Jacko Campbell and Nan Campbell and that mob from the South Coast. So it wasn't very many people but it was a good solid group of hard core people who would get up and have a go. These are also the people I think who also did things in their own communities, the ones who challenged all the time and never gave up.

And the important things about the bush meetings were also about sitting down with your family, so you'd have kids there running around, or you'd have old people, or you'd have a game of cards, or you'd have whatever you wanted to have and everybody would just be there sitting around and talking. All these things would be happening at the same time as people would be talking – and that meant you could have all these political discussions and meetings in the right kind of atmosphere. I think that's what worked a lot.

I'd always been involved with things like the Aboriginal cemetery in Collarenebri. I remember going to the cemetery, the Collie Cemetery, and doing all those things that you did there, like washing the grave decorations and telling your kids whose grave was next to whose. It was just part of life and you always connected with that.

But it was important, whenever I went to some other place to have a look at some other country, I felt you'd have to pay respect. So even when we were camping at Angledool, even though that was home, that was still different because I hadn't been there an awful lot you know. I remember when we were walking up at the Angledool meeting and Paulie was with us and Mum and Barbara and me. My daughter Cullen was a baby and I was carrying her. We stopped under this tree and Mum said 'This is the tree that I was born under'. And you know that was a real revelation about *country* for me.

***

Tombo Winters was a key leader among north-western people for many decades – a founder of the first rural legal service, an insightful analyst of rural politics, a courageous battler against racism and injustice and a deeply inspiring comrade and friend for Aboriginal people across the region. He also befriended a motley crew of white fellas who turned up in Brewarrina out of interest, offering legal, medical or research skills. He took us all under his wing, set us to work doing things he knew were useful (often not what we had first intended!) and kept us all going with endless good humour and optimism.

Tombo was the one who really pulled this Angledool meeting together, strongly supported by Isabel Flick and her nieces Karen and Barbara, by Julie Whitton from Boggabilla and by others. Tombo brought all the warring Angledool parties at least to the same campsite if not into the fold. And he and Cookie encouraged us all to see it as a big step forward.

Tombo: Now that Angledool meeting, we set up the regional land council there, just before the Act came in I think. People from all over the region came, and some of the South Coast mob, they came up.

Kevin: You chaired that, didn't you? I remember in the afternoon you said, 'I'm just going to get dinner' and you got in the car and you drove off. Then you came back about half an hour later with a sheep in the back of the car! I remember you doing the sheep with the axe.

Tombo: Yeah. Old Joe Flick was there from Collarenebri and Wee Waa. And do you remember George Rose rousing on us all when he was sitting there over the other side of the creek?

Paulie: I remember him or his brother, Teddy Guy Simpson having a go at me at that meeting. I remember George came. You know how there was this little sort of creek and we were over this side and they were on the other side. Just leaning against the car and looking for three hours.

Kevin: He stayed on the other side of the river.

Tombo: He wouldn't come across and stay with the rest of us! That was the time I got all those tents for everyone. I got them from the school and we brought them up in a trailer for everybody to sleep in. I remember that – it looked like an Indian camp! We built a big fire in the middle and it was just like those cowboy and Indian scenes, you know? They were those tents, a little square on the top and then they'd come down. A pole in the middle and they had four little corners.

Kevin: Yeah, I can just see everyone was in tents around this scene. And Essie and Doc Coffey sang the longest version of Frankie and Johnny that I ever heard! [laughter]

Tombo: Yeah, that's right. I can remember. Went on into the middle of the night. They went and camped on the other side of the road.

Despite these tensions, Angledool was a very important symbolic site. Although it was no longer inhabited, it formed a warmly remembered and treasured site in the imagination of Aboriginal people right along the upper Darling. They had been living there on the Narran River until 1936 when, in the grip of the Depression and in the middle of winter, the Aborigines Protection Board had forced the whole Angledool community, against their bitter protests, into trucks to ship them down to Brewarrina on the Barwon River, to an overcrowded and oppressively managed station to live huddled up with people from three other 'concentrated' communities. Barbara Flick explained its significance.

Barbara: There'd been a history of New South Wales and Angledool's important to me, and to our family. But its important as well as just one example of things being out of our control, of our grandparents first of all being taken to that place and then being taken away. They were rounded up and taken away from there to Bre, without choice. Children were born there in those missions, under that regime, including my mother. And then, all these years later, we were able to go back and recreate, I suppose, what that place meant to us. To reclaim that part of our history, and to make it mean something wonderful. So, you know, Georgie Rose and Mum and Tombo Winters and those sorts of people that come from there had all gone back to Angledool. And it was a different game, you know because *now* the agenda was *ours*...

Kevin: We had a *solid* camp! We had something that the government couldn't break. You know, they let the land rights issue go for a while, after the Keane Report they just put it on the back burners. But the people – there was too much support from Aboriginal people – and too much from white people as well! And that's one important thing I think, the friendships that built up over that five or six years were incredible.

Barbara: Yes, it was very broad based, very broad.

***

The much-anticipated Green Paper prepared by Frank Walker was issued on 22 December 1982 but it was not circulated widely and did not actually get published till February 1983.[3] The Aboriginal response was anger and disappointment. The Green Paper had major differences with the initial Report of the Select Committee, which had been released over two years before. The government's failure to initiate or take part in any community discussions over that time was reflected in the distance between community hopes and the very partial offerings in the Green Paper. The Organisation of Aboriginal Unity – including Tranby as well as the Aboriginal Legal Service and the Redfern organisations – stated that the Green Paper proposals were 'totally inadequate and insufficient'.[4]

The disappointments over the Green Paper will be discussed in the following chapter, 'Hard Decisions'. But it is important to recognise here that the momentum built up in those bush meetings could not be deflected by the failures of government. Over those two years, Aboriginal communities had generated their own discussions and they intended to keep up their demands.

Some elements of the Green Paper had embodied community goals. It proposed, for example, a three tiered structure which was in line with the outcome of the intensive discussions of the bush meetings, as Peter Thompson explained.

Peter Thompson: that three tier structure was roughly what people wanted, they saw the need for local ownership and that need to organise regionally and the need for some sort of state wide co-ordination.

So the next six months saw intensive lobbying as the Green Paper was hastily turned into a Bill, with still further compromises and problems. There was no reason to cease campaigning – and in fact Aboriginal activists wanted to maintain the momentum of the campaign to try to improve the final Act and then its implementation.

---

3   Wilkie 1985: 40.
4   Wilkie 1985: 44–45.

More and more of the people who attended the bush meetings, especially the older people, saw the broad discussions about land rights and protection of cultural heritage as contributing towards achieving the goals they cared about.

The Mutawintji Blockade, September 1983

This was a time when the Western Aboriginal Legal Service was instructed by Jim James Bates, May Barlow and others to intervene on their behalf with the National Parks and Wildlife Service to stop tourists from visiting Snake Cave at Mutawintji.[5] Several unsuccessful meetings, led by Jim James Bates and May Barlow, had been held to discuss the importance of Wiimpatja[6] being involved in protecting sites within the Park. At one stage the NPWS argued that their priority was protecting the Yellow Footed Rock Wallaby by holding tight control over the Park, which meant they had no choice but to exclude Wiimpatja from management decisions. Jim James Bates argued that he did not know there were any wallaby left in the area. NPWS officers responded that they were monitoring the population even though they had not seen any. When May Barlow asked them how they were doing that, the NPWS officers said they had been observing their droppings. All the Wiimpatja at the meeting burst out laughing. Jim James and May were invited to go up in a helicopter to look for these Yellow Footed Rock Wallaby but gracefully declined saying that their feet would never leave the ground. It seemed clear to them that the NPWS was more concerned about the rights of the invisible Yellow Footed Rock Wallaby than the rights of the Wiimpatja to protect their sites of significance.

The issue of control over tourists at Mutawintji flared up again in September 1983, and this became another powerful bush meeting which demonstrated the directions which communities were taking, regardless of the government focus on its legislation. This bush meeting became known as 'The Blockade', because the camp was established to demand Aboriginal control over what was then called officially the 'Mootwingee' National Park, 150 km north-east of Broken Hill. In itself, the Blockade demonstrated that the Land Rights Act, however important it seemed in mid 1983, was never going to be the only way that Aboriginal people could satisfy their interest in land justice. Peter was asked whether the Mutawintji Blockade was separate from the agitation for a Land Rights Act.

---

5   The name of Mutawintji has been spelled in a number of ways: the National Parks Service used the 'oo' adopted by early settlers to render Aboriginal pronunciations into English, so they spelled it 'Mootwingee'. Aboriginal people tried various ways to alter this spelling, firstly by adding in the extra syllable – with 'Mootawingee' and later by insisting on consistency with their spelling of other Paakintji and Malyangapa words. So 'Mutawintji' is now the accepted spelling and this is the one used throughout this chapter except in quotations.
6   The Paakantji and related language term for 'Aboriginal people'.

Figure 10.13: The people who had strong links to the important site at Mutawintji took the political step of declaring themselves a land council, the Mutawintji Local Aboriginal Land Council, with long-time activist Johnny Quayle in foreground.

Courtesy Peter Thompson.

Peter: Yeah, it was separate, but it was getting pretty mixed up together there. Because in the west, Aboriginal people in general were campaigning for the Land Rights Act. They weren't the mob who, like the old Lands Trust, were saying 'We weren't ready for this'. The Blockade happened the same year as the Act and it was being planned before the Act went through. It had seemed another obvious thing to do to keep up the politics of land rights while the government response to the politics was happening. The idea was 'Don't stop campaigning for land rights now, just because the government's done something! Just keep going!'

It was outside the Land Rights Act in the sense that everybody knew that you couldn't claim a national park under the Land Rights Act, but the aim was to use the mechanisms of the Land Rights Act to organise. So they set up a Mutawintji Land Council, to keep a little structure there.

Now this was a national park that had been managed for a long time without any Aboriginal involvement. But a lot of people had been unhappy about their ownership not being recognised and about not being consulted. Now it was the Broken Hill Centenary, and there were tourist buses running up to Mootwingee

National Park each day as part of the Centenary events. So this seemed like the right time to make it clear that Aboriginal people were the owners, not the National Parks or the Broken Hill Council.

We went out in the daytime and set up camp and made up a lot of posters. Then we went round and put up those signs on the road into the park and on the gates. They said: 'Mootawingee: Closed by the Owners'.

After that, some of us went into town and pasted up the same signs all over Broken Hill, saying 'Mootawingee: Closed by the Owners'. While we were in there, there was a big storm, flattened everyone's tents!

There was a Tranby bus that went out there and the students did a newsletter. And it was another good chance to pull in people from across the state, to be camping out ON country, with a chance to talk out where they wanted to go on Land – whether it was a national park or whatever it was.

***

In the discussion about the motivations for some of the far western people, Peter and Kevin talked over how land and employment shaped people's view of both the past and the future. Peter argued that watching the changing rural economy over even the previous 20 years in the far west had shaped the way people looked at the demand for land rights.

Peter: Yeah, that was one of the drivers of the land rights movement, for people to get control over land at a local level. And that's probably what drove the government's Lands Trust to try and stop that happening in 1974 and then eventually giving up in 1983.

Kevin: But I think the Land Rights Act has improved the life of Aboriginal people in New South Wales. There are pieces of land where they can now go onto and they've got industries. I don't know if they're making too much money, but they've still got that *land*! And while they've got land they've got something concrete. I've always said, you look at the farmer, if he's got a big farm, he's got standing in that community. And he might be the worst bloke in the world, but he's still got land and standing.

Peter: Yeah. I think that there was a memory that Aboriginal people had in the west too that when the big stations were broken up, their white mates got blocks of land and became the farmers of the next generation, from the 1940s on. But they – the Aboriginal workers – were still labourers. And there was nowhere to work now because all of the big places – where they had needed lots of workers – have been broken up and the new smaller blocks didn't want so many workers. Yet they have the same skills. So there was that memory too and it was very important in motivating people. As well as that idea of equality that you're talking about, of equal standing which seemed to have been there before when everyone worked on the same big properties. You know, there had been plenty of Aboriginal overseers and drovers, leading droving teams and teams of bore sinkers, tank sinkers, contractors. Or even just labourers working side by side with white labourers. I'm not saying everything was hunky dory but I think there was a loss of equality in the change to things now, where white people have become landholders – even though their blocks were small. And Aboriginal people saw that.

Kevin: Yeah. The loss of work, that was the main thing, they couldn't get a job.

***

And in a final reflection on how that remarkable year and a half of bush meetings had been possible, the issues of communication and resources came up:

Peter: But the networking was important. It was around a few little hubs and probably Tranby was one of those hubs in the 1970s and '80s. That was one of the places that the networking would be happening. Your work at Tranby, Kevin, made a lot of that possible. Networking's always a vague thing, it's hard to put your finger on, but it was happening! And it wouldn't have happened so well if you hadn't have been at Tranby and where you were sharing resources across the groups to support the Aboriginal Land Council before the Act.

Kevin: Yeah, you'd have to be in the right place at the right time don't you?

Peter: Hm. And be as willing to take as much action as you can.

Kevin: Well, we didn't take a backwards step I don't think, all the time we were there.

11. Hard decisions: 1983 to 1985

We didn't get everything that we wanted, and we knew when the legislation was going through that we wouldn't. But it broke a lot of people's hearts, to read the Keane Report, and then to see the legislation! What a far different Act it could have been. It could have set the stage for all States to follow… but it didn't.

Kevin Cook, looking back on the 1983 Land Rights Act

This chapter follows the experiences of the Aboriginal activists from the release of the 'Green Paper' in December 1982 to the tumultuous passage of the Land Rights Act through parliament early in 1983 and on to the formal establishment of its structures in 1984 and 1985.[1] This is not a history of the Act itself – there is already valuable work on it and new work emerging.[2] Instead in this chapter the people involved speak about their experiences of this period. They struggled first with the difficult decisions about whether to take part in the Land Rights Act implementation, and then over the practical questions as very different regions tried to set up structures that would reflect local interests as well as allowing what strengths the Act had to be best utilised.

***

After so much intensive campaigning for land rights, the Green Paper was a frustrating disappointment. The Australian Labor Party's own Policy Committee, on which Kevin sat with Bob Bellear, said that the Green Paper 'betrays the Party's commitment to meaningful Land Rights'.[3] It had fulfilled a few of the recommendations of the Select Committee Report, meeting at least some of the demands being made by communities and organisations across the state. It ensured, for example, that the outcome of claims on land would be in inalienable, communal freehold – that is, the land would be collectively owned and it could never be sold. As well it included a structure which would strengthen local and regional organising – where most decisions could be made collectively in culturally appropriate groups. And, after representations by the land council, it had limited the power of the state body so that it would only meet to ratify the decisions at regional and local level. Finally it included a feasible mechanism for building up funds to purchase land which was not able to be claimed, by drawing on a percentage of the state government's regular Land Tax.

---

1 *Aboriginal Land Rights Act 1983* (NSW).
2 Including Meredith Wilkie 1985, *Aboriginal Land Rights in NSW*, and the NSW ALC website history, drawing partially on the research for this book and on the research of Heidi Norman, 2013.
3 Wilkie 1985: 45.

But there were serious limitations to the Green Paper. In line with the Premier Neville Wran's reluctance to act on the Select Committee's advice, this Green Paper instead severely limited the amount of land which could be claimed, by allowing only those areas of Crown land to be claimed which could be defined as 'unoccupied', rather than the far larger area of Crown land which had been designated as leasehold or as national park. Furthermore it did not include a parallel Heritage Act, as the Select Committee had recommended. Another major problem was that it proposed the inclusion of the management of all housing on old reserves and new Aboriginal lands – which would burden the land councils with a complex administrative load.

Even more worrying was the failure of the Green Paper to include a plan to regain ownership of those previously existing Aboriginal Reserve lands to which Aboriginal communities had continuing links, despite the reserve's revocation. In itself, the return of the few remaining reserves to full Aboriginal ownership was welcomed because it would no longer be in the power of the government to revoke or sell them. However, the demands from many Aboriginal people – as the land claims already lodged showed – had been for the return of many reserves like Terry Hie Hie to which Aboriginal people had a deep attachment but which had been revoked as Aboriginal Reserves or sold completely since Aboriginal people had occupied them in the 1920s or 1930s. So the return of only those places which still existed *as* reserves was only a partial step to complete fulfillment.

The Land Council met at Morpeth in February 1983, and set out its demands for self-determination, self-government, a secure land base and full compensation for all land lost. The land council stated to the NSW government that the Green Paper had not fulfilled these demands and 'is not a land rights settlement'.[4]

Yet while the Green Paper was a disappointment, the actual legislation put before parliament on 24 March was shocking. The government had brought two Bills – not only the Land Rights Act, based on a modified and further compromised version of the Green Paper, but a 'cognate' Bill, saying that it would refuse to proceed with the Land Rights Act unless this was passed. This cognate Bill would validate retrospectively the revocation of over 15,000 hectares of land which had been Aboriginal Reserve land – an amount which dwarfed the remaining 4300 hectares which was all that was left for return to Aboriginal land councils.[5]

---

4 Quoted in Wilkie 1985: 45.
5 Figures cited by Wilkie 1985: 47 and derived from studies by Tobin et al 1969, who identified 22,377 acres revoked between 1909 and 1969, and Peter Read, in research commissioned by the NSW Ministry of Aboriginal Affairs.

This cognate Bill represented a direct rejection of the many demands for land which had motivated Aboriginal communities in the 1970s and 1980s in which lands lost to revocation had been a substantial part of the claim. The Aboriginal Legal Service had begun legal proceedings to test the validity of these revocations and these proceedings would be prematurely ended if the Bill were to be passed. This retrospective validation of a massive amount of revocation was a bitter blow.

To understand the full impact of this 'cognate' Bill – both legally and politically – it is important to recognise the history of Aboriginal Reserves in NSW. In the decades since World War Two, the few remaining NSW Reserves had been managed by the government like gaols, and there were very mixed memories for Aboriginal people who had had to live on them. But before this, reserves had had a very different history!

Aboriginal Reserves had been set aside from the 1850s, long before the Aborigines Protection Board was established in 1883. Most of the 31 Reserves created before 1883 had been set aside because local Aboriginal communities had been calling for the recognition of their rights to their land – they were actually a recognition of the first major Aboriginal campaign for land rights.[6] After that, of 115 Reserves gazetted by the new Aborigines Protection Board between 1885 and 1909, at least 75 – that is 65 per cent – were again notified because Aboriginal people had demanded them and planned to make them small scale but self-sufficient farms.[7] Many of these reserves were fertile lands and the records show that Aboriginal people farmed them successfully and independently for many decades, without any Protection Board or other white people controlling the management of crops and homes.

This flourishing of Aboriginal control over productive lands had been challenged from 1913, when the government's policy shifted decisively. Fearing the rising numbers of people identifying confidently and assertively as Aboriginal, the Protection Board launched a policy of dispersing Aboriginal communities and undermining their cohesion and cultural identity. Most productive Aboriginal Reserve lands were revoked and handed over to local white farmers – and particularly to white returned servicemen, as part of the repatriation policy after World War One. Aboriginal people protested and some came to Sydney, like Percy Mosely from Ballangarra near Kempsey in 1915, camping outside the Protection Board offices to make their case.[8] But the government was under pressure to find land for returning soldiers as well as neighbouring white

---

6   Twenty-seven of the 31 Reserves: Goodall 1990, 'Land in our own country', *Aboriginal History* 14(1): 9; Goodall 1996, *Invasion to Embassy*; Barry Morris 1989, *Domesticating Resistance: The Dhan-Gadi Aborigines and the Australian State*, Berg Publishers, Oxford.
7   Goodall 1990: 14.
8   Goodall 1996, see actions of protests in 1914 and 1915 from the Macleay and Manning River regions.

farmers. So this was the time that the major revocations began – as productive land was stripped from Aboriginal control. At the same time, the policy to systematically remove children was escalated. This twin-pronged assault on the independence of Aboriginal communities – through land and children – only abated in 1929, when the Depression hit. The challenges to children as well as to land continued to be met with fierce Aboriginal resistance in the 1920s in a widely publicised campaign carried out in the press and in public meetings by the Australian Aboriginal Progressive Association led by Fred Maynard, Lionel Ridgeway, Jane Duren and other coastal people, whose lands were suffering the worst of the revocations.[9]

As the Depression set in, however, the Protection Board moved to cut costs still further by 'centralising' Aboriginal populations, revoking more reserves and forcibly displacing many populations – like those of Angledool – and forcing them into the few remaining – and tightly controlled – managed reserves. Called Stations – although always popularly referred to as 'Missions' – these became the most commonly remembered experience of what reserves were like for Aboriginal people who grew up after World War Two.

The massive swathe of revocation which had taken place between 1913 and 1929 had removed 50 per cent of all the land which had ever been set aside as Aboriginal Reserve land in NSW. The remaining land held in reserves dwindled over the years. Although few Aboriginal people remembered all the independent reserves, there were some people who did, like Tiger Buchanan from near Nambucca Heads or the Davis family from Rollands Plains, who had keen memories of the productive reserves they had been farming. Jacko Campbell – who had relations in the Macleay Valley as well as at Roseby Park – was one of those who remembered the broad picture, and he had often led the outcry against the NSW Lands Trust during the early 1970s as it moved to sell off even the remaining scraps of land like Landillo and Cootamundra. (See Chapter 9.)

In a dispute in 1976 between a South Coast local government council and, ironically, the Aboriginal Lands Trust over rates owing on Aboriginal Reserve lands from 1967, the technical legalities of the revocations had been tested. The Solicitor General advised the government in 1979 that, because the Aborigines Protection Board had been set up within the government on faulty terms, then *all* of the revocations it had ordered since 1913 had been invalid. Many of these areas of Crown land had been revoked as Reserve so they could be sold as freehold, so the illegality of all these revocations threatened to unsettle many land owners' sense of security.

---

9   Goodall 1996; Maynard 2007.

In one stroke, the Crown Solicitor's advice seemed to offer full restitution to all the many grieving Aboriginal people who had fought in the beginning to stop the first revocations and then had continued the fight, as Jacko Campbell, Tiger Buchanan and Walter Duncan had done into the 1980s. Even though it was clear from all later legal advice[10] that the land which had entered the freehold system could never be restored, it seemed that the recognition that this should never have been taken out of Aboriginal hands was important as was any possibility of compensation for its loss.

Then, just as decisively, the Retrospective Validation of Revocations legislation announced along with the Land Rights Bill in March 1983 threatened to end any possibility that these lands could ever be restored.

This generated terrible anguish among the land rights campaigners, who had to weigh up the possible advantages which even a flawed Land Rights Act might bring with the losses – both real and symbolic – which the Validation of Revocations Act would definitely bring.

To this difficult dilemma was added the pressure which began to intensify as the industry lobbies escalated their opposition to any recognition of Aboriginal rights in land. The fear-mongering about the threat to suburban 'backyards' from any Aboriginal claims was repeated again and again. It drove not only conservative political groups but the right wing of the Labor Party itself to attack the draft bill. With the right-wing faction dominant in the Labor Party as well as in its union base, discussed in Chapter 7, the opposition from within the Labor government was even more threatening to the Bill than that from the conservatives.

The Aboriginal Legal Service, led by its director, Paul Coe, assessed the legislative options and early in 1983 it withdrew support from the Bill completely. The ALS argued that the Bill was so flawed and the cognate legislation so damaging that it was better to abandon the Bill altogether and start over again at a later date.

The reason the ALS could hope that there might be another chance was the 13 March federal election, in which the conservative government was defeated. The federal Labor Party came to power, under Prime Minister Bob Hawke, previously the President of the Australian Council of Trade Unions, and with a policy of returning to the goals of the Whitlam Government by finally implementing national Aboriginal land rights. In March 1983, this policy was only a promise – and everyone had seen how long it had taken the NSW Labor government to implement even a part of its own policy. And of course the Whitlam Government

---

10 Including Mary Gaudron's advice in 1982, Wilkie 1985: 48.

had been dismissed before it could implement any at all. Nevertheless, if one placed one's faith in the federal Labor Party, this new government seemed to offer a chance for real gains.

The Aboriginal Land Council was just as anguished as others. Senior activists like Jacko Campbell, Ted Thomas, Will Webster and Isabel Flick had been struggling for many years, and they were deeply saddened at being forced to consider the Validation of Revocations Bill. Yet they had seen too many promises come and go to decide to abandon the Land Rights Bill altogether. Younger people like Kevin and Barbara were painfully aware of this distress:

Kevin: But it broke a lot of people's hearts, to read the Keane Report, and then to see the legislation! What a far different Act it could have been. It could have set the stage for all states to follow … but it didn't.

Tombo Winters and Kevin talked this issue over in the recordings for this book:

Tombo: The Legal Service was worried about the Act because they reckoned it didn't meet what they wanted. They wanted to wait for further negotiations on it.

Kevin: But we talked to people at the meetings and they said, 'This is the best we can get at this particular stage. If we let it go now, it's going to be another ten to 15 years before we get anything'. They wanted something now! You know, people were dying and not able to go back to their land. Jacko died before they got their land back!

Brian Doolan talked with Kevin about his memories of watching those agonised meetings during the early months of 1983:

Brian: I remember a lot of discussions at the time of the Act coming into being about whether it was the right thing, the right way to go. Kevin, I remember you guys had meetings at Dubbo and Menindee and different places where you'd go through the whole process. A constant theme I remember through those discussions was along the lines of: 'This is a *movement* and the Act is not the end of the *movement*.'

It wasn't as though you said, 'Okay, this is the Act and that's it. There's nothing else to do'.

Even at the time when the Act was passed, there were all sorts of criticisms that it was based so much on the finances and state land tax and all that sort of thing rather than on recognising people's inalienable right to their land. There had been that important acknowledgement aspect to it. I remember that was something you guys agonised over a lot.

And you and Jacko and a whole lot of people said very clearly – 'But this is a step. It's an important step but it's not the last step. And this will change, somewhere down the track as well.'

So when, say in three or four generations, Aboriginal kids are going to be saying to people, at that stage, we want our rights to our land, that won't have been negated because of something that happened in 1983. They will still have that right and they will still have those arguments.

I remember you guys saying that.

***

The parliamentary debates over the Bill in mid 1983 were tumultuous, with bitter divisions arising as right-wing Labor members fought to water down the Bill's provisions. One of the most damaging amendments was moved by the Labor Minister for Lands – who would himself be responsible for the administration of the Act, Mr Lin Gordon – who saw himself representing white voters in rural electorates and succeeded in amending the already narrow provision that the only land open to be claimed was 'unoccupied Crown land'. The amended version restricted this still further to 'unoccupied Crown land' which were not 'needed or likely to be needed for an essential public purpose'. Even more importantly it removed the minister's decision in this matter from any judicial review. So while other dimensions of the question of whether Crown land was 'claimable' could be appealed in the Land and Environment Court, the minister alone had the final say on whether any land might ever be wanted for anything the minister might define as an 'essential public purpose'.[11] The absurdity of this amendment was to be demonstrated later in the legal battle over whether the Engonnia Common was open to claim. The Crown argued the point – and won – that the land was wanted for the 'future urban expansion of Engonnia' which is a tiny north-western town on the border between NSW and Queensland, which like most small rural towns has been declining in population for many decades.[12] The amended Land Rights Bill was passed, coming into force on 10 June 1983 – and with it, the hated retrospective Validation of Revocations Act came into force too.[13]

The key issue for claiming land was simply that land had to be 'claimable'. That is, it had to be unoccupied Crown land which had survived the test of not being needed for an 'essential future public purpose'. Land could be claimed only by a land council, which meant that membership of a land council was necessary to become a land holder under the Act. But there were no criteria for claim –

---

11 Wilkie 1985: 49–50.
12 Tony Parker and John Terry, personal communication.
13 *Aboriginal Land Rights Act 1983* (NSW) and *Crown Lands (Validation of Revocations) Act 1983* (NSW).

once the very narrow definition of 'claimable' Crown land had been met, the land should have been passed as inalienable freehold title into the hands of the claimant land councils.

There was however a preamble to the Act which responded to many of the Aboriginal demands. This preamble led to the mistaken assumption that there were criteria for claiming land, and that those criteria, if they had in fact been based on the preamble, would have been far wider than the poorly defined 'traditional ownership' of legislation in other states or indeed that in other legislation within NSW. This preamble stated firstly that 'land was traditionally owned and occupied by Aborigines' and that the Act recognised that 'land is of spiritual, social, cultural and economic importance to Aborigines'.[14] There was, however, as Meredith Wilkie has pointed out, nothing in the actual legislation which offered a tangible means of achieving any of those principles.[15]

***

The Land Rights Act had become law, but there was still no Aboriginal-controlled structures through which it could be enacted. The first step was to establish a temporary body, called the 'Interim Land Council' which would set up the structures which the Act required. Its membership was appointed by the Minister, Frank Walker, on the basis of his consultations over the previous year. He had invited organisations like the existing Land Council to suggest people who might be appointed. Barbara Flick, in a conversation with Kevin and with Tombo Winters, has recalled that difficult time.

Barbara: ... We tried to nominate people that weren't all in our camp. We tried to look around the regions and to nominate people who we thought would do a good job. Paul Coe was one of the ones on it that we had suggested, and Hewitt Whyman from Wagga. There was one person from each of the regions across the state.

Kevin: Each of the local reps went and done their own area, so you had William out the West, Tombo round Bre, Warren Mundine and Ray Kelly up on the North Coast, Barb in the Central West, Delia Lowe (Jacko's daughter) on the mid South Coast, and Mervyn Penrith on the far South Coast. I was in Sydney and Newcastle. Ann Weldon, Paul Coe's sister, was coordinator and Pat Stewart was from out there in western Sydney. But then we'd all come together as a state body and go up to the North Coast, and to the other regions. So we'd have all these meetings on a state basis too, so that everybody knew what everybody else was doing.

Kevin, as the chairperson, had a responsibility to work in each of the regions and so he often travelled with each of the other members.

---

14 Wilkie 1985: 50–51.
15 Wilkie 1985: 51.

11. Hard decisions: 1983 to 1985

From the grass roots: Setting up rural regions and local land councils

The role of the Interim Land Council was to set up the local and regional structures – this involved gathering names and signatures of local people who nominated to be in those bodies. Every member of the Aboriginal community could belong to a land council and could be a member of one over an area to which they retained an involvement, even if they did not live there, as was the case with important sites like Mutawintji from which people had been removed in the past.[16] The boundaries for the locals and the regions were ultimately to be set by the Registrar of Aboriginal Land, a position established under the Land Rights Act to be held independently of the land councils. The first Registrar was Chris Kirkbright, a Wiradjuri lawyer and later a language researcher. However, the interim land council members could pass on to the Registrar the results of consultations they had been having with the members of any local land council about the boundaries they hoped to have.

Each member of this interim council had a different experience as they worked closely with people in their region. Barbara was appointed to work in the Central Western area.

Barbara: So part of my job in the central west at that time was to go and talk to communities – Wellington, Peak Hill, Dubbo… about the legislation and about boundary issues. The people basically agreed fairly readily out in the bush about boundaries. There wasn't a big issue about that – where those lines should be drawn. A lot of people, I think, found it more difficult to organise regionally, especially closer to the east coast. But out in the bush, in the west, there hadn't been many resources over long periods of time.

And people had been moved around by government, so they had established long-term relationships with people in the areas they had been moved into. So between the River people, the Paakantji and the 'drylanders' to the east, the Ngiyampaa, who had been shifted over to Menindee on the Darling in the 1930s and then later moved back east into the central areas of the state.

I continued to work very closely with people in the far west in particular. I served on local land councils, like Mutawintji and Winbar. And we continued to organise out there. One of the examples was the Western Aboriginal Women's Council which organised bush camps which linked up women from the north-west, like from Collarenebri and Walgett – with women from the far west.

---

16   Wilkie 1985: 112–113.

That was one way in which we ensured that women and children were part of this talk about country, and getting back to country and working out what we wanted from country now.

Tombo Winters was the Interim member for the north-west. He found different problems, partly because a local land council did not just exist automatically – it could only be set up by a signed document or petition from a named group of Aboriginal people who declared themselves to have a connection with a place. This worried people because they were being asked to sign unfamiliar forms and then they found themselves asked to draw boundaries onto maps to define their areas of interest.

Tombo: '82 right through '83 we were setting up local land councils. I know all the people from Brewarrina down to Bourke and up to Goodooga. When I got over to Collarenebri – if I didn't know people, I picked old Josie Thorne up. She never said no – she'd be there every time I'd pick her up.

The hardest thing in that 12 months was trying to find the people who were willing to sign the petition to kick off the land council. They thought they were signing their lives away.

I'd take the maps to a place and I'd say to them, 'Righto, where do you reckon your boundary should start and where it should end?' And they'd look at the map but it would be hard – so they cut the thing off in Boorooma, half way to Bourke, then Bourke had the rest down from there. That was the way we worked it out. You never got it exactly.

In the far western areas, William Bates remembered they used a different approach:

William: When the Act was introduced we went all over it again you know, from [people's] memory. And we got onto the Registrar, and told him to draw a circle round each town, 20 km radius, and register them [as local land councils] until we went around and talked to all the people and worked out the boundaries, as in Paakantji and Malyangapa and Wanyuparlku and Ngiyampaa. (These were the names of the language groups to which the land and people belonged.) That's the Local boundaries. I don't know if we ever got the region right because you couldn't get together with people from across there at Cobar and Bourke and places like that.

But we did it to the best of our knowledge where the people said their Local was, you know, Balranald, Menindee, Ivanhoe, Wilcannia for an example, done their boundaries and if there was any dispute, we'd sit down with the people and work it out.

We were all over the region, Mutawintji, Menindee and Mungo was the main places we'd have meetings at, to set them up, but Tibooburra was set up a lot later on, and Wanaaring, we could never get a quorum there, although it was gazetted as an area…

Kevin: The Registrar changed the boundaries that the people put in, didn't he?

William: I don't know about other areas, but I think in ours, in the Western Region, they got through pretty well… I think because we'd sat down and talked about where they all should go…

Heather: So you actually had to keep an eye on what the Registrar was doing to make sure that what you'd worked out on the ground was translated into what went into the documents?

William: Oh yeah, you'd be arguing with them all the time. Although with Wiimpatja, they still think in that attitude that 'We know what's best for you'.

However, although unfamiliar paperwork was a problem for some people, the process of setting up the land councils did have some advantages. One was that it was flexible enough to allow people who had been displaced from an area to form a land council to care for the place they had lost. This allowed, for example, the people who felt responsible for Mutawintji or the Louth-Tilpa area, in the west and for Nambucca Island, on the coast, to come together as land councils to state their right protect that land.

Kevin explained this: Without that possibility of setting up a land council in that way, you probably couldn't have claimed some of the land that we claimed. Like Mutawintji, they set up that local land council. Nobody lives in the area now, but they set up a local land council just to look after that place. So it was very flexible, and, because people had been moved onto different lands and they'd been living there for years and years, then you have to give them the, the responsibility of looking after that land, so they could claim it.

Making Change Happen

From the grass roots: Setting up an urban land council: Gandangara

It was local people everywhere who really determined how local land councils were set up. The city Local Aboriginal Land Councils are often forgotten because it has been assumed that only rural or remote Aboriginal communities reflected 'real' Aboriginality, yet the majority of Aboriginal people in NSW actually lived in cities. So it is important here to look at how a city local land council was formed. The example is the Gandangara Local Aboriginal Land Council, which is usually called just the 'land council' in this conversation. It was formed in the Liverpool area of south-western Sydney by the women who had been involved in the NOW education course, discussed in Chapter 6, 'Tranby Reaching Out'. The women whose voices are heard here talking with Kevin about the local land council are Robyn Williams, Judy Chester and her sister, Janny Ely.

As these women became more confident from participating in their NOW program – and in the organising they had had to do to get it! – they had also become more actively involved in Aboriginal politics. They were very interested in the land rights movement and had given talks about the issue in 1981 and 1982. The hostility in these suburban areas of Sydney was intense.

Janny Ely: At that time land rights was a real big issue and TAFE[17] wanted to hold a big forum together of all TAFE students. They asked us would we be prepared to be there and answer questions. We talked to Cookie and he said, 'Yeah, go on, go for it', you know. And we gets there and they had to escort us out! The students got that wild because it didn't matter what we said, they were convinced that land rights was going to take their house away. And they got quite abusive and everything.

Judy Chester: Madeline McGrady showed them her video about Cheeky Macintosh being murdered in Moree, that was very confronting for them, you know. And those white TAFE students reckoned that she'd made the film up! You know, they just wouldn't accept anything that was put in front of them. It was really very confronting for them.

Janny: … And the bottom line was that land rights was going to take their house away from them!

Kevin: But that just goes to show you how information is stifled in this country where Moree is not that far away from Sydney and yet people don't know what's going on in that area. And so you have to say, when you go to talk to people … you have to go very slowly.

---

17 Technical and Further Education.

11. Hard decisions: 1983 to 1985

Judy: Yes, it was very confronting. But, it's a bit like the *children overboard* thing today. It's the way the government and the media portrayed land rights back in those days. I mean you walk up the street now and say, 'They didn't throw their kids overboard' and these old white people say, 'Yes they did. Oh, yes they *did*'.

Janny: We went into the march for International Women's Day in 1983 in Liverpool. There we were, just a bunch of women, kids in the pram and kids marching along with their streamers and the Koorie flag. And all these police cars pulled up to arrest us because they got a call that we were protesting!

As the women's group became more interested in forming a local land council for their area, they asked Kevin's advice, and so he agreed to come to their meeting:

Janny: Well, Cookie was on the Interim Land Council then. Robyn and I went in to town to talk to him about setting up a land council and then he came out and met with us.

Kevin: There was a fair few women there.

Judy: What he means is – there was *no* men!

Kevin: Five minutes after we get to the first meeting, and you know we'd just talked about, not even setting up a land council, it was really just the functions in setting it up – and everybody's really gung ho. I had to say to'em, 'You have to slow down. You know, you can't rush into it and do things! And there's no men here. And so you'll have to go back and talk to the Aboriginal men'.

Robyn: It was very female dominated because it was really hard getting the men involved at that time. Because there was no money… It was all voluntary. Everything we done was voluntary.

Judy: And you see a few women were married to white men too. So that's why you had a lot of the women.

Kevin: Like this was their first land rights meeting, I think! I had to say, 'You have to be very, very careful. You can't run ahead of the rest of the people, you have to bring them along slowly'.

Robyn: A hundred mile an hour, we were off! We weren't a snowball, we were an avalanche!

The women's group did widen their network with people from other suburbs becoming involved and many men, some of whom became founding members of the new Gandangara Local Land Council. Some took up active roles in building the land council's knowledge of the area, like Wayne Dargan, who took his small boat out weekend after weekend, identifying and charting the many unrecorded middens (mounds of oyster and other marine shells) piled up by the old people over many thousands of years of fishing and feasting along the Georges River.

Both before and after it was formed, this Local Aboriginal Land Council – like many others – had virtually no funds. They formed extensive networks, held meetings and made submissions on the small amounts they could glean from short term project funding or from their own pockets. The occasional funds that Kevin was able to suggest they apply for from places like the Australian Council of Churches barely kept them going. This was a further problem in urban areas because decades of government 'resettlement' projects had been carefully separating Aboriginal people in public housing, so that there could be no chance of them forming identifiable community groups. So forming a local land council – and then asking people to sign unfamiliar official-looking forms – was a huge task.

Janny: We used to do our notices all by hand, and do letterbox drops, it was so funny…

Robyn: This was BCs – before computers. We used to type up the land council notice, all the way down a page. Twelve or 13 times on a page and then we'd go down to Canley Heights to the chemist. He was the only one where you could get a photocopier. And we used to pay 20 cents a page.

Janny: We'd cut em all up…

Robyn: …Then we'd get in my old car, you both sitting in the back cutting them up! Judy jumping out and putting them in the letterbox! And me driving!

Judy: My hands were so sore from cutting up. And we'd be in that old Datsun… It had a bit of everything didn't it? A blue door, a green door. Nobody ever came near us on the road, I can tell you that now.

Robyn: Yeah – I'd just say, 'They won't hit us, they can see I've got no insurance!' We could fit 15 people in it too.

Judy: We used to even take the kids. We'd say: 'Go on, jump out and put that notice in that letterbox there'.

We knew there were a lot of blackfellas out there because we had the listing for the *Homes for Aborigines* (HFA) houses and housing commission and all those. In those days every second street had a HFA house! But we didn't have a map. They never had them next door to each other.

Robyn: It was, you know, 'assimilation'. So there wasn't a whole street of them or they all weren't clumped together.

Janny: Or they wouldn't give us any personal details, but they'd just give us the number of the house in the street, address and stuff. So, we knew which was a HFA house but not who was in it, so we'd do a letterbox drop. We slowly built up the membership didn't we?

Judy: That was amazing wasn't it? Trying to do the membership list. Now, you've got to go and see one and these government departments'd go, 'Oh why don't you just go there and get the forms filled out'. And you'd go, 'Well it's not that easy!' You've got to have a cup of tea, they want to know who your mob is, where you come from, so by the time you get through your old nan, or old mum and that, you're sitting having a cup of tea. Then they'll say, 'I want you to come back at such and such a time because I've got a son come home, I've got this one coming home'. So, you're backwards and forwards. You could spend a whole day just with one family just to get three people to join the land council. But you do, especially with the old ones. They want to know who your mob is. Where you come from. Once they feel comfortable with you, they're fine. And they'd still be very wary about filling out government forms. Yeah, those government departments, because you're living on a housing commission, they want to know who's living there, who's working.

Robyn: Once they knew what it was, they'd join the land council roll. Because it wasn't going anywhere else!

But it made it so difficult because we weren't a *community* where we were all there. You know, we had to get this information out and find everyone because we were just spread out so wide. And even when we set the land council up, you know, we were sort of Liverpool based, but we used to every month, we'd move the meeting around our boundaries. We'd have a meeting at Bankstown, at Revesby. We'd just keep moving the meeting around… Guildford… There was people out there that didn't have access to transport or anything like that. We were trying to have it in other local areas within the boundaries.

Once the local land council was funded, the questions about how to control expenditure were all new. These small land councils had to make principled decisions about directing funds only towards land – a difficult ask in communities which were all facing many social welfare and infrastructure probems which all seemed to demand money. But such difficult social decisions had also to be made in situations where local land council staff had no financial experience or training. Judy, Janny and Robyn again talk about their experiences at Gandangara:

Janny: But we had trouble, with people misinterpreting the Land Rights Act in our land council area. We ended up going to the local newspaper, the *Leader* and done a little article that said, 'Land rights is not going to take your back yard away'. But then when the land council tried to buy that house at Canley Vale, apparently all these petitions came because the Aboriginal Land Council was buying this house! We finished up going to Janice Crozio, the State Minister for Lands. And she said, 'Well I can't see a problem with it. There's a multi-cultural centre just around the corner'. So, we got the house – after a bit of a struggle!

Judy: And we hadn't spent a cent of land council money on that. We saved up for three years for that house.

Robyn: See, when we finally got the allocated funding, we just kept putting it in to a rollover investment type fund. All the renovations were done through CDEP[18] and we were building up skills and employing Aboriginal people in the community.

Janny: I'll never forget when the first cheque come out from the land rights fund. There was all these regulations about money for land councils. So, we rings up Mr Cook again! Because none of us knew how to run a cheque book or nothing. So, he's came out with his Tranby mob and sat us down...

Robyn: 'Cause those cheques came very quick didn't they? First cheque was just there. We didn't even have a bloody bank account.

Janny: That's right, because I raced up and opened an account. And we opened up that bank account with our own dollar!

Robyn: But we always had the philosophy in those days that, unless we got other funding to employ people, that that money was not there to employ one person in the community. It was there to benefit all. It was about land rights so it should go into purchasing land or an asset for the organisation and we would all continue to work voluntary. Now that happened. The money's about everybody in the community benefiting from it, rather than one individual getting a salary and a vehicle and that's the end of your money.

Judy: Actually back in those days, they just gave all of us that money. They said, 'Right, you've got land rights', but they never *trained* anyone. It was Tranby that came in and did all that. It was Tranby that actually trained every land council in New South Wales and Tranby used their own resources. And they actually went out to the communities, you know. Tranby took something out and gave people confidence about how to run their land councils, you know? How to do their books. How to be accountable and the importance of being accountable. If it wasn't for Tranby I don't know what a lot of local land councils would have done.

---

18   Community Development Employment Projects.

Kevin: It was a good program, a really good program. It's what Tranby was set up to do.

As well as learning how to do the bookwork and management documentation, the State Land Council – and Tranby – embarked on an even more important education program. This was working to produce a 'plain English' version of the Act and to demystify the whole body of legal and legislative language which clothed all the policy which affected Aboriginal people. Unlocking the key to understanding of these documents had an enormous impact on the confidence with which community members like those from Gandangara could meet with governments and bureaucrats and demand their rights.

Judy: And Tranby set up some little courses and they also set up a course on the actual Land Rights Act itself, our bible. John Terry wrote the plain English version. See you need an organisation like Tranby was back then. I mean they used to *teach* us. We could parrot that Act off. We knew every part of the legislation, the sections and that. John Terry used to take us through it, you know. We'd be sitting in there with bureaucrats and go, 'Oh well what about section such and such'. And they'd look at you, you know. We used to think we were pretty suave. You know, we could quote that Act off inside out and back to front.

Robyn: But what it did, it also educated people about how to understand other Acts and how to read Acts. Not be intimidated about going to the National Park Act or the Police Act, any other Act. Environment, Planning. You just grab it now and look through it! That's what those whitefella lawyers and politicians all do, they don't know it all in their heads, they just look through it and so we'll just look through it and read it!

Judy: That was a form of oppression. Because we didn't understand. Nobody wanted to teach people how to read legislation, it took people like John Terry to say, 'It's not really scary you know. It's bloody lawyers just write it up like that'. And he used to take us through stuff and that, you know. Send stuff over to us. We'd read it and the next day he's say, 'What part do you want me to work on?' We'll talk about it, and he'll take us through it, you know? And he taught people not to be frightened of it.

Janny: Remember when the Land Rights Act first came out? You took one look at it and thought, 'Well, shit!' Because you had the Act there but as well you had to read the Act with the regulations. It was just all jargon to us. So learning how to understand it – that was *real* learning…

12. Getting land back

The Land Rights Act 1983 'ignores many of the fundamental recommendations of the Keane Committee Report which in itself was inadequate and fell far short of reasonable Aboriginal expectations for just and equitable treatment by the Government,'

Once again Aboriginal people are left with only scraps.'

Kevin Cook, Chairperson, Interim Land Council, 9 June 1983
(NSWALC website 'Our History')

By 9 June 1983, when the Interim Land Council met for the first time, the day before the Land Rights Act was proclaimed, Aboriginal people had been forced to come to terms with the compromised Act.[1] The difficulties and challenges they then went through to set up the land council structures, described in Chapter 9, were undertaken so they could push the Act to make it work as well as possible given its shortcomings. The test for the land rights activists would be how much land it enabled to pass directly into Aboriginal control.

The restriction on what types of land were available for claim was severe, even at the drafting stage. 'Unoccupied Crown land' was expected to be minimal in the state which had been colonised longest and had had a range of ways to alienate land, including the declaration of national parks and other recreation reserves, all of which put the land they were on out of reach of any claim. The goal of the right-wing Labor members in parliament had been to restrict the land available for claim even further and they had done so by the amendment that to be claimable, any such Crown land had to be 'not needed or likely to be needed' for any possible future 'essential' public purpose, however fanciful that might turn out to be.

But in the Act had been confirmation that land which could be successfully claimed would be held in the form of title for which Aboriginal people had been calling for over 150 years – for communal inalienable freehold title. This provision held all over the state. In New South Wales, however, after a terrible drought in the 1890s which exposed widespread overstocking by the grazing industry, the Western Lands Act[2] had declared that land in the western half of the state could be held only in leasehold, protected by covenants which allowed the government to enforce conservation measures. These Western

---

1 *Aboriginal Land Rights Act 1983* (NSW).
2 *Western Lands Act 1901* (NSW).

Lands Leases were often perpetual leases and had in reality offered very little real environmental protection. Yet they were not freehold and so the Aboriginal title – if any were granted – would have been noticeably more secure.

The expectation that land claims would yield little land was the basis for the attention given in the Act to the establishment of a perpetuating funding mechanism to enable the purchase of land on the open market. Making a link between the state tax on freehold land and the rights of Aboriginal people to purchase land was a powerful symbolic statement of the fundamental nature of Aboriginal ownership of land. It was also to prove – in an unexpected outcome for both the government and the land councils – to be a substantial source of funds, which was far higher than had been allocated to the Commonwealth Aboriginal Land Fund Commission for purchasing land in the Northern Territory and elsewhere.

In general, the NSW government was clearly not expecting the claims process to deliver much land anywhere in the state. The government, however, had not counted on the inventiveness or the tenacity of Aboriginal people at grassroots and community levels to claim their rights.

This chapter looks at the two ways to gain land: by claim and by purchase. Both had unexpected successes but also deeply frustrating failures. The two areas where claims were made covered here were the Gandangara Local Land Council area in south-western Sydney and the Western Region on the Darling River and the far west of NSW. It was also the Western Region where the purchasing process was most successful, which was a direct result of the effective working of the regional land council. This was to have a very limited life: the regional councils were effectively abolished by the Greiner Government's amendments in 1990 – to be discussed in Chapter 15. This chapter looks at how they worked during the brief early years of the Act.

Claiming land

In the Gandangara Land Council area, along one of the most densely populated and industrial areas of the oldest city in the country, the idea that there would be any land to claim at all was ludicrous. But even the land rights purchase fund was unlikely to be of much use, because city land prices were so high, as the Gandangara members were acutely aware.

Robyn: We had a problem with land prices in the city too.

Janny: We couldn't even buy a bit of land with the money we got into the local land council. We couldn't do much with it at all. That's why we put it into an investment fund and we waited until we had a couple of allocations and we had enough to purchase a property. But we did a lot of research into how to claim land. Oh yes… we rang Cookie once again!

Judy: Cookie had an answer for it – he sent her down to the Land Claims Unit in the Department of Lands. See Cookie's responsible for everything! Janny always called him 'Mirrors' – cause he was always saying, 'I'll look into it!'

Janny: He did this time too – he said to me: 'Just go down and knock on the door of Colin Clague and just tell him "Colin, Cookie sent me".' Colin wasn't even expecting me. He said, 'What are you here for?' I said, 'I want you to show me how to distinguish Crown land'.[3]

I think they thought at the Land Claims Unit that it was going to be a one-day thing but I was backwards and forwards, every week. Imagine the shock of me landing on their door! I still remember their reaction that first day: 'Oh there's no-one here Aboriginal but we are going to put on a trainee'!!

I remember telling Cookie, and he was killing himself laughing! That was their reaction. 'Oh, there's no-one here Aboriginal'. I felt like saying, 'Well, I can bloody see that. But we are thinking about putting on a trainee'. I don't know if that ever happened. Anyway, I went home with all this knowledge from the claims department. Photocopies of all these maps. Bring them home and sit there and work out. You had to know what to look for.

Judy: Yeah, she had maps everywhere. You should have seen the bloody place, it was full of maps. Janny did it all, nobody else. Just with the help of 'Mirrors'. Janny just claimed everything!

Janny: Whatever was Crown land, I claimed it!

Judy: Anything that didn't have a house on it, she claimed it.

Janny: I thought well, if we get something out of it, we'll get something. If we don't, we don't.

Kevin: But Janny got a *huge* amount of land. When they were showing me the maps I'm thinking Jesus! If they can get that that's millions and millions of dollars. And there was a rubbish dump they were trying to claim… and they said, 'No, we can't give you that, but we can give you this…'. You know, they negotiated a deal through.

---

3   Colin Clague, a staff member of the NSW Lands Department, was well known to Kevin. He was the husband of Joyce Clague (nee Mercy) an Aboriginal activist from the North Coast of NSW, had once been a student at Tranby and had for many years been a senior figure in the NSW Labor Party.

Robyn: That's the only way to do it! There's always got to be an educational component to everything you do.

Kevin: And that brings in the politics. If there's no politics in education then it dies.

One of the strengths of the 1983 Land Rights Act was that it had not identified particular criteria for claimants in the claiming of land. It had also been a weakness that the Preamble which did recognise the broad bases of Aboriginal goals, had not been carried through in the legislation itself. However, Aboriginal people had watched the narrow definition of 'Traditional Owners' used in the Northern Territory Land Claims Court hearings to exclude claimants who clearly had a strong and enduring affiliation to land. So NSW people reasoned sensibly that in their state, where so much land had been put out of reach of any claims and where so many Aboriginal people had been relocated and displaced from their traditional lands for many reasons over 200 years, it was going to be difficult to establish an interest in terms of 'traditional ownership' to the fragments of remaining claimable land.

The NSW Land Rights Act had reflected these concerns only in its preamble, where it had referred to the fact that 'land is of spiritual, social, cultural and economic importance to Aborigines'. However, the only issue was whether or not the land was indeed 'claimable' under the Act. It meant that Aboriginal people did not have to prove either traditional ownership or historical association or economic need. They just had to prove that the land was 'claimable' in the terms of the Act.

The broad approach to recognising the legitimate interests of Aboriginal people in a heavily colonised state was however lost on most of the public servants with whom Aboriginal people had to deal. As the Gandangara women recall, they faced repeated challenges as they tried to claim land.

Robyn: And they used to come out, like from the Department of Housing, and say: 'But there's no Aboriginal sites on it'.

We had to tell them: 'Well, there hasn't *got* to be!'

Judy: The Department of Housing were bloody rife on that, weren't they, they were always saying it! 'What do you want all this land for?', they'd say. We'd have to say:

'Because its our *right* to claim it!'

Robyn: How many times did we have to say it?

'We can claim it! Its *vacant* Crown land.'

'We can *claim* it. It hasn't got to be a site!'

Figure 12.1: Demonstration to stop the rubbish dumping at Lucas Heights in a continuing process of getting land back after Janny Ely's Gandangara claims. Urban land gains have been under constant pressure from sale or encroachments like residential development and waste disposal. This is a 2000 demonstration – but the process of claiming and protecting the land has been ongoing.

Courtesy Judy Chester family collection.

The eventual success of the claims put in by Gandangara was unusual – the rate of processing claims has continued to be best described as 'glacial'. Figures were very difficult to obtain in the early years, but even by 2009, when more than 20,000 claims had been lodged, over half were still awaiting determination. Of the 10,000 which had been determined, more than 5000 – over half – have been refused. Only about a third of those 10,000 determined claims have been granted, that is, a success rate to date of only one sixth of those submitted.[4]

While this may have resulted from a lack of preparedness among public servants in the Lands Department and elsewhere, it was widely suspected by Aboriginal people that in fact the government was simply reluctant to fulfil its obligations to pass land over to Aboriginal people. This reluctance was seen as the cause of the delays. Government reluctance became very obvious when the largest

---

4 NSW Aboriginal Land Council figures, 2009, <www.alc.org.au/about-nswalc/our-history.aspx> accessed 13 January 2013.

claim in the state was organised in 1984 by the Western Regional Land Council over a block near the Darling River at Winbar. Peter Thompson was acting as an adviser to the Western Regional Council and William Bates was a member of the Interim Land Council and the regional council.

Peter Thompson: It's 23,000 hectares. We knew this bit of vacant Crown land was there when the Land Rights Act came in.

The property had been earmarked for a nature reserve in 1970s. But it was surrounded by other leases, and all the cockies around it kicked up a big fuss. They all said, 'We don't want bloody National Parks and Wildlife owning next to us! The government should do what they've done with previous expired leases and cut it up for neighbours to build up their blocks!', blah, blah, blah. So they stopped the nature reserve proposal going ahead but they didn't get around to doing the carve up before the Land Rights Act came in. I think we saw it advertised for carve up for additional holdings and that's when we lodged the claim.

So Winbar Land Council was set up as another one where people didn't live, because we knew we were going to try and get this bit of land. The people who had ties with that land lived mostly at Bourke or Wilcannia or even further up and down the Darling River, so to give it to Bourke would have been unfair and to give it to Wilcannia would be unfair too. So there was a logical reason to set up that as another non-residential land council to claim the title to that big area of land.

So that's how the claim got started and then it took a long time to go through court, so then the government changed the act in '86!

William Bates takes up the story: Yeah! Labor done that in 1986! The same crowd that introduced the Act!

They'd brought in the inalienable freehold title in the Western Division in the '83 Act. All the rest of the land out there in the Western Division is Western Lands Leases. But all the land we got in land claims was inalienable freehold.

Now we'd claimed Winbar, and I've got all the documents from that... and tapes... even the stuff when we were doing the archaeological surveys...

But then they repealed those certain sections of the Act.

We was bang in the middle of that land claim in Winbar! So we appealed it in the court! John Terry did that case. And it was still goin'.

Then the Premier, Barry Unsworth – well 'Gunsworth' as we call him – when he knew he was going to lose that election in 1988 to Greiner, he turned around and said, 'Well that section of the Act has already been repealed. We'll give you the land, it'll be in leasehold, it'll be a Western Lands Lease'.

And we went along to the court … Henrietta Dean from the State Land Council, and John Terry for us, the Far West Regional and the barrister… We appealed, and we told them that we was only going to accept what it was *at the time of the claim*, that is it had to be inalienable freehold.

Well, Bang, we got it!

Its still owned as inalienable freehold! But unfortunately for the local land councils, its still owned in the name of the State Land Council … it never got transferred.

Peter Thompson was skeptical: That's what the Winbar case proved – the Labor government in 1986 went to parliament and amended the Land Rights Act, to try and stop Winbar being granted, because it was too big.

Buying land back

While claims had a low completion and even lower success rate, the purchase of land was dogged by the high prices of land across NSW, not only in urban areas but wherever land was demonstrated to be productive. While the amount of income the land councils received from 7.5 per cent of Land Tax was substantial, half of that had to be reserved each year for a capital fund, to allow continued funding following the sunset clause ended the allocation after 15 years. This left 3.75 per cent of Land Tax each year to be distributed. If it went directly to local land councils, it meant dividing up the funds that came in each year between as many as 113 locals. If each local decided to have an office, employ staff and run a car, this amount would rapidly be dissipated.

Most often, each land council not only faced such running costs but had suddenly become the only organisation in an impoverished community where many people faced urgent financial demands. Requests to fund medical costs or pay for funerals were difficult to resist, while calls for aid to meet rent payments or pay fines were almost as hard to refuse. On top of these demands – which were not legitimate expenditure in the terms of the Act but which were understandable in community terms – there were examples of fraud and negligence, in which individuals were able to pocket funds themselves or channel jobs and other advantages to allies and relations. Such problems make the decisions of organisations like Gandangara even more striking – their refusals to use the land rights fund for salaries and on office infrastructure were not just sound management – they were in fact heroic restraint! In the far west, the Western Regional Land Council did the same. No-one was paid a salary, the locals took a minimum amount and almost all the money was pooled in a land fund.

Given high land prices, the possibilities of buying a whole block of land in any local area was slim, even before the calls for help which were so hard to knock back. The only real way to buy back significant amounts of land was going to be if regional land councils could be used to pool the annual funds from all the locals in their area. This would allow them to accumulate enough for a property in one area for one local land council and then, when more funds had accumulated, to buy another property for another local. This required a high degree not just of planning and negotiation but of trust. Whose land was to be purchased first? Would the last local land councils on the list have any confidence that the regional land council would eventually get round to giving them a fair turn? Did they trust their fellow local land councils enough to wait till their turn came? In this situation, the benefit of a regional council was that it was made up of people well known in each local land council area, who were each living close at hand and had to face daily the responsibilities of the regional council decisions. Unlike the old Lands Trust, these regional councils were not remote and they were not peopled with unfamiliar faces from distant parts of the state. They were all from just down the road, more or less.

In this section, Barbara and Kevin talk about their observations and experiences with regional land councils, then we turn to William Bates talking about the Western Regional Land Council and their strategies for buying land back.

The regionals: Collaborative planning

Kevin: I think what really impressed me about the regional land councils, the way it was set up. … It was set up primarily to get land. But it also enabled the region to come together to say, and tell people, what problems they had in their locals, and their region. And that was important too.

We had the Sydney region doing things on a regional basis. Not as much I would've liked, but they were doing things. We'd say, 'X' amount of dollars, and if there was any over it would go to one land council so that they could do something with it. Say there was one land council setting up an oyster lease, we could give them extra money to be able to do that. It took away from the money that could've gone to the other land councils, but then the next time it'd be someone else's turn.

Barbara: In the west of the state, people had been moved around by government, so they had established long-term relationships with people in the areas they had been moved into. Say between the River people, the Paakantji and the easterly desert mob, the Ngiyampaa, who had been shifted over to Menindee on the Darling in the 1930s and then the Ngiyampaa later had moved back into the central west.

So, people were used to and related to each other. It was a big region. But they were able to negotiate without any trouble at all, about how the money into the region would be spent. Everybody agreed that we'd buy properties that came on the market, to acquire a land base. And that we'd try and ensure that if we bought a property in the north, that we'd buy the next one in the south, or in the middle. So people agreed to that. There was a lot of money going into the region, and it was shared on that understanding. And we were able to spend big blocks of money to acquire property.

Now where that didn't happen, and I think what's happening to a large extent now, is that when you get a much smaller amount of money, that you can't do much more than employ a couple of people and buy a car and run an office, you don't actually have the potential to think more broadly about spending $3,000,000 on a property. So I think that's what's limiting things now. Hopefully people will go back to this idea of thinking regionally. The government departments should be dealing with supporting and housing and all those other things. Housing in particular was always a contentious issue for us. We didn't want anything to do with it at all. Just like the land council must deal with land, the government departments have other responsibilities to people in the state and they should fulfill those.

Kevin: Out in Wilcannia they never had any problems with that. They just didn't have the overhead expenses. And you know William was the banker… [laughter] … Yeah honestly, he'd ring up and want to talk about interest rates! I can remember William ringing up and saying: 'Look, we've got all this money…'. I said: 'You put it into IBDs.[5] You have to go to the bank and say: "I want so much interest"'. And I found out for him how much interest we were getting at Tranby on our money.

He was wheeling and dealing in a matter of seconds… you know, 'Chung!' and he had the best sort of deal. He was just incredible how he worked so quickly about money.

William: Oh yeah! We used to be experts on buying commercial bills: we made enough money to buy all the plant and stock on Weinteriga and I think we bought some on Auley too, and Appin. We'd buy mainly 30 day ones – 'Bills'

---

5   Interest Bearing Deposits.

they used to call 'em – because interest rates were high in those days. We made lots of money out of that so we could pay over $100,000 for all the plant and stock at Weinteriga.

The Commonwealth Bank got that way, when it was run out, if we was late, the staff'd run over and get us to sign the documents because if you catch the morning or the afternoon markets, whichever had the highest interest, those 30 day ones used to be the highest interest ones. Used to be 30 days, 60 days and 90 days. And they'd deposit the money straight into your account, that was the secure thing about it. It'd go straight into your account, the minute you sign the document, but you weren't allowed to touch the money for that 30 days. So it was probably one of the most securest ways…

Kevin: Yeah, and so that was really good… that people who'd never dealt in that field, got to be the experts. They'd ring up a bank and say, 'Oh the other bank's giving X amount of interest' so, if that was right, then the first bank'd come up to that level. So it gave a lot of skills to the region. And if they were getting into enterprises, the regional council could make sure there wouldn't be two enterprises in the one region, competing with each other.

So the regionals could do all of those sort of things… So that when the regions went, that whole dynamics left too. The regionals would mean you had people with experience coming together with people with not so much experience. They'd sit down and they'd say: 'Oh you're doing this, what happened to you?' So all the time, people were learning off one another. And you'd bring in experts to your regional meetings, that could teach you, or tell you things you wanted to know, and then you could take that advice if you wanted to use it, or chew it over. If you wanted to use it you could use it. If you didn't, well you didn't have to.

So that's what I thought the region was for. And then the locals. Well, locals are nothing now, are they? These days [2005] the locals have got no say in what happens, the state's got the all say, its top heavy. Originally, what we had wanted was for the state to meet only about three or four times a year, just to make the policies, so the regions and the locals could enact them. And just to give the money out, say here's the money and see you later, Jack!

William: To look at what we used the money for, I'll start from the top:

We'd claimed Winbar of course, and we ended up with that in freehold, inalienable freehold at the time of the claim. There's 56,000 acres. The land at Tibooburra was 24,000 acres – its called Mokely paddock I think. Then there's about 300 acres on the eastern side of the river between Tilpa and Wilcannia. There's Weinteriga which is 86,846 acres and 46 km of river frontage.

There's Appin station at Menindee. Its got 22 km river frontage and I think about 62,000 acres. It's around the size of Winbar, I think. Then there's Auley station at Balranald, that's about 4000 acres, with 5 km river frontage in it...

When the Greiner Government brought in the amendments in 1990, they just took everything the regional land councils had... and the regions had been the only ones that was saving the money really, the only ones that was doing things. We used to pool the money out home way, and so we was able to buy land.

Gees imagine the acreage we could have had today! We'd have been like Sir Kidney Sidman,[6] as Barbara used to call him! The locals would have all had a property by now, every one of them. But when they got those amendments through, it just took away everything the regional land council owned and left it with nothing. They're just a skeleton advisory committee today that no-one listens to anyway.

The saddest thing, and its still happening today, they're mainly concentrating on houses instead of on land. Through claims and purchase, we achieved over a quarter of a million acres round Wilcannia... The western region.

Figure 12.2: Weinteriga Opening: ceremony marking the purchase of Weinteriga by the Western Regional Land Council. Tree carved in celebration – covered in Aboriginal flag until official opening.

Courtesy Heather Goodall.

---

6   This was a local joke about Sir Sidney Kidman, an Australian pastoralist who controlled huge tracts of land in the Northern Territory, Queensland and north-western NSW.

Making Change Happen

Figure 12.3: Crowd begins to gather round carved tree to hear speeches for official opening.

Courtesy Heather Goodall.

Figure 12.4: Tree carving unveiled.

Courtesy Heather Goodall.

Figure 12.5: Close up – carving is traditional form of marking places as sacred and significant.

Courtesy Heather Goodall.

Ozne of the frustrations for land rights activists was that the Select Committee's Report had recommended that a parallel Act to allow Aboriginal people to manage Aboriginal heritage should have been introduced with the Land Rights Act. This was not incorporated into the 1983 Bill and although there was a Task Force established to move towards its later creation, on which William Bates sat and contributed heavily, the Heritage Act never came into being.

Kevin: The other Act that never came in was the Heritage Act. We had pushed very strongly for that. We wanted a dual thing so that the Land Rights Act and the Heritage Act should work in tandem.

Barbara Flick: I think that would set principles, guidelines. We'd made a list of things and that was circulated. So if there was going to be heritage legislation, we said it must include these things. We had a list of the completely protected sites – which allowed for people being excluded from particular areas in protection of fauna and flora. But our plan was that the Heritage Act should be focused on joint management.

Kevin: And on intellectual property ... We've always pushed for that. That's what was especially happening in the regions – when regions were allowed to be involved.

Barbara: See people were still all involved in negotiations with National Parks. Both the far western people and the north-western mob were really interested in and involved in that issue. In the first instance the national parks and heritage issue was almost thrown out of the ballpark for us on the Interim Land Council. It was identified as something that we shouldn't be worried about! As if it had nothing to do with us!

But we always *had* identified national parks as being part of our right to claim or to help manage. So we always wanted an involvement with it that would be negotiated.

William Bates explained why he and the people in the western region felt it was so important to have a Heritage Act.

William: Its important because it's about having Aboriginal ownership recognised!

What really stirred me up was that National Parks would have Advisory Committees on their parks in our area. And you'd go to these meetings with them and they'd put these files down in front of us and they'd say, 'This is what we recommend ... and we expect you to agree with it' ...

So they just wanted us to rubber stamp it!

And I said, 'Go away, what do you think we are?'

And one of them run out the door crying one morning in Canberra. But I said, 'We need a chance to read through them', and they'd say, 'Your insulting me!'

Well we'd say, 'Stiff Shit! If we have to insult you to get it through your thick head, well fine'.

We were having some of these conversations around Mungo Lady[7] at the time… We were trying to get her remains returned back to Mungo, as well as them other skeletal remains they found there at the time that's a lot older.

We talked in them days I think about keeping places, we talked about putting one there at Mungo, building it into the side of one of the hills, not on the sand dunes, but back near the park quarters. We wanted to be able to control heritage, and everything else that came with it.

They'd say, 'Why should you take them remains and artefacts?'

And we'd say, 'They're ours, give em back!'

'Oh', they'd say, 'We have to look after them!'

All of a sudden after 200 years we're not capable of looking after anything!

Tibooburra's got a keeping place up there. Mutawintji we're still messin' around, but we're hoping to start doing something there, like building a keeping place or something like that there. We are just making the decision that we need to make and then we can go ahead and do it, because with the rent we get, there's no problems with financing it to do it and that.

There's a lot of interest in it there at Mutawintji. We've got buses. If I can get these guides to sit down and start taking it a bit more seriously and talk about it, we could get a coach and take tourists around the country, with camping trailers and things like that…

Well then the Labor Party got voted out in '88 and Greiner was in, taking apart the Land Rights Act.

But his Environment Minister Tim Moore first introduced the National Parks Hand Over Bill, after he'd been to the Northern Territory. We thew it back at him and said, 'You've got to be joking!'

And he said, 'Well give us a hand to polish it up'.

And it amazes me that it took a Liberal minister to do that!

Cause Chris Hartcher got hold of it and he didn't want to have anything to do with it. And it was in limbo there until Tim Moore come along with a Bill and they flew us out, they run around the region with an Aero Commander, it come to Wilcannia and picked us up, and Aunty Dorrie and Aunty Tibby, and he had the cameras there and said: 'We're going to give you Mutawintji back!' And we

---

7   The ancient remains of a woman found at Lake Mungo, who had been buried with ceremony involving decoration with ochre, as well as cremation. Widely dubbed 'Mungo Woman' by the media, she is referred to here more respectfully by William Bates as 'Mungo Lady'.

looked at the Bill and said, 'Not with this you won't!' [laughter] ... But the good thing is it took ages and ages, we worked on it slowly and for a long time, and now its probably the best Act, the best Aboriginal ownership Act in the world! Not that its perfect! But I mean – it's workable! You've still got that thing, with National Parks, it's like a disease if you like, or a culture. They just don't seem to want to acknowledge Aboriginal ownership. We're for everlastingly fighting with them, and they're still trying to pull the wool over our eyes. We're still in the middle of a battle with them at the moment, but if it's not one thing its another.

Kevin: If the Heritage Act was in, that would override the National Parks and Wildlife Act,[8] that's what we wanted it to do.

William: Actually we might start bringing it up again, cause the way they're changing things around again now, there's no reason why you couldn't revive that and start the campaign up again. 'Cause National Parks are useless...

Reflecting on the Land Rights Act post-1983

Barbara: I think that at the same time that all this political activity was happening on the ground, there was the old Land Trust structures in place. And I think it's important that that'd be acknowledged by history that there were certainly difficulties between the views of both of those groups. The NSW Land Council, before the legislation, was firmly of the view that people on the ground, in the communities, understood what they wanted in terms of land. And really it was about land in those days. And that the Lands Trust wasn't seen as representative. It looked like it was doing a lot of deals with government without consulting with people. And I think that they in fact were isolated from a lot of the communities. And their resistance was a major thing that needs to be acknowledged. And I think that we had some difficult times in trying to resolve those differences. I don't think we ever did.

Kevin: Well we knew that. But now, years and years later, some of the same people who worked for the Lands Trust are now members of the NSW Land Council and in very senior positions. Now, it's good in a way that they've come on board and are looking after the land councils now. Because I don't think they ever wanted to consult when they were on the Lands Trust. If they had done that, people would have seen no use in setting up the land council! Because of the way the Act was structured, the Lands Trust then, it was doing no good for Aboriginal people.

---

8   *National Parks and Wildlife Act 1974* (NSW).

I think we should look at the Act, not the people, but the Act. And that's what we were fighting – we were fighting that Act, not the Aboriginal people involved in it.

Barbara: Well I don't know whether I can agree fully with those comments. But I think that they had enough power to make things fairly difficult from time to time. And I think there were even compromises that we made during the negotiations and it worried me then and it still worries me how much legislation changes the political environment in which you work. When you're struggling for change or struggling to win back land – we were all being driven by a passion about land and about country, about history and about relationships. But when the legislation came into place, I think it was moving very quickly back into becoming a bureaucracy that the government was much more comfortable with. But I felt it moved away from the people – even though we tried really hard to stop that from happening.

For one thing, we tried to limit the role of the State Land Council, right from the beginning, to ensure that people, local land councils and regional land councils, had the money to buy back the land or acquire land, and to control the State Land Council.

But somehow or other it started to shift back to a lot of central management and control. And I'm still sad about that. And although I think it would have been much harder to maintain the local and regional control, I think that would have been well worth the effort.

I think it's the nature of the beast. We tried to resist it. I remember meeting at Dubbo *after* the legislation, in the Council Chambers. One of the things that made the organisation powerful *before* the legislation was that we were out in the bush with people, we weren't sitting under fluorescent lamps. We were down the South Coast, we were out in the far west, we were up in the northwest. But I think legislation does something to Murris. You know, sitting under the fluorescent lights affects us somehow. And when you're trying to meet government requirements and reporting requirements, sometimes it takes away the focus of what you set out to achieve.

Kevin: I think we've always said that the easiest part of the struggle is before legislation comes into being. Because you can go out and say and do nearly anything that you want before it comes in – and that's what we did. We said: 'These are the wishes of the people' and we didn't go away from that. But when the legislation came into being, it wasn't what we wanted, it was far short of it.

It was a compromise. But it was the only thing that we were going to get.

And people said that they wanted to go with it. You'd see people crying and saying, 'I want to be buried on my land'. And they were saying, 'We want land rights, we want to get that land so we can be buried out there. We don't want to be buried on someone else's land'.

And so that carried the day.

Barbara: Before the legislation we met out at the farm. But when we were the Interim Land Council, we met at the Town Hall. Because the farm had burnt down. I think it's got to be said that Kevin's leadership at that time was crucial for a lot of things happening. There were a lot of people on the ground that wanted things to happen, but the catalyst was Kevin and his connections, and his passion for the struggle for land. And those of us that worked in the region were able to bring, I think, a more structured approach to that.

But if there had been no Kevin Cook at that stage, or no base, which was Tranby College, with all of the things that that brings with it, there wasn't any way in which any of these things could have been articulated. So on the one hand you had bush people being able to talk about land and land acquisition, and on the other hand you had an organisation and a person, that was Kevin Cook, who already had access to the political environment in the state at that time. Whether it was through the trade unions with all of those contacts, or though the politicians, and mainly on the Left.

So those things were present at the time and it didn't seem to me that there was anybody else. Even with the Lands Trust there wasn't enough confidence in those people, one, to understand what was happening on the ground and the wishes of the people, and two, to be able to articulate that to politicians or to other political organisations in the state. And Kevin's willingness to go and sit on the riverbank and travel to Menindee, or go down the South Coast. And that's where he was from so he already had a lot of that trust people had, and their relationship with the people up the North Coast enabled that to happen. But old people would see that.

Kevin: I think in the end, people have got something, you know.

But I think we should never have given away inalienable freehold title. We should never have given that away. Because whatever lands are sold, you'll never get back. People are not going to buy lands unless they're going to make a profit out of it. And so they're making a profit out of you, and you're prostituting yourself. So I don't think you should sell land.

PART 4
NETWORKS 1980s

13. National networks

Aboriginal voices were heard powerfully at state, national and international levels in the 1980s. This was largely because there were networks of support and solidarity which were operating. In the earlier chapters about land rights activism we have seen the way that local campaigns in NSW developed into regional networks of grass roots organisations and that these in turn provided the base for networks across the state. Similar processes had occurred in many other states during the 1970s but there were few bonds between grass roots communities – or even land rights activists – across state borders, despite the earlier existence of national peak rights bodies like FCAATSI, the Federal Council for the Advancement of Aborigines and Torres Strait Islanders.

From the early 1980s, Kevin played a central role in establishing and fostering new networks which crossed state borders. Emerging in 1980, these became the Federation of Land Councils, most active till 1985 and the National Coalition of Aboriginal Organisations, which continued into the 1990s. The Federation and the Coalition in turn developed links with international networks. Ultimately, these national and international networks shaped the responses to the Australian High Court's Mabo decision in 1992 and then the federal Native Title Act in 1993.[1]

In this chapter Kevin talks about his memories of how those early interstate networks got started. In a series of interviews for this book, many of the people from across the country who worked with Kevin in the Federation and the Coalition have explained how these networks looked from their point of view and what they were all trying to achieve.

This chapter is not so much about what the networks did, as about how they worked. Tracing the story through networks gives a new way to look at the contributions of people like Cookie and his fellow activists: their time, energies and thought was turned to building and consolidating not just the formal organisational structures, useful though they were, but the human relationships which underpinned them. And while the relationships between them have been the focus of their recollections, they each took seriously the idea that they served a specific local and regional community.

This involved very different types of relationships to those developed only in formal, organisational meetings or in bars, which had been the frequent meeting places of the men who were the leading activists in past years. While women like Kath Walker had been well known to a broader public, the majority of

---

[1] *Native Title Act 1993* (Cwlth).

Aboriginal political leaders had been men.² This changed in the 1980s, when networks more often involved activists sharing time and friendships as they travelled long distances on shoe string budgets, talked frequently on the phone, stayed with each others' families, camped out and shared cheap hotel rooms with each other in order to meet face to face across the enormous continent. The very informality of many of these networks, and the experiences which generated them, meant that men often worked closely with men and women with women, in an echo of continuing traditional relationships. But Kevin, notably among a strong group of active people, was in constant touch with women as well as with men and fostered supportive home backup for the people with family responsibilities who nevertheless took up the arduous demands of travelling, either across the nation or overseas.

These person-to-person relationships explain the emergence of the networks which built on them – the networks of collaborating organisations which had friendships at their base. Taking this approach allows us to understand at least some of the underlying reasons those networks came into existence, flourished and changed.

Getting started: 1980 to 1983

When Kevin came home from the Coady International Institute at the beginning of 1980, he brought a strong sense of the value of networks between activists of all sorts, as well as between their organisations. His work in NSW in both Tranby and in the land rights campaigns had all involved building stronger networks between local campaigners and between groups across regions.

There was already a model for regional bodies which had emerged in the 1970s from the federal drafts for land rights in the Northern Territory which had set up the Central and the Northern Regional Land Councils, conceptualised partly on the basis of shared traditional cultural relationships but also on the basis of contemporary economic and social associations. Their role was expected to be both to support and to lead the activities of the local communities of each region. These two NT bodies, formed in 1974, had continued to operate but they were separated by long distances and flooded with the demands of the first few years of the NT land rights procedures; they had not formed strong bonds between each other. On this model, however, Aboriginal people in North Queensland and in the north of Western Australia had set up regional political campaigning bodies, the North Queensland Land Council and the Kimberley Land Council, both of which operated totally independently of the deeply conservative state

---

2   As 1930s and 1940s activist, Pearl Gibbs commented, at times bitterly (interviews with Heather Goodall, 1981).

governments which controlled property law. These two bodies were outspoken advocates of Aboriginal demands for land rights in Queensland and in Western Australia.

Kevin had barely settled back into Tranby again after returning from Canada, when the Western Australian land rights struggle flared into national headlines when the Kimberley Land Council (KLC) supported local Aboriginal land owners at Noonkanbah who were opposing mining on their sacred lands. The WA government in 1978 had decided to push through mining exploration on the Aboriginal-owned Noonkanbah pastoral property, against the wishes of the Yungngora owners. This land had only recently been returned to the Yungngora community by purchase through the one section of the federal land rights apparatus which was able to operate to acquire land outside the NT.

In mid 1980, after a bitter two year struggle, the mining companies despatched a convoy of trucks to begin the long journey from Perth to the Kimberley – with government-provided police protection – to deliver the drilling rigs needed to begin the exploration. In an inspired decision, the KLC organised a demonstration by the Noonkanbah community to take place in an open paddock near the mine site. This occurred thousands of kilometres removed from the urban streets where most demonstrations took place but film of the Noonkanbah march was beamed out into television sets across the world, and its symbolism of chants, banners and placards was instantly recognisable.

Peter Yu, then a young activist involved with the KLC from the start, remembers: In those days we had nothing in the Kimberleys. Basically we were just one or two people and a lot of senior people in the community who were giving the direction with a lot more hope and trust than anything else, I suppose.

Kevin began to look for ways that Tranby and the NSW land rights campaigners could mobilise support for the KLC as well as for the activist North Queensland Land Council where his old friends like Joe McGinness were based. One strategy was developed by a supporter of the land rights cause, Guy Morrisey, an art dealer from Paddington. With the support of renowned artist Arthur Boyd, who loaned new work to be exhibited, Morrisey was able to encourage well known artists to donate works to be auctioned to contribute to funds for land councils. The audience for this and later land rights auctions was developed not only from the expanding land rights support movement, but also from the trade union networks which Kevin had been building on through Trade Union Committee on Aboriginal Rights. Kevin here talks about the fund raising auction Morrisey had organised in the Paddington Town Hall, an area of Sydney known both for its interest in art and for its middle class affluence.

Kevin: We made $21,000 and so out of that. We gave $7000 to the Kimberley Land Council and $7000 to Mick Miller from North Queensland and we kept $7000. Well, that $7000 lasted us and we still had money in the bank, which we gave to Deaths in Custody when we finished. And the amount of people we got to that art sale was incredible, we filled the Paddington Town Hall. Not only were we raising money, but we were getting the message out! We gave them the Aboriginal flag from Tranby that they raised at Noonkanbah. So we knew what was happening all over Australia.

At this time too, Kevin found another source of support and communication. He had already joined Gary Foley as a member of the Aboriginal Advisory Committee of the Australian Council of Churches (ACC),[3] taking up Bob Bellear's membership when Bob needed to focus on his law studies. When eventually Gary also had to take up other commitments, Kevin became Chair of the committee, a role he fulfilled for the next ten years. The people Kevin had come to know so well at Coady International Institute in Canada had showed him how valuable the networks of churches and related organisations like co-operatives could be in supporting and expanding the political movements of the Philippines, India, South Africa and Zimbabwe. A substantial number of Aboriginal activists from each state were invited onto the ACC advisory committee. As Kevin recalls, this decade in the ACC was an important one in allowing him to work with sympathetic churches to support Aboriginal advocacy organisations.

Kevin: I think how we got everything through was with the Australian Council of Churches. Now what we'd been saying in the NSW land rights movement was that we had to get the trade union movement, the churches, and other groups, other forward-thinking groups, to support us.

So I went in there to the ACC and here we were – we had a line right to the Australian Council of Churches. And soon as we got in it, we were able to direct funding to Aboriginal organisations that would never, ever have been funded. Particularly like the Kimberley Land Council. And there were a number of other groups who would never have got funded, only through us. We didn't fund the medical centres or things like that, because they were getting funded already.

The Australian Council of Churches was an incredibly good organisation to work with at that particular time. You could go into the office and see the coordinator of the Australian Council of Churches and just sit down and say, 'Look these are the issues that we want the churches to support'. And here was one fella that could just send out a fax to every church.

---

3   The Australian Council of Churches changed its name to the National Council of Churches in Australia – NCCA – in 1994.

So then, after a while on the Committee, I took on that job as chairman and I was chairman for ten years. We had ten years of having that direct contact with the churches. I don't think we 'used' them: we worked *with* the churches and it went really well.

Figure 13.1: Cookie and Tory in Tasmania.

Courtesy Tranby Archives.

One example was 1984 when the Labor Party was meeting in Tasmania and they were in government. We had the Australian Council of Churches Advisory Committee meeting in Hobart at that same time. That helped bring a number of people down. After each of the meetings people stayed on for an extra week and went to the other meetings and lobbied all the politicians for that week. It was a long time being away.

When an Australian Council of Churches meeting of the Aboriginal Advisory Committee was on, you could always bet your life in the next two days there would be a Federation or a Coalition meeting. And you'd have an ACC Advisory Committee meeting in Broome or somewhere like that and you'd get most of the participants over there.

You've gotta learn to survive. That was one of the things we learned in the NSW Land Council struggle. That was a good struggle and we used everything that we knew. We used the trade union movement, the churches, and a heap of prominent non-Aboriginal people, to get that through. The Catholic Church played a pretty big role in talking to the members of parliament – and in the Labor

Party there were quite a few Catholic members. So with the parliamentarians, like we were able to do with the churches, we always tried to work with these people. Yeah, but we didn't have much success with the Liberal Party.

Peter Yu has remembered the role the ACC – and Kevin himself – had played in this early period.

Peter: We were getting a lot of our money from overseas. Most of our money came through contact with the World Council of Churches, and the Australian Council Churches and all those contacts that Cookie had and put us onto. The only reason we're still going today is because of that period.

But what that also did was also contribute to building the culture of the organisation. It's not only that it kept us alive and able to do something, but what it did was reinforce the spirit and the principles upon which we were established. People in that period, if you talk to Johnny Watson [a key leader in the KLC], they just remember with such pride how we survived on nothing basically. We had people coming to work for us who'd given up their jobs and whatever like that because they saw this thing happening.[4]

I think Noonkanbah played a role in the sense that up to that time, our world view in the Kimberleys was just within that region. And then when we started to get support from the blokes in the Territory like Pat Dodson and Rossie (David Ross) and others down around here in Sydney, it opened up people's perspective. Particularly when there was a public campaign when people started to move around during Noonkanbah to speak in different states, because as an organisation the KLC was really still young, we'd really only just been born...

But I think it was that realisation, not only that people were actually supportive and prepared to do things, but also because people they had begun to get to know like Cookie were down here. That made that connection. People felt comfortable. There's always the situation where people are uncomfortable when they move out of their region anyway, and they'd come down here and met blokes like Cookie who just made everybody feel at home. There was an immediate connection, I think.

People in the Northern Territory had begun to hear about Kevin's role in NSW before they actually met him. John Ah Kit was one: he was usually referred to by Kevin and others as 'Jack' which will be how we will see him in the rest of this book. He was Director of the Northern Land Council from 1984 and later a senior minister in the NT government. He has explained this process.

---

4   See later section, this chapter, in which Karen Flick talks further of going across from NSW to the Kimberley to work with the KLC, an experience already mentioned in Chapter 6, on Tranby explorations of learning possibilities.

Jack: Before I met up with him, I'd started to check out this 'Kevin Cook'. Who the hell is this Kevin Cook? He was at various functions in NSW. You'd come down there and take over the office of the Land Council and meet up with Judy Chester and Karen Flick who were there in the early days. And these people would say; 'Oh Cookie is not a bad bloke'. So you'd check him out and he was highly spoken of.

Activists like Jack Ah Kit had long been aware of the problems with poor communication between the NT land councils.

Jack: I became a member of the Northern Land Council, representing the Katherine Aboriginal community back in June 1983. It appeared to me fairly quickly, even though it was early days, that the three land councils in the Territory weren't meeting as much as they should have or working together as much as they should have. I had some connections with the mob in the Central Land Council: I had known David Ross and Patrick Dodson for a while and I'd been born in Alice Springs, so I could start working towards making sure we established a relationship with each other.

The three land councils met about once a year back in those days. They had won land rights but they didn't have a common co-operative relationship. We had two distinctive regions but if we were to go anywhere and if we were to maintain a position or formulate a position, then if we had to defend that position – we needed to defend it collectively.

So I thought that that was something that I had to work on and so it was good that David Ross was there at Alice Springs and we started to work closely together. It was from there that we began to look at the federal scene. And we knew that there was a need to ensure that the picture that was painted of the Territory Aboriginal people and the Land Rights Act was a real one. The historical position we were in was one that wasn't really clear to people on the eastern seaboard. This was in 1984, a year after I'd become a member of the Northern Land Council and I took on the director's job in March '84.

Jack: The Federation was virtually born out of the Noonkanbah situation. It was always going to come, but that's when it started to consolidate itself. When people started to share concerns and that there was an enormous need for support from right around the country. And then if there were any issues of major importance then we tried to get the meetings around to different parts of the country so that the Federation could be seen to be ensuring that it's not just down in the eastern seaboard, that it's in the Territory, that it's in the west… and to educate what the Federation of Land Councils stood for.

Figure 13.2: Jack Ah Kit (from Darwin), Clarrie Grogan (from North Queensland) and Cookie at Oenpelli during a meeting in the Top End.

Courtesy Kevin Cook family collection.

Figure 13.3: Cookie and Judy with Gail Ah Kit, Jack's wife, and their children.

Courtesy Kevin Cook family collection.

Such personal contacts became important in the formation of the new Federation in September 1980, just months after the climax of the Noonkanbah crisis. Pat Dodson has discussed the earlier difficulties on interstate communication and the challenges of building both personal and community relationships.

Patrick Dodson: It certainly started out that the Federation's concern was very much with a land focus, with getting land legislation in at the national level, although the agenda moved outwards a bit later.

Prior to that there was always a sense of the support from the south given to Vincent Lingiari and the Gurindji in the Top End over the strike in 1965 and the battle to get the title leases for them. And the role that the trade unions played in that background, there's a sense of that support that came, not necessarily knowing where it came from, but it came from the southern states.

But there was no-one in the communication chain though, until Cookie, and those people came through to dispel some of the myths and misperceptions that we had, about what comprised NSW in a sense. Because the previous days it had been the Legal Service that was very much the corporate representation of NSW.

The complexity of it wasn't known to us. It might've been known to a few people but not to the main players. And similarly the complexity of the Territory and the Kimberley and the west and South Australia wasn't known to the people from the south. So there was a mutual learning there and an understanding of the strengths and weaknesses, I suppose, that we all went through.

A lot of the organisational stuff was pretty much unknown in the bush in the early days. Like raising funds and getting the word around. Cookie knew about it from his interactions in the city, but them other old fellas, certainly in the Centre, didn't know about it and so they got a sense of what was happening from the city end of it.

But even if they didn't know all the things about that organisational end, they did have this ability to share with other people, to be concerned about the other people, to provide opportunity so that they could do things with whatever their skills were or whatever the dough that Cookie could bring to bear on those things. So I think that there was a complementarity about the Federation, there was a meeting of the minds in some ways, about many of those things. Which had never existed [before] in terms of the structured movement. Shared things like the movement for national land rights that was part of the Federation's agenda, and the sustaining of land councils as a vehicle to assist people in the advocacy of their rights. The bodies that were supposed to be doing that, didn't appear to be doing those things.

So, there was a very important way in which I think the influence of what Cookie and Tranby were trying to do in the city, actually influenced some of these things in the bush. I remember Cookie would ring up and say: 'Oh, you've got to get someone over to this meeting somewhere. It's really important'. And I'd say: 'Why is it important?' 'Oh, you've just got to get someone over here. Someone should be at this meeting'. That's what Cookie would do because he was good at it. And then we'd have to say: 'Jesus, someone's got to go. We don't know what it's about but Cookie reckons we got to go.' We'd know it was important for us to be seen there – then we'd see Cookie and he'd say, 'Oh, just go along and tell them what you want to talk about'.

Kevin's involvement with North Queensland had even longer roots through the links he had built up in the trade union movement, his early Tranby work with the North Queensland co-operatives and emerging from both of these, his friendship with Joe McGinness and his community. Through the ACC and then the Federation, Kevin became close friends with another Queensland activist, Terry O'Shane, whose sister Pat, a teacher and then a lawyer, was already a well known political figure in Sydney from her work in the 1970s movements. Terry has described how his early meetings with Kevin deepened into the supportive friendship which came to characterise the networks Kevin was fostering:

Terry: My involvement with Cookie started with the Australian Council of Churches. There was concern about how to get resources to the right people. You didn't want to be just putting money into some sort of a project that benefited one person, or a little group of people. So Cookie got in touch with me about Queensland, and said, 'Mate, how's all this work?'

And it didn't take long for us, when we got involved at the political level, to sort of gel, because of our similar backgrounds, like my father being a wharfie.

I remember one time I had to come in one weekend for a meeting – he said come a bit early and we'll go for a drive. And he took me down to Wreck Bay. As we drove through, he was just telling me this and that. It wasn't a bad settling down time for me. He must have thought, 'Oh I'll take this lad for a drive and show him my country, and at the same time I'll give him a few clues about how things work, so he'll be a bit at peace with himself when he's doing business with others'. But oh well, I grew up in a different climate, in North Queensland, where the way in which you got on at school was to fight your hardest! So it was a good exercise.

His involvement and my involvement in trade unions taught us a discipline. I think the key point to it all was that his analysis of things was not about it being a black issue – it was much bigger than that. It was about an issue for all of us, it was about justice and human rights and things like that. And so we needed to involve a much larger portion of the community to achieve what needed to be achieved. Because it wasn't just a thing for blackfellas. It was a thing for all Australians.

I was with another high profile person just recently at a trade union conference. And he got up and asked the ACTU how they can assist us, like what would they do for us? And I thought to myself, 'Well that's exactly what you shouldn't be asking!' You should be saying, 'Well there's an area here we can work together on. And we need your support'. Do you know what I mean?

The trade union movement gives you your influence within the Labor Party, 'cause that's what the Labor Party should be about, the political wing of the trade union movement. And with all due respect to some of my old mates, at the end of the day, the realisation's not there of what the linkages are. Whereas Cookie understood it, you know, in the same way I'm apt to myself, from being *in* it.

As you can imagine it wasn't going to be easy, bringing together people from the diversity of backgrounds. Well Paddy Dodson came out of a Catholic background, he was in the priesthood when he first came along. Jack Ah Kit was out of the North Australian Workers' Union and David Ross coming out of Central Australia. But you had the Tasmanians, who, you know, thought that the centre of the universe was Tassie and you had the West Australian mob who always thought they were isolated. So to bring them all together and say, listen, we need to develop a uniform position. I mean it wasn't easy! And especially not to someone like myself who was a cane-cutter, you know, like this crazy troppo from the tropics! You imagine trying to bring that together and saying: 'Well, we all had our different backgrounds and all had different upbringings but at the end of the day there is a focus. You need to all come together in that one focus. And identify the goal and identify the way in which we go forward on that.' Outside of something like that, we're more than likely go down the street and agree to disagree! But we actually all ended up hanging out together in the end.

Kevin thought the quality of genuine friendships was important: What I thought was really good, was the ability for that friendship to develop – you know we came from very diverse backgrounds and had not too much in common at the beginning. And then when you went through it – went through the issues and went to all the different meetings – people started to know how you thought. And if it was a trade union issue they'd look straight at Terry and they'd be waiting for him to say something.

There was another dimension however to the friendships outside of the meetings. Kevin's partner Judy Chester felt that the personal relationships not only between Federation activists but their families were crucial in sustaining the communications and support.

Judy: I think the important thing about the Federation and later on the Coalition, was because we had so many meetings. And it was the women who were the backbone of the families for the blokes involved. We're all got to be really good friends. We're family. All their kids call me 'auntie'. We've just formed this relationship. And yet I've only met a couple of the wives. But we stuck fats because there was a job to be done.

Terry O'Shane also thought that the roles women played and the lessons he learnt in his family had all shaped how he approached the Federation relationships. But he thought it went beyond even these, to the principles they all shared:

Terry: Actually the links for me to the union movement were through my mother, Gladys O'Shane. On the waterfront, from the Waterside Workers' Federation and the Seamen's Union. My mother was very active in the women's committee and she joined the Communist Party, so we had links there too. And Mum was very active in the Aboriginal Advancement League regionally. So my background was with my mum, you know.

But from my dad too. Dad come out here to Australia as a 14-year-old boy and never saw his mother or any other family for another 50 years. He was sent out from Ireland and indentured to a farmer in Western Australia.

I think one of the things that connected me very strongly to Cookie was the way in which he did an analysis of things. It was never done on the basis of race, and never done on the basis of gender. It was done on the basis of what was right and wrong. And it's a thing that I actually related to all the time.

I think it would have come from my family: my mother and father being married – your non-racial household – and I had a mother and two older sisters who could all beat me in a fight. So you never had a gender problem, because they were the ones who grew you up and looked after you. So it was a non-racial, non-sexist sort of house that I grew up in, you know. And so that's just the thing that's happened in my teaching – that's just the way it happened. So when I first ran into Cookie, we just sat down and talked. And I listened to how he analyses things, and then how he develops a strategy from there and a way to plot a course – well, it fitted in to how I believed in things anyway.

Figure 13.4: The developing connections between activists from different states were visible in the Eva Valley meeting in Central Australia. This photo shows Terry O'Shane (Queensland) and Kevin Tory (NSW) at Eva Valley.

Courtesy Kevin Cook family collection.

Figure 13.5: Eva Valley meeting with Joe McGinness (Queensland), Michael Mansell (Tasmania) and Josie Crawshaw (NT).

Courtesy Kevin Cook family collection.

Because we were never on about the size of us. People sometimes thought Cookie must be ten foot tall and bullet proof! And look at the size of him!!

But we didn't worry about how big we were. We've been talking about the Coalition, which is a very small group. And as Judy articulated, it was the back up – you know the support group that was behind them – was just enormous. There was a lot of dedication in terms of the support group. There was a lot of dedication from the people who were out front. But that's the thing a lot of people don't understand. They think, 'Oh, we'll bowl this bloke over with that person'. But the movement was much bigger than one or two people. It wasn't based on Cookie or Terry O'Shane or Paddy Dodson. It was based on how best we had advanced this issue on behalf of the Indigenous peoples and the broader community. Now, that's an ideal that we don't have a right to walk away from. It wouldn't matter how bad it got, you can't walk away from it.

So our premier activity was not only organising at a national level. There was actual participation in all those little meetings up in far North Queensland. That was the attitude that prevailed right throughout the whole Federation period, you know. Never to be stood over, never to be put aside, never to be aggressive in terms of trying to oppress or push someone down for the purpose of getting our own way. Cookie always said it. It was about creating an awareness and developing a friendship. Those friendships, let me tell you, exist today! They're still here. With the Dodsons and the Peter Yus and all that sort of nonsense, you know.

Moving people in the Federation

The links in the Federation did not only form between the individuals who were taking leadership roles. Instead the Federation was characterised by the extensions of these personal relationships out into community level networks. While the movements of people were constantly limited by funding shortages, the organisations still opened up possibilities for moving people into places and communities into which they had never ventured before. Kevin travelled to Victoria, Western Australia and to Central Australia at various times to be at Federation meetings. He has talked about his growing feeling that this process of travelling and meeting people was a critically important part of building the future. There were misunderstandings and conflicts among those who attended but the meeting at least allowed a space for the beginning of discussions to work out solutions.

Figure 13.6: Bruce McGuinness, a major activist from Victoria who was active in the Federation meetings, including Eva Valley, speaking in 1983.

Courtesy Gary Foley collection.

Kevin: We got on really well. From the first time when we went up there and met people and they came down to Sydney. The next minute, you'd be on the phone! I think it was because of the communications that enabled us to keep in contact on a regular basis. People were moving around more. Before then people from NSW had never been to the Northern Territory. They'd never been to Alice Springs. So people were going up there, and the people from the Territory were coming down. You'd stay at people's places, and when they came down they'd stay at your place. There was a lot of friendship formed in those early years. …It brought the people together. Now inside that we had arguments on the way forward, but the end goal was always the same. And I found that quite remarkable, that everybody agreed on where we were going, but we couldn't agree all the time on how to get there.

Making Change Happen

Opening the way

Soon after the formation of the Federation, senior NSW community members from the South Coast of NSW decided to make the long journey by car up to Central Australia to meet senior people from those communities in the context of a Federation meeting. Jacko Campbell, his wife Nan and Mervyn and Shirley Penrith drove all the way from Nowra to Alice Springs, and into the memories of the people gathered there from Central and Top End communities. Patrick Dodson has talked about what this meant to people in Central Australia:

Patrick: It began with those early trips. Prior to those Federation meetings the only communication between the Northern Territory mob and the cities would've been the efforts made through the trade union movement. That's how the Gurindji campaign worked really. And the disastrous church relationships with some of those mob in Arnhem Land.

So providing the communication link was pretty important. And the fact was that there were *senior* people who came from the south, from this part of the country. I don't think that ought to be discounted, that it was a pretty big thing. You've got all these senior bosses[5] out of the desert, out of the Kimberley and the Top End and then come these senior old blokes from the South Coast, who I suppose just spoke about their life experience. They just talked about the challenges, the difficulties, the loss, the hopes and the odds that they could see to achieving anything.

And it was the commitment, of old Jacko and Nan and all that mob coming by car all the way to Alice Springs that impressed most of the centre mob, and most of the other people… I mean people travel by cars all the time, drive from the Kimberleys to Alice Springs… But the fact that out of NSW came a little old bomb, that Geoffrey Shaw had to fix up, or try to fix up, when the muffler or something fell off it. It left a lasting impression about the commitment of the players there.

Kevin has recalled that trip, not knowing if Mervyn's old car would even get them there, but even more apprehensive of the reception they would get.

Kevin: When we went up to that Federation meeting, we didn't know what to expect up there. We went up with Jacko and Mervyn that first time. And then we just kept sending people up there just to continue that link. We wanted to get people to come down, and talk about what was happening up in the Centre and in the Territory and Western Australia and then for us to go there.

---

5 'Boss' is an Aboriginal English term for senior ceremonial leader – who therefore has the right to give directions to others.

Everyone was saying, 'Oh people from the south are going to do this, people from the south are going to do that, when they go into other people's territory'. And it *wasn't* like that, you know? We didn't go up there and say, 'Look, we're going to do this and do that' or 'We've done that down here, so you should do this'. It was just good to get that talking between the groups going. And when I say the groups, I mean Western Australia, Northern Territory and South Australia were one group, then from NSW and Queensland and we had a lot of strong contacts with Victoria, so that was another group, and then there was the Taswegians, so there were another group that more or less linked in with Victoria.

Patrick explained how these personal, face-to-face interactions had changed the broader community perceptions of distant regions:

Patrick: I think that's a real point. It is the human encounter, not the issues. We probably knew what these issues were, but it was these *people*. These people who represented people in some other place, who were there. And in another way it's similar to Rob Riley in Perth because that's the southern part [of the State] from the Kimberley, a personality who represents a whole region of people plus all sorts of national issues at the time. But who created a sense of… well, when you thought of Perth you thought of Riley, and when you thought of Sydney you thought of Cookie, you didn't think about anything else. You just said, well, 'They're the people that you got to see, when you go there'.

It's very much akin to the traditional way of operating. You go and see the people who will then look after you or tell you what you had to do and introduce you to whoever it is and would look after your interests, in a constructive way. So you could talk to them about whatever your business was, and I think that was the link that was made. And that gave that mob then a path from the centre through the Federation affiliates, the land council affiliates, to here. That gave them a path into here. Before that there was no path.

There was no path, there was no road to come in because there was no-one in Sydney. I mean there were people here, but from the protocol point of view there was no-one *there* to open the place, if you're opening a meeting someone from the place has got to open it. So that's what happened then, it was opened for people. It's a very important thing because if you lose people out of these systems you've got to make sure that that path is still opened, it remains open so long as that person is there, once that person is no longer in that situation it gets shut again.

Making Change Happen

Learning journeys in both directions

We have already seen that Kevin had encouraged Karen Flick to travel to the Kimberleys (see Chapter 6) which had reflected the strong Tranby commitment to links to far flung communities grappling with similar questions of social justice. Patrick Dodson argued that there was a need for everyone to travel, including the people from Central Australia. He had pointed out that south-eastern people from NSW or Victoria had no idea of the variety and complexity of Aboriginal communities in the Northern Territory or Western Australia. But he also pointed out that he had not had any idea of how complex and varied Aboriginal cultures and societies were in south-eastern Australia. Only when he came into the south-east as a friend and family member was he introduced to different types of non-urban communities and began to realise that any one or two 'representatives' could not even begin to really reflect the complex nature of the wider communities they were said to represent. He has recalled his own journey into south-eastern Australia.

Figure 13.7: Travelling to the coast from the Centre, the people whom Patrick Dodson (NT and WA) was able to meet when he travelled in rural NSW included Tombo Winters, shown at home in Brewarrina, in an unusual break from his own travels in this period to other regions and other states.

Courtesy Heather Goodall.

13. National networks

Patrick: I reckon the problem is that I never knew anything about NSW until I went to the back country with Barbara Flick. To that little town out in the back sticks there, Wilcannia, next to Bourke. I met all those wonderful people in that place.

When I brought Adrian, my son, through there, he said: 'Do any white people live here?' I said: 'No mate, these are all black fellas around here, they run this place.' He had no idea see, because NSW was over 'here' somewhere, on the coast. This bloody Botany Bay is the NSW symbol. But if you go from Botany Bay and travel all that way, you end up at Dubbo and you go up to Brewarrina or Goodooga and these other places.

That's where you run into all that sort of family section of Barbara's – Sonny Orcher and Old Joe Flick and all that mob. It's a different world there. But it doesn't have a voice. It might have a voice here inside New South Wales but it doesn't have a voice in the national arena. The voice in the national arena is going to be whoever's elected as your ATSIC commissioner – he's going to be your voice. Your voice for so long, before Cookie was around, was Paul Coe in the Legal Service, he was the voice.

So it wasn't until someone like me went through and met all those other people in this other part of the country who have a different set of priorities, that anyone from the outside hears about it. Those are people who don't have the same set of allegiances as the 'spokespeople'. And they have a whole different world view about many things, but that isn't known out there.

Whether you live in Alice or you live in Broome or you live in Meekathara or wherever else you live, you've got no idea – zero, zilch – about the bush in NSW. In the same way that people in the bush in NSW probably don't have any idea about what the go is over there. And what happened when Cookie and Old Jacko and all that mob came up to the Centre was that that gulf was covered. No-one else has picked up the candle since Cookie had to drop out of that.

Making Change Happen

Figure 13.8: Joe Flick (Mutawintji Hand Back) when meeting Patrick Dodson.

Courtesy Heather Goodall.

14. Onto the streets

There were two important national demonstrations in the first half of the 1980s which brought together Aboriginal people from key areas across the country. The first, in 1982, used the occasion of the Commonwealth Games being held in Brisbane to focus the anger that Aboriginal people felt towards the Queensland state government which kept them trapped under century old 'Protection' laws but at the same time, changed the land laws to make it impossible for them to gain recognition of their rights to land. These demonstrations focused national attention on the State of Queensland. The continuing racism of policies about Aboriginal and Islander people was paralleled when the conservative state government attempted to shut down all political dissent by banning street marches and other forms of peaceful protest. The interests that Indigenous and non-Indigenous communities both shared were brought starkly into focus. In many ways this powerful experience – of high support between Aboriginal and Islander communities and between them and white Australians – ushered in the national perspective which made the Federation of Land Councils possible.

The second of these big demonstrations, three years later in 1985, was organised through the networks established by the Federation. This was the protest held on the steps of Parliament House in Canberra to protest at the federal government's betrayal of its promise to enact national land rights laws. As frustrating as the government decision was, the Federation's nationally organised mobilisation generated new strategies to make the demands for recognition of land rights visible not just around Australia but around the world.

The Commonwealth Games, 1982

Kevin through Tranby had already had a long association with Queensland since the mid 1970s. Alf had earlier been excluded from church work in northern Australia by the Anglican Archbishop of the Carpentaria Diocese who had rejected Alf's militant support for Aboriginal and Torres Strait Islander rights as they developed self-managed cooperatives to free themselves from dependence on the exploitative pastoral industry. So Kevin inherited a staunch tradition of supporting Aboriginal demands for independence and, increasingly, for an end to the oppressive Queensland Act.[1] This was the last surviving legislation in any state from the 'Protection' regimes of the early twentieth century. The Act

---

1   *Aboriginals Protection and Restriction of the Sale of Opium Act 1897* (Qld); *Aboriginals Preservation and Protection Act 1939* (Qld).

had been amended several times, most recently in 1965,[2] but still interfered in the employment, residence and personal lives of all Indigenous people in the state, most of whom were 'under the Act'. The conservative Country Party state government under Joh Bjelke-Petersen had recommitted Queensland to this Act when it used its power over land law to savagely oppose the attempts by the Whitlam Government in 1974 to establish recognition of Aboriginal land rights in Queensland. To the demand for an end to the Queensland Act was therefore added the explicit demand for land rights in Queensland.

One of Kevin's first roles at Tranby in 1976 had been travelling to North Queensland to stay with members of the communities running co-operatives there. By the early 1980s, he had already developed close friendships with Joe McGinness and then Terry O'Shane and he was in frequent touch with activists in Queensland like Mick Miller in the far north of the state as well as Bob Weatherall, Ross, Lilla and other members of the Watson family and Cheryl Buchanan in Brisbane. So Kevin had built up the links between the newly formed Federation of Land Councils and the Queensland land rights movement, including FAIRA, the Foundation for Aboriginal and Islander Research Action, based in Brisbane, in which Weatherall and Buchanan were involved.

After Noonkanbah, the coming Commonwealth Games which were to be held in Brisbane in September/October 1982, looked like a good opportunity to focus world attention on Australian conditions and particularly on those in Queensland. This was topical for both the Left and the Right in Australian politics. The anti-Apartheid struggles in which Kevin and the Builders Labourers' Federation, along with Gary Foley and many of the Sydney Aboriginal activists, had been involved, had focused attention on the politics of sport. There continued to be bans arising from these campaigns which kept Apartheid South Africa out of all international sporting events. More recently there had been a boycott called by the federal Liberal government on the 1980 Moscow Summer Olympic Games, resulting in Australian athletes marching under the Olympic rather than the Australian flag and undermining the conservative parties' traditional 'keep politics out of sport' arguments. So through 1981, a campaign built up across Australia to use the Commonwealth Games in Brisbane to focus attention on both the Queensland Act and the state government's refusal to recognise Aboriginal land rights.

The Federation, with its strong interest on international links, through the World Council of Churches as well as through Kevin's links with co-operative and political movements around the world, hoped to mobilise those international networks to organise a boycott of the Games. In April 1982, the Federation sent Les Malezer and Bob Weatherall to Africa to try to convince

---

2 *Aborigines' and Torres Strait Islanders' Affairs Act 1965* (Qld).

the Commonwealth countries that the racially discriminatory Queensland government should be boycotted. There was a disappointing response to this Federation call – by this time Malcolm Fraser, the Liberal Party Prime Minister, had made strong public statements condemning Apartheid South Africa and so the Commonwealth African countries were reluctant to impose a boycott, despite the Aboriginal appeal. The Federation turned its attention to building media attention and nation wide Aboriginal support for the protests planned at the Games themselves.

The Bjelke-Petersen Government passed draconian security legislation, banning street marches and indeed, any gathering of individuals which could be defined as a 'political gathering'. The years of abuse of public civil rights by Queensland's conservative Country Party government had been enacted very visibly in these new public order laws. So the broad civil liberties movement, not only in Queensland but across the country, was organising to support the Aboriginal protest. At the last moment, Bjelke-Petersen attempted to short circuit the coming protest by announcing a complete redefinition of Aboriginal Reserve land to become local government areas, but, as every aspect of these new land categories remained under the control of the government, this move fulfilled none of the Aboriginal demands for independence and ownership.

Kevin mobilised his many links in New South Wales to bring people to Brisbane for the Commonwealth Games demonstrations. The whole land rights network was alerted across the state and not only the Aboriginal activists like Barbara and Karen Flick were preparing to go, but so too were the long time trade union supporters like Rod Pickette and Hal Alexander. Many of the Tranby students and staff wanted to go and were organising all sorts of transport to get there.

I was a part of all those events. I remember I was flat out trying to finish my doctorate – a scarecrow living on coffee and cigarettes. Paul couldn't get time off from the hospital to come to Brisbane but he shouted me an airfare so at least one of us could make it.

Cookie and Brian Doolan were going to drive, leaving late on the night of the Grand Final Rugby League game. Cookie's team lost, so he'd had a few beers before they left – quite a few beers – so he slept heavily while Doolan drove into the night. Cookie remembers Doolan waking him, groaning that he couldn't drive another inch. When Cookie had woken up enough to see, he says Brian's eyes were hanging out, so he agreed he'd better take over the wheel. When he'd woken up enough to see the road signs, he found Brian had already got them to the border with Queensland, and so he only had a few hours comfortable drive to bring them in to Brisbane.

In the weeks preceding the Games, a huge camp had blossomed in Musgrave Park. This big park in inner city south Brisbane had long been a place where Aboriginal people had taken temporary shelter if they had just arrived in the city or had been newly released from gaol. Although often harassed by the police, Aboriginal people had continued to come to Musgrave Park for refuge, temporary shelter and as a familiar meeting place. It had come to have powerful symbolic significance as a place in the heart of the city which was nevertheless claimed by Aboriginal people.

I met up with Kevin when they arrived at Nikki's house. Nicole was an old nursing friend of Barbara Flick's and had a house near Musgrave Park. So she was putting a lot of us up on her lounge room floor. Cookie told us he'd driven most of the way while Doolan dozed in the back, so we all felt sorry for him and made him tea while poor Brian shuffled off to get some more sleep.

Musgrave Park had became the nerve centre of the organising which FAIRA and other Queensland Aboriginal and civil rights groups were doing for the Games. There was extensive union support in Queensland, NSW and nationally, to assist with transport and food for the thousands of people who were going to be camping out in Brisbane.

There were a series of major gatherings in the park, with high profile national figures lining up to talk. Senator Neville Bonner, a member of the conservative federal Liberal government, feared the marchers would be subject to police violence, but he was compromised by his party allegiances. Senator Susan Ryan received a better response. Then Labor Shadow Minister for Aboriginal Affairs, she pledged that the ALP, if it should win government under Bob Hawke in the coming elections, would ensure that Queensland joined all Australia in the new government's implemention of the firm Labor Party policy for national land rights. But the strongest applause was for the Aboriginal activists from Queensland, like Mick Miller, and those who had travelled such a long way to be there, like Gary Foley.

The government had dismissed most applications to march but it had approved two. The first one was held on Sunday 26 September 1982, when 3000 Australians, both Aboriginal and non-Aboriginal, gathered in Musgrave Park and marched along the approved route, although they made a series of unauthorised sit-ins on the street along the way to voice their protests. Two days later they marched again for the only other authorised march, but they faced continuing police harassment.

14. Onto the streets

Figure 14.1: The Commonwealth Games demonstrations: 'We have been carrying Joh long enough'.

Courtesy Tranby Archives.

Making Change Happen

Figure 14.2: Mick Miller speaking to a rally during the Games.

Courtesy Tranby Archives.

Figure 14.3: The (illegal) street march at the Commonwealth Games, Brisbane.

Courtesy Tranby Archives.

14. Onto the streets

Figure 14.4: Marcia Langton surrounded by other demonstrators carrying Aboriginal flags.

Courtesy Tranby Archives.

Making Change Happen

Figure 14.5: Tranby students with the Flag at march (visible in the background in Fig 14.1).

Courtesy Tranby Archives.

At the close of the Games on 7 October, as the Queen officiated only blocks away, the Musgrave Park crowd formed into rows to move onto the streets in an illegal march. Aboriginal activists announced on the loud speakers that they were going to fill the front lines of the march. They wanted no-one else there to distract attention from the key goal of land rights and freedom for Aboriginal people from the hated Queensland Act. They vowed, as one activist said, 'To march where and when they want'. All the marchers knew they were facing mass arrests, and in the preceding days, after calls over a local radio station, $8000 had been raised to pay bail for those arrested. Kevin Cook and Gary Foley held half of the bail money each – they planned to keep away from any area where they might be arrested so that they would be able to bail people out as soon as they were put into the cells, so they wouldn't have to stay under the control of the distrusted Queensland police. Cookie moved over to the side of the road, waiting where he hoped it would be safe so he could move as soon as the expected arrests began.

I moved off the road, taking notice of the call for all whites to get out of the way and leave the front lines to the Aboriginal and Islander marchers. But as the lines started to form up, Karen and Barbara Flick caught sight of me and called out, 'Hey, get over here. You're with us!' So I raced over to link arms with them and we all moved off towards the main street. The streets were echoing with chants of 'Land Rights Now', 'No Police State' and 'End the Racist Queensland Act'. Within minutes, the police moved in, seizing marcher after marcher and throwing them all into the waiting paddy wagons to be hauled off to the city watch house.[3] Our turn came and the three of us were shoved into a waiting van with dozens of others. Shouting orders, the police waded through the crowd, grabbing whoever they could reach.

Kevin was watching anxiously from the side of the road when a mate rushed up and shouted that Foley had just been arrested. 'He can't have been', Cookie remembers gasping, 'he's got half the bail money!' Then a big cop barged into Cookie, shouting at him to move on. Without thinking, Cookie turned and shouted back: 'Get fucked!' The next thing he knew, he'd been lifted bodily and hurled through the open door into a wagon – with the rest of the money!

Inside the watch house, there might not have been any more violence, but the police derided and humiliated us wherever they could. Everyone who was arrested was kept in jail for over eight hours, with no food at all for the men. We women were given cups of a thin Salvation Army curried soup. Hungry as we were, many of us felt afterwards that we would have been better off without

---

3 Personal observation. Among many papers to cover the story, *Daily Sun*, 8 October 1982. See 'The Koori History Website' for an accessible selection of scanned newspaper clippings and photographs: <http://www.kooriweb.org/foley/images/history/1980s/82games/gamesdx.html> accessed 10 January 2013.

it. Kevin was one of the very last released, with the bail money handed over intact – eventually – but too late to have made it any easier for anyone to be released! They ended up letting us all out on our own recognisance – knowing that none of us would come back and that they weren't going to put any effort into bringing us back. The whole thing had been a show to bolster the Bjelke-Petersen Government's pretense of defending public order!

The demonstration might not have stopped the Games but it had been shown across the television screens of the world as the reporters who were covering the Olympic Games rushed to film the police carving through the demonstration in the government's denial of any right of assembly. Moreover the demonstration called even more attention onto the discriminatory abuses of civil rights to which unions and all civil society organisations had been facing in Queensland, along with Aboriginal and Islander communities. Ultimately, it heightened the scrutiny able to be brought to bear by investigative journalists like Chris Masters with the ABC *Four Corners* program 'Moonlight State' in 1987 and led to the Fitzgerald Inquiry into possible Police Misconduct (1987–89) which exposed the extensive corruption within the Bjelke-Petersen Government.

Perhaps most dramatically in the short term, it contributed to the momentum which swept the ALP, led by Bob Hawke, into federal power in 1983, bringing with it the pledge to implement national land rights for Aboriginal people in every state.

'National land rights': The false promise, 1984 to 1985

The networks of personal confidence which had been built up in the years from 1980 to 1984 became critically important in 1984 and 1985. The Labor Party policy guaranteeing National Land Rights specified five key land rights principles:

- inalienable freehold title for Aboriginal land
- full legal protection of sacred sites
- Aboriginal control over mining on Aboriginal land
- access to mining royalty equivalents
- compensation for lost land

The new government set up a National Land Rights Working Party and after meeting with it, the Hawke Government yet again recommitted itself to those five principles and began drafting new legislation which would apply nationally. The mining companies launched a heavily funded national advertising campaign against any extension of land rights, with Western Mining Company magnate Hugh Morgan arguing in 1984 that land rights meant a return to 'paganism'. Divisions emerged within the federal government between those who supported the mining companies and those who wanted to stand by Labor Party policy. Then the WA Labor state government, under Brian Burke, head of a mineral rich state where the 1980 confrontation at Noonkanbah had been characteristic of the government support for mining, argued that Labor would face electoral defeat at the coming state election if the 'Five Principles' were imposed from the federal level.

There was no longer any structure existing at the national level to express a collective Aboriginal view – the Whitlam Government established National Aboriginal Congress had been disbanded and the incoming Hawke Government had set up the National Aboriginal Consultative Committee (NACC), which was regarded as having little real power. The Western Australian government succeeded in pressuring the federal government into severely watering down the proposed National Land Rights legislation. When the government revealed its draft legislation in February 1985, as its 'Preferred Model', four of the five principles that the government had outlined in 1983 had been dumped. The new model:

- required no Aboriginal consent for mining on Aboriginal land
- prevented land claims over stock routes, stock reserves and Aboriginal-owned pastoral leases
- restricted eligibility for excisions (the establishment of living places for Aboriginal traditional owners where full land claims could not be granted over pastoral holdings and other alienated land)

The National Federation of Land Councils and the National Aboriginal Conference walked out of the next Land Rights Working Party meeting in protest.[4]

The way Kevin remembers it, the position for people in NSW was awkward but the national Act would in the end have worked out well for the state.

Kevin: The Five Point Plan wouldn't have watered down what was in the NSW Act. What it would've done is that the federal Act would've overridden the State Act, and so it could have. But the Act that was going in would've been the Act that we recommended. And although it was above what was happening in NSW, we would be able to keep what we wanted of the NSW Act and then we could've taken the best of the federal Act. Like you know that the freehold title was one of the things that they wanted in the Five Principles. But now that's gone anyway from NSW.

---

4 Koori History Website has a concise and accurate summary of these events: <http://www.kooriweb.org/foley/timeline/histimeline.html>

The reason why Burke could stop the national Land Rights Act was that he had a state election, and he said: 'Look, squash that or we won't win the election'. They had no state land rights at all in Western Australia, and he was trying to win the election by blocking the national plan. He didn't win the election that year even though he quashed the land rights thing.

It became clear that the government further intended to amend the NT Land Rights Act to make it consistent with this weakened 'Preferred Model'. From being an eagerly awaited victory, 'National Land Rights' had suddenly turned into a bitter defeat. It became urgent then for the NT Aboriginal leaders to call for support and unity from Aboriginal groups across the country. But their pleas could now be interpreted as a self-serving call to defend the NT Land Rights Act at the expense of other states which had no recognition of land rights at all and for whom even the weak 'Preferred Model' might have offered something. In the absence of a credible Aboriginal voice directly to government, the Federation of Land Councils – independent of government and now with strong bonds of personal confidence between its key participants – offered a network which could carry the complex arguments about why it was to the advantage of everyone to defend the earlier version of the National Land Rights model.

Jack Ah Kit, then newly established in his role as the Director of the Northern Land Council, argued in this interview that it had become urgent to strengthen the networks which the Federation had begun to build. He explained that there were divisions among Aboriginal people both inside the Northern Territory and between the 'traditional' northern areas and the more heavily colonised people in the south.

Jack Ah Kit: The National Land Rights model would've been great for this country. It had been an election promise of the Hawke Labor Government in 1983 and they'd come up with this Five Point model, but then in 1985, before they could implement it, Burke from Western Australia tried to torpedo it. Now we're seeing that bastard doing time in gaol, thank God, for being corrupt, even though he was with the Labor Party...

Then that Burke played us off. He came up with his state election ads about bricking off Western Australia. He had a model too, but the Burke one was about lowering the Northern Territory Land Rights Act. It was about taking rights away from that group of people and then extending a real watered-down version to everyone. Bob Hawke, the Prime Minister at the time, wasn't strong enough to say, 'Sorry Brian. Not on. We can't wear it'.

So we knew we had to fight long and hard to convince our countrymen down the eastern seaboard, South Australia, Western Australia and Tasmania that: 'What's this country on about? Taking away rights the Territory Aboriginal people have under the Land Rights Act? Going to the lowest common denominator? To something that hasn't got any teeth in it? We can't do that!'

So we decided – the NT mob like Patrick Dodson, myself, Galarrwuy Yunupingu and David Ross – that it was really an important matter to build up relationships with people in the eastern seaboard.

Cookie played an important part in ensuring that we were involved and that we had every opportunity to come down here and put our case.

Because there was a lot of animosity towards Aboriginal people in the Northern Territory, there was a lot of jealousy and misunderstanding. And we worked with and through Cookie in ensuring that the National Federation of Land Councils, and after that the National Coalition started to have a focus, and we started to get the message out to people – to radical elements in the Aboriginal community in the eastern states – who were saying: 'The Territory Aboriginal people, they're all right, they're spoilt. They've got their Land Rights Act, they don't care about us.'

It was hard in those days to come and talk at forums, and to ensure that we got the message across to people that we understood that, yes, we may be in a better position that they were. We had a Land Rights Act that was given to us. It was a Land Rights Act that was to be the first, and it was one that we understood was going to be extended to other states and territories within the Commonwealth. But we never got to that, as Whitlam, as you all know, got thrown out of office. But we had to put a clear concise message to Aboriginal leaders in the south, and especially on the eastern seaboard, that Territory Aboriginal people want you to have the same Land Rights Act that we have, to have the same benefits that we have, and that we would continue to fight for that so that we had equal land rights.

It was hard in the Territory too. I found it very hard because there was this misunderstanding out there. People had local or regional historical perspectives, there was never this bigger picture of Australia as a colony being colonised and historically what happened when the country started to get invaded. And the churches and native welfare commissioners… I don't know who developed or influenced this… or whether it came from the elders … but there was this fear. I lived through it in Darwin in the '50s and '60s where you could be called 'a yellow-fella' or you were 'mongrel'. And if you didn't have the balls to cope with that and if you didn't have your language, then you didn't have much at all – just the colour of your skin.

I saw people have some terrific fights over this, some of them tribal Aboriginal people. They played sport together, but it came down to this lack of understanding, I think, through not knowing people's background in terms of the stolen generation and everything we know today. And there was this fear of the unknown, especially from the people from the bush that was really a way of protecting themselves. It was hard for me when I went to the land council in 1984, to start working on influential Aboriginal people to get them to understand that we were all one. We had no choice whether we were taken away or who was or wasn't taken away and then what happened to us. And the sooner we came to grips with that – and understand it and respect that – the better it will be, not just in this Northern Land Council area or the Central Land Council area but in this whole country as a nation.

So to try to get some sort of national strength some of these issues on both sides had to be tackled. It had to be done. Because if you looked at the other option, there was every likelihood that the gap was going to be widened further, and somebody, somewhere – whether it was going to be black or white politicians drawing a line between Geraldton and Townsville and saying: 'Everything south of that can go and get lost', because of the historical nature of the colonisation we were in. And that was the last thing that I wanted to happen, and that was the last thing that Dodson and the others wanted to see happen. And looking back I think we made the right decision.

And we had to start getting this round. We had to start showing our faces and inviting people to come to the north and ensuring that we attended the meetings that were happening down south, down the eastern seaboard, whether they were at Brisbane where FAIRA was co-ordinating the meeting or whether it was down at Oyster Cove with Michael Mansell and Jim Everett and others, we'd be there – in Geraldton, Perth, in the Kimberleys… I think that was really good and it gave a focus.

But for us in the Territory, in those early years it was getting these European advisers away from these Yolngu leaders and starting to talk to the Yolngu leaders about understanding Yolngu people in the south, Yolngu people who had been taken away with the stolen generation. Yolngu people who were abused. Once that started to happen, once 80 land council members came together with a lot of bosses[5] on it, a lot of understanding developed… A lot of them knew it, but as a council they had to arrive at a position that they felt comfortable with and a position that their leaders were going to advocate, that we need to look after our countrymen in the south. And they in turn need to support us.

Galarrwuy said on a couple of occasions, very strongly, 'We go back to one mother and one father…'. You know, whichever way you come off that, you

---

5 'Boss': an Aboriginal English term for senior ceremonial leader – who therefore has the right to issue directions to others.

come off the one mother and one father. And I think that's one of the things that I will always remember as something really important to me. It's been that to bring about a change that was for the good of Aboriginal people.

The tensions Jack Ah Kit talked about were very real for Aboriginal activists in NSW. Barbara Flick, who had taken a major role in regional and interim land councils, recognised the importance of overcoming the divisions which in the past had split the overall Indigenous population. She has explained how she saw this period from the NSW perspective.

Barbara: The national links at that time were important too, with the Federation... we were really at the cutting edge of trying to develop policy in many areas, at federal, state and territory levels, for government to consider. And very quickly we gained credibility as negotiators and we tried to develop ideas around national legislation – the 'preferred model'. We were trying to get the best deal for everybody. We wanted to build up unity across the country and get beyond this artificial 'real Aborigines' versus people who live in the city – who somehow weren't 'real Aborigines', all that division kind of syndrome. I think the Federation of Land Councils was important, with people like Jimmy Bienderry from the Kimberley, when the Noonkanbah dispute was on. Before that it had been the Gurindji people from Watti Creek who had been making those links with people across the country. We thought it needed to be done again and this time both at a personal level – just getting to know each other and to understand each other – but also at a national level, on the organisation side I think, to make those important links.

In response to the threat to the land rights campaigns in all states, the Federation of Land Councils convened a major demonstration on the steps of Parliament House in Canberra. David Ross, the Chairman of the Central Land Council, described at an interview in Sydney the way the demonstration was organised across the country.

David Ross: I remember it was organised quite efficiently at the end. The NT Land Rights Act was under attack and the organisation and abilities of one Mr Riley from WA and Dodson and Ah Kit to an extent, who organised the protests up there – along with Cookie and the mob who organised people from this part of the world. All those things were brand new to me. We all rocked up to Canberra in '85 and we had big protest marches and people were trying to break down the doors of Old Parliament House and so on.

Those were the first big convoys out of the Territory and into the southern parts of the country. People talk about the '88 marches and the convoys that came through for that. But I suppose the first lot was in '85 for that big protest. And that was all a big eye-opener to a lot of the old people who were the real staunch supporters of the Land Rights Act, the land councils, who had really put the effort and the energy into getting the Land Rights Act in place, in the Territory back in them days. And it was under attack. And they wanted to keep it in place, and so people just piled into motor cars and whatever the best way it could possibly done and headed for Canberra.

And as I say, I don't really know the ins and outs of how things were done, but they were certainly done and it turned out very well. It was successful. The Land Rights Act is still in place today. There were changes but in '87 a couple of years after the original changes that they were trying to put in. But then we moved on after that and had that Federation of Land Council's meeting in Cairns.

Kevin asked David Ross about the relationship between Federation meetings and the campaigns to influence international opinion:

Kevin: I think that those early meetings led onto things like that overseas push, when you went over a couple of times didn't you Rossie?

David Ross: Eventually – very reluctantly – I did. I suppose my first thoughts and knowledge of overseas trips, especially to the UN and the working group was probably that very important event in '85 before... I only went overseas eventually – and very reluctantly. But the first thing I knew about the UN, not even thought about the working group, was the protest in Canberra.

Then after that me and Dodson drove across from Alice, and shot some nice big, fat turkeys along the way, and that was when we decided, at that meeting, that, yes, these fellas should go to Geneva. Supported by the Federation and what not, through that process.

Building the next stage: The National Coalition

There were many more people and organisations besides the land councils who wanted to defend the national land rights opportunities which the Hawke Government had seemed to be promising. Soon after the 1985 demonstration, discussions started among activists in many places about a way to extend the strengths of the Federation to the broader base of Aboriginal organisations.

In a conversation recorded for this book, Jack Ah Kit talked about how he remembered this process.

Jack: I think the Coalition was really important because the Federation of Land Councils was seen to be exclusive to land councils and it was cutting out other people. So the idea came up that we needed to start getting really organised and that the way we could be seen as inclusive was to start the Coalition up. The

Coalition would bring to its membership national Aboriginal representation – across the legal services, across the childcare services, across the land councils. So that we would be seen as more representative and a truly Aboriginal representative body.

We were relaxed and there was no: 'You're barred. If you're not representing anyone, get out of here. You mug…' you know? A person was qualified to come to the meeting and stand up and talk just by their own Aboriginality. We didn't disallow that. If a person was representing and had a gripe against the national organisation, from the state childcare, they were entitled to get up and say their bit. But we did have to keep it focused. We didn't lock anyone out. It was really good at that time to ensure that the message was filtering back and people were understanding what the Coalition was on about. And that it was there to advocate Aboriginal people's rights and to bring notice to the struggle.

Kevin pointed out that there were plenty of debates in the process of forming the Coalition. But the dense network of communications which had now been set up across the country with the Federation was able to serve the new Coalition even better now that more people had a say.

Kevin: We didn't always agree. We had some really good meetings where people were jumping up and down. But it ended-up all right, it didn't come to fisticuffs.

One of the main things was the Makarrata, the idea for a treaty. It was being touted around, that was one of the things that was on the go and people came together and disagreed with it and started formulating their own treaties. And so people were having meetings all over the country. And it was that communication, you know? Within days you'd know where the meetings were on and you'd organised for as many fares as possible to get there. It was incredible… the fundraising that you had to do to get them! But we did a pretty good job.

We were always thinking about how important it was for us to get what we wanted to say down pat so that we were all coming from the one direction. There was a lot of work put into getting people to compromise their positions. And there were a lot of people with a lot of different ideas, but when it came to the crunch there was one voice, that's what we call it, 'one voice'. And at all our meetings we had one voice. The things that we didn't agree on, then we came back later and discussed them out fully. And the decisions that were made at the meetings! … you'd have to sit down and get some materials and have a look at the things that were being discussed.

So all that sort of stuff where the hard work went on. And I think behind the leaders back in those days, where people were pushed up, where their organisation and their councils and their elders who haven't been recognised because those people, some by choice, some not by choice, were pushed up to the front line whether they liked it or not and had to represent their people and their people's interests. And they took a lot of flack, but managed to hang in there and continue to be a part of an important push to ensure that we're moving forward rather than sliding backwards.

Jack Ah Kit thought that as well as all these things, humour had got them all through:

Jack: And I think the biggest thing – and the beauty of it all –was our sense of humour. When you get to know them a lot of Aboriginal people will tell you about the sense of humour that we're born with, it's like an Indigenous trait, it's handed on. When you live in an oppressed situation for that long, you don't just develop it, you're born with it and it's handed down as with our spirituality, and that gets us through. Because you can be anywhere in this country or outside this country but as long as you're together and you have an opportunity to sit down and discuss the good things that happened throughout the day and the frustration of the day.

But at the end of the day you start talking about humorous things – whether they happened that day or before or whether you've heard it from somebody else. And we look forward to sitting down and having a yarn and joke, and it's something we can all relate to, and that keeps us going. It really does. And any Aboriginal person in this country who's lost that sense of humour is a person who hasn't got much to live for as far as I'm concerned.

Responding to Jack, Cookie had agreed completely.

Kevin: That's incredibly good how you've put that. It's like Aboriginal culture, everybody has got a place and a job to do. And the Mansells, Foleys, Coes and that… they were seen as the radicals and they were pushed there, and did a fantastic job. And other people who were just as radical moved in a different direction also had a part to play. And I think everybody was given kudos for what they did. And I think it was a very good team effort.

15. International networks

Aboriginal people had been speaking up on the international stage since at least as early as Anthony Martin Fernando had walked the streets of Italy in 1913. He had spoken in Geneva in the 1920s in the first days of the League of Nations and then demonstrated in London in the 1930s against British settler brutality towards Aboriginal people. The forces of Imperial power had of course been very evident to Aboriginal people: they had been appealing to the British monarchy from the earliest days of the British invasion. And when William Cooper had spoken to the press in the 1930s, he had pointed out the parallels which Aboriginal people saw with the theft of the land of Native Americans and with the Nazi racial discrimination faced by the Jews and others in Europe. There had been Aboriginal involvement with left-wing international networks in the 1950s and 1960s: Ray Peckham from north-west New South Wales, for example, had travelled on a Youth Study Tour to the Soviet Union and the first Australian delegations to the People's Republic of China had been the Aboriginal representatives who went there in 1972.[1]

Since that unprecedented trip in 1972, however, although Aboriginal activists had been very aware of Maori activism in New Zealand and the anti-Apartheid struggle in southern Africa, there had been very little travel outside Australia by Aboriginal spokespeople. The co-operative movement at Tranby had continued to host visits from Papua New Guinea and the Pacific Islands like Vanuatu, where the leaders of the Nationalist movement like Walter Lini and Barak Sopé had supported the Tranby co-operative goals. But there had been very few trips overseas by Aboriginal activists which meant there was simply no experience in the major forums of international debate like the United Nations. So the trips made to the Coady International Institute by Tranby student Charles French in 1964, on a Sydney University scholarship and then by Kevin himself in 1979, again through Tranby, were unusual and important sources of information and contacts.

***

The mid 1980s saw a new wave of very targeted Aboriginal interventions into the formal structures of the international community. Kevin Cook was in the centre of this re-emergence of an international voice, although he seldom travelled overseas himself. The push into international representation reflected

---

1 Fiona Paisley 2012, *The Lone Protester. AM Fernando in Australia and Europe,* Aboriginal Studies Press, Canberra; Maria Nugent 2012, '"The queen gave us the land": Aboriginal people, Queen Victoria and historical remembrance', *History Australia,* 9(2): 182-200; Andrew Markus (ed) 1988, *Blood from a Stone: William Cooper and the Australian Aborigines' League,* Allen & Unwin, St Leonards; Goodall 1996, *Invasion to Embassy.*

all three major influences in Kevin's life: his commitment to Aboriginal land rights networks, his union experience and his networks through the national liberation movements' connections to co-operatives.

In retrospect, what is often stressed about this period is the flowering of the links between indigenous groups in many different countries. But we can see from Kevin's involvement that there were at least three different sets of contacts – indigenous organisations, unions and the churches – which all came into play to enable indigenous activism to be heard so strongly.

Memories can help us see even more about the processes. Hearing from Kevin and his activist colleagues we get more of an idea of how it felt to be setting up these links. Firstly, it was a huge learning task for the people who eventually became well known as international representatives of Australian Aboriginal people on the world stage. Secondly, they were often stricken with anxieties and self-doubts, as well as concerns about whether they were really representing the broad collective opinion well. And finally, despite the glamour supposedly attached to overseas trips, it turns out that most Aboriginal activists were reluctant to travel away from home. The imagined 'globetrotting spokesperson' disappears in the details of how these trips were actually accomplished when funds were always short and the reception which Aboriginal people might receive at an overseas forum was not by any means assured.

***

When Kevin returned from Canada, he maintained contact with the many people he had met there from the co-operatives and liberation movements in Latin America, the Philippines, India, South Africa and Zimbabwe. But his energies were focused on putting into practice his ideas about adult education at Tranby and in the community and with the rapidly escalating campaign to achieve land rights in New South Wales. He was working at this local level with old friends like Barbara and Karen Flick and William Bates, under the direction of senior activists Jacko Campbell, Isabel Flick and Tombo Winters. Yet, as the last chapter has shown, not only his work at Tranby but his support for the Aboriginal campaigns in other states, meant that he turned to his role with the Australian Council of Churches to achieve the funds and the networks to deliver that support. The ACC was eager to take an active role in the World Council of Churches meetings and Kevin, as Chair of its Aboriginal Advisory Committee, was one of the people the ACC called on to travel to those meetings. He made some of these early trips with his friend and fellow activist, Barbara Flick, including a trip to London where they connected with the British Land Rights Support group and were able to add to the mounting international pressure on the NSW government to deliver on the land rights promises of its policy.

15. International networks

Figure 15.1: Cookie and Barbara in London.

Courtesy Tranby Archives.

Through the 1970s, the political focus around the world had turned to the concerns of the 'Fourth World', that is the indigenous peoples who were trapped inside nation states, like Native Americans, First Nations Canadians and Indigenous Australians. At the Coady Institute in Canada, Kevin had been very aware of the political movements of indigenous North Americans but he had also been meeting Adivasi from South Asia, a number of indigenous people from the Philippines and from Latin America and as well those from the activist groups in Africa – none of whom were well recognised as indigenous by the better organised movements in the 'First World'.

Only one international body had a legally binding convention of the rights of indigenous peoples – this was the Indigenous and Tribal Populations Convention 107 of the International Labour Organisation (ILO), declared in 1957. The ILO, established in 1926, was a forum for representatives of unions, employers and governments from every member nation. Very aware of the long history of labour exploitation involved in slavery and indenture under colonialism, the ILO assembly had recognised that indigenous people were particularly vulnerable to economic and labour exploitation. Yet while working conditions were the focus of Convention 107, it was related to far wider issues of civil rights and freedoms. Although there was no representative place for indigenous peoples *as* peoples, they were welcomed at the ILO as members of union or other delegations, as long as the formal delegations were prepared to give them some of the representative positions to which they were entitled.

In the early 1980s the ILO begin the process of revising and updating Convention 107. At the same time, the United Nations (UN) – which is a related but quite separate organisation to the ILO – also began to consider a declaration which would recognise the overall rights of indigenous peoples, and attempt to combat discrimination against them. A UN Declaration, however, could not be legally binding in the way that ILO Conventions are. The United Nations could not, by its charter, allow representation of any delegates other than those which represented sovereign nations, so 'Fourth World' Indigenous peoples had no voice there. However, the United Nations took the first steps towards the drafting of a possible Declaration when it set up a 'Working Group on Indigenous Populations'[2] in 1982, to which NGOs and indigenous colonised people could send representatives. This group began active meetings only after 1985, and the Declaration was not voted on until 2007, but it became a continuing focus of attention for indigenous people's movements in many countries.

The ILO process was much more concrete and tightly organised. It had a strict time limit – the new ILO Convention 169 had to be completed to be voted on in mid 1989. As it was also legally binding, it was to become the core of the eventual UN Declaration which added weight to the ILO discussions about how to amend the early convention. The major redrafting work had to done during ILO meetings in 1986 and 1987, but before these occurred, there needed to be extensive meetings with Aboriginal people around the nation so that when the ACTU (Australian Council of Trade Unions) amendments were first taken to the ILO in 1986, they had already been discussed and endorsed by Aboriginal people. So while the UN Working Group on Indigenous Populations continued to draw much attention, it was the 1980s redrafting of the ILO Convention – with its meetings in Australia as well as those at the UN itself – which was critical to the real impact of the much later, non-legally binding UN document.

The role of trade unions was of key importance in the ILO and therefore in the revision of Convention 107 to make it the Indigenous and Tribal People's Convention 169, of 1989. So it was Kevin, with his long established union relationships from his own experience and that of Tranby, who was ideally

---

2   There was a long dispute at both the International Labour Organisation (ILO) and the United Nations (UN) about the use of the term 'populations' rather than 'peoples'. 'Populations' was deemed not to indicate political or cultural cohesiveness in opposition to that claimed by the nation state, whereas 'peoples' was thought to offer some challenge and therefore its use was resisted for decades. Pat Anderson and Kevin both recalled bitterly that they lost that vote both in relation to the new ILO Convention 169, partly due to lack of support by Australian government delegates but also due to anxieties on the part of the African delegations. Today, however, in 2011, both the ILO Convention 169 and the UN Declaration have been amended to use the term 'indigenous peoples' rather than 'populations'.

placed to contribute to the process. He had to organise to inform and then consult with Aboriginal people across the country to develop their preferred amendments to the old Convention 107. He did this with the support of Patty Anderson, an Aboriginal member and employee of the Australian Teachers' Federation (now the Australian Education Union, the AEU) originally from Darwin but based in Melbourne in the early 1980s. Kevin was able to draw on the networks of communication which had been established over the previous four years between members of the Federation of Land Councils and then the National Coalition. Tirelessly circulating drafts and taking endless phone calls, Kevin and Patty talked the Convention clauses over and over with Aboriginal people all round the Coalition network to develop a set of amendments to be finally drafted by Robert Blewer and put to Simon Crean, the ACTU President, for approval before they were taken to be negotiated yet again at the first ILO drafting session in 1986.

Kevin has mainly talked about the experiences he and others had at the ILO sessions, but Pat has described the role she, Kevin and others played in those early, crucial lead up discussions of the amendments in Australia as well as the Geneva sessions.

Figure 15.2: With the Victorian Teachers Federation, showing Patty on left, next to Kevin Tory (representing TUCAR).

Courtesy Kevin Cook family collection.

Patty Anderson: So the first time I met Cookie was when he was going to go with Robert Blewer to the International Labour Organisation in Geneva, where they were amending that extraordinary convention, the 107, and now it's become 169. It was an extraordinary convention, because it was really to do with human rights. I would say the backbone of the ILO convention is a human rights issue. It wasn't about freedom of association, like conventions to protect trade unionism. There wasn't anything around in 1957, when they put that convention on the books. The ILO thought that that would be good to have an international convention about indigenous rights, and it was the very first one. And it's stayed on the books all those years. So I think that was about 1984 when I met Cookie.

They decided it would be a three-year process before it got amended. And the ACTU were going to be involved, and so Simon Crean asked Robert Blewer from the Teachers' Union to go as a delegate in his place. So it was just Cookie and Robert Blewer that year.

It was before the heavies like Simon went because all the work had been done in the first part of that three-year period.

Now the ones who went to the ILO had to be from three groups: the government, the union and the industries. All the amendments that got put up were the ACTU amendments and they came out of all that hard work done here in Australia. Blewer and Cookie had been negotiators and they were very good. They talked to the Coalition of Aboriginal Organisations. I sent out all the stuff to everybody on it so we could have meetings. We had a big meeting of the Coalition at the ACTU – we were all there – and Simon Crean was up one end and all of us from the Coalition down around it.

The ACTU were very good over that three year period, particularly that first year. Robert Blewer really did an excellent job with Cookie, they did all that work for Simon Crean. It worked so well because it was through Cookie, with all Cookie's contacts and with me sending it all out and making sure everyone saw it, and the meetings and co-ordinating everything. So Cookie and Robert started it all off.

One of the things was trying to change the words 'indigenous populations' to 'indigenous peoples'. We argued for three whole weeks for that. So that was really important, I think. That was some of the work that had to be done, and then Robert Blewer did the drafting.

Then Robert and Cookie went over there, from the ACTU. Now the following year, the ACTU rep was Terry O'Shane and I went too to make up the numbers. But I'd won an overseas study award year from the old Commonwealth Education, so I worked in Geneva for three months, which was really interesting for me because I was able to find out how all of that worked.

At the same time, I was there for the Coalition, for the three weeks of that second year of getting that new Convention up. So there was myself, Geoff Clarke and Terry O'Shane from the Coalition. Also we were able to influence the industry representation, from the Employers Association. So they sent an Aboriginal bloke there too! He was a bloke from the Northern Territory, Margot Weir's nephew. I think that would've been the first year we had Aboriginal people with the union delegation and with the employers. Not with the government of course, but that was interesting as well.

But they had already got through a lot of work in the meetings with the Coalition of Aboriginal Organisations and it was Cookie's direction and guidance that made all of that happen. So that was an important little timeslot there, with the formation of the Coalition and the work with the ACTU, specially in amending that Convention 107 to Convention 169 at the ILO.

When I was at the Teachers' Federation in Melbourne, I had lot of do with Cookie specifically, but not so much with Tranby. I would come as a visitor from time to time, and knew what was happening at Tranby. But it was mainly that political stuff. Cookie was really supportive and important to me, because I would ring him up and say, 'This is what's happening'. He'd give advice and direction and guidance, but what's good about Cookie is that he would never tell you what to do. He'd say: 'Well, there's this and there's that'. He never said: 'I think you should do X or Y'.

Then he'd leave it up to you to make your choices, make your own mistakes and doing your own learning. But his advice was always quality! That was because he knew the trade union movement really well. Although I'd been a unionist all my life, I'd never really worked in that arena before, so it was really useful to have that bit of guidance and direction. I'd ring up and he'd say: 'Yeah, well, you know he's from the Right…' or this or that. I was always really grateful for that direction and advice.

Characteristically, Kevin ensured that the chance to get to Geneva in 1985 was shared around. He hoped to be travelling to the ILO meeting for the ACTU with Robert Blewer, the Teachers' Federation representative, but he encouraged the NSW Aboriginal Land Council to fund representatives from regional land councils, William Bates and Norma Walford from far western NSW and Delia Lowe from Roseby Park to be NGO observers at the meeting of the UN Working Party on Indigenous People, during the discussions on a future Declaration of Indigenous Rights. But while their fares were secured, Kevin's was still in doubt. When he and Judy Chester drove the Land Council representatives to their plane – the first trip overseas for any of them – none of them knew whether he might be there as well. After they had left, the news came through that Kevin was on the next flight. As William, Norma and Delia left their Geneva hotel in a day or two, the first sight they had was of Kevin was as he sailed past in a Mercedes with the Teachers' Federation representative. They hadn't realised by then that all the Geneva taxis are Mercedes vehicles. Kevin hugely enjoyed watching their shock. He shared his time between contributing to the ILO sessions, sitting in with the NGO team at the UN, talking strategy and sharing the sights of Geneva as they made their way around the tiny city.

Figure 15.3: The International Labour Organisation foyer – Cookie with Norma Walford, Delia Lowe and William Bates.

Courtesy Kevin Cook family collection.

Figure 15.4: ILO meeting – Cookie and Robert Blewer at the 'Unions' table.

Courtesy Kevin Cook family collection.

15. International networks

Figure 15.5: ILO meeting – Cookie talking with Simpson, Delia, Norma.

Courtesy Kevin Cook family collection.

Figure 15.6: ILO meeting – William foregrounded in NGO group.

Courtesy Kevin Cook family collection.

Kevin was intensely frustrated at the disinterest of the Australian government delegation, whom he felt were not taking the amendment process seriously. But he found the potential to talk with other unionists and the representatives of Indigenous people in or around the ILO extremely valuable. He was also alert to how challenging the session environment was in demanding strong speaking skills and intensive negotiation around the actual sessions. The experience made him feel that the people to represent the Coalition at the next meeting had to be able to speak formally from the floor as well as carry on the tough negotiations behind the scenes which would be needed in the second and third years to get the Aboriginal position up at the vote in 1989. There were people in the Federation and Coalition whom he thought could do it, even though they were at that stage unfamiliar with these international arenas.

Kevin: When you have a look at all the names of the people that were mixed up with the Federation and the Coalition, I reckon they're probably our best orators.

Kevin came back to Australia to continue the consultations through the Coalition, but he started straight away to recruit the people he thought would benefit from the experience and be able to meet the challenges of that gruelling and very public stage.

One of the people Kevin believed combined the trade union knowledge and the capacity to speak well with the grit to hold his ground on principle was Terry O'Shane, who takes up the story:

Terry O'Shane: Yeah, the ILO was doing a review of Convention 107, which dealt specifically with the conditions of indigenous peoples. And there'd been representation at UN and other forums by Aboriginal people in Australia but there was never a coordinator or anything. So Cookie rang up and said, 'Oh mate, you're on your way to Geneva. You're going to have to go to the ILO'. I said, 'Oh, Jeeze!'

So I got over there and I got in because I was associated with the Maritime and Seamen's Union in those days – the Maritime Union of Australia today. I knew Simon Crean, of course, who was the president of the ACTU then. And his policy adviser Mike Macleod was there. So I actually went and sat in there with Mike Macleod as an official delegate, representing the ACTU as an Indigenous person.

We were there for three weeks, four weeks. What you've got to understand is that the ILO was made up of governments, employers, and trade unions. And there was no NGO status for anybody. If you were someone outside those three areas, they weren't allowed in. It was a couple of days after we were there and started discussions, that there were these women from Bolivia who were held out. They weren't registered as delegates, but there was no women from Bolivia in the conference. And the men from official delegations from Bolivia had gone and told the chairman of the ILO session that the women shouldn't be allowed to attend because they weren't official delegates. So I just took my union delegate badge off and gave it to her and said, 'Well, you're now a delegate from Australia. You're welcome to attend. They can't keep me out!'

And that was just the way it went. Because of how we operated here in Australia, we tried to become all-inclusive. We weren't going to then go to an international forum and be restrictive in terms of our participation. If we could assist any group, then we would. And as Cookie said, it was then that people we'd met at the ILO wanted to come to Australia and get to identify who this Coalition was who'd been standing up for them. And of course, out of that, you've had numerous delegations come over here and go through to Tranby and say g'day!

So after that, we went to the President of the ILO – we organised a delegation, half a dozen of us – and let him know that we were unhappy that while this international forum was discussing a convention that dealt with indigenous peoples, when in actual fact there was no indigenous peoples sitting in the conference, in the UN, and having a say or having an input into the discussions. And so the ILO couldn't actually take it on board. Though we were there, it was because we were actually representing the union movement. We weren't representing indigenous peoples as such – even though we were!

So we got him to agree to give indigenous peoples a time allocation after every day of an hour – I think it was half an hour originally. So he'd formally close the session at five o'clock religiously, even if we were going to progress on that evening. Then he'd ask everyone to stay. And then he'd allow indigenous peoples to speak, just from the collection of people there. There was a group of them – 15 or 20 from around the world – he just allowed them to get up and do a presentation about the issues that they heard being discussed during the day and give their opinion about it. That had a big impact on how things went.

In the end, at the end of the two-year process, indigenous peoples were not happy about all of it. But I thought that we had made a great advantage.

The fact remains this: that we went there. We participated. And we made changes!

And we made changes to a convention that had been in place for 20-odd years or 30 years. And not only did we made changes – I thought they were positive changes! And then it actually made it very difficult for the UN in their Declaration of the Rights of Indigenous Peoples to have a lesser condition than the new ILO Convention 169, because they were part of the international conditions.

But maybe even more important was it brought indigenous peoples into a forum for the first time, where we'd have been excluded for all the time that it had taken place in the past. So for the very first time we were able to put a challenge to it — and it was successful! We had been successful and we had brought indigenous people into that forum and were being able to express our opinion freely on the floor.

So enormous changes happened, but it happened because of a reason. It happened because there was discipline in the ranks, amongst ourselves. We caucused before we went. And basically, the rules of engagement were laid down for us, *by* us. We were going there to do a job, and we needed to do it and participate. And, yeah, – you use your footwork when you get there, and use a bit of commonsense, and we'll make some progress. And that's what we did!

Kevin's confidence in Terry O'Shane was more than fulfilled and he found the other people he encouraged to travel to these meetings were just as impressive. He was able to see them in action at one of the next meetings, when Kevin was also in Europe for a World Council of Churches meeting and he talked about what he saw.

Kevin: You'd just marvel at people's skills level when they went over there. I went over there once to the ILO, and to me that whole experience was mind-blowing. After that, Clarkie and O'Shane were the two mainstays. I went over with World Council of Churches later and there was an ILO meeting going on. So I got to look at Clarkie and O'Shane – they were really incredibly good!

I could see how they manoeuvred – they used it like a trade union meeting! And they not only used that for us but to involve all the indigenous peoples. They did everything from knowing very little about the protocol at first – they had to learn very quick, very quick! And they ended up being able to get up and talk at that level. They'd be up to two and three in the morning trying to scribble down notes for speeches. But it's very daunting, because when you do get up to speak, you're looking up and people are looking at you. There's 30 to 40 interpreters interpreting, and the Aboriginal delegates would be on their feet there, they'd have to think on their feet all the time.

There were some indigenous people there, like the Native Americans, who had the resources that a small country would have, while our mob didn't have much at all. Then you get people who are worse off than us – who didn't understand one thing about the mechanism of how the things worked or even how to get into the session room. And they were lost. I could understand them. I was one of them. But it was just cruel to see them over there and to see what they were trying to do. Some of them were getting shot because they were protesting about the army putting roads through their country. They were getting shot out of the trees!

Clarkie and O'Shane took away the myths. There was still the protocol there but they were doing things that nobody else had ever done before, and it was just incredible. I always found it amazing to hear about. After they came back from Geneva, I made sure I never missed a meeting cause I'd just hang onto every word!

Going over there was a hard thing to ask people to do. There were a lot of funny stories but there were a lot of serious things going on. And people were just not used to other countries. I can remember people going over to Geneva and I'd get a phone call about three o'clock in the morning. I pick up the phone and it's a reverse charges call. The operator wanted to know: 'Will you pay for this?' And then when they got on, I'd hear: 'I'm lonely!' And I could hear the country and western music playing in the background. 'I feel like coming home.' I'd be saying: 'Please don't do that. You've only got two more days to go'.

And when you're overseas you often think you're not doing a good job. You ask yourself: 'Will I go again?' or 'I don't think we gained any ground'. Everyone tosses those ideas around. But you have to keep at it. You're not going to take a great chunk out of the wall. You might just knock on a door. But you have to be there. And I believe you have to have some continuity – that's what I used to say to O'Shane: 'Terry you'll have to go again'. He'd say: 'I don't want to go'. He used to yell at me! 'I don't want to go!' … But you know, he loved it.

I think the trade union experience was a big help to all of us. See, if you had to do something, you needed all the troops to be behind you. And really what had happened, nine out of every ten times, was that the Coalition had made a decision. It was really healthy that way, too. Because we would have already gone through the arguments to and from and we'd have come to an agreement, then we'd go with that. You'd hear things from Geneva the next day, about what was happening over there. People would ring up and say, 'Look this is what we've done!' And it'd be fantastic, you know? And when they came back, you'd say, 'How did it go?' And they'd always say 'Oh yeah, WE did this and this and this'. You know 'WE can …'. It was never 'I did this' or 'I did that'.

We happened to get this into place and next time anybody goes over, it makes it a lot easier for them. And not only for us, but for any Indigenous people going across there! Like that woman from South America. O'Shane just said to her: 'You take mine in! Now you're a delegate'. They really *were* with us – and so in they went!

Terry O'Shane also believed the union movement had given people like Kevin and himself valuable experience, but he thought there were deeper reasons.

Terry O'Shane: That was never luck. I gotta say this. Cookie, because of his background in trade unions, he knew very clearly the need to forge international links. It was exactly the same rule he applied to having us address the process of reconciliation. Or have Australia address the issues of social justice for Indigenous peoples. We needed to forge those links with the broader community. It was important for us. If they were coming to Australia they needed to talk to us. Cookie forged links so that at the end of the day, when they did visit, the first place they visited actually was Tranby College. Now that wasn't by luck they turned up at Tranby College. If you just took some luck, you'd end up in Kings Cross, or you'd end up in Woolloomooloo! It wasn't luck. It was that someone – Cookie – had an understanding that that was needed to happen, what was going to develop an awareness, not just within the domestic community, but in the international community. And so it was because of that, that we had those links. The trade union movement has been important. But at the end of the day, we take on a responsibility. At the age of maturity, whether it's 18, or whether it's 28 or whether it's 38. And Cookie has taken on that responsibility and he's given that thing direction. That's what's happened. Not for himself, but for all of us.

Kevin drew in a number of people to take the long trip to Geneva. One of the those he recruited was a young woman from Arnhem Land, Jacqui Katona, who like Karen Flick was just finding her way in political life, coming to Tranby as much a student as an interested worker and contributor. Kevin encouraged her to go to one of the UN meetings of the Working Group and saw her confidence and experience blossom. She was to come back to Australia and play a major role in the organisation of later political campaigns and then to become the national and international spokesperson for her community in their battles against uranium mining on their land at Kakadu.

Another of the people on whom Kevin leaned hard to attend meetings was Jack Ah Kit, who began to take on the travel to Geneva late in the 1980s, after the new ILO Convention 169 had been accepted and the focus had shifted onto the UN. By this time, those who had been involved with the ILO over the past five years had a fund of experience which they could pass on. Jack remembers it this way:

Jack Ah Kit: Cookie was the one who dobbed us in for a lot of this travelling – he was the mastermind. He'd just sit there – and I'd sometimes wonder if he had a little bit of a draughts board there. On one side he had – Patrick Dodson here, Ah Kit up there, Rossie in Alice, Bob Weatherall there, Terry O'Shane up there. And then he had this other side, with a map with international meetings and so forth …And he played draughts with us! He'd tell you what he wanted you to do and where you had to go and, when you said you didn't want to go, he'd say 'Don't fuck around, you've got to go'. And you'd be left saying, 'Oh gee, hang on Cookie'. He'd say he was just delegating, but you can't delegate if you're not the mastermind.

He never moved too far out of Glebe, out of Tranby, he was always hovering around that area. But he had all the contacts and he was genuine in wanting to see Indigenous people in this country united. Because if we weren't united we would be perceived by indigenous communities outside of Australia as a fragmented group of people who didn't really know what they were on about. So Cookie was the organiser. He was the bloke put it all together. He organised people to go and he had all the contacts. That's the role he played, and he played it really well.

There's no doubt in my mind that he sat and he looked and he watched and he started to pull it all together. And that is a credit to him and to Tranby and to Judy Chester! Because somebody had to pull it together. Somebody had to get it organised. There wasn't a lot of concentration on the big picture in the international arena. And this bloke was the one that had all the knowledge and experience.

When people came to Australia they came in through Sydney and it was through Tranby and his connections with the Labor Party, through his connections previously with the Builders Labourers' Federation that it's all happened. He used to say it was just because we wanted to go overseas!

But we all used to buy him a beer to fuckin' *not* go overseas!

Jack continued: What was very important in those early days was that the Indigenous representation from Australia at the UN was really astounding. I'm thinking of Cookie, Geoff Clarke, Terry O'Shane, Mick Mansell, Josie Crawshaw, Pat Dodson, Helen Corbett, Marcia Langton and there were others – they were all very important in ensuring that we had a place at the UN, we had an opportunity to contribute and participate. I went across in '91 with the experienced Indigenous representatives. I saw them hold the floor of the convention for an hour and a half – almost two hours. They had orchestrated a situation where Indigenous peoples were on the agenda one after the other, so they had the then Aboriginal Affairs Minister, Robert Tickner, confronted with these Indigenous people all dobbing in the Australian Government, saying how bad they were treating the Aboriginal people. It was basically having the Aboriginal Coalition, the Federation, the land council and others all putting their case. And they participated in the UN working group – to understand the processes of the UN and to respect the protocol just amazed me! And they got so much respect from other indigenous representatives, like the Ainu people I knew from Japan.

There was no doubt in my mind that the Indigenous delegation from Australia were the cheeky mob. They took it up to their governments and they couldn't give a damn! It wasn't a case of us just saying: 'Let's go over there to embarrass them'. It was to highlight the problems that were happening back home. And I think that the Coalition and the Federation in the early days played an important role in that.

A lot of those delegations and a lot of the people who went overseas in the '70s and '80s, they didn't know what they were going into. They had an idea, but they were prepared to put themselves on the line for the struggle. And that was something that made me very proud of them. Because it was like me when I came onto the scene in the early '80s as someone wanting to learn. So I admire the way people learned about what they needed to do … and a lot of us had no understanding of how important it was to let people know in the international community what the situation was like back home.

For a lot of people going over that far was a really big thing. And if you went over by yourself it would kill you. There's nothing worse than that feeling in your body and in your mind and your heart than flying out over Darwin at 36,000 feet and looking down and seeing just on dusk the lights of Darwin, the Melville and Bathurst Islands, and not knowing where you're going to end up, how long you're going for you do know, and wondering whether you're going to come back… your spirit is in chaos.

I often had a little giggle there… Like when I gave Bob Weatherall and Clarkie a big feed in Darwin one time and they were ready to take off. Bob turned around to Clarkie and said: 'This plane we're on tomorrow to Indonesia, do we have to wear parachutes again?' Apart from the funny side of it, that was one of the serious things. They hadn't thought about that: 'If we die, we die, but will they bring us back here to bury us?'

It's a really frightening thing. The people who have been overseas, our ambassadors, it must have crossed their minds: 'Goodness if anything happens to me over here, if I get ill or get hit by a truck my body has got to get home. I've got to be buried back in Australia, where I come from.' It's adventurous… 80 per cent of you is thinking how exciting it is to be on a jumbo jet but when you look down you start to wonder… and you start to run into foreign places where in most cases people are friendly and in some other cases not so friendly. It really is a cultural shock.

That feeling of not knowing if you were doing any good was really just like the work here. The Aboriginal political push, the Indigenous political push in the 1980s that came out of the Federation. It was inspirational but it was also like you were sitting in the corner with the Dunce cap on. You didn't know if you were going anywhere. You didn't know what you were doing – whether it was going to win you any Brownie points anyway.

But we sat there and we persisted. We didn't realise the strength that we had as individual representatives, representing a region of peoples with thousands of constituents. Until we started to realise what power and responsibilities we really had, then we started to play ball and get the show on the road. We were a group of Aboriginal leaders who were wondering how the hell do we stem the tide? How do we turn it back around? Given these arses who'd kicked us around for so long. How did we get on the front foot?

There were some tensions which developed in the broader Aboriginal community around the frequency with which some people travelled and also about the boys-club atmosphere among the group of men who had become such close friends through the Federation and Coalition days. As Jack Ah Kit saw it, the deep personal friendships were important to sustain people in the high pressure environments of the big international meetings.

Jack Ah Kit: I think it was a situation where… not excluding the ladies, but it was a brotherhood. It was a feeling of very strong camaraderie. We all knew where we were coming from. We all knew the stories and the situation and the struggle. The stories that went out with our representatives were common stories. There was no bullshit about it being worse in Victoria than what it was in Western Australia. Everyone knew what the message was that had to be passed on to anywhere we went around the world.

That's one of the reasons why it seemed like we were an exclusive old boys club or something, but it wasn't. It was never intended to be. I mean, there were strong Aboriginal women who spoke up and later on started to come on these delegations – Josie Crawshaw, Helen Corbett, Marcia Langton in the early days and a few others. It was about them finding the time to participate and go off onto these trips. But I think with us blokes anyway, it really formed us up into a bunch of brothers. I think I'm right in saying this, but I can ring just about anyone of the Aboriginal leaders around the country who were involved back in the '70s to '80s and even still involved, if so, to a lesser extent. I can track them down and be able to talk to them, and I think that's something I'm proud of.

But Geneva was a good place to be getting to know people from other countries too. That was the other thing that I thought was really important – political people who were just coming in to make contacts – like Ron Layman and others from the Canadian Indian territories. We'd made the contacts at the UN and then we started to get invitations to go here and there, and participate a lot more. It was always reciprocal, and we encouraged them as much as we could to come into Australia.

***

Meeting new people who shared ideals and experiences was an important part of the travel to Geneva for everyone. Tranby was able to be a doorway into the Indigenous networks in all states of Australia through Kevin's role in the Federation and the Coalition. Jack Ah Kit has talked about the way he could direct people to Tranby so they would have an orientation and then from there he knew that Cookie would be able to direct them to the Kimberley or Queensland or Tasmania, wherever their interests seemed to lie. This added to the networks which were operating already, as discussed in earlier chapters, from the old Co-operatives network, from Kevin's time at the Coady Institute and then later with the Australian Council of Churches. For Jack and others it meant they had somewhere to invite people to come, and for Australian activists like Karen Flick, it meant that Tranby opened up a doorway in the opposite direction, to a whole world of activist and indigenous contacts.

Kevin has explained the way he saw the importance of Tranby in this process of interchange:

Kevin: Tranby had a really good reputation so you got a very good reputation. Anybody who was anybody used to come and stay at Tranby if they were passing through Sydney – they'd always call in, come and have a cup of coffee and a talk. It was a neutral place. And it was really good.

***

But the doorway worked the other way too. Karen Flick has talked about how she saw Tranby as a place to meet and learn about international agendas as well as very local ones:

Karen: I got involved at Tranby once the land rights campaigns were underway, and I came down to Sydney with my baby and worked there for a year. That was good because Tranby has always been more than just a meeting place. It was a place that allowed ideas to grow and develop. It allowed people to say whatever they wanted to say, supported a whole lot of people who would not have access to any other forum. And also it opened us up to meeting a whole range of people, not just from other countries, but from other struggles.

Being at Tranby and working with Cookie meant you were getting your strength from people like that, but also knowing that we played a role – just that little bit – in the support stuff. We could play a role through them connecting them to resources and getting their message out.

For me, Tranby allowed me to meet the Maoris and the mob from Vanuatu, from the Philippines and from Kanaky, in fact the whole South Pacific and then Asia. And of course there was a long term connection with Africa through Tranby too. It meant I got to meet people like Eddie Funde and people who were working here locally, but then, people who'd come and visit – you know Oliver Tambo came to Tranby and Bishop Tutu came to Tranby. And then I had the opportunity to meet Nelson Mandela because Cookie gave me his ticket. It was just amazing, I think I cried the whole time I was talking to him and I didn't say an awful lot.

Bringing international politics back home

Like Karen's story, the international work was connected with the local work for Kevin and all of the people he was working with. Jack Ah Kit has talked about how the ideas about developing an international campaign became more important to the regional land council activists as a means of adding pressure for change at home.

Jack: Another angle was coming at it from the international arena with a representation over there. It was working in tandem. And governments were feeling the pressure, and they will continue to feel the pressure because they haven't been able to understand yet that Aboriginal people are not going to go away, they're not going to stop trying to educate all levels of government and the people in this country that there's a few wrongs that have gone on in this country that have to be rights. And when you stop bull-shitting around and seriously start addressing these concerns that we may end up being a very proud nation that can stand up in the international community's eyes and be accepted as a nation that will be seen as doing things for the Indigenous people and non-Indigenous people that we can all be proud of. And that's not happening at the moment.

PART 5
BRINGING IT ALL TOGETHER

16. Bicentennial

We turned it around, so as it wasn't 'them and us.' We said, 'YOU are doing that but what WE are doing – despite everything that's happened to us – WE are still here.'

I remember that it was a conscious decision not to make it just a protest, but rather to make it a celebration of who WE are, and that we're HERE.

Patty Anderson, Director, Medical Service, Darwin

Getting ready

In 1938, William Cooper had thrown down a challenge. It was 150 years since the landing of the ragtag British 'first fleet' in Sydney Cove on 26 January in 1788. As white Australians were preparing to celebrate, Cooper had branded that landing as the beginning of 150 years of invasion, dispossession and exploitation. Cooper dared white Australia to recognise that their 'Australia Day' was no celebration but instead a 'Day of Mourning' for invaded Australia.

Over the decades since 1938, Aboriginal Australia had echoed that challenge, using 26 January to mourn their losses and marking the landing of Captain Cook in Botany Bay in 1770 with the laying of wreaths at La Perouse. So by the mid 1980s, after the Hawke Government's betrayal on national land rights there was a determination to make 1988, the Bicentennial of the British invasion, into an event which would drive home the recognition of Aboriginal Australia which Cooper had demanded.

The Australian Government had established the Australian Bicentennial Authority (ABA) in 1980 to prepare for what was expected to be a year-long celebration of the nation's unity. The Liberal Party Prime Minister Fraser was aware that this had to be a very different view of 'the nation' than in 1938. Even a conservative leader like Fraser could see that the Bicentennial had to recognise the presence and contribution of Aboriginal Australians. But he was clearly expecting this would all be wrapped up in glowing praise for a unified nation.

A Labor government was elected in 1983 and after some ambivalence it redefined the Bicentennial to be an inclusive working people's celebration. Yet before long, as earlier chapters have traced, the Labor Party had betrayed its promise of full national land rights and had retreated so far that it seemed about to destroy the Northern Territory Land Rights Act.

So Aboriginal people were just as angry as William Cooper had been when the ABA announced in 1986, that its goal was:

> to commemorate the 200th anniversary of permanent European settlement in Australia ... The 1988 program offers Australians the opportunity to contribute effectively to their own national celebrations and to use the year to extend their range of ideas and experience about what it is to be Australian. The Bicentenary will encourage Australians to develop a unity and common purpose as a nation. It provides an ideal opportunity to focus worldwide attention on Australia in tourist, economic, social and cultural terms.[1]

The world's media would turn its attention onto Australia and onto Sydney for that Bicentennial. This offered an opportunity that was too important to lose.

As early as 1986, Aboriginal people – including those involved with the Federation of Land Councils and the National Coalition – were considering how to mark the Bicentennial. The burning issues were already taking them to the international forums of the world to be heard. How were they going to make white Australia listen?

As David Ross has pointed out (Chapter 14) the big demonstrations in the previous ten years had brought people from across Australia. These had all offered models for how Aboriginal people could take action: the Commonwealth Games in Brisbane in 1982, then the Canberra demonstrations in 1985 in protest at the betrayal of national land rights. So it was not surprising that the idea that eventually caught on drew its inspiration from those powerful events. This was to organise a gathering of Aboriginal people from all over Australia – and this time to focus it on the place where the British had first begun their invasion: Sydney.

The Bicentennial Long March idea was raised first by Reverend Charles Harris. He was President of the Aboriginal and Islander Christian Congress, a body in 'covenant' or partnership with the Uniting Church in which Harris was a minister. The challenge was how to deal with the enormous distances between Australian places as well as between its communities.

Patrick Dodson, living in Alice Springs where the Uniting Church had a strong following, has warmly remembered the conversations with the Rev Harris – although Patrick joked about the details of the strategy:

---

1 Australian Bureau of Statistics, *Year Book 1986*, <http://www.abs.gov.au/ausstats/abs@.nsf/featurearticles bytitle/46EAD83E7FF09E21CA2569DE001FB2DF?OpenDocument> accessed 10 January 2013.

Patrick Dodson: Charlie Harris, the minister, wanted the great march, from Uluru to Sydney. He was a good man, Charlie. He had no concept of where the money was going to come from but he had his heart very much in the right place. He had a vision.

But he didn't have any idea of the distance!

Now we weren't walking from here, I'll give you the drum!

No-one was going to *march*! We said, 'Lets get on a truck! We're coming *down* here, but we're not going to march, no way in the world'.

What was needed was confidence that things in Sydney would be arranged – and more importantly, that the many people coming from other places would be welcomed. This was made possible by the networks already set up through the Federation of Land Councils and through Kevin's role at Tranby. Patrick had earlier explained that the Federation contacts had opened the way to feel comfortable about coming to Sydney, opening a path in protocol so that people felt welcomed. He explained the decisions to come to Sydney for the Bicentennial demonstration in the same terms.

Patrick: You don't do things unless you have trust in the people who are asking you to do something or that you believe you have a sense of obligation to them, and then you'll do it. Or you'll approach them first and say: 'Do you want a hand? What's going on? Can we do something?'

But you won't do that unless you have some sense of it and unless the interaction is there. We thought: 'Ring up Tranby, find Cookie!' or if we needed to talk to trade unions, 'Ring Tranby, Ring Cookie!'

We were coming down to see Cookie. We'd have found Cookie if he was on the other side of the world, but all the same, we weren't *walking* for it!...

So it really was a significant link. And then when we came here in '88, when all the mob came in and you guys had got the market gardeners and whoever else to put a feed together for everyone and got the hostels. And then the convoys rocked in with Rossie and all this other mob from the Territory – again making sure the people were looked after properly in that situation. So they had the confidence that the welcome was going to happening, and that wouldn't have been there, if it hadn't been preceded by these earlier encounters. There's no way in the world you would've got the mob coming together under any other sort of arrangement, they'd feel very uneasy about it.

***

Kevin explained how he had became involved in the campaign after Charles Harris' suggestion that the churches could assist with the funding.

Kevin: We got onto the Long March committee because we were with the Australian Council of Churches. Charles Harris just said: 'God will provide'!

Anne Patel Grey from the Australian Council of Churches was there, and Australia-wide networks of the ACC were critical to the success of the campaign. Some of the campaign was run through Tranby and Kevin Tory and Judy [Chester] had a lot to do with that. There was the Uniting Church as well.

There was quite a lot of people situated all over Australia, in Queensland, there were little bodies in each state, all organising... People wouldn't have been fed without them! People wouldn't have been housed without them! Especially people in South Australia. They made the T-shirts up and they were a very good source for fundraising. Those people came through some of the church groups down there.

Then you had people from the NT, like the local land councils. All we did was say: 'Look this is happening, are you coming?' We got money for some people to come down. We had money to get people to go back. (We paid some people three times to go back! That was really funny.)

There was a lot of negotiations to give people the confidence to know they could come and that they would be welcomed. That there'd be a network to support everyone.

The whole campaign was run like a military operation. We were in constant contact with the mob in South Australia who were in contact with the NT organisers, figuring out travel stops, food and petrol costs along the way. The organisational skills were phenomenal!

You'd get a telephone call from the people in South Australia – and they were saying: 'Look we want to do this' – say it was making T-shirts. So we were saying: 'Oh well, do it! And send the T-shirts up here when you're finished making them!' They did the design with all the footprints – but they designed it first without Tasmania on it!

Well, we said 'You'd better not do that or Mansell'll get the shits. He won't come!' So then they just designed them again!

And so when they said, 'We've got places for people to stay', we reckoned it was fantastic! ... So everyone had a role to play – everyone communicated to make sure it all worked out!

So I reckon with the '88 thing, once it got momentum nothing would've stopped it.

By 1987, Patty Anderson, who had worked with Kevin on the International Labour Organisation motions when she was with the Victorian Teachers' Federation, had returned to her home in Darwin to take up the position of director of Danila Dilba, the Aboriginal Medical Service. She remembers how the early discussions about the Bicentennial flowed through Tranby where Kevin developed a hub for information passing in all directions.

Patty Anderson: Now '88 was pretty important. That's not going to come again in such a spectacular way. And that was Cookie's idea to have Tranby work that way …Cardinal Cookie, with the World Council of Churches. He was sort of guiding all those people as well.

Paul Torzillo, Tranby Board member and activist in the NSW movement, pointed out that the national and cross-cultural networks of communication which Kevin held together in the Bicentennial organising worked in the same way as the links between regional Aboriginal communities had worked earlier during the NSW land rights campaigns.

Paul Torzillo: That need for someone who was providing the communication and the importance of trusting in someone who is doing it… that's exactly the process that happened in the '70s with making the land rights movement here into something that was state-wide as opposed to little groups.

The key thing was linking the South Coast mob of Jacko Campbell, Mervyn Penrith and those people with what was happening out west.

The key meeting was at Angledool, out of Walgett when all those north-western people were there. Mervyn did the same thing as he did getting up to Alice Springs, broke down six times on the way, but he got them all to Angledool, right up in the north-west. And that's where those South Coast mob could meet up with all those north-western people, where Tombo Winters had basically organised everyone to get there and pulled all the people who were blueing into shape. Then he and Joe Flick basically held those people together.

And the only reason they were able to do that and to have that meeting is that Cookie was there in the middle. So Jacko and Mervyn were talking to Cookie. And then Tombo and those people were talking to Cookie, and that was exactly what happened. So it was a sort of rehearsal of what was going to happen a few years later in 1988 – absolutely, no doubt about that. The meeting in Angledool was just like that. If Cookie hadn't been there then I don't think anyone would've ended up talking to each other.

Kevin Tory was involved in both the Federation/Coalition meetings and in mobilising the extensive network now operating out of the Trade Union Committee on Aboriginal Rights which Cookie had set up in 1977. Tory took part in many of the early discussions at a number of Aboriginal events to try to hammer out what strategies would be best for the Bicentennial. As he remembers those discussions.

Kevin Tory: For the first time it brought a lot of different Aboriginal and Torres Strait Islander people together, that had really different points of views and I think that was really important. And I think people didn't think we could get it together. And then we did! We did organise the caravans, as we called them, coming down from the west and the north and the Top End. And when they eventually got in to Sydney and La Perouse, we had those big containers, refrigerated containers, we got donations of food from the fruitos, the bakers, we had everything, we had cooking teams out there. We had the lot!

The unions had been mobilised through TUCAR: news would flow through TUCAR union representatives and contacts, then into the newsletters and job site meetings of each of the member unions. So the networks were already there and word flowed back and forth, with Cookie and Tory both speaking on jobs and delegates' meetings so that the word got round and donations flowed back in. Badges, T-shirts and posters all blossomed in the process.

Yet while some networks were long established, there were others which were created in the process of organising for the Bicentennial protest. One example was *Migrants for Aboriginal Rights*, which drew together both individuals and organisations in the union and the immigrant arenas to engage them with Aboriginal activists and with each other in new ways.

As *Kevin* has recalled it: The people who helped organise the '88 March were the migrant communities… you know, they had that night where there was 23 different nationalities, they put on a show to raise money for us. Twenty-three different nationalities! I reckon that was incredible.

I've always said that in the metropolitan area there's a lot of support if we tap into it properly. And we have to do a lot of work, which we have over the years, it hasn't been white people going out and doing the work for us, we've gone out, we've talked to people, we've introduced them to the Aboriginal way, and they've come along. And you know like, I've still got friends from that era, from '88. It's years now – and we still talk about 'the march', still talk about how they helped organise it. And it was a really good thing to be able to do that. To be able to give them the responsibility of being part of the '88 March. It's just incredible.

Kevin had continued to be in close contact with his old Builders Labourers mates like Joe Owens and Roy Bishop. But he had made other new friends through the unions, like his meeting early in 1979, before he went to Canada, with Serge Sereno, in the Federated Engine Drivers and Firemen's Association, whom Cookie had met at a workshop run by TUTA, the Trades Union Training Authority. Serge was often at Tranby in the years afterwards – not only contributing to the teaching program about trade unions and labour economics but also lending his ute when Cookie needed it for Tranby business. It had been Serge who had introduced Kevin to Frank Panucci, another Italian. Frank was a member of the activist organisation FILEF,[2] which had been founded on the principle that immigrants should be contributing to building social justice in their new countries. Between them, Serge and Frank had supported Cookie in strengthening the Aboriginal voice in Leichhardt Council (Chapter 8). So they were both on hand to offer support and extend the debates about Aboriginal rights in the Bicentennial into migrant communities.

In the early discussions, when it was still unclear what form the protesting Aboriginal voice at the Bicentennial would take, there were heavy pressures exerted by government on immigrant organisations like FILEF to contribute to the Bicentennial celebrations to demonstrate successful integration of 'new' Australians into the nation being celebrated. There was just as much pressure on high profile Aboriginal personalities, like Ernie Dingo, as the Bicentennial Authority strove to make it clear that the celebrating nation welcomed cultural and ethnic diversity. Yet as Aboriginal people were already pointing out in the bitter aftermath of the failed National Land Rights campaign and the grim statistics of the increasing numbers of young Aboriginal people dying in custody, there had been little recognition that 'White Australia has a Black History' as one Aboriginal Rights badge stated.

FILEF was torn between wanting to take an active role in shaping the way the nation saw itself in its Bicentennial celebrations, and its growing awareness that their role if they wanted to contribute to social justice in their new country had to be to support Aboriginal people's demands. Frank Panucci has talked about this struggle.

Frank: Of course a lot of people were worried about whether you should engage with that publicity for the Bicentennial, so that somehow you managed to get your view in there. Some of us were looking at Ernie Dingo and saying, 'What a cop out, he shouldn't be doing that!' But other people were saying, 'Maybe not, but maybe yes, because you never know what he might be able to say, to present, to the audience'. And so obviously it was a negotiated thing.

Kevin's advice to us was good advice. It was, 'Well, here are all the positions, now go away and work it out yourself'!

---

2   Federazione Italiana Lavoratori Emigrati e le Loro Famiglie.

But as it got nearer to '88, it became more and more obvious that the engagement with that funding body was going to resist us doing some of the things we wanted to do. Like to address the Bicentennial in terms of colonisation and where migration fits into the colonisation process…

So there came the famous day when we made a decision – to actually say no to the money and reject it – which wasn't an easy thing to do! It was still a commitment to the idea of the project we wanted to do… And we talked to Kevin again, and he said, 'Well if that's what you've decided to do, then people in Indigenous communities will see it as a positive thing if that's your reasons…'. So we made public announcements, went on SBS and got interviewed, and tried to say what we thought it was all about. I remember sitting through an 11 hour meeting down at the Wharf theatre with the three parties involved and they flew a negotiator down from Brisbane… So we said no.

So we got involved with a number of people around FILEF who were setting up Migrants for Aboriginal Rights, which was about where migrants fitted into this whole '88 thing, and where we sat in terms of supporting Indigenous people and trying to highlight those 200 years of colonisation and dispossession.

And it was a thing that was supported inside FILEF, but it also brought in people who weren't in FILEF – members of the Italian community. A lot of those people were younger people, second generation, third generation kids, but there were also a lot of the older comrades, who'd arrived here post war and some were Communist party members. Also a couple of them were old ex-wharfies and still remember some of the stuff that the wharfies did around Indigenous issues and stuff like that. So it was almost a continuation for them of a moment of struggle which was something which was always sitting in the back of their mind, but maybe they didn't know how to articulate it that well before. So basically out of the offices of FILEF we contacted a whole lot of migrant community organisations across Sydney and New South Wales. I think at the end there must have been about 30 or 40 different organisations which became part of Migrants for Aboriginal Rights.

One of the big meetings that Migrants for Aboriginal Rights (MAR) organised was in the Tom Mann theatre, in the Metal Workers' building. Judy Chester has remembered how important that event was for her and for other Aboriginal people. It began as a fundraiser, but became much more.

Judy Chester: They said they were going to do a fundraiser for us. It was not just FILEF, it was other migrant groups too, they all chipped in. And we said: 'We can get Aboriginal dancers and that', and they said; 'No, we're doing a fundraiser for *you*! You are all going to sit there and watch all different cultural things from other parts of the world'. There would've been at least six to seven people with every cultural group. It was really big, and they had kids performing. There were the Chileans, the Nicaraguans, the Vietnamese, the Argentinians, the Italians… They were just amazing! It was a brilliant concert. Never saw one black fella on stage. It was amazing.

Frank Panucci has explained why this Tom Mann concert had such special significance for him and others in the Italian community.

Frank Panucci: It was a big thing but for us it was not only the number of acts and the fact that it was such a joyful event as well! But also for a lot of us, and me included, it was one of those rare events, where you actually had Indigenous people in the audience, and migrant people in the audience, *together*, enjoying something *together* and actually interacting, in a way that for most of us is not going to happen again, because of the way the communities are constructed and their interactions. So it's never going to happen! And there were things that came out of that, spin offs, where people kept relationships up, kept their activities up. People are still – I think – sensitive to and supportive of Indigenous issues which most probably wouldn't have happened.

Frank felt there were had been some key issues where the differences between Indigenous people and migrant groups had become clearly apparent. He felt that he and others from Migrants for Aboriginal Rights had learnt lessons from these conflicts which had continued to shape all their later relationships with Aboriginal people. One was the style of the Aboriginal activists with whom the migrant groups were interacting. Some were particularly confrontational and accusatory, which as Frank pointed out was always useful – it was good to be 'constantly challenged and pushed' so as not to get 'complacent about what you are doing'. But he felt that it was even more valuable to have Kevin's advice.

Frank Panucci: Kevin in his own way does it much more subtly. Just when you think you got there, there's always something else on the plate, something else that you need to do and there's something else you need to look at. So as we thought we were moving along the path and stuff, Kevin would say, 'Well, we're running some courses at Tranby and it might be a good idea if a few people come along'. So some of us would go to the courses, to help Tranby on the night on some of the issues around, and we'd end up learning more about Indigenous culture and Indigenous issues.

Another point of real tension was the Aboriginal insistence that the march in protest about the Bicentennial be led by Aboriginal people.

Frank Panucci: The thing that struck me was when the organisers of the march said: 'This march is going to be led by Indigenous people, anyone who is not Indigenous starts when the Indigenous people stop.'

Now I said, in my heart of hearts, for a lot of people it didn't make sense. They were thinking, 'Aren't we in this together?' But at the FILEF meeting, everyone accepted it as, that's the way it has to be and should be.

I think the reason that was clear to us was because of what people had learnt – to use that terrible term – because of the journey we'd all gone through in terms of learning stuff. Our relationship had been built up over time as one of interaction and discussion, but at the end of the day, we knew who was leading it.

I think that was the hardest thing for all of us to understand. That no matter how supportive we are of the issues and how close our hearts are to that issue about resolving it, it's their decision about how it's led and about how they will interact with us.

The thing that Kevin taught me, is that it's always been an issue about power, and I shouldn't try and undermine that building of their power. And that's the important lesson that I think that we all took away from that, and still carry with us today.

The change which the Bicentennial organising brought which Frank Panucci had not expected was the dramatic increase in the networks of communication which were achieved through Tranby and particularly through working with Kevin there.

Frank: What was interesting was that all of a sudden, even through we had all made our own networks of like-minded people across the place, Cookie sort of – how can I say it – he *web*-spun!

He would spin out to a whole lot range of smaller webs out there that – really – people didn't know about. So these people mightn't know each other till then but it would turn out that they had things in common. Even today, these are still people that I can pick up a phone to talk to about different issues, and our paths still cross at times because of work and stuff. And it would amaze you how often one of the constant reference points is a certain Kevin Cook! Tranby in general, but Cookie in particular.

FILEF and Kevin were also able to draw in the Italian labour movement to support the Aboriginal rights movement. Judy Chester described one occasion.

Judy: Kevin organised for Karen to go over and meet the Italian who was like the leader of the ACTU in Italy. He'd come out here. I went with her to meet him in a little office they had behind Norton Street there. It was packed! She was petrified, but she was brilliant! They were interpreting to him from what Karen was saying. And at the end he got up and spoke. Panucci was interpreting to me and Karen. This man's saying: 'You people have to get behind the Aboriginal struggle. You're living on their land!' ... and he was going for it! He was saying how wonderful Karen was! I've still got an Italian magazine with Karen's face on the cover. I've kept it. And there was another one with Foley on the cover, cause he talked to him in Melbourne.

The FILEF members came to feel that their goal of contributing to the building of social justice was well served by their role in this campaign. Frank Panucci has summed up the effect on them all.

Frank: FILEF was an organisation that was interested in ensuring, that was basically – to cut all the crap out it – about ensuring that Italians and people of Italian origin played an active role in the way this country moved forward towards being a more progressive, open, equitable country.

It meant that you did that with issues which were day-to-day bread-and-butter stuff within your community and then with the broader issues.

So that's why the '88 experience was so important to us. Actually, I think it was a fundamental shift for us, to understanding this place a lot better.

And we saw that unless you address Indigenous issues that you would never actually achieve the transformation of this country that we all wanted.

***

While the Migrants for Aboriginal Rights group flourished in the months leading up to the Bicentennial, there were other networks which were born at the very end of the campaign, emerging in its final days but going on to blossom over the coming years. The Building Bridges musical relationships were an example of this network, which really came into being just as the Bicentennial arrived.

Jacqui Katona was the young Djork woman from Arnhem Land who, through Tranby, had contributed to the international campaign of taking Aboriginal views to the United Nations. In 1987, she was back at Tranby, working there with her friend Karen Flick on the campaign to build the Bicentennial protest. There were a growing number of people offering their help after coming to the Migrants for Aboriginal Rights meetings which were being held at Tranby – or just coming directly to Tranby which, as Patty Anderson explained, had become a central organising point for contributions to the Bicentennial campaign. As it became clear that more and more people were planning to join the convoys of trucks and cars heading down to Sydney from across the country, it was increasingly urgent to organise funds to support their travel and then to help them with food, bedding and general support while they were in Sydney. So fundraising was a priority and it was the goal of many of the Migrants for Aboriginal Rights events and many other support groups.

Aboriginal activists across Australia were also making plans to support the coming events in Sydney. Gary Foley, although by then living in Melbourne, was a frequent visitor to Sydney and Tranby, often speaking to the Migrants for Aboriginal Rights group there. Foley was in touch with many of the musicians in Melbourne, Sydney and elsewhere, and there was a growing interest in mobilising their support for the fundraising needed to bring the convoys to Sydney. One model was the Rock Against Racism events which had occurred in the United Kingdom and which were well known among many musicians and others involved with the live music scene in Sydney and Melbourne. Two of these music activists were Tony Dukes and Jim George who had become associated with Tranby and the Migrants for Aboriginal Rights group. With Foley and Kevin they had begun the planning to hold a concert with Aboriginal and non-Aboriginal performers both to welcome the incoming protesters and mainly to raise money to support them.

But at the same time, the tensions were building between the Bicentennial Authority and the swelling protest movement. There was rising media scare mongering and hysteria about Aboriginal activism and 'Black Power'. The tabloid press accused Aboriginal organisations of plotting violence against the athletes and the games venues. These wild accusations inflamed an already hostile section of the public and it was Aboriginal people who suffered violence. Tranby College was targeted by a racist group identifying as neo-Nazis who smashed the windows of the old building, and daubed crude abuse on its walls.

As *Tony Dukes* recalls: Jim George and me and others had been going to the anti-Bicentennial protest meetings. We'd booked the Bondi Pavilion on the weekend before the Long March to do some fund-raisers. And then we got a call through Foley about how a whole lot of negative press was starting to build up around the Long March: 'All the blacks are coming to town, lock up your daughters, lock up your sons!' So there was a need to refocus those events as an event to bring people together and to try to capture some positive media in the two days before the mob hit town for the big march.

So the planning shifted towards how to make this concert a positive event – David Bradbury and Peter Garrett had both become involved, interested to contribute their time and resources to the campaign. The concert was happening, some good bands were booked, the text of the poster was written but it didn't have a name. Everyone knew that all concerts have to have a name. Jacqui Katona has talked with Jim George and Tony Dukes about how they found a name for the concert that turned into the name for what became an ongoing musical anti-racism movement:

Figure 16.1: Kevin at Tranby behind one of the broken windows left by the neo-Nazi attack.

Courtesy Tranby Archives.

Jacqui Katona: We had this conversation in the café in Glebe. You were there Tony – come on! What happened? It was in 1987, in November or December, leading up to the Bicentennial and the big march.

Tony Dukes: Right – so there was you, me, Jim, Foley, and Gillian, the state manager. I forget her last name. We were sitting around because we had to do a poster. Braid Mix had done the design for the poster. Walt had done the words for it but we didn't have a name. We were going round and going round, going what are we going to call it?

Jacqui: And someone said: 'What about "Building Bridges"?' And I said, 'Oh God, you can't mean it!' I said, 'That's disgusting. Don't be so soft!'

Tony: So we said we should call it 'Planting Trees'. And Jim goes, 'Oh, why not Plucking Chooks?' And then we all pissed ourselves laughing! And we said, 'No, no, no, we've got to have a name! – We've got to get to the printers!' So that was it! We picked *Building Bridges* and away it went!

Figure 16.2: The Building Bridges campaigns kept on going.

Courtesy Kevin Cook family collection.

The journey

Meanwhile, people all over the country had begun to move, heading down to Sydney. Patty Anderson was coming from Darwin, in just one of the convoys which had started out for the long trip. She has remembered what a difficult journey it was for that Top End mob.

Patty Anderson: It was amazing that time. There were all sorts of stories about people just taking their swag out and standing on the road and saying, 'Well, someone will come along'. And sure enough, somebody did come along. Pensioners were saving up their cheques for train fares. There's lots of those sort of stories about how people came to Sydney.

David Ross, from the Central Land Council in Alice Springs, was also on buses, coming down through South Australia and across. They had planned the camp sites all the way across, keeping in touch with the organisations Kevin was talking to in Adelaide and western NSW. Each place they pulled up, everything had worked like clockwork, the food was there, the fires were burning and the swags prepared.

16. Bicentennial

David Ross: I was the mug who was in charge of the troops and getting them from Alice to Sydney, and looking after them while they were in Sydney and getting them home without losing anyone or getting anyone into trouble. That was my job. I had nothing to do with any of the rest of the organising or the meetings or anything, that was Patrick's job. [Patrick Dodson]

I don't know what it was like for the mob coming from Queensland. But certainly for us, we came around that South Australian way and we had camps organised along the highway. It was all fixed. All done. So you know, people got here and they were quite happy and contented and got on and done whatever had to be done at the time.

My job was looking after the gang, and boy, what a job that was. I had people from the bush who'd never been to the city before who were wandering around the city, and looking after themselves and you'd find them hanging around out a cafe or a pub somewhere. We'd pile them back into a car and get them home. God, what a job that was. I needed a holiday after that.

Patrick Dodson has talked about that journey down too, joking with Kevin about why everyone was so sure it would all work out:

Kevin: It was just incredible… I wouldn't say it was incredibly *well* organised.

Patrick: No, no, nothing was ever *well* organised, Don't think of it as well organised, but it was *organised*!

Kevin: You could say it fell into place!

Patrick: And we knew if it got stuffed up, then Cookie would fix it! 'So don't worry about it, if it's not organised, we'll talk to him, it'll be sorted out.' Bang!

Kevin was waiting at La Perouse with many others, who had been sleeping out overnight waiting for the convoys. It was raining and it was unseasonably cold for January, but people had been sleeping on the ground so they wouldn't miss the moment when those buses arrived. As word came through that the convoys were coming through the western Sydney suburbs and getting closer, the crowd at La Perouse got more and more tense. For Kevin, the overwhelming memory was the emotion everyone waiting felt as the buses finally rolled into La Perouse. 'People were just crying' he says, 'just crying'.

Patty Anderson has described what it was like for her and her mob, getting off the Darwin buses.

Patty: Yeah, it was very emotional when those buses came.

Because there'd been two deaths, and really important deaths for my mob up in the Northern Territory.

They had all came on the big cavalcade with buses and then an old man had died. He was a really important man and really by rights they should've turned around and went back. But they had a meeting and they said, 'No, We're still coming'. And then there was another death! And they thought, 'No, we're still going to come'.

They had ceremonies along the road and so by the time we came to La Perouse, all the buses had been ochred up.

And there were all these people … seemed like thousands and thousands of people at La Perouse. And these buses came in, blowing their horns. They went driving around the block – around and around – blowing their horns. And then when the people got out of the bus – with all this excitement, I don't really know what happened – but we sort of just stood and then all the people from La Perouse came up slowly. Then they started slowly walking towards each other, these huge groups of people.

And we got to a point and then everybody just ran and hugged each other. It was very emotional, everyone was crying.

Jack Ah Kit from the Northern Land Council was already in Sydney, waiting with Kevin.

Jack: That was evidence of what the Coalition could organise! I mean, we had people coming from Western Australia, from the Kimberleys. The land councils all coming down in convoy. I was down earlier as sort of head of the advance party getting accommodation and food, which Tranby helped with, shopping at a co-operative.

To be in touch with that convoy when they were coming through Liverpool, and then to see this convoy drive into La Per was something that I'll never forget.

It was sprinkling with rain and to see all these Aboriginal people – *countrymen* – down here waiting and cheering as the convoy started to drive in. People were crying with happiness. And to see grown men crying with happiness – it brought tears to me eyes also because it was such a wonderful feeling. People's hair stood up… There was goose bumps everywhere. The rain was sprinkling… and if you mentioned it to a few blokes… you might say 'Touching isn't it?' 'No, no', they'd say, 'it's the rain. I'm not crying. I'm not crying!'

It was just so wonderful. Everyone was so emotional – so proud to see this convoy coming in. They had travelled all this distance to be together. It was magnificent.

***

Some of the buses drove directly to the Building Bridges Concert at the Bondi Pavilion on the beach, joining the already overflowing crowd as Tony Dukes, one of the concert organisers, remembered.

Tony: The biggest mob turned out. And then on top of all of them, there were the buses arriving from the bush, with people just hopping off, never seen the beach before! I remember that we had a reasonable price on the door – around five dollars. It wasn't much but we had wanted to raise a bit of money for the march.

But for safety reasons we just had to throw the doors open.

There were just too many people. We weren't ready for it or able to deal with it. And of course just the spirit of the event was about the connections of bringing people together. Why wait at Bondi Beach on a beautiful day for half an hour to try to get in? Just come in! And so we walked around with the buckets. We ended up with a couple of grand in the buckets at the end of the day. And that was the start of Building Bridges! I remember then talking with Kevin, and it was like 'Well, what can we do now? We've got some money and we've got a lot of interest'. So we started to organise then for the concerts later on.

Jim George remembered Bondi that day: David Bradbury the filmmaker came and documented the concert. We had five cameras and we got 120 hours of footage from that first one at the Bondi Pavillon. I remember it had a strong black lineup. We had Roger Knox there. And it was Yothu Yindi's first gig – we billed them as Koori Dancers! They were down working with the Swamp Jockeys doing some stuff. We had Black Lace and we had to turn the power off, 'cause they wouldn't get off stage!

We were all scared of course! Because of all that stuff about 'the blacks were coming to town' – so we weren't sure what to expect from the police or the general community either! So the concert really gave everybody the push to keep going with stuff and take it positively forward.

Cookie's memory of that first concert was again the overwhelming emotion.

Kevin: It was very emotional, that gig at Bondi. You know, when you seen all the people coming in, your heart swole up. Talking to other people later, some of the musicians, they got caught up in that too. But from an Aboriginal perspective, everybody was pumped up. Really pumped up about the concert and later on, the march.

***

But once everyone had arrived, the day-to-day organising had to be ramped up another notch. All these people had to be fed and, especially for those people from the hot summer in the northern states, they had to be kept warm in the unexpectedly cold Sydney weather.

First of all they had to be found a bed out near La Perouse. There were a lot of buildings not too far away, often used in the past as migrant worker hostels. So they all had names like 'Endeavour House' or – as Patrick Dodson joked – 'Some other First Fleet name! Some Captain Cook name! We thought "What the…?" And then we had a good laugh at that!'

The ones who didn't find a bed, slept outside despite the cold. Often as Kevin remembered they were Sydney Aboriginal people who had come out just to be with the mob who had all come down. But they couldn't all fit at La Perouse and many people had made their own way down, ahead of the convoys, so they could be in Sydney in time. As Patty Anderson remembered, they were billeted all over the inner suburbs of Sydney, in Aboriginal and non-Aboriginal homes, wherever there was a friendly bed.

Patty Anderson: As well as putting up people in these hostels and that, most of the Sydney people had someone staying with them. Say for example, Cookie and Judy – they had what we called 'an elastic house'! There was that many people there, half the Northern Territory was there. There was Old Nanna… Nan Campbell was here, Delia's mum from the South Coast. And a few other old girls from there too. Then there was me and my nephew from Darwin and there was Jimmy Everett and Michael Mansell. A whole bunch of people in and out of Kevin and Judy's house!

Now one night about ten o'clock, these Tasmanians came in wanting to cook mutton birds. They brought this big bag of mutton birds and they came in, insisting that we all eat it. They got the stove on and they're cutting up these birds and putting them under the griller!

They were just like everyone – there were a lot of people who were doing, in their own way, as much as they could.

They were putting people up or taking people around to Op shops, or… you know, serving cups of tea… there was a lot of people. In fact, a lot of non-Aboriginal people too did quite a bit.

Then once people could be found a bed, they had to be fed. This was just as great a logistical task – hundreds of volunteers made tea as Patty Anderson remembered, and organised coffee and biscuits and sandwiches out of the little kitchen at La Perouse. Others made daily runs to Flemington Markets, where many of the produce sellers donated food for the protest camp. A big cool room had been hired from the markets and there were 'stacks and stacks of fruit and vegetables in there'. Between the tea makers and the market shoppers, Patty says there were 'Lots of people… old people, young people, kids… pensioners, people on the dole, people working – everybody. Lots and lots and lots of people came from all over.'

A special addition to the food was made by William Bates from Wilcannia, who had spent so much of the last decade supporting land rights in his far western region. He knew how to run a bush camp! He arrived with three fresh kangaroos and a hand saw. He butchered the meat there at La Perouse and they hung it in the coolroom, so it could be cooked up later in big pots of stew to feed all the mob camped around. Patrick Dodson remembers the enthusiasm that the Northern Territory people had about the preparations once they knew William would be bringing the kangaroo meat for the camp.

Kevin talks proudly of the extraordinary management job they all did:

Cookie: I've always said that we're probably the best organised group in Australia. And nobody'd believe you. But I reckon we can do anything. Who else could've got people from all those remote areas in that short time for less money? You know, it would be physically impossible. But we did it and we did it easy! Fed them. Clothed them. We looked after everyone!

The next priority was to organise the public statements of the demonstration. After all, this was what so many people had travelled all this way to do – to make sure their voices were heard. There was meeting after meeting to plan the march and the press releases, and with so many different states and organisations represented, there were also lots of arguments! So there was an understandable reluctance to allow the press into these meetings. Kevin has pointed out the irony of this – the demonstrators wanted press coverage but at the same time they wanted to control it – so they spent much of the first five days of the camp chasing journalists away – and then suddenly wanted them to come back to report the final Aboriginal press release.

Cookie: There was a couple of film crews that had come in from overseas especially to cover what we were doing. That was their brief! Not what was coming steaming up the harbour!

One reporter came in to a meeting and they all threw him out. And then what we were all talking about was how could we get the press to get our message across? 'How could we get our message across?' they were all asking!

I was just roaring laughing. The first thing you do is to throw all the reporters and television crews out. That had a good effect! They came back. They thought there must be a story there! So that was fun, throwing them out for days and days and then it was 'How are we doing to get the press'!

Patrick Dodson has pointed out that not only the press but the Aboriginal demonstrators were all waiting to see what this ALF was going to do! The imaginary Aboriginal Liberation Front had been the centre of frenzied media scare campaign, and so everyone was uneasy!

As *Patty Anderson* has remembered the dilemmas: There were thousands of us. We had these enormous meetings, thousands and thousands of black fellas on the hills at La Perouse. So of course we had the biggest fights and everything! And then you had people on the go again, because the press were frantic to talk to us! There was even a team from Alaska and everything! One time we were all having this meeting and this van drove down the side of the fence there, with one of those long-distance sort of speaker things to try and pick up what people were saying. So we were getting a bit toey about that, because we were arguing something bad, you know, just normal sort of stuff.

In the end, Karen Flick organised the press! She'd been talking to the press all those years for the Black Deaths in Custody mob and she knew people.

The final part of the organisation was planning the March itself. Given its high profile and the many other events of the day on 26 January, the Aboriginal protesters needed a permit. This had been worked over many times but the final meeting with the police was one where Kevin Cook had to be at another crucial meeting about the Co-operative, so he asked Kevin Tory to go. Cookie was confident about Kevin Tory's resolve but he remembers giving him final instructions: 'We've got the route all organised, so just tell 'em!'

Cookie was full of praise: Tory did an incredibly good job... He went in there, and the bloke was one of the heavies in the coppers, and he's got a map drawn and he tries to say, 'Youse all have to go here!' Tory said, '*Here*'s where we're going – and that's it! You can agree with it or you can disagree with it but this is the way we'll be marching'. And he said, 'We'll have hundreds of thousands of people'. And the copper laughed! Well, they didn't laugh on the day!!

Not only did Aboriginal people confidently take over managing the route, but they were organised as marshals and ran the march to ensure the police did not have any chances to intervene. Patty Anderson watched Karen Flick defuse a potential problem.

Patty: There was about eight to ten of these young fellas all running into the pubs and started running out with cans to rejoin the march. Well, Karen was right beside me and she said: 'Hey!' And I thought: 'Oh, here's a go' and I pulled back a bit, thinking there was no way anyone was going to manage these lads. But she said: 'Look, go and put that back. You'll give us a bad name. There are coppers here everywhere!'

And the whole lot of them ran back to the curb, just had one sip and put the cans down, and then joined the march. Well I couldn't believe it! Karen looked at me. We *both* thought 'We're in for it now'. But they had been really, like 'Oh, sorry Sis!'

Cookie reflected on the whole day: You know, something always has to go wrong. But there was not a thing! Nothing at all went wrong with the whole march.

The march

The Aboriginal marchers gathered in two places. Many came to Belmore Park, just outside Central Station where they had already filled the park for many hours ahead of the assigned time for the full march to start into the city.

The many people who had arrived in Sydney from all over the country in convoy and stayed at La Perouse had all piled into their buses again and came into Redfern, where they formed up in rows to march along Regent Street towards the railway tunnel under which they had to walk to join the crowd at Belmore Park. The marchers coming from Redfern could not see the park until they had passed right through the tunnel, but the crowd in Belmore Park could hear them coming – the sound of their clap sticks and the songs they were singing in language were echoing and reverberating all across the park, bouncing off the tall buildings around it and washing into the streets beyond. The Redfern marchers did not know what to expect when they came out of the dark tunnel into the blinding light.

Figure 16.3: The Wilcannia group formed up in Redfern to march to Belmore Park at Central Station.

Courtesy Heather Goodall.

Figure 16.4: Waiting: Julie Whitton from Toomelah with some kids in the park with the growing crowd. They gathered to wait for the interstate visitors staying at La Perouse to march into the park from the east, through the tunnel which passed under the railway line.

Courtesy Heather Goodall.

Patrick Dodson has explained what they saw: We came through the tunnel there… and we'd talked about what we were going to do, we were going to have a rest at this park, you know, sit down and have a drink and everything. And then we couldn't even get into the park, hey. They were all standing there – clapping.

We just couldn't stop crying, because we didn't expect it. We didn't expect anybody there. We thought we were just doing it ourselves.

And from then on they just lined the streets and there was people holding put banners. They read: 'Chile' and 'the PLO' and 'Argentina' and 'Timor' and… every country in the world just about! The Greeks, the Italians… everybody! And we didn't expect that. There was no way we had expected that many. That was really really good.

Jack Ah Kit came out of that tunnel too: The paper recorded it as 30,000 at that time, but I would've sworn there was 50,000 people there. I was telling a friend today, the echoing of those ironwood clap-sticks as we walked under that bridge was just incredible. I can still hear it today. It just makes my hair stand up.

Figure 16.5: The Northern Territory mob had painted up for ceremony and they sang as they marched in. We in the park heard the song echoing out from the tunnel even before the people themselves came out, with songs and clapsticks – and many tears.

Courtesy Heather Goodall.

Cookie remembered it that way too from the Belmore Park side: ... There was a number of things that was going on under that tunnel... seeing all those migrants and white Australians, all standing there clapping like that. And people crying – blacks just crying – and people were saying, 'The sun's in me eye!' and they wipin' the tears away!

***

And for *Patty Anderson* it was a sign of a lasting change, even if only a slight one: That feeling just sort of tapped in, like, with all those people waiting for us at the park... but there were people all along, all along. And then when we got almost to the end, like there was a Teachers' Union, I remember just along the side of the road waiting for us, and there must've been about a couple of hundred of them. It was really impressive – they were waiting, just waiting, for all of *us* to come!

I think it gave people a lot of confidence, and it reaffirmed who everybody *was*: politically, emotionally and – the other missing ingredient – spiritually as well. It was a very emotional time, but I think people were doing a lot of things from their heart. They knew it intellectually... they knew it in their head that it was politically important, but then when it came, we went into another space and it just sort of evolved. It sort of just happened!

We turned it around, so as it wasn't 'them and us'. We said, '*You* are doing that but what *we* are doing – despite everything that's happened to us – *we* are still here'.

I remember that it was a conscious decision not to make it just a protest, but rather to make it a celebration of who *we* are, and that we're *here*.

And that was a conscious political decision to turn it around.

I think our lobbying against 1988 was one of the most positive things we've done because it really did take all the oomph out of that 'celebration of the nation' that they were planning. There were non-Indigenous Australians really stumbling on the word 'celebrate'!

In the end, *we* were the ones using the word 'celebrations', because it came to be a bit more difficult for them, than they first thought. So it did take a lot of that oomph out of the big party, the big bang kind of things. And I think it's made them... at that time at least, a little bit more thoughtful.

It seemed to me that after 1988, we heard them say more often: 'the time of the invasion', and 'the first inhabitants'. So the language kind of changed a little, it shifted just a bit. You don't hear so many people saying: 'This explorer found this river'... or 'climbed that mountain'...or 'The first man to cross this river or climb that mountain'… That real sort of 1950s language has disappeared. I noticed it anyhow, after '88. And even now people don't use that language anymore.

Figure 16.6: The march moving off from the park and on down into the city streets.

Courtesy Heather Goodall.

***

There are many white Australian analysts who have written about the Bicentennial celebrations. Some of the most thoughtful accounts were by historians in the later part of the year. Peter Cochrane and David Goodman wrote about the attempts by the curators of the Bicentennial Travelling Exhibition, one of the major products of the long preparation years, to incorporate everyone and everything – including Aboriginal people and their concerns. It did so however by 'levelling' them into being 'immigrants' like everyone else, all on a 'journey' in which they were just like all the other citizens of the nation.[3]

Peter Spearritt wrote about the politics of the Bicentennial Authority, and agreed with Patty Anderson that the Aboriginal protest had rubbed at least a bit of the gloss off the Bicentennial celebrations and certainly off the day itself. The Bicentennial he writes, was burdened throughout for Aboriginal people

---

3   Peter Cochrane and David Goodman 1988, 'The great Australian journey: Cultural logic and nationalism in the postmodern era', *Australian Historical Studies*, 23(91): 21–44.

– and many other Australians – by the Hawke Labor Government's betrayal of national land rights and its floundering attempts thereafter to make up for it. The Australian Bicentennial Authority tried repeatedly and anxiously to 'include' Aboriginal people in its 'celebration of the nation'. In the end, however, it was the peaceful dignity of the Aboriginal protest which was remembered, causing many Australian people to reflect on the prior ownership of the land in a way they had never done before.[4]

None of these writers, however, was aware of the impact of that day on Aboriginal people and their white supporters. But then, they did not know the whole story.

Kurnell

Sometime during the evening before the March, Aboriginal people in the camp at La Perouse had began to talk about what would happen at the end of the next day. Many people there came to think they should go to Kurnell, on the southern side of Botany Bay, into what is now a national park but which in 1770 was the place where James Cook first landed and plunged a post flying a British flag into Australian soil. I asked Cookie about it:

Heather: Kevin, had people been planning for a long time to go to Kurnell that night after the March?

Kevin: No. It only happened, I think, the night before. People were saying… sitting down and saying: 'What can we do? What's the most symbolic thing that we can do?' And you know, Cook sailed in there! So we sailed out there from Redfern and off we went. We even got permission to use the park to put our flag up. We pulled the flag down, the Australian flag, and put our flag up! We had permission to do it, while the ceremony was going on. That was an incredible statement, you know – just putting our flag up! *For me, that was the highlight of the whole thing.*

Heather: I was there that night at Kurnell, I'll never forget it as long as I live. I watched that dancing all through the night, through those big fires and in their glow, with the people all around. This is how I wrote about it in 1996:

> Anyone who doubted that relations between land and people remain at the centre of Aboriginal politics and symbolism need only to have been there that night on the hillside at Kurnell.

---

4   Peter Spearritt 1988, 'Celebration of a nation: The triumph of spectacle', *Australian Historical Studies*, 23(91): 3–20.

On January 26th, 1988, many thousands of Aboriginal people from all over Australia marched in Sydney to celebrate their victory in surviving a long and violent invasion over the last two hundred years. The hosts were Murris, Kooris and Wiimpatjas, the Aboriginal people of NSW, who had suffered the longest and most intense impacts of colonisation.

The event commemorated on that date is the founding of the colony by Phillip and the First Fleet at Farm Cove in Sydney Harbour, but the Aboriginal organisers chose another site for the climax of their business that day. They said their work was about restoration and new beginnings, so they would go to the place where the story of the invasion had really began, to Kurnell, the landing site of James Cook in 1770 on the southern side of Botany Bay.

At sunset, as white Australia celebrated with fireworks, the Aboriginal people of Australia began to restore the links which had been ruptured by the invasion. At the invitation of NSW Aboriginal people, the men and women from commmunties where traditional ceremonial life has been able to be upheld, began to dance and sing the stories which begin in their lands but travel across the country towards the east. As Central Land Council Chairman, Wenten Rubuntja explained it,

'When the English people found our country and Aboriginal people, they put their cities and their culture all over our country. But underneath this, all the time, Aboriginal culture and laws stay alive.

'In Central Australia... our culture, our laws and the song in the land has a voice – the Walpiri voice, the Arrernte, the Luritja, the Pitjantjatjara, Gurindji – many voices....

'The Aboriginal people living along the coast where the white people took over first, they might not know their language any more, but the emu story and the snake story goes all over Australia.... When they see us dance we can celebrate that we all belong to the songs that go across the whole of this country.' [*Land Rights News*, 2[6] January 1988]

Many Aboriginal people and their white guests spent that night on the slope above the water at Kurnell. It was an unseasonally cold clear night, with the water of Botany Bay reflecting the bright moon above, the still glow of the oil refinery and the eerily silent lights of planes landing and taking off beyond hearing range. The trappings of white Australia were not denied, but had been made powerless by distance and the intensity of the ceremonies which began with the dusk. All through that night, the dance fires burned. Young and old, men and women, defiantly, joyously, they danced the stories for the country.

At sunrise, exhausted but elated, the dancers ceased, and Aboriginal people from Sydney and the south-east spoke to us about what had happened on that land and what it meant to them. Then, quietly, Aboriginal leaders from across the country shepherded people into lines to walk through the smoke of smouldering green branches, a ritual cleansing and protection which can be used for many purposes. On that morning, it was said to be to release people from the sadness of so many past deaths and pain and to protect us all there from the powerful forces now able to move again in the land.

Most saw that dawn through tears, Aboriginal and non-Aboriginal people there both profoundly moved by the power of the night and the ritual of care and protection.

The custodianship of the land had been made again a public thing.

Invasion to Embassy, 1996

Jack Ah Kit remembered it this way: The dancing and smoking ceremony at Kurnell was really spiritual… and it was proper. There was no half measures. There were white people there too, and that made it really nice for me to see. Because when I asked Galarrwuy, 'Shall we invite all this mob?' He said; 'Yeah'.

I think there must've been four to five thousand people there that night. It was on the spur of the moment, and it was cold. But to see the smoking ceremony in the morning and to see people coming through being smoked, was something unforgettable.

Patrick Dodson recalled that as they travelled, the people he had come with from Central Australia had discussed the big questions about how the long Dreaming tracks had traversed Australia. They knew those tracks would have passed through the eastern states. They had talked over which ones would have passed through Sydney. Where would they have entered the sea? He put that night at Kurnell into the context of those discussions.

Patrick Dodson: It was because prior to that, all the good work that Jacko and all the old people had done, had created a sense of solidarity, and a sense of respect. And there was appreciation too for what the people at La Perouse were doing. We'd had those discussions about where the Dreaming tracks went. Where they might've come in – was it through Brewarrina? Or through Wilcannia? But anyway we thought they could have come in through that country and we were trying to find ways of connecting all of these things together.

And in the '88 stuff, Galarrwuy was talking over at the Cove there. And he was talking about the shark and the porpoise meeting in these countries. And so those four message sticks were to say: 'here they are'.

Me and Mr Shaw, we were catching the plane the next day, still with ochre all over us. And the hostess was sort of looking at us on the plane as we went back to Alice Springs… We were all blurry-eyed with ochre all spattered all over us. We were saying: 'Don't worry about that, we just come from the great south land'…

Patty Anderson remembered it as she talked with Kevin: We slept on the beach at Botany, remember Cookie? You know, that's never really been looked at, what actually happened. It's very very interesting and very symbolic. Its extremely important spiritual symbolism that actually happened, and very few people got it. There wasn't a big crowd of people at Botany anyhow. Because… I don't know why because. But there was this – not exactly transference, but the people from the NT came down and brought certain artefacts and what have you, and the whole object of bringing that was – not impose it on people here in Sydney in particular, but rather to help regenerate it. Bring the old and… you know, the stuff that was all there, put the spirits to rest, and begin to make it anew. And there was a big ceremony all night, and I don't think that its been looked at, nobody has spoken about it, myself included. And well, I hope it hasn't disappeared. The people who were there – I think it is in those people's minds and hearts.

They started talking about it during the day and they said to people… (that's exactly what they said, eh Cookie?) 'No dancing in sandshoes', 'no jitter-bug' was the word they used… those skinny old women, skinny old ones that nobody notices, but they notice everything.

Kevin: Them old folks, they really made me laugh when they were talking about 'No dancing in sandshoes', and 'no jitter-bugging tonight'… all of this. Yeah, proper stuff and no jitter-bugging.

Patty: And no sandshoes!

But they didn't make such a big thing of it either, it was just… it was almost like: 'Well, if you hear it, you'll come. And if you don't hear it, well, you won't come.'

That's in retrospect, that's how it seems to me now.

Kevin: Looking back and looking at the different groups, they were very competitive when they danced.

Patty: Our mob are the biggest show-offs, Cookie!

So there was a bit of a competition! And they'd get really shitty if people don't do it properly or they're just slack because they're mucking around! Everybody gets onto them because they want to be as good as – if not better! – than that other mob. Because you're on show, I suppose.

But that thing at Botany, it was to put the spirits to rest. The ones that had been… you know … had all that terrible torture and atrocities. It was to put them to rest. Like, to say, 'It's all okay'.

But also to help regenerate and bring the spirits back and make it sort of new and strong again.

I think everybody who was there felt it, but it's not been talked about.

Now those old fellas, they sang all night. Just non-stop. There was two campfires, the Top End mob and Centre. But between them, they sang all night and played sticks. All night. And thinking about it now, it was a kind of soothing thing to have sung like that. It was saying to the spirits, 'It's all right, you can go now, you can rest'.

And then at the end that really big smoking… that purification ceremony. That was pretty powerful too… it was very, *very* significant.

Kevin: You know people still talk about that at the Top End and people still speak about it down here in New South Wales. Because it grabbed them. They'd never had anything like that ever happen to them before.

Patty Anderson: There was lots of sharing, you know. People were really anxious and really keen to come together in some co-ordinated way – and also a very spiritual way as well – which we don't do enough. We do a lot of head stuff, but we don't do that – to look after the spirit, if you like, as much as we should do.

Thinking it over, *Kevin* summed it up like this: For me it meant, it's the first time that we've ever had a ceremony on that particular land for a very long time. And it meant that we're part… everybody that was there was part of that ceremony, and that'd live with you forever and ever. It's just incredible. I felt sorry for people who didn't come out there, you know? You talk to people after, and they say, 'Oh, I wish I would've been there'. Anybody that was there, they'll say that that was the highlight of '88…

It was just such a terrific feeling.

Figure 16.7: The morning: smoking ceremony at Kurnell, as the sun came up, and after a night of dancing, to heal the pain of the invasion which had for so long severed the songlines. Once again, they stretched across the continent.

Courtesy Heather Goodall.

Figure 16.8: At Kurnell – Warlpa Kutjika Thompson, Edna Hunter's and Peter Thompson's son had spent the night like my daughter Emma rolled up in a swag on that cold hillside. As the sun came up and the smoking ceremony took place, the flag was at half mast. We were mourning losses but also celebrating renewal.

Courtesy Heather Goodall.

17. Beyond the Bicentennial: Victories, defeats and more struggles for change

The Bicentennial March had been moving and impressive. It had demonstrated unarguably the passion and conviction of Aboriginal people themselves in demanding justice but also in insisting their goal was celebration of survival not retribution or revenge. It was a moral triumph as well as a political one. And it had demonstrated the widespread admiration and support of many Australians of all backgrounds for the Aboriginal struggle.

By the end of 1988, many things had changed. Some could not have been imagined at the beginning of the year. Some of them had arisen because of the huge impact generated by the Long March. Others had been born in the emotions of the march and the life changing events of the Bicentennial and the night at Kurnell. Others were attempts to patch up or bandaid over the bitter disappoints of the past decade.

All of them were to shape the next decade and beyond…

On the positive side, Gerry Hand's attempt to set up a more genuinely representative and independent national Aboriginal body, ATSIC (Aboriginal and Torres Strait Islander Commission), was being circulated during 1988, as were discussions about modifying the Australian constitution to better recognise Aboriginal people's rights. The continuing protest into the rising numbers of Aboriginal deaths in police and prison custody resulted suddenly in a federal government decision to launch a Royal Commission into the tragedies. The Hawke Government's attempt at compensation for its betrayal over national land rights led to the announcement of a formal 'Reconciliation' process which, loaded with confusion and contested definitions, and without offering anything specific, nevertheless was to be funded to promote dialogue and 'reconciliation' between whites and Indigenous Australians.

But as well as these attempts at restitution, there had also been rising anger among rural interests and other conservatives ever since the Aboriginal Land Rights Act had been passed in NSW in 1983. Once the Australian Labor Party lost the state election in 1988, the new coalition Liberal-National Party government under Nick Greiner was determined to dismantle the Land Rights Act by seizing the funds already granted to land councils to purchase land. The government attempt to do so was blocked because such action in fact threatened the bank holdings of all incorporated bodies. Forced to retreat on that front, the Greiner

Government pushed through amendments which attacked two key elements of the 1983 Act – the existence of regional land councils and the inalienability of Aboriginal freehold title.[1]

Regional land councils had been established to strengthen the local land councils by allowing them to come together in culturally appropriate groups, usually with common histories and economies, to share strategies and pool funds. While some regional land councils had not always performed as well as they could have in this role, their existence offered the opportunity for local land councils to make considered decisions in an accountable setting which was not too far removed from grass roots discussion. The State Land Council had initially had little more than a formal role, as a platform for regional land councils to confer on strategies and policies. Amending the Act to remove regional land councils had the effect of reducing the power of local land councils: all 113 would now be competing to be heard at the single, state land council, which was now to hold final decision making power. The old systems of centralised power appeared to have been replicated.

Even more troubling was the removal of inalienability. This meant that Aboriginal land could be sold, although this would require consent by a vote of local land council members. It was promoted as a path to equality, because it allowed Aboriginal organisations to seek bank loans by mortgaging their land and so enter the market and raise development funds like any other land owner.

Kevin believed that the pressure arose from the Aboriginal side because local land councils were the only organisation in many areas and so communities were relying on them to offer all sorts of welfare support. In order to keep the local land council offices running, there had to be funds to cover wages and equipment, and that wasn't going to be covered by the annual land council share of Land Tax which was supposed to be earmarked to purchase land. So there was pressure to sell land to cover wages – but once that was all gone, there would be nothing left. Evaluating the outcomes of the Land Rights Act years later, Kevin had said when talking with Barbara Flick:

Kevin: I think, in the end, people have got *something*, you know.

But I think we should never have given away inalienable freehold title. We should never have given that away. Because whatever lands are sold, you'll never get back. People are not going to be able to buy land back because it will cost too much. So I don't think you should sell land.

In practice, losing inalienability meant that Aboriginal land was again vulnerable to being lost. Aboriginal activists had consistently argued for inalienability since

---

[1] Further reading for these events includes Norman 2013 and Wilkie 1989.

the 1880s, fearing that any land they gained would be lost if it was vulnerable to later sale. In Kevin's view, 'Inalienability was the number one issue when we went to Wran on' when the negotiations started for a Land Rights Act. Judy Chester discussed contemporary support for inalienability at the state-wide land conferences open to all Aboriginal land council members.

Judy: At most of the state conferences, and at the last state conference they had up in Dubbo before the Greiner changes, people overwhelmingly said that they didn't want the inalienability lifted. At every meeting I went to, nobody wanted the inalienability lifted.

Paul Zammit, the Assistant Minister to Premier Nick Greiner, was empowered by formulating amendments to enact these changes and to 'consult' with Aboriginal communities around the state to gather their views. Zammit was abrasive and many people found interactions with him to be difficult. As *Judy Chester* explained:

Judy: Paul Zammit was an extremely aggressive person. A lot of the meetings that they went to weren't 'consultations', they were *confrontations*!

He was trying to dictate to us about what was going to be in the new legislation. He nearly got thrown out of the meeting at Redfern when they had to remind him that he was actually on the Block and there was no guarantees for his vehicle to be intact when he went outside! He was a horrible man.

As the reaction against Zammit – for both his style and his message – escalated, Greiner employed the senior Aboriginal public servant in the federal government, Charles Perkins (originally from Alice Springs) to conduct a further round of 'consultations' on the government's amendments and issue a report. Perkins' conclusions mirrored those of the government, arguing that the sale of Aboriginal land would enhance land council funds by enabling mortgages, allowing private property and commercial development by Aboriginal people. This view was widely disputed by NSW Aboriginal people, as Barbara Flick recalled.

Barbara: I have strong memories of me and Cookie meeting with parliamentary staff and Charlie Perkins to appeal desperately to them not to remove the inalienability status and not to change the role of the local, regional and state land councils. I was really angry that Perkins would break the ageless cultural protocol of involving himself in making decisions about country that was not his but which would have an impact on peoples from the east coast forever.

The government needed support from some form of NSW Aboriginal voice and the passage of the Amendments hinged on whether the State Land Council would accept Perkins' conclusions. Around 80 community members, including many long time land activists like Isabel Flick from Collarenebri and Nan Campbell, Jacko's widow from Roseby Park, gathered in the park near the State Land Council offices in Liverpool as the full Council was meeting. The members had split: long time campaigners like William Bates and Tombo Winters were holding out against the Greiner Government but others in the State Land Council were wavering – while some actively supported the move to saleable land. Kevin was in hospital at that time, with lung problems. Judy Chester, then on the executive of the Gandangara Land Council, remembered these events:

Judy: The State Land Council was meeting to decide whether they'd accept the Zammit proposals. So we all went out to Liverpool. There was a big mob of us down at the Park and we listened to what a few people had to say. Then we all marched up to the State Land Council.

But they didn't want to discuss it in front of us, they wanted to do it in a closed meeting. They tried to lock us out of the meeting.

So we all barged through. We said, 'We have a right to know what the decision is, because there wasn't proper consultation with the local land councils'. We said: 'You don't have a mandate to make decisions'.

Aunty Is told them that they didn't have a right to make decisions. And that we fought for land rights too. She was very angry, Isabel, because she could just see that nothing was happening in her community, even though we had land rights, that it was just a few who benefited from everything. You know Isabel would give you her shirt if she could get it off, so would Nan Campbell, these are people that knew what it was like to have nothing and still share everything that they did have. They didn't believe in wealth and that, you know.

I just felt that they wanted to lift the inalienability. We said, 'Once you do that, you're just going to desecrate the whole Land Rights Act'. Because we always said, we're just the custodians of the land, it has to be there for the future generations.

One of the members on the State Land Council from the South Coast was sitting around the table and he didn't see Nan Campbell, from Roseby Park. She walked up and she grabbed him by the ear and she said to him, 'You don't talk for me boy! You don't come from my country'.

Then they tried to get the police and have us removed. Isabel Flick and Nan Campbell were the mainstays of the occupation and they just said, 'This is our land council, we're entitled to be here'. And the police wouldn't chuck us out.

So when the police didn't arrest us or do anything about it, we stayed the night. We had swags, and they had a kitchen there, and we got take away and everyone just chucked in. We just all looked after each other, not everybody stayed out there, there was only a few of us. Karen Flick was there – and her cousin, Gavin along with Nan Campbell's daughter Delia and her kids.

And I was getting instructions from Isabel and Nanna Campbell, telling me what to tell Kevin when I drove back into the hospital to see him each night.

Despite the protests, the government pushed ahead, trying to gain the consent of even a small number of the NSW State Aboriginal Land Council members. This would lead the Labor Party opposition to vote to pass the new laws as well. A large crowd assembled outside Parliament House to support the existing Act and to encourage the land council members.

Figure 17.1: Joe Flick seated on the edge of the fence outside Parliament House.

Courtesy Heather Goodall.

But the mood became angry when elders who attempted to enter Parliament House to speak to politicians were physically thown out. As it became clear that some members of the State Land Council had decided to support the Amendments, a hush fell over the crowd. People stood shocked and silent as the vote was taken – activists from across the state who had been fighting for land rights over many decades stood in silence as some of their hardest won victories were dismantled.

Deeply disappointed, many echoed Judy Chester's bitter reflection:

Judy: What we fought for in 1983 was we wanted an inalienable title on our land. Especially the Sydney mob because we didn't have that much land mass to claim, and we were thinking well, you know, it's too precious.

We fought for land rights but we got land councils.

This was a defeat, but it was not the end of land rights campaigning. Not only did the day-to-day management of local land councils call for energy and attention, but the urgent need continued for a Heritage Act which would recognise Aboriginal people's ownership and management control over all significant landscapes. Ironically, it was a member of the Greiner Government, the Minister for the Environment, Tim Moore, who soon afterwards took the unexpected step of the adopting the Northern Territory's concept of Aboriginal ownership and joint management of National Parks (discussed in Chapter 12). In May 1991, Moore introduced a Bill into NSW State Parliament which promised to hand ownership of national parks to Aboriginal owners, on the condition they leased them back to the government, and entered into a joint management agreement. Eight years after the Blockade, Mutawintji was to become the first park handed back to Aboriginal ownership. The Bill had a long and stormy passage, with a watered-down version finally being approved in December 1996. Enacting ownership and management of national parks has itself been another long and difficult process with many severe problems remaining unsolved, referred to by William Bates early in this book (see Chapter 12). Yet this step has nevertheless expanded the range of ways in which Aboriginal people's rights over lands were recognised in NSW.

Figure 17.2: When Joe and his nephew Gavin attempted to enter Parliament House to deliver a message, they were unceremoniously forced down the steps and off the grounds.

Courtesy Heather Goodall.

Figure 17.3: The mood was angry as it became clear that a slim majority of the land council members were about vote to support the amendments. Delia Lowe, Jacko Campbell's daughter, stands here shocked in the middle of the crowd.

Courtesy Heather Goodall.

Making Change Happen

Figure 17.4: Mervyn Penrith, another long time South Coast campaigner, in the crowd, with Steven Gordon from Brewarrina behind him.

Courtesy Heather Goodall.

Figure 17.5: The hushed crowd as news of the vote is taken to pass the amendments and rescind inalienable title. Greg Davis from Nambucca Heads, clearly visible with his shock of white hair, can be seen standing grimly among the dispirited crowd.

Courtesy Heather Goodall.

17. Beyond the Bicentennial: Victories, defeats and more struggles for change

Figure 17.6: The ceremony to mark the formal return of ownership of Mutawintji back into Aboriginal hands. William Bates holds up the deeds of the land at the ceremony to mark its return.

Courtesy Heather Goodall.

Figure 17.7: Warlpa Thompson, Peter Thompson's son, explains the beautiful and ancient hand stencils on the rock walls of Mutawintji.

Courtesy Heather Goodall.

Soon after Moore's announcement, the long High Court battle to challenge British sovereignty across all Australia came to fruition in 1992 with the decision which carried Eddie Mabo's name, in honour of his untiring commitment to the fight to have the rights of Torres Strait Islanders – and therefore of all Indigenous peoples – acknowledged. This judgement accepted the Common Law reality of Aboriginal rights in land as property in pre-colonial times, and therefore the potential for residual rights to exist beyond the British claim to sovereignty in 1788. While this judgement has borne little fruit for Aboriginal people in the heavily settled south-east of the country, it has delivered access to substantial tracts of land in the northern half of the continent. At the time, the judgement and the ensuing federal Mabo Native Title Act of 1993 were major symbolic victories, opening once more a promise of recognition of land rights across the country.

So this was a tumultuous period, bringing with it new challenges as activists had to face the demands of becoming administrators, coping with the difficulties of managing organisations and of meeting the rapidly multiplying bureaucratic demands for financial accountability from governments unwilling to allow Aboriginal communities to make decisions about their land. Isabel Flick at Collarenebri, for example, was one fellow activist who, despite her disappointment over the amendments to the Land Rights Act in 1991,[2] threw herself completely into the day-to-day complexities of managing a Local Land Council. But the energies of many of these land rights campaigners were drained by the administrative burdens this imposed and there was a growing sense of frustration as the momentum of the 1980s appeared to have been diverted into endless audits, reports and acquittals.

Figure 17.8: Willie Bates, William Bates' son and now a ranger with the National Parks and Wildlife Service at Mutawintji, making *new* hand stencils to celebrate the land's return and to demonstrate the continued community presence and role in the custodianship of the land.

Courtesy Heather Goodall.

2   *Aboriginal Land Rights (Amendment) Act 1993* (NSW).

Kevin talked this over with Patty Anderson from Darwin:

Kevin: People were getting snowed under – that's the problem. They're working for an organisation, and then it's not funded properly so you don't get enough people to run the place. So you're running around doing too much work and you can't go out. That's how governments keep you down.

Patty Anderson: I think you're right. I think that's what's happened, that people are really busy protecting their organisation. So there isn't that luxury, if you like, of taking it to the next level. You're so busy with your nose to the grindstone, so you haven't got time to lift your head up and look what's there or what might be coming, because you're so focused on maintaining and keeping your organisations afloat.

Kevin: And that's what people want you to do! So that you can't stop to work it out!

You think that if you push yourself to go to that next level, then you might have time to go to a meeting. Because if you go to the meeting, maybe you'll find extra money to employ a person so that people have got more of a chance to get out and about, and to see what's happening in other areas.

Figure 17.9: Kevin with his family – his older aunty Mary, then Grace, Joy, Ronny and his aunty Kit.

Courtesy Kevin Cook family collection.

17. Beyond the Bicentennial: Victories, defeats and more struggles for change

Figure 17.10: When Norma Walford was badly injured in a car accident, with a brace bolted into the bones of her skull and backbone, she came to stay with Kevin and Judy in their 'elastic house' so she could be properly looked after close to the city hospital where she needed regular check ups until she could eventually have the brace taken off. Norma, Aunty Kit and Kevin visiting Grace.

Courtesy Kevin Cook family collection.

Figure 17.11: Barbara Flick and Judy Chester welcomed our daughter, Judith Torzillo (who was later to do the image research and database for this book). Judy is holding her in this photo at our house with Emma Torzillo in the back in pixie fancy dress, and Patty Anderson's grandson.

Courtesy Heather Goodall.

Tranby: Making change happen in the 1990s

Kevin's illness was diagnosed around this time as emphysema, which would increasingly limit his activities in the future. But his pace didn't ease off noticeably at first. Instead, his attention returned to Tranby, where the challenges of making Aboriginal-directed education work in the new environment were being tackled.

But the immediate problem, as it always had been, was how to protect the students at Tranby.

Protecting students

As Kevin explained, the students who came down for Tranby's courses were often very young, perhaps only 18. Some of them had barely been off the reserve before, let alone to the city. Now they were in Sydney for a year or more, sometimes staying at a quiet suburban hostel managed by Tranby staff but as students at Tranby, they were socialising in Glebe. Cookie not only felt responsible for bringing them down to Sydney, but responsible for their well-being while they were there.

As in many areas of Sydney, there was racial tension in the pubs, and early in the 1980s, the students had reported to Kevin that they were being harassed in the local hotel, the Toxteth. So Kevin and Robert Stanley went down there one day – to try to find out who was standing over the young students. After a bit of talking, they worked out it was the heavies in the pub, all tattooed up as Cookie remembers. So he says they went up to them to have a talk: 'Just Robert and I. See I wasn't a threat to them – you know – five foot nothing!'

He explained that they had students at Tranby from all over Australia, who just wanted to have a drink, and asked the drinkers to lay off. After a bit of arguing about who had started the trouble, Cookie negotiated a truce. Then an old bloke drinking there, who was 'a bit of a knockabout', invited himself over and joined in the discussion. So, Cookie says, 'We had a drink with them, and in the end we got on all right with the blokes'.

Kevin had taken the same approach of fronting up directly with the local police, who had a history of conflict with Aboriginal people in the inner city. So he went down to the Glebe police command centre, although the conversation turned out to be more difficult than at the pub.

Kevin: So I went down there to talk to them and they gave me a hard time. Yeah, they talked about Redfern and how they'd like to police. And I said, 'Look, we can go up and dig up Hitler and put him in charge of the police force out there.

Would you like that?' And the Commander was up there and he said, 'No. Come on. Steady down'. It was only two or three of the young coppers having a go at me. But it was good to get up and talk to them, even though you wouldn't do much good.

The upshot was that there had been reasonable communication – within limits – for some years. But in 1989, that all fell apart.

On 26 April, a young police officer was shot dead in a city street while arguing with an Aboriginal man, already known to police. The Aboriginal man apparently escaped in a cab which he directed towards Tranby in Glebe. Somewhere on Glebe Point Road, he had jumped out and disappeared. Soon after, in Tranby at Mansfield Street, Kevin heard distressed students screaming and shouting: 'The coppers are everywhere!'

Kevin: So next minute the coppers just swarmed into Tranby, and the head of the squad came up and said, 'We're looking for…' and we said, 'No he's not here'. And they all had shotguns, and the students were really scared. Some of the staff were scared. In fact, I was a bit toey too!

And he said, 'We're going to look in every room in the place'. I said, 'Righto, there's a building out the back'. I said, 'But there's no one here'.

So we go up the stairs of the double storey out the back. We hear this boom, boom, boom. Well there's about eight people at the door you know. And I started to get a bit worried with all these shotguns around. So I opened the door and just slung the door open, and all these shotguns came past my ear. So they all raced in and there's no one there. So I got the key out of the door and said, 'Look, this is a master key, it can get you into any room that you want to go into'. And I just let them go because I thought someone was going to get shot, because they were really nervous.

And after the coppers went all the way through the joint, and they come back. And they were really annoyed that he wasn't there. You could see it, you know? Real hatred because one of theirs got killed.

After the police had gone, Cookie looked for the students who all disappeared – some had gone straight to the pub, but some just packed up and headed home – all the way home, out of the city – and those students never came back.

Worse was to come. In the early hours of the next morning, the Police Special Weapons Squad raided the Redfern home of an acquaintance of the man they were chasing. Without asking questions and with all their shotguns loaded, they broke down a door and shot the man asleep in the bedroom inside – who turned out to be the innocent David Gundy. He was a young Aboriginal man, living in the inner city with a Tranby student, Dolly Eatts, the mother of a young son. Both Dolly and her son were in the house when David Gundy was murdered. Dolly appealed to Tranby for help, and the students rallied round to give her some support, while the Black Deaths in Custody committee, still operating out of Tranby, organised legal advice and helped her on the long road to justice.

But the impact on Tranby students was a lasting one. Throughout 1989, the police were involved in one violent incident after another. Police were often shown to have drawn their weapons and fired in situations which were dangerous to many Aboriginal people including children, like their raid in plain clothes with guns drawn – and fired – at a large picnic of Aboriginal people in Redfern just a few months later on National Aboriginal Day in July.[3]

As *Kevin* has described the aftermath at Tranby: Well Dolly was never the same after that… She needed a lot of support. She nearly went to pieces. But that little fella, you know, to see all that. He's got to carry that with him for the rest of his life.

It affected the young Aboriginal students here, you know. We've always told them, if you get into strife here, go to the cops. But make sure two or three of you go, you know?

But after that they had no trust.

Sustaining learning visions

Tranby had developed three basic programs through the 1980s: the Tertiary Education Preparation Course (to enable Aboriginal students to enter Tertiary Education), the Business Studies course (arising from the earlier Cooperative studies program) and the Skills course (for basic literacy and numeracy skills). Accreditation and funding had been won – after hard battles in the 1980s – from the NSW government through its Technical and Further Education department (TAFE) which however also demanded a high level of control over content and management. Tranby's community programs (Chapters 7 and 8) had been largely unaccredited, giving skills but not certificates. In the 1990s, the College pushed out in many directions.

---

3   These events were documented soon after by criminologist Chris Cunneen and later by Justice Hal Wooten, Royal Commissioner into Black Deaths in Custody: Chris Cunneen May 1990, *Aboriginal-Police Relations in Redfern: with special reference to the 'Police Raid' of 8 February 1990: Report Commissioned by the National Inquiry into Racist Violence*, Human Rights and Equal Opportunity Commission, Sydney.

What stayed the same: Learner-directed learning

A decade earlier, Kevin had worked with new teaching staff like Brian Doolan, Terry Widders, Chris Milne and myself, who were exploring strategies for teaching and learning which recognised and respected the knowledge of students.

This was an important result of thinking about the knowledge Aboriginal people learned in their communities – about past traditional life but also about very contemporary, collective Aboriginal cultures in which places and kinsfolk mattered, along with working to build communities. So at Tranby, the Aboriginal-directed education which emerged had done so from an interaction of the experiences of students enrolled in the courses, of the Aboriginal and trade union activists who came into the College and of the academics – both Aboriginal and non-Aboriginal – whose research was being called on to contribute to teaching.

In many ways also, it drew from Kevin's experience in democratic, rank-and-file unionism in the Builders Labourers' Federation as well as in his international networks at the Coady Institute. So this focus on linking the experiences of learners to the building of new capacities – not only capacity to get work or further education but capacity to make change in communities – was a political as well as an educational commitment.

This approach is called 'student-directed learning' in some places, but the emphasis at Tranby from my memories of teaching there in the early 1980s was on the fact that the people enrolled were *adults*: to be recognised for – and encouraged to be – making their own decisions. So the words we used were 'participant-directed' or 'learner-directed learning' – because the Tranby environment also emphasised that we were *all* learning.

While this 'learner-directed learning' approach was developed with innovative teachers in the early 1980s like Brian Doolan and Terry Widders, Kevin had encouraged incoming teaching staff who joined the College afterwards to follow along these same approaches to building learner-directed learning into Tranby programs both in the courses in Glebe and in community settings like the land councils and local government training courses. So the later directors of studies or particular programs who worked at Tranby, like Helen Corbett, Jack Beetson and Yvonne Jackson, had all followed up and expanded aspects of this strategy. Despite changes in staff, Kevin was able to sustain the vision he had that *real* education had to recognise *politics* to contribute to continued learning and change.

Christine Kerr, who came to Tranby as a teacher in 1993, explained the impact she could see then at Tranby:

Christine Kerr: Anybody who'd been in any political life both state-wise and federally knew of Tranby in terms of Aboriginal Education. It was the longest surviving and the most radical of the Aboriginal-controlled educational organisations!

Tranby continued too with its outreach programs into the non-Aboriginal community. As well as more formal interventions through Black Books in its sales to school libraries and educators, there were the 'Dreaming and Dispossession' seminars – running as a free, community education course held once a week in the evenings over a semester. These were widely attended and drew in many people – including those like Chris Kerr, from an activist and educator background, who became interested in joining Tranby once she had attended this program. But the seminars attracted a far wider audience than those who, like Chris, already had some knowledge of Tranby. When I was researching community environmental relations in the Georges River area, for example, I came across a number of people from Bankstown who had taken the course. Some were employed in Aboriginal-related work but others were suburban housewives and community members who had enrolled just out of interest.

Figure 17.12: Yvonne Jackson, Director of Studies at Tranby, during the 1990s, with Robyn Ridgeway, Head of Tertiary Prep and Sylvia Scott, Wiradjuri elder, long-time supporter of Tranby and close friend of Judy and Cookie.

Courtesy Tranby Archives.

17. Beyond the Bicentennial: Victories, defeats and more struggles for change

Figure 17.13: Yvonne (third from left) and Judy (fifth from left) carrying the Tranby banner.

Courtesy Tranby Archives.

Figure 17.14: Patrick Dodson with Judy Chester and Kevin's nephew, Gregory Streets, at Tranby. The brass King Plate in Patrick's hand had been found in the family holdings of Louise Taylor, left, from Canberra who had repatriated it to Tranby.

Courtesy Tranby Archives.

Figure 17.15: Bob Bellear was among many long time friends of Kevin's and supporters of Tranby who were regular guests at Tranby barbeques.

Courtesy Tranby Archives.

Figure 17.16: Tranby welcomed elders of the community and Kevin's uncle Stan was a regular visitor.

Courtesy Tranby Archives.

17. Beyond the Bicentennial: Victories, defeats and more struggles for change

What changed? Courses, accreditation and people

The circumstances of the early 1990s had changed greatly after 1988, as the first pages of this chapter have shown. So it was important for Tranby to continue to bring community goals for education into the way Tranby's learning programs were developed in this new environment.

Kevin: Our community has always dictated what was going on at Tranby and they were looking for more courses that involved actual academic learning, rather than job creation as such. And I think that's the direction where we were headed. And I had great support from within the organisation too – not only from academic staff but from administrative staff like Greta North.

Figure 17.17: Tranby Secretaries with Kevin in the main office. Lorelle Corderoy on the right.

Courtesy Tranby Archives.

Tranby not only began to strengthen its academic education by developing new higher level diploma courses but also to demand recognition of its right as an Aboriginal-controlled education body to accredit and manage its teaching programs. To do this, Tranby had to undertake long battles with the NSW Vocational Education and Training Accreditation Board (VETAB) to secure accreditation for its three new programs, Diplomas in Legal Studies and in Development Studies in Aboriginal Communities and the Advanced Diploma of Applied Aboriginal Studies.

Kevin explained the old TAFE control: It made it hard. We'd have someone come out and tell us how we had to teach the course and we refused to do that. And they all went, 'If you don't do it this way, then you don't get any money'. So we were always under the strap of conforming to their way of thinking and it wasn't Tranby's way of thinking. So then we decided that the only way out of it was to get out of TAFE funding. And so that meant we had to design our own courses, and that meant bringing in new people, looking out for new money.

Through all the new developments, Kevin continued to stress literacy and numeracy: he was determined that the old Tranby strengths of basic literacy skills were critical underpinnings to reinforce in all the new programs.

Figure 17.18: Cookie shared his passion for following the racing with Judy's brother-in-law, Tommy Ely. Cookie bought a number of trotters, including this one, in partnership with Tommy and although the horses did not win much, Cookie and Tommy took a lot of pleasure in following their progress.

Courtesy Kevin Cook family collection.

New staff: Discovering learner-directed learning

Chris Kerr had trained in primary education and had worked teaching young children. She had been involved in the Nuclear Free and Independent Pacific movement in Sydney in the 1980s, so she had been aware of Tranby. In the earlier years of the decade, she went to work in the Northern Territory, employed on Bathurst Island with the Aboriginal community. Only on her return to Sydney in the early 1990s did she come to Tranby to work – although as she explained, she was also 'looking for community'. Employed as a part-time teacher at Tranby, Chris found teaching adults with the Tranby approach to learner-directed learning to be a huge shock:

Chris: I knew nothing! It was just the thought of teaching Aboriginal adults who were much more than the children I'd taught before. After the first three weeks, I'd offered my resignation. I thought, I can't do this, it's just far too hard.

But Cookie said to me, 'Just hang on. Just give it a little time, give it another few weeks'.

That's when I really came to understand that Tranby education was a process of facilitation not teaching. The people there weren't students they were participants. And they were such informed adults – and they were very angry! I can still remember one of the students in the Tertiary Preparation Course one day. We had a TAFE curriculum so we all tried very hard to do it differently, and to find relevant sources. I had remembered this one poem that I thought would be good. It was based around a Welsh mining town where there'd been a mud slide across a school and it was very emotive. So we were discussing it as a class and one of the blokes pushed back his chair and said, 'Well it doesn't move me at all'. He said, '*My* story hasn't moved anybody'. He was saying he had this whole other story that he'd never even had the opportunity to tell, so others had never had the chance to be moved by it. That was a reminder to me of the pain of other people's stories and the enormous desire for different lives that enabled people just to get out of bed just to come to Tranby – if they had a bed. There were no 'learning curves' at Tranby – they were all huge learning *precipices*. There were no 'curves' at all.

What was different about Tranby was that you were not set with a curriculum because it was about the students bringing their own issues into the discussion, their own knowledge and skills base. Then it was built upon and extended where that was required. So while all the foundation stuff was covered, the way we did that that was developed from the student groups' own experience. And in any of those groups you might have Elders and then you've got the young ones beside them – so it was a very powerful teaching and learning environment.

Kevin was a key figure even for new staff, as *Chris* recalled: I was terrified of Kevin when I started out. I was absolutely terrified. I'd think, 'Heaven help me if he calls me into his office!'

His office was at the front as you came in the door. So it was a visual thing, about where he sat and how his office was positioned. You'd wonder if you could sneak past that door without getting sprung or he'd just be going to say: 'I'm looking for you'.

But even so, they were very exciting days. I know I wasn't alone in feeling that. For many of us who were non-Aboriginal workers, we came from such different arenas and different experiences. But we had all come with the profoundly strong sense of why we were there. And of course the challenge for all of us was: 'Well, what would it have meant if you couldn't have got paid to stay there?' And at that time – all of us would have stayed there! That was just how it was.

There was always the vision that was really strongly present and the vision was talked about, it was articulated for all of us. So even for teachers who might come in two hours a week, everybody had a sense of the importance of the task at hand and nobody was excluded from that. It was the energy that grew out of that place and the importance of continuing the process of getting justice, particularly around education.

I was often asked: 'Well why are you working here? You're white!' And I would say, 'Well I'm employed here because maybe we can build something together'. There was a sense of the struggle being for all us to benefit from. We felt this belongs to all of us. So there was incredible good will and it wasn't even about having a job – it was that this was your *life*, so you just lived your life. It was a sense of being part of a community, of respect for each other, and what that meant. So there was no holds barring anybody. The aim was to enable everybody to shine, that was the opportunity – and it was Kevin who provided that opportunity.

New diploma courses: Legal studies

The first of the new diploma courses was National Aboriginal Legal Studies, funded initially by HREOC, the Human Rights and Equal Opportunities Commission. The diploma was later renamed to be one in National Indigenous Legal Advocacy. It enabled a broad and different sweep across the legislation and legal processes of the times.

But although the content was new to Tranby, the people were not. This new diploma allowed a more structured interaction between students and lawyers who had already had a long involvement with Tranby, like John Terry. John had helped to write the 'plain English' version of the 1983 Land Rights Act and had taught into the land councils and local government community courses. And the lawyers from the various Aboriginal and general legal services, like those at the Western Aboriginal Legal Service who had supported Barbara Flick and William Bates, or those at SCALS – the South Coast service – who had supported Jacko Campbell and Ted Thomas in their land rights campaigning.

Development studies in Aboriginal communities

The second major new course was the Diploma in Development Studies in Aboriginal Communities, which was launched in the mid 1990s. Development which took account of social, cultural and political dimensions of community life as well as economic advancement had always been a central goal for Tranby. This had been the focus of Alf Clint's work with co-operatives and it had been the focus of Kevin's work at Tranby and in his work at the Coady International Institute in Canada. The course was aimed at equipping Aboriginal community members to return home with real, effective skills and with confidence in their analysis of the challenges and opportunities facing their communities. Kevin and Chris Kerr talked about the course goals and outcomes

Kevin: Although a lot of political stuff was going on, it seemed to enhance what was happening at Tranby and I think vice versa too. People said, 'Oh, all of these students that are leaving here were going to lead the armed struggle!'

Well, that didn't happen! A couple of students got really involved in politics but the majority played a more important role in community when they went home. For the first time they could read the accounts, where the community organisations were spending money, they could go through the accounts book and say, 'Hm, we're spending too much money here, stop it'. Before that, the accountants had had all the say and they could dictate. But when students left Tranby, they could go back home and then *they* would be able to dictate where the money was spent.

Chris: People were politicised in a very different way. Their role was to bring the capability for positive change in community. Particularly through a course like Development Studies, which tried to articulate a bit more clearly about what was happening for people on the ground. It talked about the history of new legislations and policies and put it into perspective, so it brought people a greater understanding of why we're all in the position that we're in today. It taught people about the ability to change things and then *how* to change them, what sort of capabilities you need for change.

Figure 17.19: Suzie with her first son, Jake.

Courtesy Margaret Munday family collection.

It was also interesting because some people would start off in the Aboriginal Studies course and then complete that and then move to Development Studies. It was an opportunity for building skills and certainly for building confidence and self esteem. And as well, to build a communal esteem about what it meant to be doing what they were doing and studying at Tranby.

The edge of difference that Tranby provided was that it was aimed at students who would take the information back home. So often there was a spin-off effect: people would come down for the first time to do a course and then go back home. Then others from the community would come down because they either knew of the benefit or they could see the changes.

There was a real mix of ages too. There were some very young ones who would come in. And again Elders from Sydney – people like Esther Carrol, from a Wiradjuri family of activists, who was an incredible benefit to the group and to the learning that went on in the group. We had lots of people too from around Maclean, Lismore way.

Among the people who came down, everybody has different stories to tell. So we used to deliberately use the stories – and the places in the stories – in building the curricula. So while the curricula didn't change, the content of it certainly did! We built the tasks and experiential learning of the courses on the people's own stories. We'd find out if anybody was visiting Cookie and we would try and get them into the classrooms, even if it meant the arrangements had to be done that day and we changed whatever else was happening. People like Christine Christopherson, the artist and community and environmental activist, would always be part of the classes when she was in town from the Northern Territory. And people like Gary Foley and Terry O'Shane and other people when they were in town visiting Cookie.

Figure 17.20: Judy and Jody's younger daugher, Yamirra, who often stayed with Judy and Cookie – her Nanny and Poppy.

Courtesy Judy Chester family collection.

Aboriginal Studies and block programs

Being put together at the same time as Development Studies was another important program, the Advanced Diploma in Aboriginal Studies. This program built on the recognition that students already had a powerful body of knowledge from their lives within the Aboriginal community on which to draw and build.

It was also a key aspect of the way Tranby College began articulating with universities. Terry Widders was teaching Aboriginal History at Macquarie University from 1989, drawing on his recent research with Indigenous peoples in Japan and China, as well as Australia. I was at the University of Technology, Sydney (UTS), in the Public History program, which built on my experience working in legal research for Aboriginal communities in Royal Commissions like that in British Nuclear Testing and Black Deaths in Custody as well as my time spent teaching in the Tertiary Prep course at Tranby with Terry in the early 1980s. One of Tranby's goals was that it would be able to offer this program not only to its own students but would be able to feed into the university programs. To this end, a network was formed which linked Tranby with interested academics, like Terry and myself, along with others who had a long commitment to working with Aboriginal people.

A great deal of information flowed in all directions, and many Tranby students graduated from the Tertiary Prep program and then the diplomas and then enrolled in degree programs at universities like Macquarie and UTS. A number of Tranby students and staff went on to make important, continuing contributions as university staff members, like Christine Evans, who became a long term member of the teaching staff in the Education Faculty at UTS. A key innovation which developed at Tranby and also flowed into university programs was the intense commitment Tranby had to encouraging course participants to return to their communities.

To meet this goal, Tranby introduced the strategy of *not* taking people out of their communities in the first place. Students were able to enrol for Tranby's new Diploma courses in Development and Aboriginal Studies by undertaking them in 'Block' mode. So instead of having to leave their community to live in the city for the year or two that it would take to finish the course, Tranby students could come for intensive 'blocks' of teaching over two weeks, which was repeated once or twice a semester, and then return to their communities to work on assignments.

Kevin explained the logic of the strategy: Well we were always fighting for people to be able to come away from their communities for short periods of time and then being able to go back. So that their community wouldn't miss out on their expertise. Because the people doing the courses used to run the communities. So if they were away for a length of time the communities would suffer.

To run the program, both funding and accommodation had to be rethought. Previously students who had come from rural areas to do Tranby courses had stayed over the semesters or years in hostels, some run in close association with Tranby itself. But for the short term accommodation need for 'Block' modes, a new arrangement had to be worked out. Chris Kerr who was teaching in the Development Studies course in 1996 has described the process of putting it all together:

Chris Kerr: The block program got started coinciding with the Development Studies diploma starting because I remember Christine Evans was coordinator of the Tranby program (before she went to UTS). And teaching in it was Les Meltzer from South Australia, and then also Bob Maza, the actor and arts activist, who was working there at the same time, both as a teacher and as a resident consultant to the students and staff. That always had enormous value, because it allowed people to reflect and provide that opportunity for enrichment. There was Tex Skuthorpe too, working there as an artist in residence and teacher.

When people came down on block release they were mainly staying I think at that stage at the Glebe motels close to Tranby. That's when there was a really wide sweep of people coming in. We had successful applicants coming in as course participants from Western Australia – from north-west Western Australia to the south of Perth. I'm not sure if there were people from South Australia, but there were certainly students from southern and far North Queensland, including Palm Island. There were a lot of people from the Torres Strait Islands. Tranby had had a long connection with the Torres Strait Islands from the old Co-op days, and Josephine David-Peter was the head teacher of the Business Studies course when I first started too. So there was already a strong connection with Torres Strait Islander mob to build on. So there's this constant renewal of history in the people who were coming to the college.

Kevin has recalled the interaction with Macquarie, which had been the first university in NSW to adopt the block mode: Macquarie picked it up after we had a meeting with them. Then we were running a course in conjunction with Macquarie for about two years.

The difficulty became funding – not only was Tranby struggling to pay teaching staff but so too was the university. Once it became an issue of who would be paid for the teaching hours, the university had all the bargaining power. Tranby found that the hours, and the funding, all went to the university – which made it impossible to sustain Tranby's side of the course.

Later on, as *Kevin* remembers: We were always invited to the end of the year 'dos' and we kept pretty close contact with the Aboriginal teachers and a lot of the white teachers who were teaching in that course. But once money became involved...

I was teaching at UTS at the time, and I can remember the impact which Tranby was making on the thinking of universities. Inspired by Tranby's lead, we at UTS put a lot of time during 1993 into establishing a cross-Faculty Aboriginal Studies Major, with a planning committee on which Tranby representatives sat to give us advice. This major was strongly supported in the Faculty of Education, which utilised the strategy of block delivery of courses, which enabled Aboriginal students to undertake the degree while remaining in their communities. So Tranby's lead had generated a major change in tertiary education, but as Kevin remembers, Tranby was left with little else but the invitations to the 'end of year dos'.

Accreditation

There was an initial delay in establishing the Advanced Diploma in Aboriginal Studies because Tranby was determined to establish the principle of Aboriginal control over accreditation of Aboriginal Studies courses. Kevin talked with Chris Kerr about the process:

Kevin: What we were trying to do was trying to get accreditation in our own right and not have to go to anybody else. We fought very hard and long for that.

Chris: The last one to get accredited was the Aboriginal Studies one because it had been formed deliberately to challenge the NSW Vocational and Educational Accreditation Board (VETAB). The whole point was to become an accreditation body in our own right and become part of the Federation of Independent Providers. Who else was better placed to be in a situation of accrediting independent providers? It still doesn't seem right that a non-Aboriginal, very bureaucratic agency would seek to accredit an Aboriginal Studies course, developed by Aboriginal Elders and community members from across NSW.

Kevin: There was some good people on that VETAB. But the issue wasn't with the people, you know, but about the course being accredited in the end by a non-Aboriginal group, which is crazy. A lot of the people who had input into the design of our Aboriginal Studies course were people with high standing in their community – like Isabel Flick, and Chicka Dixon and Sylvia Scott. And there was a number of other people too who helped frame the course at that stage.

Chris: Yeah and that was the irony. Kim McConville was the one who was employed through Tranby to pull together the Advanced Diploma of Applied Aboriginal Studies and she'd done a great job. She'd consulted with you and worked closely with Aunty Is and others. But the first time it went up to VETAB, they didn't accredit it. They said, 'No, no, you know it has to look like this and behave like this and so on'. So you had all of these Elders involved … everybody working with Kim on getting the content right and the delivery structure of it right. I remember Aunty Is saying, 'We want this to be delivered to *both* Aboriginal and non-Aboriginal people. It should be delivered differently to non-Aboriginal people, but none the less they can do it'.

So it always struck me as extraordinary that a non-Aboriginal bureaucracy could say 'That's inappropriate'.

But Kim reworked it in such a way that it still maintained the integrity of the original purpose – and in the end it got through.

Networking: 'a national reach'

The extensive networks which Kevin had built up across the 1980s continued to bring people through Tranby's doors during the 1990s when Cookie was there, because as Chris Kerr laughed, '…oh trust me, they all came in to see Kevin, they weren't coming in to see us!'

But there were many such contacts which went on to be with Tranby more generally, because Kevin continued to ensure that education was political.

Kevin: Everybody that came in there, it didn't matter who, there were no airs and graces about them. Like Doddo [Patrick Dodson], he'd come in and say g'day to everyone, have a cup of tea with all the students. There was Jack Ah Kit and Rossie [David Ross], these incredibly high powered blokes from the big Northern Territory land councils…

Chris: there was such incredible good will at Tranby and it was such an open vibrant place. People would just drop in for a cup of tea. Not only the high profile people like Pat Dodson and David Ross who came to see you Cookie, but everyone. It was welcoming and it had this energy about it…

These visits, as *Chris* explained, were directly engaged in teaching: And so with this huge energy and people communicating about local and national issues and from such different communities, it meant that the diploma courses had a national reach, a grasp of national issues. It has enormous benefit for students from outside of New South Wales because it's still a lesson that people are often surprised about to learn – about the radical nature of politics in New South Wales.

Networking: Trade unionists

The people enrolled at Tranby were not the only ones who benefited. Kevin and Judy Chester, who became an organiser in the Public Sector Union (variously called the PSA or the CPSU in NSW and the Commonwealth), talked about the way union organisations drew on the opportunities Tranby offered to engage with Aboriginal people in a relaxed setting:

Judy: Cathy Block worked with the ACTU and she was involved with the TUTA[4] training programs. Cathy used to love using Tranby. She'd come with trainee organisers all from different unions and from all over the country. So here's these young gung-ho organisers – or trainee organisers – all going to change the world! They'd get stopped in their tracks pretty smart! They found they had to rethink their priorities, keeping Aboriginal issues up front. Cathy would take them over to Tranby and me and Kevin Tory would go and talk to them about Aboriginal involvement in the trade union movement. We'd tell them about Cookie in the Builders Labourers and all that.

Kevin: See, they'd never heard of a blackfella being involved with the trade union movement, like Terry O'Shane and all those blokes, who'd all been in unions all their lives!

Judy: Yeah, but it was interesting for our students too. They'd hear from the trade unionists in the session before lunch, and then come lunch time everybody would intermingle, you know. And the Tranby students would be curious, about who are these white fellas. And the white fellas would be there too, wanting to know something about the students, what they're doing there. Most of the TUTA mob had been through university and so most of these trainee union organisers would want to know what the education was like. So Cathy did a good job. These gung-ho trainees would get to talk to the students, and they'd walk away with a different perspective you know.

The strong friendships which Kevin had built up over the years across the country did not only now benefit Tranby. As far as he was able, Kevin continued to sustain the flow of support to Aboriginal education projects. He took a special interest in linking Tranby with IAD, the Institute for Aboriginal Development in Alice Springs, where his friend, the Pitjantjatjara activist Yami Lester was

---

4   Trades Union Training Authority.

director and with the broad movement for Aboriginal education in Victoria. There he supported Gary Foley and Bruce McGuinness to defend an Aboriginal secondary school from being closed down in the mid 1990s.

As *Kevin* saw it: ... Whatever they did to any education organisation, whether it be in Victoria or the Northern Territory, they could do the same to us in New South Wales. There was always a fear that the government was trying to close Tranby down on some excuse. I don't believe that any of us should have been closed down because we were serving a real purpose.

Networking: International

Kevin also was able to continue to encourage the international connections which he had found valuable. The new national representative body, ATSIC, was expected to contribute funding for Aboriginal international political travel and communication, but the application process was cumbersome and the body's priorities were not always those of more compact, Aboriginal-controlled bodies like Tranby. Chris Kerr has related her memories of an example where Kevin's intervention ensured the networking continued. Yvonne Jackson, despite being Director of Studies had never attended an international education meeting. She had applied for ATSIC funds to go to a UN gathering in Germany, but it became clear that the decision, even if it was positive, would be too late to organise the trip.

Chris continued: It was the Friday before they were to leave on the weekend and Kevin said, 'Right, exactly what's the situation?' and I had to explain: 'Well I know Yvonne has organised her passport, but we still haven't heard from ATSIC and I know Yvonne's been shopping to make sure she has some clothes to go. This is her first time overseas'. And Kevin's response was, 'Well she will go either way'. In the end, Kevin organised to cover the fare and ATSIC eventually paid it back.

It was a big thing for me to learn, because here was an organisation that wasn't flash for funds. It was not only Kevin's individual compassion but his broader understanding of what it means for others to be part of a movement that was greater than even Tranby was itself at that period of time. There was an enormous commitment at Tranby to broaden the level of struggle and that meant working out how people could get involved. What I learnt then was that Cookie believed that if ATSIC wasn't going to fund it, it was the responsibility of our organisation to see that the trip still happened.

The international networks themselves were important to Kevin. He kept in touch with the African National Congress representative organisation in

Australia, and continued to play an active role in the campaign against the Apartheid government. For example, Kevin and Barbara Flick had attended a 'Free Nelson Mandela' rally of over 250,000 people in London in 1984 where they made new contacts and developed strong international links. By 1990, Kevin took an active part in organising the trip in which the triumphant Nelson Mandela came to Australia in October 1990, after being released from gaol, although many Aboriginal people were frustrated that the African National Congress would make no comment on Aboriginal demands during the visit. Judy Chester was able to meet Mandela, who had become the symbol of hope for continuing justice for many. Kevin sustained his networks in the Indian and Pacific Island nations as well, supporting the emerging Pacific Islander and Australian NGO meetings to which Kevin Tory was able to go as a representative of TUCAR and Tranby.

And the role of Tranby was well known internationally. *Chris Kerr* remembers a surprise visit: I still remember very clearly the day that Danny Glover turned up. He said to us: 'I have to come somewhere first to pay my respects and I've been told this is where to come to announce that I'm in Sydney'. People at Tranby said, 'Well now you've gotta go to Redfern and go down to the Block'. So he signed everybody's books and papers at Tranby, and then he went over to Redfern. Tranby was an incredible focus then and I suspect it still is.

Figure 17.21: Tranby graduates Eddie Galleghan, Laurel Johnson, Ted Budd with Judy Chester on right.

Courtesy Tranby Archives.

17. Beyond the Bicentennial: Victories, defeats and more struggles for change

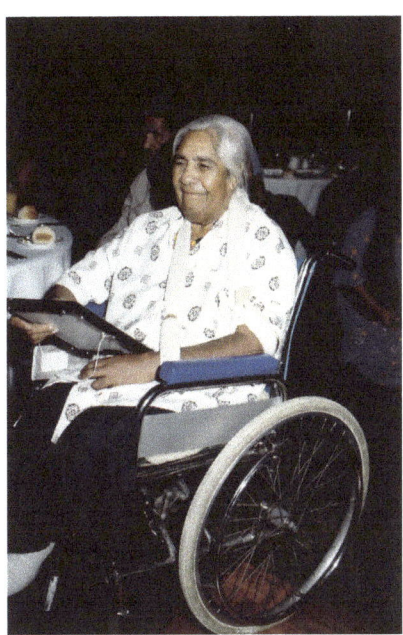

Figure 17.22: Nan Campbell, a heroic land rights campaigner and Jacko Campbell's widow, recognised with an Honorary Doctorate.

Courtesy Tranby Archives.

Figure 17.23: Those acknowledged for their extraordinary contributions with Honorary Doctorates, including Kevin, Sylvia, Isabel, Nan and others, along with a number of Tranby staff members. (Others in this photo include Rossie Fisher (far right, now deceased) and staff members Reid Strachan, Jack Beetson, and Josephine David-Petero.)

Courtesy Tranby Archives.

In 1994, Tranby initiated a program of recognition of the sustained contribution of key senior people in the Aboriginal community to the local, national and international movements for education and social justice. To be chosen for an Honorary Doctorate by Tranby was widely regarded as an honour within the Aboriginal community. Judy Chester discussed the program, explaining how important these awards were within her own community in Wellington.

Judy: The Doctorates acknowledged the work that people did in their communities. And they were very well sought after. Because Kevin was making sure that a lot of people that didn't usually ever get acknowledged *were* going to be acknowledged for the work they were doing. So people like Isabel Flick, Bob Bellear and Sylvia Scott got all the first ones. And Nan Campbell got one, Joe Flick and Joe McGinness.[5] I think the last ones that were given out were to Justine Saunders and to Bruce McGuinness. It was just before Bruce died and so he was too sick to come up. Naomi Meyers came to accept the award for him because Naomi was really stoked that Cookie acknowledged Bruce and he was really proud of that.

And my Auntie Joyce got one for the work that she does in the western area of New South Wales, around Wellington. For these old people, that doctorate is the most important thing. They're really proud of it you know. I went to Nanna Latham's funeral and you know, the minister got up and talked about Tranby College acknowledging Nanna Latham and that and how proud she was. So it meant a great deal.

The Honorary Doctorates program brought together the many strands of Tranby's activity over the 1980s and 1990s. It recognised community knowledge and power, drawing on the extensive networks into Aboriginal communities across the country which had been built up through the learning networks of students and staff and the political networks in which all of them had been involved. In honouring heroes among Aboriginal communities in the form of a doctorate, Tranby was demanding that the non-Indigenous world recognise too the standing of continuing Aboriginal culture and community.

---

5   The full list of people honoured by Tranby in this way included also Naomi Meyers, Gary Foley and – eventually, after his illness had forced him to retire – Kevin Cook himself.

18. Reflections: Networks, hubs, pathways – and leadership

Heather Goodall

The photographs of Cookie's 70th birthday in 2009 tell a great deal about his life. They all show Judy Chester beside him. Cookie is sitting in a wheelchair, older of course and more frail, but around him as always are the family, mates and campaigners who had stood shoulder to shoulder with him in the exciting process of making changes happen. In front of him was a big cake, iced in the Aboriginal colours of black, red and yellow and next to the cake, a huge plate of oysters!

Figure 18.1: Cake with oysters.

Courtesy Heather Goodall.

Making Change Happen

His aunty Kit is sitting on one side and on the other side is Sylvia Scott, long time friend of both Judy and Cookie. Standing next to Cookie are Joe Owens, presenting Cookie with the last remaining Life Membership badge of the Builders Labourers' Federation and Pat Geraghty, towering leader of the Maritime Union and a friend from way back, talking with Cookie about memories of Alf Clint and then all the times with Cookie at helm of the Co-operative. The Tranby people were there, along with those others who have shared Cookie's vision of education for change: Brian Doolan, Linda Burney, Chrissy Kerr, Robyn Ridgeway and Derek Mortimer. The old friends from the early land rights days: Meredith Burgmann, Nadia Wheatley, Rod Pickette. And those stalwart unionists – Hal Alexander, Russ Herman and Tony O'Bierne. There are close friends: Paul Torzillo, Janny Ely (Judy's sister) and her husband Tommy, Norma Walford and Greta North. And there are many younger people – Judy's children and grandchildren, Rod Pickette's children along with Paul's and my daughters. Those young people were there as family, but beyond that, each of them was a friend of Kevin in their own right, drawn into the enthusiasm and enjoyment for life that he has continued to nurture in all of us.

Figure 18.2: Joe Owens presents Cookie with the last remaining BLF life membership badge. Brian Doolan and Sylvia Scott sitting on left.

Courtesy Heather Goodall.

18. Reflections: Networks, hubs, pathways – and leadership

Figure 18.3: Pat Geraghty, long time secretary of the Seamen's Union, shaking Cookie's hand.

Courtesy Heather Goodall.

Figure 18.4: Patty Anderson speaking.

Courtesy Heather Goodall.

Patty Anderson, who had come down from Darwin, made the final speech, one that had everyone in tears one minute and laughing the next, about the times Cookie had brought people together despite distances and languages, and, even more amazingly, how he had somehow made sure that everyone got on. He'd given them all things to do, got them to go overseas when they hadn't wanted to, always been there to listen to midnight reverse charges phone calls from god knows where. Cookie is not well these days, but for all of us, he has continued to be generous with his time and warm companionship no matter how far away he is or how much it costs him in effort and energy. 'Mirrors' Cook – that's what Janny had called him long ago – is still using the phone to 'look into' many things for many people, fixing them when he can, helping to make new plans when he can't fix things, and never giving up.

***

By the time of that party in 2009, 20 years had passed since the Long March to mark the Bicentennial of January 1988. The defeats and the victories of the 1990s, in land, heritage and learning, discussed in the last chapter, had all played a role in shaping the ongoing momentum of the years to come. But the bigger questions were about how to nurture the storytelling which had been at the heart of Tranby.

In Kevin's later years at the College, with the expansion of Tranby's teaching program, it became clear that the old, dilapidated buildings would not be adequate for the students, let alone for the associated resources like Black Books. So he was involved in the planning for an ambitious building and renovation program. Not only were there the new programs, but there were as well some emerging opportunities which needed space, like the possibility of extending the library with a well-organised archive of Tranby's history, which the supporter and archivist Julia Mant had proposed. Kevin's lobbying skills became crucial to funding the plan, which he did with characteristic ingenuity by offering a personal invitation to federal ALP Minister for Schools, Vocational Education and Training, Ross Free to visit Tranby to see the state of the old buildings for himself. Perhaps even more important, because Kevin knew the building industry so well, he took a high role in negotiating the construction contract and then in liaising with the building unions to ensure there were Aboriginal workers on the job and that the Tranby students learnt about the building industry while the new College areas were being built.

But it wasn't just about the bricks and concrete. There was a central structural element of the old building which needed to be preserved for much more than its architectural value. This was the old sandstone fireplace in the dining room.

I remembered its importance in the early 1980s when I had worked there, and recently, in 2012, Chris Kerr described her memories of the way that fireplace was working in the early 1990s.

Christine Kerr: It was at the fireplace that everybody got to tell their stories in that building and they were stories that were shared. I still can point out that spot where it used to be. Somehow, metaphorically and symbolically, the whole of Tranby is the fireplace.

In the reconstruction of the new building there was a place left for the fireplace, but because of some council regulation, the fireplace couldn't be put back in there. I'd been worried that when it wasn't not a fireplace any longer then the stories would get lost. How were the young ones learning when those stories weren't getting retold around that fireplace?

I know better now.

Kevin too had been increasingly concerned about the stories of the place and the struggle. He had wanted to sustain the focus on cultural activities which had been generated during the Bicentennial. A developing program around the music industry expanded Building Bridges to become a major mentoring program for young Aboriginal artists, which linked high profile and politically active singer-song writers like Paul Kelly with Kev Carmody and others. Kevin had fostered the Aboriginal Writers Festival through Tranby, nurturing the storytelling in which he was increasingly interested. In the early 1990s, Kevin had encouraged his old friends to tell their stories. Joe McGinness was already underway with his story. On trips down from Cairns, Joe enjoyed Cookie and Judy's 'elastic house' in the evenings, with a lot of back up from Kathy Kennedy, Kevin's cousin, who was staying with them too while she studied at Tranby. During the day, Joe could be found in Cookie's office at Tranby, dictating his life story to Chrissy. It blossomed into his book: Son of Alyandabu: My Fight for Aboriginal Rights.[1]

Out of that process, Kevin looked for practical ways to encourage Aboriginal history makers and story-tellers, and this was the genesis of the Rona-Tranby Trust, the collaboration between the Jewish community and Tranby. With applicants chosen under Aboriginal control, the funds were able to foster the telling of stories in forms which otherwise could not have been published and circulated.

Cookie was able to be at work less often from 1997, as his emphysema got worse. He made it into Tranby on some days, sitting in the office like he had always

---

1   Joe McGinness 1991, *Son of Alyandabu: My Fight for Aboriginal Rights*, Queensland University Press, St Lucia.

done. But increasingly, he was working from home, with Judy managing his days and liaising with Chris Kerr who kept up the flow of work papers between Kevin's house and Tranby. Kevin kept in touch with Tranby staff and his far flung network of comrades by phone – the handset seemed to be attached to his ear.

At Tranby itself, the office still looked the same but Cookie's chair was often empty. The office was busy, however, not only with staff but because Isabel Flick, after a bout of illness, had decided to retire from the local land council in Collarenebri and was now often at Tranby, talking with students, undertaking outside talks and representing Tranby visions in many ways. And she had a new project. Cookie had encouraged her to take up the opportunity for funding support from the Rona-Tranby Trust and she had decided it was time now to get on with her story. She asked me to help with the research and writing but she wanted to use the money mainly to help her travel to talk with the people who had been close to her throughout the many struggles she had been in to gain justice for the people in north-western NSW. The Rona-Tranby funds made her story into a very strong community conversation – with the people she had worked with all featuring strongly alongside her as she tried to answer the questions she had about why her life had worked out the way it had.[2] Chris Kerr described to Kevin what the office had looked like in those days:

Chris Kerr: Aunty Is sat in that big pink chair. I can see her sitting there to your left side. You occupied the centre position at that desk whenever you could be there.

But it was probably after 1997 when you were spending a lot more time working from home. There was constant movement at Tranby, and lots going on, there was absolutely no doubt about that. But whenever I came into that office, I'd get the feeling as if you were there, Cookie, as a figure that was spiritually certainly very present even if you couldn't be there so much physically.

The only other person I knew to sit there solidly in your chair for any length of time then was Auntie Isabel. No-one else could fill it!

Kevin and Judy's home space now became even more important to Kevin as he became ill. Judy was tireless not only in making him comfortable and organising the medical visits and treatments. She was a committed activist and unionist in her own right, and her companionship and support for Kevin in his political work was just as important for him as her homemaking and carer role.

---

2   Published after Isabel's death as the co-authored: Isabel Flick and Heather Goodall 2004, *Isabel Flick: The Many Lives of an Extraordinary Aboriginal Woman*, Allen & Unwin, Crows Nest. It was launched at Tranby.

Judy built a whole environment that celebrated Kevin's political as well as his family life. Kathy, Kevin's cousin, had begun to trace their family's stories through her Tranby coursework, which allowed her to build a collection of old photos and letters which were exciting and moving for everyone. Judy had them framed and organised around the house, and composed in collages on the bedroom mirrors. She ensured throughout this time that Kevin was able to re-engage with Susie and Mereki, his children, through contacting Margaret and the kids to gather photographs of their lives so Kevin could keep in touch despite no longer being able to travel. The photographs of Susie's four children, three boys and a girl, were up there among the rich display of family pictures for Cookie to enjoy.

Judy's own children had become very close to Kevin in the early years of their relationship, when the kids all came to live with Cookie in the inner city. All of them have continued to be often around. Talea and Karana, the daughters of Judy's son Peter, lived with Kevin and Judy for a time in their 'elastic house' in Burwood and recent photos show Cookie delighted to be meeting Talea's new baby daughter, Rose. Janette, the youngest of Judy's three children, lived with Kevin and Judy for many years, sharing in the supportive family life as well as generously supporting Judy in looking after Kevin when he needed it. Judy's middle child, Jodi, got married and moved up to Wellington, but has been constantly in touch. Jodi's three children, Tjanara, Ngahla and Yamirra, were often in the house or on the phone to talk not only to Nanna Judy but to their Poppy. Kevin and Judy followed all their growing up – Tjanara's traditional dancing, talented artwork and her determination to graduate from high school, Ngahla's exciting independence and his football games and Yamirra's exuberant childhood visits to stay with her grandparents. A steady presence in Cookie's life have always been his sister Joy, and Judy's sister Janny, with her husband Tommy, who enjoys following the trots and racing as much as Kevin. Along with them, there has been Kevin's brother, Ronnie, still in Perth but often over visiting Sydney to keep in touch, while Kevin's cousin Kathy would bring her mother, Kevin's Aunty Kit, up for visits as long as she was well enough to come.

Figure 18.5: Mereki and his wife, Miriam, on the South Coast where Cookie himself grew up.

Courtesy Margaret Munday family collection.

Figure 18.6: Linda Burney and Judy.

Courtesy Judy Chester family collection.

18. Reflections: Networks, hubs, pathways – and leadership

As Kevin was spending more time at home, the idea that he himself might get a book together began to take shape. At the same time as friends were wanting to drop in and yarn over old times in this comfortable setting, Cookie began to think he could use these opportunities to record the histories of the movements they had all worked for in a crucial political period. He talked it over with the Rona-Tranby Trust – and kept insisting he wanted to gather a history of the movements, not of his own life – and once they agreed to offer some funding, he asked me to help with the writing. So from then on, we used the grant to fund people's travel from all over the country, to bring those old comrades down to yarn about the ways they had tried to make change happen. The long lunches and dinners started to happen, with good friends enjoying the time together as they recorded their memories. Judy and I were usually there, and often Paul Torzillo would be there too. I would work the recorder and Judy would produce magic food and endless cups of tea – and each of us asked some questions as a back up to Cookie. All the chapters of this book arose from those recordings of discussions, reminiscences and debates, although often the funniest stories have had to be left out. There was a lot of good cooking with Judy's many roasts and seafoods and salads although sometimes the guests cooked too. Jack Ah Kit's great curries are memorable!

Figure 18.7: Cookie with Terry O'Shane and Paul Torzillo.

Courtesy Kevin Cook family collection.

Figure 18.8: Cookie with David Ross (Central Land Council, Northern Territory) and Kevin's nephew, Gregory Streets, Joy's son.

Courtesy Kevin Cook family collection.

Figure 18.9: Bruce McGuinness, Gary Foley, Tim Anderson and Cookie, 2002.

Courtesy Tim Anderson.

18. Reflections: Networks, hubs, pathways – and leadership

Figure 18.10: Cookie with activist and union mates Eileen Haley, Russ Herman and Hal Alexander.

Courtesy Kevin Cook family collection.

Figure 18.11: Cookie with Kevin Tory and Heather Goodall.

Courtesy Kevin Cook family collection.

Making Change Happen

Figure 18.12: Cookie with Karen Flick.

Courtesy Kevin Cook family collection.

Figure 18.13: Cookie with Jack Ah Kit and his wife Gail.

Courtesy Kevin Cook family collection.

18. Reflections: Networks, hubs, pathways – and leadership

Figure 18.14: Cookie with Peter Thompson.

Courtesy Kevin Cook family collection.

Figure 18.15: Janny, Tjanara (Judy's granddaughter) and Judy at Salt Pan Creek on the Georges River, Sydney, February 2010, where Janny and Judy spent some of their childhood. This was a great day and almost the last outing Judy had before she suddenly became ill and passed away in April 2010.

Courtesy Heather Goodall.

Figure 18.16: Judy and Cookie in the early 1980s.

Courtesy Kevin Cook family collection.

Judy passed away very suddenly in May 2010 and left a deep sadness among all of her many friends and her family. The sessions which led to this book were all shaped by her presence and her warm enthusiasm for the project, so in very many ways, this book reflects her from all its pages.

Each of these sessions with old friends was unique but there were themes which kept recurring and these have shaped the ways the edited segments of transcript are arranged in this book. Those key themes can be drawn together here to close Cookie's book. These are themes which shaped the movements but also they are characteristic of Kevin's contribution to them.

Firstly, *learner-directed learning* at Tranby was sustained and encouraged through Kevin's time there. It has not only shaped the educational experiences of countless students but has made all of us who worked there into better teachers. This idea – which was an important outcome of the collaboration between Brian Doolan, Terry Widders and Chris Milne in the early 1980s – picked up the cutting edge thinking of Adult Education researchers and activists at the time. But it was so right for Tranby because it met Cookie's conviction that Aboriginal-controlled education at Tranby should recognise, respect and build on the knowledge of the Aboriginal people who came there as both learners and activists. Before he came to Tranby, this idea had flourished in the rank-and-file movement of the Builders Labourers' Federation and before that, it has arisen in Cookie's learning as he grew up in the working environment of Wollongong and within the Aboriginal community of the South Coast. Kevin's commitment to this idea was sustained through changing staff at Tranby and different cohorts of students. So while Kevin always worked in collaboration with teaching staff at Tranby, he was also shaping the ways they developed the learning environment of the college, so that it met the goal of valuing and building on the knowledge of the learners and the whole Aboriginal community. This was the approach Kevin took in all his political involvement.

Secondly, in all of the movements in which Kevin has been involved, his contribution in *building alliances* was central. It was the alliances across left and right unions and between black and white supporters which strengthened Tranby as an adult education provider with whom the labour movement felt it could work. Then it was the alliances between regions in NSW which Kevin helped to build which enabled the successful campaigns which forced through not only the flawed Land Rights Act of 1983 but the broader gains of the Heritage movement. Then, crucially, it was the alliances between states and the very different Aboriginal movements in each which enabled the national push for land rights in the 1980s. As Patrick Dodson had said, Cookie was able to welcome people and enable them to come into the spaces they had not previously felt comfortable entering.

Then it was the alliances between the labour movements not just in Australia but overseas in the ILO with indigenous movements which enabled the interventions of Aboriginal Australian unionists like Kevin and Terry O'Shane into the international Indigenous Rights movement which led from the ILO to the UN and the more widely recognised steps which led to the UN General Assembly Declaration on the Rights of Indigenous peoples in 2006.

Thirdly, all these alliances involved *crossing borders* – not just those between states or nations but across accepted divisions of factions and racial divisions. It took great courage to be able to make those leaps, but without the links across right and left in the ALP at various times, the political decisions which offered some support to Aboriginal people would not have been made. Similarly it was the links between atheist socialist unionists and the religious bodies of the World Council of Churches which not only drew funds for Tranby but generated support for campaigning organisations like the Kimberley Land Council or the North Queensland Land Council. These were the borders which often it was only Kevin who could cross, because he had won the trust of all sides.

Crossing borders for a specific question was fruitful, but all of the movements depended on far longer lasting connections. One of the outstanding needs was for *networks* which would be formed by strong personal friendships and confidence as well as political affilations. When the movements discussed in this book were working at their strongest, it was usually because such networks were alive and functioning to pass information around and enable communication and decision making across the obstacles like distance or factions or even languages. As so many of the people, whose words are recorded in these pages, say – Kevin was often the glue which kept those relationships active and functioning.

There have been many different metaphors to describe the way Kevin works. But when Chrissy Kerr speaks here about education, she is echoing the endorsement of Patrick Dodson, Brian Doolan, William Bates, Isabel Flick, Pat Anderson, Terry O'Shane and many others who all speak about Kevin's role about different movements, from the NSW land rights movement to the national one or the trade union movement.

Chris Kerr: That small player Tranby had become a very large player that provided that hub of the wheel that keeps things turning. And it was Kevin who maintained that and kept the hub well greased and oiled and smooth so that this other wheel could keep turning – which had much broader implications for Aboriginal education nationwide.

That process was the networking of comrades and friends with whom Kevin was constantly in touch. Patrick Dodson put the same thing in another way, with another vivid metaphor (Chapter 11) when he talked about opening a pathway.

Patrick Dodson: It is the human encounter, not the issues. We probably knew what these issues were, but it was these *people*. These people who represented people in some other place, who were there... who created a sense of... well, when you thought of Perth you thought of Riley, and when you thought of Sydney you thought of Cookie, you didn't think about anything else. You just said, well, 'They're the people that you got to see, when you go there'.

These are different images but they add up to the same idea. The basis for this capacity for Kevin to be a 'hub' or the person who was able to 'open' a place for visitors was his universally acknowledged *integrity* in all senses: his personal integrity, his financial integrity and his integrity of principle. These are rare qualities separately and are even more rare together, but all the people interviewed for this book have commented that these – all of them – were characteristic of Kevin's involvement with them and whatever campaign they shared with him. These were qualities which Kevin has put together uniquely with warmth, generosity and humour – endlessly patient and always able to steer a diplomatic pathway though uncomfortable situations. This confidence in Kevin – to act as a hub or to open pathways – has been solidly based on a belief in his unshakable and unquestioned integrity.

The final theme which recurs in all the conversations is *leadership* – as an important but elusive quality of which all the activists were appreciative but about which they also had reservations. Many of the contributors to these conversations stressed how frustrating it was to see individuals cut themselves off from the grass roots or the rank and file movements (depending on whether the speakers were Aboriginal activists or unionists). Both meant the same thing – they saw leadership as important for building movements but also as causing problems when people got carried away by power or separated from the source of their movement, the people who were making the day-to-day changes. Yet all of the people who came together to share their many and monumental contributions to different movements all deferred to Kevin – many spoke of him as always offering that valuable sense of direction but never seeking to put himself into the limelight or take any of the glory. In fact it has often been difficult to give Cookie his rightful share of the credit for the many things he has been involved in.

'Leadership' is such a sought after quality that learning programs have been established around it, such as the Australian Indigenous Leadership Centre in Canberra. The series of interviews in this book have often reflected on the qualities which inspire and support communities and organisations – and Kevin's approach has invariably been described as achieving just that – of embodying leadership. Kevin has not ever presented himself as leading nor has he seized the highest profile roles or the spokesperson's mantle. Most often he has been encouraging other people to step into those roles and has supported them when they did so. Chris Kerr has pointed to the adage of Lao Tzu as embodying how Kevin has worked:

> The greatest leader of all is one when, after the work is done, the people will say 'we did it ourselves'.

In his own words, in all his work in movements and in education, Kevin has carried out what he regarded as the key principle of the Coady International Institute about leadership. Cookie remembered it as:

> *you have to bring people along with you – you can't lead by being out in front.*

It has been that approach to leadership which has allowed Kevin to continue to open the pathway to the many people in the many movements of his life.

Appendix 1. Interviewees

NOTE: these groupings are rough guides only.

Everyone on this list is an activist.

Most of them would say their work contributed to a number of these different groups.

The grouping names will just give you an idea of which chapter each person has contributed to.

The names are listed in alphabetical order in each group.

Indigenous activists

John Ah Kit
Patty Anderson
William Bates
Jack Campbell
Judy Chester
Pat Dodson
Janny Ely
Barbara Flick
Isabel Flick
Karen Flick
Jacqui Katona
Bruce McGuinness
Terry O'Shane
David Ross
Guboo Ted Thomas
Kevin Tory
Robyn Williams
Tombo Winters
Peter Yu

Unionists

Bobby Baker
Paddy Crumlin
Russ Herman
Joe Owens
Rod Pickette

Other activists

Tim Anderson
Meredith Burgmann
Frank Panucci
Peter Thompson
Paul Torzillo

Tranby staff

Brian Doolan
Heather Goodall
Julie House
Yvonne Jackson
Christine Kerr
Chris Milne
Dave Morrissey
Terry Widders

Building Bridges

Tony Dukes
Jim George
Paul Kelly

Family

Jannette Chester
Jody Chester
Janny Ely
Kathy Kennedy
Joy Steep

Appendix 2. Glossary and abbreviations

Glossary

Dharawal	Aboriginal Language group, speakers of which are understood to have extended from the Georges River to around Wollongong.
Indigenous	In Australian usage, this indicates the owners of the Australian lands prior to British colonisation. So it refers to both Aboriginal people and Torres Straits Islanders. When used in Australia it is usually capitalised as 'Indigenous'. Internationally, the word at times is used to describe the original inhabitants of any country, in, for example, India or Canada, where it may be used without capitals, as 'indigenous'.
Koorie	Term used widely today in Sydney, the South Coast of NSW, the south-west of the State and Victoria, to mean 'Aboriginal person'. A similar word, sometimes spelled 'goori', is common on the northern coast of NSW. The word meaning the same thing in north-west NSW and Queensland is *murri* and in far western NSW it is *wiimpatja*. Each of these words has various spellings.
Rife	Used by Judy Chester in phrases like 'He was rife on that', indicating irrational and vindictive pursuit of some perceived infringement. A dictionary definition is close to the way Judy used it – as an adverb about something unpleasant - 'in an unchecked or widespread manner'.
'Sticking fats'	A colloquial term Kevin uses frequently and which he remembers from his childhood. He understands it to mean sticking by someone or something through thick and thin, that is, maintaining solidarity with friends and comrades and adhering to principle.
Wandandian	Aboriginal language group, speakers of which are understood to have extended from Wollongong to the far southern coast of NSW.

Abbreviations

ACC – Australian Council of Churches

ACTU – Australian Council of Trade Unions

ADU – the Action Development Unit

AECG – Aboriginal Educational Consultative Group

ALP – Australian Labor Party

ALS – Aboriginal Legal Service

ANC – African National Congress

ATEA – Australian Theatrical (& Amusement) Employees' Association

ATEU – Australian Theatrical Employees Union

ATSIC – Aboriginal and Torres Strait Islander Commission

AWOL – Absent Without Leave

AWU – Australian Workers' Union

BLF/BLs – Builders Labourers' Federation (NSW)/ Builders Labourers

BWIU – Building Workers' Industrial Union

CAE – College of Advanced Education

CBD – Central Business District

CDEP – Community Development Employment Projects

CDP – Community Development Program

CFMEU – Construction, Forestry, Mining and Energy Union

CLC – Central Land Council

CPA – Communist Party of Australia

CPSU/PSA – Commonwealth Public Sector Union

FAIRA – Foundation for Aboriginal and Islander Research Action

FCAATSI – Federal Council for the Advancement of Aborigines and Torres Strait Islanders

Appendix 2. Glossary and abbreviations

FEDFA – Federated Engine Drivers and Firemen's Association

FILEF – Federazione Italiana Lavoratori Emigrati e le Loro Famiglie

HFA – Homes for Aborigines

HSC – Higher School Certificate

ILO – International Labour Organisation

MAR – Migrants for Aboriginal Rights

MBA – Master Builders' Association

NACC – National Aboriginal Consultative Committee

NCCA – National Council of Churches in Australia

NGO – Non-Government Organisation

NLC – Northern Land Council

NPWS – National Parks and Wildlife Service

NSWALC – New South Wales Aboriginal Land Council

NTEU – National Tertiary Education Union –

SPA – Socialist Party of Australia (a Soviet-affiliated splinter group after the Australian Communist Party split in 1968 in response to the Soviet invasion of Czechoslovakia)

SUA – Seamen's Union of Australia (later amalgamated with the Waterside Workers Federation to form the Maritime Union of Australia, the MUA)

TAFE – Technical and Further Education

TEPC – Tertiary Education Preparatory Course

TUCAR – Trade Union Committee on Aboriginal Rights

TUTA – Trade Union Training Authority

UTS – University of Technology, Sydney

VETAB – NSW Vocational and Educational Accreditation Board

WALS – Western Aboriginal Legal Service

Appendix 3. Bibliography and further reading

This is a small selection of accessible readings to follow up the themes in this book.

Library and museum holdings

AIATSIS library

The Australian Institute of Aboriginal and Torres Strait Islanders library has a wide range of important holdings. Those used for this book include:

Ted Thomas, Jack Campbell, Max Harrison and Terry Fox 1980, *Report on Wilcannia Trip 27.11.80 – 6.12.80*. Travelling as representatives of the N.S.W. Land Council. Itinerary of trip by members of N.S.W. Land Council to Wilcannia and Menindee; and including land rights claims by Toomelah/ Boggabilla people; submission to N.S.W. Parliamentary Select Committee on need of N.S.W. Aborigines for land rights; see also AIAS slides in Resource Centre, AIATSIS Library, PMS 3322.

National Museum of Australia

Relevant holdings consulted include:

South Coast Land Rights campaign information lodged by Terry Fox.

<http://www.nma.gov.au/collections-search/results?search=adv&ref=coll&collname=Terry+Fox+collection>

Websites

Gary Foley, 'The Koorie History Website', <http://www.kooriweb.org/foley/images/history/1970s/china/chinadx.html>

Redfern Oral History, <http://redfernoralhistory.org/>

A History of Aboriginal Sydney, <http://www.historyofaboriginalsydney.edu.au/>

Barani: the City of Sydney Indigenous History, <http://www.cityofsydney.nsw.gov.au/barani/>

NMA, The National Museum of Australia, <http://www.nma.gov.au/history/australian_history_and_society_since_1788>

Books and articles

General

Cadzow, A and J Maynard (eds) 2012, *Nelson Aboriginal Studies*, Nelson Cengage Learning, Australia.

Parbury, N 2005, *Survival: A History of Aboriginal life in NSW*, NSW Department of Aboriginal Affairs, Sydney.

Aboriginal culture and politics

Attwood, B and A Markus 1999, *The Struggle for Aboriginal Rights: A Documentary History*, Allen & Unwin, Sydney.

Bellear, Robert W (ed) 1976, *Black Housing Book*, Amber Press. Extracts available at the Redfern Oral History site, <http://redfernoralhistory.org/OralHistory/BobBellear/tabid/150/Default.aspx>

Maynard, J 2007, *Fight for Liberty and Freedom: The Origins of Australian Aboriginal Activism*, Aboriginal Studies Press, Canberra.

Unions and the NSW Builders Labourers' Federation

Burgmann, Meredith and Verity Burgmann 1998, *Green Bans Red Union: Environmentalism and the New South Wales Builders Labourers' Federation*, UNSW Press, Sydney.

Burgmann, Verity 2003, *Power, Profit, and Protest: Australian Social Movements and Globalisation*, Allen & Unwin, St Leonards.

Co-operatives

Australian co-operatives

Clint, Alf 1964, 'The Rochdale principles on co-operation', *The Aborigine Welfare Bulletin* 4(1): 13.

Loos, Noel and Keast, Robyn 1992, 'The radical promise: the Aboriginal Christian co-operative movement', *Australian Historical Studies* 25(99): 286–301.

Friesan and Taksa 1996: 'Workers' education in Australia and Canada: a comparative approach to labour's cultural history'. *Labour/Le Travail/Labour History* 38(71): 170–197.

Fairbairn, Brett 1994, *The Meaning of Rochdale: The Rochdale Pioneers and the Co-operative Principles*, Occasional Paper, Centre for the Study of Co-operatives, University of Saskatchewan.

International co-operatives

Coady International Institute

Reports are accessible in Coady newsletters and other documents, digitally archived on the Coady website at <http://coadyextension.stfx.ca>

Welton, Michael 1995, '"Bolsheviks of a better sort": Jimmy Tompkins and the struggle for a people's Catholicism, 1908 – 1928', paper delivered at 36th AERC, University of Alberta, Edmonton, Canada, May 1995.

Other international cooperatives

Rogerson, CM 1990, '"People's factories": worker co-operatives in South Africa', *Geodournal* 22(3): 285–292.

Taimni, KK 1994, 'Asia's rural cooperatives origin, evolution and emerging challenges', *Annals of Public & Cooperative Economics* 65(3): 469–489.

Bara, Joseph 2007, 'Colonialism, Christianity and the tribes of Chhotanagpur in East India, 1845–1890', *South Asia: Journal of South Asian Studies* 30(2): 195–222.

Education and children

Fletcher, JJ 1989, *Clean, Clad and Courteous: A History of the Aboriginal Education in NSW*, Southwood Press, Sydney.

Haebich, A 2000, *Broken Circles Fragmenting Indigenous Families 1800–2000*, Fremantle Arts Centre Press, Fremantle.

Land rights and native title

Goodall, Heather 1996, *Invasion to Embassy: Land in Aboriginal Politics in NSW, 1770–1972*, Allen & Unwin, Sydney.

MacDonald, Gaynor 2004, *Two Steps Forward, Three Steps Back: A Wiradjuri Land Rights Journey*, LhR Press, Canada Bay. (edited by Julie Marcus) <http://www.lhrpress.com.au/catalogue_pages/two_steps.html>

Maynard, John 2007, *Fight for Liberty and Freedom: The Origins of Australian Aboriginal Activism*, Aboriginal Studies Press, Canberra.

Morris, Barry 1989, *Domesticating Resistance: The Dhan-Gadi Aborigines and the Australian State*, Berg Publishers, Oxford.

Norman, Heidi 2013 (forthcoming), *From Activism to Enterprise: A Political History of the NSW Aboriginal Lands Rights Act, 1983*, Aboriginal Studies Press, Canberra.

Ritter, David 2009, *The Native Title Market*, University of Western Australia Press, Crawley, WA.

Weir, Jessica 2009, *Murray River Country: An Ecological Dialogue with Traditional Owners*, Aboriginal Studies Press, Canberra.

Wilkie, Meredith 1985, *Aboriginal Land Rights in NSW*, Alternative Publishing Cooperative Ltd in association with Black Books, Chippendale.

Index

Page numbers in **bold** refer to images, page numbers in *italics* refer to transcripts of conversation involving the individual.

Aboriginal Advancement League 286
Aboriginal Affairs 103, 191
   Office of 155
Aboriginal Advisory Committees, council 172
Aboriginal and Torres Strait Islander Commission (ATSIC) 293, 367, 399
Aboriginal Educational Consultative Groups 149, 150
Aboriginal Housing Company 1, 50, **51**, 53, **54**, 55, 176
Aboriginal Land Council Sydney march, 30 October 1981 213-218
Aboriginal Land Rights Act 1983 (NSW) 84, 123, 157, 158, 234, 237, 243, 244, 253, 255, 258, 270–273
   amendment to stop land acquisition 261
   amendments by Greiner 269
   before Act/outside Act 226–229, 233
   cognate Bill 238–239, 241
   course 253
   potential 242, 243
   proposed Heritage Act that did not happen 267, 268
   strength 258
Aboriginal Land Rights (Northern Territory) Act 1976 (Cwlth) 176, 180, 190, 216, 417
Aboriginal Legal Service (ALS) **50**, 53, 157, 176, 209, 231, 283
   legal challenge 239, 241, 242
   split of WALS from ALS 226–227
   Western Aboriginal Legal Service (WALS) 178, 193, 194, 195, 218, 391
   involvement in Mutawintji blockade 232
Aboriginal Medical Service 54, 176, 339
Aboriginal Progressive Association 240
Aboriginal Reserve lands 13, 136, 238–240
   attempt to keep/regain control of by Aboriginal people 175–176, 180, 202
   attempt to take control of by government 297
Aborigines Act 1969 (NSW) 175
Aborigines (Amendment) Act 1973 (NSW) 175
Aboriginal Land Rights (Amendment) Act 1993 (NSW) 377
   protest against 370
Aborigines Protection Board 13, 230, 239–240
Abschol 55, 68
Action Development Unit (ADU) 159–161
African National Congress (ANC) , 399–400
Ah Kit, John (Johnny/ Jack) 106, 127, *280–281*, **282**, *306–309*, *331*, 411, **414**
   Building Bridges 350, 357, 362
   ILO 326–330
   National Coalition 310–312
Alexander, Hal 162, 297, 404, **413**
Anderson, Patty 316, **317**, *348–350*, *352–354*, *358–359*, *363–364*, *378*, **405**, 406
   ILO 318–320
Angledool meeting, July 1982 226–232
Apartheid 33, 47, 48, 49, 64, 83
   demonstrations 47, 82, 296
   government protest 297
Australian Bicentennial Authority (ABA) 343, 349, 354, 367–368
Australian Communist Party 129, 184, 188, 286
Australian Council of Churches Aboriginal Affairs Committee 278–279
Australian Council of Trade Unions (ACTU) 132, 285
   ACTU support for ILO amendments 316, 318–319, 322
Australian Labour Party (ALP) Conference, June 1982 186–192
see Select Committee

Australian Manufacturing Workers' Union (AMWU) 185
Australian Seamen's Union 63, 67–70, 129
Australian Workers' Union (AWU) 39, 59

Baker, Bobby *33–36*, *41*, 58, *59*, 65
Barlow, May 219, 232
Bates, Brian (Briany) – Bourke 215
Bates, William 193, 219, **220**, *221-224, 246-247*, 314, 319, **320**, 353, **375**
  importance of proposed Heritage Act 268-270
  Winbar Land Claim 260-261
Bellear, Bob **182**, 199, **207**, **386**
  Aboriginal Advisory Committee
  Australian Council of Churches 184, 278
  Aboriginal Policy Committee ALP 190–191
  Tranby Board 102, 105
Belmore Park 355–358
Berkeley, Wollongong where family lived 22–23, 63
Bicentennial event 335–366
  Bicentennial Long March 336–360
  Bicentennial Travelling Exhibition 367
  Building Bridges 347–351, 407
Bienderry, Jimmy from the Kimberley 119, 309
Bishop, Roy 24, 25, 33, 37, 53, 340
Bjelke-Petersen, Joh 296, 297, **299**, 304
Black Books 102, 110–111, 117, 126, 145–148, 384
  McKell, Maria 147
  Lambkin, Joyce 148
Black deaths in custody 135–142
Black Defence Group 65, 178–180, 184
Black Theatre 1, 56–58, **182**, 213
Blewer, Robert 317–319, **320**
Block, Cathy 398
'Block, the', Redfern 49–50, 52, 369, 400
Blockade, Mutawintji 372
Bonner, Senator Neville 298
Bostok, Gerry 57, **183**

Bostok, Lester 56, **72**, 164
Boyle, Helen 121, 139
Briar, Tibby 218, 225
Briggs, Alice (Taree) 181, **212**
Buchanan, Cheryl 296
Buchanan, Tiger 240, 241
Builders Labourers Federation (BLF) 33–44
  ban on demolition at the Block 50, 56
  connections between migrants and Aboriginals 40–41
  end of NSW branch 58
  Green bans 30, 33, 37, 52
  impact of Sydney high rise development on 25, 27
  life membership badge 404
  rank and file control 29–30
  support for Aboriginal campaigns 39, 53
  social status 31
  women members 53
Building Workers' Industrial Union (BWIU) 25
Burgmann, Meredith 25, 27, 48, 61, *55, 57*–58, 65, 76, 129, 131, 167, 178, 186, *189–190*, 207, **404**
  Black Defence Group 65, 178–180, 184
Burke, Brian WA Premier
  influence on land rights 305–306
Burney, Linda 404, **410**

Campbell, Jacko 105, 118, 133, , 314, 339
  Sites course 152–155
Campbell, Kathy 96, 98, **99**, 110, 115, 145, 147
Campbell, Keith in TAFE 94
Campbell, Nan 35, 105, 118, **134**, 370, **401**, 402
Carrol, Esther from a Wiradjuri family of activists 393
Cavanagh, Jim 52, 53, 54
Chester, Judy 4, *40*, **124**, *139–140*, **143**, *148*, 248, **379**, **385**
  Black Deaths in Custody 139–140
  daughters Jody and Jannette 132

FILEF 342–343, 344–345
Honorary Doctorates 402
inalienable title 369–372
NOW 150–152, 157
Clague, Colin 257
Clague, Joyce 181, 190
Clint, Alf 20, 61, 62, 63, 66, 91, 102, 129, 429
   development studies 391
   co-operatives 73
   international links 165
Coady International Institute 64, 78–84
   founder Moses Coady 79
   influence of teaching on Kevin Cook 87, 200, 284, 286, 419
   links forged 164, 321, 315
Coe, Paul 53, **216**, 241, 244, 293
Commonwealth Games, 1982 Brisbane protests 295–302
communal inalienable freehold title – *see* inalienable freehold title
Communities, Aboriginal
   Huskisson 10, 13, 14
   Cringila 9, 13–17
   Roseby Park 13–14, 183, 199, 202
Cook, Kevin (Cookie) **16**, **17**, **19–22**, **23**,
   Aboriginal Housing Company 53–56
   Bicentennial Long March 338, 349, 351, 353–355, 360, 363–364
   Black Books 147–148
   Black Theatre 57–58
   BLF 29–35, 32, 59
   Coady 76–84, 80
   co-operatives 75–76
   dogman 25–27, 28–29, 33–34
   early years 9–24
   Land rights 368–369
   National service 18
   Tranby 112
      Board 102–106
      courses 152–158
      funding 93–100
      international links 165–168
      international reputation 330
      joining Tranby 61–63
      NOW course 151–152

TUCAR 132
Cook, Ronnie 17, 18, 23, 409
Cooley, Harry 87-87
Coonanberi Mountain 198
Co–operatives 63–64, 73–76, **74–75**, 79, 87, 116, 160, 314
see Coady International Institute, Tranby College
   boomerang manufacturing 87–90, 88–89
Cooper, William had spoken to the press in the 1930s 313, 335, 336
Corbett, Helen 327, 329, 383
Crawshaw, Josie **287**, 327, 329
Crean, Simon 317, 318, 322
Crimes Act 1900 (NSW) 198
Crozio, Janice the State Minister for Lands 252
Crumlin, Paddy *67–69*, **67**
   Tranby Board 102–103
Curtis, Brian 18
Cwata, Maria Zimbabwe **80**, 82

Davis, Greg from Nambucca Heads **211**, **374**
Deaths in custody – *see* Black deaths in custody
Department of Aboriginal Affairs 155, 179, 201, 210
   Clyde Holding (Minister) 99
   Susan Ryan (Shadow Minister) 298
   Robert Tickner (Minister) 327
   Frank Walker (Minister) 210, 214
Dodson, Patrick *283–284*, 336, *337*, *349*, *352–353*, *357*, 362–363, **385**, 417, *418*
Dogman 25, **26**, 29, 33
Doolan, Brian 76, 87, 91, **110**, *125–128*, 151, *242–243*, 383, 404, 416, 418
   Commonwealth Games 297–298
   International linkages 165–168
   Tranby 92, 93–101, 107, 110–111, 120
   Tranby Board 102
   TUCAR 129
   Wilcannia 195
Dukes, Tony *346–347*, *350–351*

Eatts, Dolly the mother of a young son 381–382
'elastic house' 125, 352, 379, 407, 409
Elliott, Eliot V 63, 68
Ely, Janny 152, 157, 166, *256-257*, 404, 406, 409, **415**
   Gandangara Land Council 248–253, land claims 256–257
Ely, Tommy **388**
Engonnia Common 243
Eva Valley meeting **287, 289**
Everett, Jim 308, 352

Federal Council for the Advancement of Aborigines and Torres Strait Islanders, the (FCAATSI) 133, 275
Federation of Land Councils 118, 119, 275, 281, 283, 288–291, 296, 306, 317, 337
Federated Engine Drivers and Firemen's Association (FEDFA) 52, 53, 64
FILEF 41, 162–163, 341, 342, 344
Fitzpatrick, Stephen a WALS lawyer 218
Flick family 227–228, 293
Flick, Barbara 76, 105, 106, 125, 128, 135, 178, *184–186, 193–194,* 195, 198, *201–205,* **217,** *217–218,* **224,** *230–231,* 268, *270–272,* 303, *309,* **315,** *369–370,* **379,** 391, 400
   Interim Land Council 244, 245–246
   Menindee meeting, 1981 218–221
Flick, Isabel 1, 2, 3, *111–115*, **114,** 135, 137, *138–139, 141,* **197, 204, 224,** 370, 376–377, 396, 402, 408
Flick, Joe 178, **197, 210, 224,** 359
Flick, Karen 116, *117–119,* 123, **147,** *168–170,* **216,** *228–229,* 303, *330–331,* 354, 371, **414**
   Aboriginal Land Council Sydney March, October 1981 213-214
   Black Deaths in Custody 136–141
Foley, Gary **48,** 278, 296, 345, 346–347, 393, 402, **412**
Foundation for Aboriginal and Islander Research Action (FAIRA) 296, 298, 308
French, Charles Coady 76, **77,** 313

Galvin, Bill 222–223
Geraghty, Patrick 68, **70,** 131, 404, **405**
George, Jim *351*
Gibbs, Pearl 1930s and 1940s activist **204,** 276
Granny Kate – *see* Speechly, Josephine Kate
Greiner, Nick Liberal Government 265
   attack on land rights Act and inalienability 367–372
Green bans 30, 33, 37, 52
Goodall, Heather 1, 107, 360–362, **413**
Gooriala buttons 97–98, **97, 98**
   funding for Tranby
   designer Dick Roughsey 97
Gordon, Lin Labor Minister for Lands 243
Gordon, Steven 183, **374**
Gundy, David innocent 381–382
Gurindji people from Watti Creek land rights campaign 30, 31, 290, 309

Harris, Reverend Charles President of the Aboriginal and Islander Christian Congress 336–338
   Bicentennial Long March 336–338
Harrison, Max 14, 200
Hawke Labor Government 241, 285
   betrayal of land rights 368
   National Aboriginal Consultative Committee (NACC) 313
   promise of National Land Rights 314
Heritage Act, proposed 238, 267–270, 372
Herman, Russ 66, 69, *73–75,* 90, 404, **413**
Holding, Clyde 99–100, 140
Holland, Sekai **47**
Homes for Aborigines (HFA) 250–251
House, Julie 87–88, 90
Human Rights and Equal Opportunity Commission (HREOC) 390

Indigenous and Tribal People's Convention 169, of 1989 316, 318–319, 323, 326
Indigenous and Tribal Populations Convention 107
   declared in 1957 315–322

Interim Land Council 84, 244–245, 255, 272
  role in setting up local and regional land councils 245–247
Interim Report on Aboriginal Land Rights 200
International Labour Organisation (ILO) 315–325, **320–321**

Jackson, Yvonne Director of Studies at Tranby 383, **384**, **385**, 399
Jerringa claim for Roseby Park 183, 186, 202

Katona, Jacqui 326, 345, 346–347
Keane, Maurie 177, 192, 199, **217**
Kelly, Alice **152**
Kelly's Bush 52
Kelly, Ray on the North Coast 155, 181, 244
Kennedy, Aunty Kit (Kitty) 10, 14, 15, **378-379**, 404, 409
Kennedy, Father Ted 55, 92–93
Kennedy, Kathy cousin 10, **24**, 407
Kerr, Christine 4, *384, 389–390, 391–393, 395, 396–398, 399–400*, 404, *407, 408, 418–419*
Keys, Harry Margaret's father 20
Keys, Margaret (Munday) 19, **20**, **21**, 22, 24
Kimberley Land Council 277, 278, 417
Kirkbright, Chris Registrar of Aboriginal lands 245–247
Knott, Bill Margaret's uncle 20, 63, 193
Knox, Roger 351
Kurnell 360–366

Lambkin, Joyce 148
Land claims 183, 186, 200–203, 255–261
Land councils, Aboriginal 155, 158
see Interim Land Council, local land councils, regional land councils, State Land Council
Land rights 131, 136, 175–207, 219–235, 237–253, 255–272
  Green Paper 128, 211, 231, 237–238
  National Coalition 310–312

National land rights 304–310
  Preferred Model 305–306, 317
  Five Point Plan 305–306
  training courses 157–159
  National Coalition 310–312
Land Rights Conference, 1977 Sydney 181–182
Land Rights March, July 1981 210–218
Land Rights Support Group 146, 185–186, 202, 213
La Perouse 349–350, 352–355
  Building Bridges accommodation 349–355
  land claim 200
Lavender, Bobby from the FEDFA 52
Layman, Ron and others from the Canadian Indian territories 329
Legislation – *see* under individual Acts
Local land councils 248–253
  Gandangara Local Land Council 248–253, 256–262
  Winbar Land Council 260–261, 264
Lowe, Delia (Jacko's daughter) 105, 133, 244, **373**
  ILO meeting 319, 320, 321

Mabo, Eddie 275, 376
McConville, Kim employed through Tranby 397
McGinness, Joe 106, 115, 117, 124, 133, **134**, **287**, 402, 407
McGrady, Madeline filmmaker 136, 248
McGuiness, Bruce **289**, 399, 402, **412**
McKell, Maria **147**, 148
Malezer, Les 296
Mandela, Nelson 83, 331, 400
Mansell, Michael (Tasmania) **287**, 308, 327, 338, 352
Mant, Julia 406
Mason, Jacqui **114**, **197**
Master Builders' Association (MBA) 58
Masters, Chris
  ABC Four Corners program 'Moonlight State' in 1987 304
Mazibuko, Sophie South Africa **80**, 82
Menindee meeting, 5 December 1981 218–226

Middleton, Hannah 130, 131
Migrants 39, 41, 162–163, 358, 359
   BLF 41
Migrants for Aboriginal Rights (MAR) 340–346
Miller, Mick in the far north of the Qld **182**, 278, 296, 298, **300**
Milne, Chris 96, 107, 110–111, **120**, 120–122, 151, 157, 171
   learner-directed learning 383, 416
Moore, Barry 156
Moore, Tim Minister for the Environment, first introduced the National Parks Hand Over Bill 269, 372, 376
Moree Special 209, **210**
Morrisey, Guy an art dealer from Paddington 277
Morrissey, Dave 96, 107, 110, 146, 151, 152, *153*, **154**, *155–157*, *158–160*, 170, *171–172*
   Land Rights Support Group Black Books 147–148, 186, 213, 215
Mosala, Monica 82
Mosely, Percy 239
Mumbulla, Percy from the South Coast **183**, 216
Mundey, Jack 30, 31, 45, 52, 62, 202
Mundine, Warren 244
Musgrave Park 298
Mussing, Wally **99**, 105
Mutawintji **376**
   Blockade, September 1983 232–234
   handback 185, 372, 375
   Land Council 233

National Aboriginal Consultative Committee (NACC) 305
National Coalition of Aboriginal Organisations 275, 288, 307
National Land Rights Working Party 304
National Parks and Wildlife Act 1974 (NSW) 270
National Parks and Wildlife Service (NPWS) 152–153, 260, 377
Native Title Act 1993 (Cwlth) 376, 275

networks 129–130, 275–331, 417–418
   international 165, 313–331, 399–400
   national 275–294
   see Australian Council of Churches (ACC)
      Federation of Land Councils 317, 337
      Migrants for Aboriginal Rights (MAR) 340
   unions 129–130, 398–399
Noonkanbah 119, 277–283
NOW course 150–152

Oliver, Charlie from the AWU 66, **130**, 132, 184, 191
O'Shane, Terry 106, 115, 127, 132, 284, *286–288*, **287**, 393, **411**
   ACTU representative 318
   Coalition 319
   ILO 322–323, 324–325, 326
outreach – *see* Black Books, Tranby
Owens, Joe 2, 27, 28, *29–31*, **29**, *36–40*, **43**, 45, *50*, *52–53*, *62–66*, **404**

Panucci, Frank, 41, 64, *162–163*, *341–345*
Parliament House in Canberra protest 1985
Penrith, Merv and Shirley 125, 133, 185, 201, 290, **374**
Perkins, Charles 369
Peterson, George 188, 193
Pickette, Rod **66**, **189**, 297, 404
   Black Defence Group 65, 178–181
   land rights 186
   TUCAR 129, 131–132
Pringle, Bobby **29**, 30–31, 33, **42**, 47, 55–56, 58, 61, 202

Quayle, John(ny) 199, **233**
Quayle, Vinno 223

Redfern **34**, 49–50, 57–58, 355
see the Block
Regional land councils 262–270
   attack on 265, 368

Central Land Council in the Northern Territory 163, 276–277
Far Western Regional Land Council
Kimberley Land Council 277, 278, 417
land purchase power 262–265
NT models 276
North Queensland Land Council 276, 278, 417
North Western Regional Land Council 118, 226–229,
Western Regional Land Council 195–197, 198, 218–223,
Registrar of Aboriginal Land 245–247
Reserve, Aboriginal 161, 175, 239–241
Coomaditji 13
loss of reserve due to legislation 241
Ridgeway, Robyn Head of Tertiary Prep at Tranby **384**, 404
Rona–Tranby Trust 2–3, 407, 408, 411
Rose, George snr **227**, 228–230
Ross, David 280–281, 285, *309–310*, 336–337, *348–349*, 397, **412**
Ross, James Liberia **80**, 81, **82**
Royal Commission
Aboriginal deaths in custody 140–142
Rutter, Sue 194
Ryan, Senator Susan, Labor Shadow Minister for Aboriginal Affairs 99, 298

Salt Pan Creek on the Georges River, Sydney 133, **415**
Saunders, Justine 402
Black Theatre 56, 58
Scott, Dick (AMWU) 104, **128**, 131, 185, 191
Scott, Sylvia Wiradjuri elder 105, 384, **396**, 402, 404
Select Committee, chaired by Maurie Keane 192, 199–201
report and recommendations 131, 177, 210, 216, 231, 237–238, 255, 267
Sereno, Serge 340–341
Sharkey, Stan 30, 65, 104, 131
Socialist Party of Australia (SPA) 62, 65, 184
Socialist Workers Party 188

Speechly, Grace 9
Speechly, Josephine Kate 9
Speechley, William 10, **11**
Stanley, Robert 87, *90–92*, 380
State Land Council, NSW 155, 181, 183, 200, 201, 368
Land rights rally, 1981 209, 213–218
local and regional council controls 271
support for Amenments to Act 370–373
St Francis Xavier University – *see* Coady International Institute
Stringer, Wendy 45
Sutton, Evan 93

Tent embassy 52, 55, **56**, 61, 93, 175
Terry, John lawyer working with WALS 140–141, 157, 194, 222, 253, 260–261, 391
Terry Hie Hie, south–east of Moree [reserve] 176, 180
land claim 177, 186
Tertiary Education Preparation Course (TEPC) 109–110, 116, 170
Thomas, Guboo Teddy 133, **153**, **204**, 216
Thompson, Lyn **48**
Thompson, Peter *194–199*, 202, *225–226*, *231–235*, *260–261*, **415**
Thorne, Colin (Chittles) from Collarenebri 136, 215
Tory, Kevin **124**, 130, 132, 165, **279**, **287**, 317, 339, *340*, 354, **413**
Torzillo, Emma **379**
Torzillo, Judith **379**
Torzillo, Paul 27, *54–55*, 65, 101, *102–104*, 197, *230*, *339*, 404, *411*
BLF 36–41
Tranby Board 101–104
Trade Union Committee on Aboriginal Rights (TUCAR) 123, **128–132**, 184, 194, 340
Trades Union Training Authority (TUTA) 64, 341, 398
Tranby College 61–74, 92–106, 107–122, 380–402
fireplace 406–407

Honorary Doctorates program 401, 402
influence on local government 161–164
international links 164–170
learner–directed learning 383–384, 389–390
links to community and bush 111–119
networks 164–170
participant-directed learning 121, 383
union/ist support 65–68, 72
Tranby Board 102–106
  Board members – see Bob Bellear, Nan Campbell, Patrick Crumlin, Isabel Flick, Delia Lowe, Wally Mussing, Dick Scott, Sylvia Scott, Stan Sharkey, Paul Torzillo
  Clancy, Pat 65, 104
  Foley, Cliff 105
  Hassam, Jack 68
  Hope, Justice Bob 61, 102
  Knott, Michael 102
  Mawley, the BWIU rep 104
  Perumal, Peru 103
  Short, John 102
  Stanley, Robert 105
  Sweetenson, Pat Seamen's Union 68, 104
Tranby courses
  Aboriginal Studies, Advanced Diploma 394–396
  Co–operative Course (first Tranby course) 71
  Development Studies in Aboriginal Communities 391–393
  Land council training 157–159
  National Aboriginal Legal Studies, Diploma 388, 390–391, 416–417
  NOW course 150–152
  Sites Course 152–155
Tulladunna 136, 141, **224**
Tutu, Desmond **130**, **166**, 167, 331

Unions – *see* ACTU, Builders Labourers Federation, TUCAR
  Australian Manufacturing Workers' Union 185
  Australian Workers' Union 39
  supporting Aboriginal causes 12–13, 53, 61, 67, 126, 129–130, 283
  supporting inalienable freehold title 190–191
  support for ILO 316–319
United Nations (UN) 316
  Working Group on Indigenous Populations 316, 319, 326
University of Technology, Sydney (UTS) 394–396
Unoccupied Crown land 159, 231, 243–244, 255–260
Unsworth, Barry 261

Vietnam War 24, 30, 33, 49
Vocational and Educational Accreditation Board, NSW (VETAB) 396–397

Walford, Norma from far western NSW 319, **320**, **379**
Walker, Frank 188, 193, 210–211, **214**, 221, 222, 231, 244
Wandandian 9
Watson, Johnny 119, 280
Weatherall, Bob 296, 326, 328
Webster, Big Will (Thartu) 93, 218, 219, **220**, 223, 225, 242
Wee Waa 135, 138, 178
Weinteriga Opening 263–265, **265–267**
Wellington, Nan 13, 133
Western Aboriginal Land Council 195, 198, 260, 262
  establishment process 220
Western Aboriginal Legal Service (WALS) 193, 218, 226, 232, 391, 425
Western Lands Act 1901 (NSW) 255
Western Lands Commission 194
Western Lands Leases 255–256, 260–261
Wheatley, Nadia 404
Whitlam, Gough 175

Whitlam Labor Government 53, 296, 307
    effect of fall 176, 188, 241
Whitton, Julie from Boggabilla **224**, **256**
Widders, Terry 92, 99, 149, 150, 383, 416
    Tranby 107–111, 115–117, 170–171
    Macquarie University 394
Wilcannia Common 194, 198
Williams, Foxy Wilcannia 93
Williams, Gary **50**, **212**
Williams, Joyce Judy's aunty **166**, 167
Williams, Aunty Lotte 223
Williams, Mervyn / Crow 195
Williams, Michael 111
    Macquarie University Aboriginal
        History course 111
Williams, Robyn 27, *45*
    Gandangara Land Council 248–253
    outreach for TAFE 117
    NOW 117, 150
Wilson, Eric one of the WALS lawyers 55, 222
Winters, Tombo **203**, **210**, *229–230*, *242*, 244, *246*, **292**, 314, 339, 370
    Brewarrina Legal Service 193, 227
Wran, Neville Labor Government 183–184, 192, 209
    Select Committee 131–132, 201, 238
    land rights 199, 205, 213–4, 216

Yolngu people 308
Yothu Yindi's first gig 351
Yu, Peter *277*, *280*
Yunupingu, Dr 307

Zammit, Paul the Assistant Minister to Premier Nick Greiner 369–370

www.ingramcontent.com/pod-product-compliance
Lightning Source LLC
Chambersburg PA
CBHW041248240426
43669CB00034B/2989